States and Strangers

BORDERLINES

A BOOK SERIES CONCERNED WITH REVISIONING GLOBAL POLITICS

Edited by David Campbell and Michael J. Shapiro

Volume 11 Nevzat Soguk, *States and Strangers: Refugees and Displacements of Statecraft*

Volume 10 Kathy E. Ferguson and Phyllis Turnbull, *Oh, Say, Can You See? The Semiotics of the Military in Hawai'i*

Volume 9 Iver B. Neumann, *Uses of the Other: "The East" in European Identity Formation*

Volume 8 Keith Krause and Michael C. Williams, editors, *Critical Security Studies: Concepts and Cases*

Volume 7 Costas M. Constantinou, *On the Way to Diplomacy*

Volume 6 Gearóid Ó Tuathail (Gerard Toal), *Critical Geopolitics: The Politics of Writing Global Space*

Volume 5 Roxanne Lynn Doty, *Imperial Encounters: The Politics of Representation in North-South Relations*

Volume 4 Thom Kuehls, *Beyond Sovereign Territory: The Space of Ecopolitics*

Volume 3 Siba N'Zatioula Grovogui, *Sovereigns, Quasi Sovereigns, and Africans: Race and Self-Determination in International Law*

Volume 2 Michael J. Shapiro and Hayward R. Alker, editors, *Challenging Boundaries: Global Flows, Territorial Identities*

Volume 1 William E. Connolly, *The Ethos of Pluralization*

States and Strangers

Refugees and Displacements of Statecraft

NEVZAT SOGUK

BORDERLINES, VOLUME 11

University of Minnesota Press
Minneapolis
London

Portions of the Introduction and chapter 6 were previously published in "Politics of Resistance and Accommodation: Managing Refugee and Immigrant Movements in the Post–Cold War Era," *Current World Leaders: International Issues* 38, no. 2 (April 1995); reprinted by permission of the publisher. Portions of chapter 5 were previously published in "Humanitarian Interventions as Practices of Statecraft: Re-crafting State Sovereignty in Refugee Crises," *Refuge: Canada's Periodical on Refugees* 15, no. 3 (June 1996). Portions of chapter 6 were published in "Predicaments of Territorial Democracy and Statecraft in Europe: How European Democracies Regiment Migratory Movements," *Alternatives: Social Transformation and Humane Governance* 22, no. 3 (July–September 1997); copyright 1997 by Lynne Rienner Publishers, Inc., and used with permission of the publisher. Lines from the poem "The Border," by David Chorlton, were originally published in *Outposts,* by David Chorlton (Exeter, England: Taxus Press, 1994), and are reprinted here by permission of the author.

Published by the University of Minnesota Press
111 Third Avenue South, Suite 290
Minneapolis, MN 55401-2520
http://www.upress.umn.edu

Library of Congress Cataloging-in-Publication Data

Soguk, Nevzat.
States and strangers : refugees and displacements of statecraft / Nevzat Soguk.
p. cm. — (Borderlines ; v. 11)
Includes bibliographical references and index.
ISBN 0-8166-3166-2 (hc : alk. paper). — ISBN 0-8166-3167-0 (pb : alk. paper)
1. Refugees — Legal status, laws, etc. I. Title. II. Series: Borderlines (Minneapolis, Minn.) ; v. 11.
K3230.R45S66 1999
341.4′86—dc21 98-40329

Printed in the United States of America on acid-free paper

10 09 08 07 06 05 04 03 02 01 00 99 10 9 8 7 6 5 4 3 2 1

Contents

Acknowledgments

I owe thanks to many people for their support and encouragement during the course of this study. Special thanks are due Richard K. Ashley, who rigorously and patiently engaged this study, enabling it to develop into the body of work that it now is. Thanks also to Roxanne L. Doty, with whom I had converging interests around the larger theme of international migration, of which refugee movements constitute a face. She has offered many critical insights that have been of inestimable contribution to this study. I cannot pass without thanking Stephen G. Walker, who lent his intellectual and administrative support, without which the research for the study would have been impossible. I also thank the editors of the series, Michael J. Shapiro and David Campbell, for their support and encouragement, Nicholas Xenos, Patricia Molloy, and an anonymous reviewer for instructive comments and suggestions, and Carrie Mullen and Robin A. Moir of the University of Minnesota Press for their guidance and help. Tammy Zambo and Laura Westlund of the Press are to be thanked as well—Tammy Zambo for her meticulous copyediting, and Laura Westlund for making the process as painless as possible. Last, R. B. J. Walker, Brian J. McCormack, Daniel Warner, Jon Goldberg-Hiller, Manfred Henningsen, and numerous students offered their comments on the whole or parts of this study in direct and indirect ways—thank you all. My greatest debt is to Clare for her unabated support for and enthusiasm about this work. This was no surprise, considering the fact that she has worked with refugees for years. Her sensitivity to the practical human realities of displacement has greatly shaped this study. Finally, I dedicate this study to my mother, Neriman Soguk, who has been my lifelong inspiration for inquiry. She has taught me how to ask questions.

Abbreviations

CCIH	California Commission of Immigration and Housing
EU	European Union
HCRFG	High Commissioner for Refugees Coming from Germany
ICEM	Intergovernmental Committee for European Migration
IGCR	Intergovernmental Committee on Refugees
ILO	International Labor Organization
IRO	International Refugee Organization
LNHCR	League of Nations High Commissioner for Refugees
NIOFR	Nansen International Office for Refugees
OAU	Organization of African Unity
OHCAR	Office of the High Commissioner Responsible for All Refugees under the League of Nations' Protection
UN	United Nations
UNHCR	United Nations High Commissioner for Refugees
UNRRA	United Nations Relief and Rehabilitation Agency
USCR	United States Committee for Refugees
USEP	United States Escapees Program

Introduction

Such is your present removal from what you take to be your native land. For by nature there is no such thing as a native land, any more than there is by nature a house or farm or forge or surgery, as Ariston said; but in each case the thing becomes so, or rather is so named and called.

—PLUTARCH

Narratives on Refugees

Along the Austrian-Hungarian border, winding through the fertile Burgenland region of south Vienna, the gaunt steel watchtowers on the eastern side are deserted, relics of the Cold War. On Austrian soil, new look-out platforms have sprung up, manned by army conscripts in sheepskin coats. They are watching not for the march of communism, but for the travelers from Turkey, Romania, Sri Lanka or Bangladesh seeking illegal entry. . . . Most are economic refugees, adds Karl Barilich, Austrian gendarme on patrol in his van. Captured border crossers are taken into an impromptu reception center in bleak rooms at a disused sugar refinery. They are questioned, photographed and given medical checks. After a few hours, those without a *prima facie* case for political asylum are sent back to Hungary.

Financial Times, May 1992

At the close of 1992 the embassy of Denmark in Moscow sent a verbal message to the Russian Ministry of Foreign Affairs. It said that on a dark, misty night a motor vessel without identity markings landed 129 refugees on the Danish Island of Bornholm in the Baltic Sea.

When checked the detainees were found to have neither passports nor entry visas. As it turned out, the citizens with no passports to boast about found themselves on a lifeless patch of land, having completed a fatiguing and dangerous route: Iraq-Jordan-Turkey-Moscow-Tallinn-Bornholm.

Moscow News, February 1993

Four weeks ago, Camill and Michele Iliescu turned out the lights in their Bucharest apartment and set out on an odyssey with their 8-year-old daughter, Ana-Ruxandra. With $100 in their pockets, they rode a cramped train 675 miles through Hungary and Czechoslovakia to Prague, then hitched a ride to the border 70 miles away. At nightfall, the Iliescus set out on foot through the woods to Germany. Thirty-five miles and 20 hours later, they walked into Dresden. The German Red Cross sent the family to a camp. . . . Among the hundreds of Romanians, Bulgarians, Soviets, and other refugees crammed into a former hospital, the Iliescus spend their days waiting for a decision on their request for asylum.

Atlanta Journal and Constitution, May 1991

REFUGEE SCENES, DISCOURSE INCITEMENTS

In recent years, refugee events have unmistakably come to the fore, demanding ever more attention. Contributing in some measure to this visibility is the mobility of millions of peoples in the Middle East, the former Soviet Union and Yugoslavia, and in regions of Africa and the Americas. Enormous political, social, and technological changes and transformations are triggering mass movements of people in search of "better" and "safer" places. Suffering or affected by poverty, famine, natural disasters, military coups, civil wars, or slow-working societal disjunctures, or enamored with the "imagined possibilities" of other "homelands" in distant places, a steady flux of people is expanding the world's "refugee" population. Contributing also to the visibility of the refugee is, ironically, the immobility of people in relation to catastrophic developments. The case of Bosnia and Herzegovina, with thousands of people "immobilized" in towns like Goražde or Tuzla, is a testimony to the "visibility of immobility" as an element of "refugee situations." In other words, novel "refugee" images, thriving in scenes of movements and "nonmovements," continue to proliferate in the face of the traditional conceptualizations of "refugee," gradually blurring the imagined clarity of identity borders and boundaries. They all point to the complexity of the refugee events.

What is most apparent is that the complex reasons for people's movements—their displacements, replacements, banishments, and/or permanent exiles—make it increasingly problematic to speak of refugee events and issues in categorical terms, privileging one or the other refugee image as more worthy of consideration or more deserving of response than others. The categorization of refugee experiences into clear-cut "conceptual incarcerations" no longer elicits unquestioning loyalty, as people themselves infuse into and attribute to their movements crosscurrents of meanings, identities, and objectives (Appadurai, 1988): "Behind the phenomena of moving lie deeper and often interrelated patterns of political, economic, ethnic, environmental, or human rights pressures, which are further complicated by the interplay between domestic and international factors. . . . There are as many reasons for moving as there are migrants" (UNHCR, 1993b: 13).

In their "beginnings," the movements of bodies across as well as within borders might be no more than the quest for a "better" life, however that "better" is defined in the image of the participants. Better, of course, might mean safer, more secure, more peaceful, more plentiful, or even more productive in terms of work, and so on. Whatever it might mean, however, it is lived as real by those who choose to take to the road or are forced to do so.

The realness of the experience of moving the body toward a better life can be seen in an escape from a bullet to the brain in Rwanda, Bosnia, Cambodia, Kurdistan, or Chechnya, or in a piece of bread finding its way to one's stomach. The whole objective of the move could be as simple as "dropping an honest day's sweat on the fields" in distant lands to earn a living (Kearney, 1991: 60). For those who become refugees, moving reflects life's overwhelming necessities for survival.

For instance, for the person on the Rwanda side of the Rwanda-Zaire border, the single most important move at such a specific moment might be to cross to the other side of the river into Zaire. For the Bosnian women in Srebrenica, the act of the moment might be simply to get into a UN truck headed out of a death zone, for to stay behind might mean to face murder or, even more insidiously, rape, a gendered instrument of power employed with brutal regularity against refugee women across cultures and places. For a group of Kurds, men and women about to disembark onto Denmark's shore illegally, the overriding incentive might be the chance to start their broken lives over again. "When I see the shore of Sweden," one such Kurd remarked aloud to an accompanying reporter, "I think it is my motherland, and the day we arrive, I feel, is my birthday" (Kamm, 1993). For the elderly refugee woman, the "illegal refugee" from Guatemala, life's choices boil down to selling a couple of necklaces or a pair of earrings to tourists on a crowded beach in San Diego, California.

There is, in other words, no commonality to the refugee experiences, save the experience of displacement. Similarly, there is no intrinsic paradigmatic refugee figure to be at once recognized and registered regardless of historical contingencies. Instead, it could be argued, there are a thousand multifarious refugee experiences and a thousand refugee figures whose meanings and identities are negotiated in the processes of displacement in time and place.

Amid the ever complex pastiche of refugee events, there is an emergent attitude that poses the question of the refugee precisely from this standpoint, that is, from the standpoint of the complexity and multiplicity of refugee experiences as negotiated by refugees in displacement. This attitude is oriented to comprehend the refugee events and experiences in their polymorphism, in their complexity, by posing the question of the refugee from the standpoint of the ways in which the displaced people, the refugees themselves, labor to constitute and define their experiences of displacement.

This attitude affords a space for the refugees by listening to a plethora of refugee voices. It affords a space, for example, for the testimonies of Bosnian women and children in the UN trucks leading out of Srebrenica, the Chechen men and women tracking their way back to Grozny, or the Rwandan refugees lost in Zairean border towns such as Goma and Bukavu. For these people, the question of the moment is one of life and death just now and just there. For them, uninterested in the familiar official and popular narratives of the "true" refugee, "refugee" means themselves, wanting desperately to get into the UN trucks for transport to "relative safety" out of a death zone or struggling to secure a piece of bread. They cry out hurriedly, "That is all we want to be for now, that is all we can afford to be."

The emergent attitude takes these people seriously and reflects their sense of being and becoming refugees, displaced persons, or something else. In addition to their deprivation and vulnerability, however, this attitude also takes seriously the powers and resourcefulness of these people to remake their lives even in displacement, for example, in a refugee camp, or in re-placement in new places with unfamiliar names, speeches, and mores that are fast familiarized in their determination to survive. It invites one into a richer world of the refugee—"resilient, resourceful and [sometimes even] heroic—of which we know so little" (Peteet, 1995: 177). So, one hears the voices of the Palestinian refugees who, for example, adopt the term *returners* instead of refugees in an attempt to inscribe their identities in their own terms (Peteet, 1995: 177).[1] Among the people of Grozny in Chechnya, Kurds in refugee camps in northern Iraq, Kurds in asylum centers and/or "refugee neighborhoods" in France and Germany, Palestinians in Lebanon, Guatemalan Mayans in Chiapas, Mexico, Bosnians all across Europe, Hutus in Zaire, and Tutsis in Burundi, one realizes, is manifested the capacity of refugees to affect the contours and the quality of their lives even in displacement. Their capacity for agency against all odds in turn manifests new possibilities of living found in the interstices of dramatic changes that nowadays go under the multiple names of interdependence, transnationalization, globalization, and postmodernization of the world in a political-economic sense.

The emergent attitude recognizes the resilience of the refugee but is also sensitive to the relative specificities of refugee experiences along a number of markers such as race, ethnicity, and gender. Doubtless one of the most significant of such markers is gender, which dramatically shapes the countenance of life in displacement. Both men and women are displaced and become refugees, but their "refugee" experiences can be drastically different. While refugee men and refugee women similarly endure many difficulties common to displacement, they also face unique circumstances that reflect gendered historical sociocultural and political practices that often afford more voice, more agency, and more privileges to refugee men largely at the expense of refugee women, their voices, and their agency. Typically, for example, refugee women are seen and treated as already subordinate to their male counterparts. As Jacqueline Bhabha and Sue Shutter put it, they are perceived as a mere "appendage" to refugee men (1994: 6). This perception amounts to depriving refugee women of the meaningful capacity to shape their "refugeed" lives.

Their perceived subordination is harnessed to practical processes of refugee governance, whether in flight or in refugee camps, by which refugee women are left almost without agency. If refugee men suffer from the reality of a single displacement—a physical displacement—refugee women suffer from a double displacement—a physical displacement from the home community and a symbolic and at times violent displacement from agency altogether.

The emergent attitude urges a reconsideration of territorializing national, ethnic, economic, cultural, and aesthetic identities amid the transversal ambiguities of a world ever in ferment. It reminds one that there are a thousand different ways to be and to feel displaced in the exhilarations of the world. It does so through increasingly persistent voices that remind us, as Julia Kristeva (1991) and Daniel Warner (1992, 1994) do, that in a sense we are all refugees and strangers: we are all "strangers to ourselves" even in the heart of the imagined spaces of identity and difference we call "fatherlands and motherlands." Long ago, preceding Kristeva, Friedrich Nietzsche forcefully argued the same point in *On the Genealogy of Morals* (1969). William E. Connolly (1989) takes up Nietzsche's line to suggest that we are deeply "homesick" for the identity "homes" (of the cultural, political, and aesthetic kind) that we have never had and are likely never to have (see also Warner, 1992; 1994: 167–68). In the midst of imagined communities, Connolly (1989) and Benedict Anderson (1994) assert that, inasmuch as we are not "men and women of knowledge" with respect to ourselves, we are in some sense nomads, wanderers, that is, refugees, though driven by different concerns and circumstances. Guillermo Gómez-Peña generalizes this view by arguing that in our search for ourselves in a thousand acts of deterritorialization, we are all becoming "border-crossers," though never finally leaving our familiar old places and never finally arriving in familiarized new places (1996: 102). Ours, one might suggest, is an impossible politics of nostalgia, one of "returning to a world of equations and alignments that never was and can never be" (Warner, 1994: 168). "Every refugee," K. C. Cirtautas writes,

> regardless of nationality, race or creed points to the refugee within ourselves. . . . By maintaining that the refugee points to the refugee within ourselves, we mean that man is often not at home within

> himself, within his family, within his city, within his country or within his society. . . . The life of the actual refugee is much closer to nonrefugee than it appears to be at first sight. His nightmares and travails, his misery and courage reflect the traumatic experiences of every human being who is in perennial search for "home." (1963: 13–14)

Edward Said might call this "perennial search" the state of permanent exile. But the Caribbean Edouard Glissant has a more optimistic reading, in which the state of permanent exile is seen not as disempowerment in displacement but simply as a "tale of movement, a tale of errantry" that affirms life precisely in displacement, in exile, or in refugeeness. "The tale of errantry," Glissant suggests, "is a tale of relation," in which identities are "no longer completely within the root but also in Relation" and there is a certain poetics to the "Relation" born in migratory encounters. This poetics of relation intimates that human experiences are about the "thing relayed as well as the thing related": "It is not merely an encounter, a shock, . . . a *metissage,* but a new and original dimension allowing each person to be there and elsewhere, rooted and open, lost in mountains and free beneath the sea, in harmony and in errantry" (1997: 34). Glissant's is a practical ontological shift informed by an epistemological rethinking of movement that, instead of focusing exclusively on the borders and roots, focuses on the moments or events of "relaying" one's stories and "relating" to others' stories in a "relation," in other words, in the "borderization" of life. It is at these moments or events that we become border crossers—refugees, exiles, tourists, transnational laborers, or the like—and realize, as Trinh T. Minh-ha articulates, that "other than ourselves, our rooted selves, is our other selves, our migrancy, our refugeeness" (1997: 9).

Of course, this is not to argue that the experiences of men and women in Grozny, Chechnya, or Goma, Zaire, are the same as those of Kristeva in Paris, Said in New York, or Connolly in Baltimore. Rather, it is to suggest that the identity of the nonrefugee—for instance, the citizen—is always contingent, never fully fixed—"always mobile and processual, partly self-construction, partly categorization by others, partly a condition, a status, a label, a weapon, a shield, a fund of memories . . . a creolized aggregate" (Daniel and Knudsen, 1995: 6). It is to argue that just as the identity of the refugee is always contingent, so is the identity of the nonrefugee.

When one thinks of it, there are a thousand different ways to be and to feel displaced in this world. The emergent attitude takes all this seriously.

This attitude might be called a genealogical attitude, an attitude that poses the question of the refugee not from the standpoint of a single paradigm that "conceptually incarcerates" the refugee, but from a standpoint that recognizes the contingency, multiplicity, and complexity of refugee events and experiences in order to be able to hear and to take seriously the muffled but persistent voices of refugees themselves in Bosnia, in Chechnya, in Rwanda, in Iraq, in Turkey, in Kosovo, and in Burma and Vietnam.

As refugees occupy an ever more visible place in everyday landscapes locally and globally, the genealogical attitude is brought to bear upon the question of the refugee, however marginally and tentatively.[2] Although this is increasingly the case, the prevailing conventional discourse on the subject of the refugee remains rooted in a certain paradigmatic hierarchy of interpretation that negates the multiplicity and polymorphism of refugee events and experiences. The prevailing discourse on human displacement, on human estrangement, seems, in fact, very strange, and by strange I mean an estrangement that is always in the process of being effected, day in and day out, in a mélange of displacement events and occurrences. It is a strange discourse of displacement, for it has no place for the displaced humans, a discourse on the question of the refugee that affords no place for the refugee and the refugee's voice. Indeed, it is largely blind to the refugee herself as a subject who might be capable of initiating and leading a resilient and productive life even "in displacement," as is indeed the case everyday across the globe.[3]

Who is a refugee? What are the causes of refugee flows? What are the effects of refugee events? What instruments might be effective in bringing refugee situations under control? How might people be made to understand the need to do what must be done if the problem of the refugee is to be managed? These are the questions that have undergirded the refugee discourse in the past and that continue to do so today. Yet in this discourse the refugee remains silent, voiceless, figuring only as a lack. Suspended indefinitely in a void without a homeland, as one United Nations High Commissioner for Refugees (UNHCR) representation puts it, the refugee's life is desperately simple, and empty. No home, no work, no decisions to take today. And none to take tomorrow. Or the next day. Refugees are the victims of persecution and violence. Most hope that, one day, they may be able to rebuild their lives in a sympathetic environment. To exist again in more than name. (UNHCR, 1993a: 48)

This, the voicelessness of the refugee, I want to argue, is the *effect* of the refugee discourse, not the refugee's essence or the peculiarity of the refugee's existence in life, whether in flight in Bosnia, in inertia in cities like Grozny, in camps in northern Iraq or northwestern Zaire, or in the provinces and metropolises of Europe and North America. I want to ask *how* this effect is made to happen and, even more importantly, for what purposes. Still more importantly, however, I want to ask what the discourse on refugees does, once it is articulated and put into circulation. How is it that the discourse of the refugee announces itself as a privileged discourse oriented to helping the refugee yet all the while manages to afford no place for the refugee? This is, I would accentuate here, a question of power.

How, then, is this discourse one in which the refugee figures prominently only to be subjected to a treatment, a regimentation, that deprives the refugee of a place, a voice, and an agency to effect contingent changes in his or her life? This is the question I want to pose. However, I am interested in much more than the question of how this discourse is produced. Theoretically, I am also interested in the question of what the discourse does "in the real" once it is in circulation in multiple fields of policy and conduct, including national and international security, democracy, economic and social welfare, human rights, and humanitarianism. What does it do?

REFUGEE SCENES, CONVENTIONAL DISCOURSES: REFUGEES AS OBJECTS OF THE CITIZEN/NATION/STATE HIERARCHY

Studies that represent the conventional discourse (or attitude) on refugees start from the premise that the modern citizen, occupying a bounded territorial community of citizens, is the proper subject of political life: the principal agent of action, the source of all meaning of value, and the point of decision to which, ultimately, all matters of political uncertainty must recur.[4] In turn, these studies understand the modern state as a creature of representation. Not grasped as a metaphysical source of meaning, the state is understood to derive its powers from the citizens it represents, the citizens who author the state by way of a covenant or social compact that accords certain powers to the state, the citizens for whom, in return, the state deploys law, force, and rational administrative resources in order to guarantee certain protections.

These studies comprehend the complexities of political life and offer solutions to arising problems in terms of participation, representation, and protection in the bounded space of presupposed particularity and difference, that is, in sovereign territory of which, presumably, the citizen is the constitutive agent and the state is the representative agent. According to this understanding, it is the community of citizens (the nation) that empowers the state, and it is the community of citizens (the nation) that the state claims to represent and protect within the clearly demarcated locale called the sovereign national territory.

Starting from this premise, these studies then, and only then, define the refugee as one who lacks the citizen's unproblematic grounding within a territorial space and, so, lacks the effective representation and protection of a state. While the citizen remains rooted in the territorial space, the refugee is seen as uprooted, dislocated, displaced, forced out, or self-displaced from the community of citizens. This is the refugee's identity—his ascribed identity. The refugee is one who lacks affinity with the national community.

Narratives on Refugees

> A man's status as a refugee is determined, first and foremost, by the factors which led to his condition: expatriation and the breaking of [the] ties that bound him to the state of his nationality. The emotional reaction of a social group to the refugee is both complex and ambivalent. There is not only pity, but also an element of anxiety. The refugee is, in the first place, a symbol of *instability*. . . . The refugee symbolizes, in the second place, *isolation*. Social groups react almost with an instinctive mistrust of those who have been cut off or who voluntarily cut themselves off from the community to which they belong by origin or by adoption. Lastly, the refugee is the *unknown*. . . . He is no longer on his land, he has fled his country, he has been cast out by his group, or by those who speak in the name of the national group of which he was a member. The refugee is therefore one whose ties have been doubly cut, both his territorial ties and those with the national group, or, rather, with the state which is its legal expression.

> What stamps the refugee as a man apart, justifying his classification in a specific social category, is his *inferiority;* he is inferior both to the citizens of the country which gives him shelter and all the other foreigners, not refugees, living in that country.
>
> Jacques Vernant
> *The Refugee in the Post-war World* (emphasis added)

In a world imagined to be composed of mutually exclusive, territorially bound spaces, the refugee figures only as an aberration of the proper subjectivity of citizenship; lacking the posited qualities of the citizen, she does not properly belong anywhere. She remains homeless even if she dwells in a house, "a helpless casualty, diminished in all circumstances, the victim of events for which, at least as an individual, [s]he cannot be held responsible" (Vernant, 1953: 3). Her relationship to a space of sovereignty must be redefined so that she may once again belong in this or another "national" space properly through either repatriation or resettlement (both of which are forms of reterritorialization), so that she can "once again enjoy protection as [a] full-fledged [member] of a national community." (UN General Assembly, 1993: 2.3). Thus, conventional studies attribute the proliferation of refugee bodies (and, hence, the emergence of the refugee problem) to the rise of circumstances that exceed the limits of action within the realm of individual territorial states. They argue that refugee bodies, by virtue of their movements and inertia, overflow the boundaries of the individual state and so exceed the capacity of the state to deal with them unilaterally within the sovereign space (Hope-Simpson, 1939; Stoessinger, 1956; Robinson, 1953; Gordenker, 1987; Gallagher, 1989; Dacyl, 1990).

From such diagnoses, conventional studies then proceed to consider how the emergence of international regimes might work to solve the problem, still within the context of sovereign territorial states but at a different level (Skran, 1995; Dacyl, 1990). In other words, in the face of the limitations of unilateral activities to resolve the refugee problem, the range of possible responses or solutions is seen in the emergence of international regimes (Krasner, 1982; Kratochwil and Ruggie, 1994; Haggard and Simmons, 1987; Ruggie, 1993a), which, as mechanisms of policy coordination and harmonizing among states, might work to rectify the refugee-generating conditions and circumstances and, in so doing, reaffirm the "normal" territorial order of life activities around the constellation of citizen/nation/state (Gallagher, 1988; Dacyl, 1990; Rogers, 1992; UN General Assembly, 1993: 2.1).

Consider, for example, the following introduction to a 1993 UNHCR study on refugee protection entitled *Note on International Protection,* which was submitted to the General Assembly, articulating the problems of refugee protection and policy alternatives in order to address these problem areas. The note is useful in that it conveniently summarizes the history of the international regime for refugee protection, of which I have thus far spoken in theoretical terms. It is important further for, with its peculiar assumptions and postulations as to the proper subjects, objects, and agents and the rules, norms, and principles that regulate the activities and identify the tasks, it embodies in its representation of the refugee problem the cardinal postulation on the territorially rooted hierarchy of citizen/nation/state.

> The international response to the plight of refugees—culminating in a virtually universal consensus that people forced by violence or persecution to flee their countries should receive international protection—is one of the most remarkable humanitarian achievements of this century. Building on foundations laid by the first High Commissioner for Refugees, Fridtjof Nansen, beginning in 1921, the international community has progressively developed the structure and practice of international protection, elaborating and consolidating a system of legal principles and norms and, most importantly, providing asylum to millions of refugees.
>
> The international legal framework for the protection of refugees now has the explicit support of 121 State Parties to the 1951 Convention Relating to the Status of Refugees, its 1967 Protocol, or both. Many of these states are also parties to the 1969 OAU [Organization of African Unity] Convention governing the specific aspects of refugee problems in Africa, or adhere to the principles of the 1984 Cartagena Declaration on Refugees. The vast majority of States confronted with refugee situations observe the fundamental principles of refugee protection in granting asylum to persons in need of protection. Having entrusted to the High Commissioner, under the auspices of the United Nations, the task of ensuring the international protection of refugees, States regularly extend to the office the cooperation and support that are essential to the discharge of its functions. The human solidarity thus manifested by governments is inspired and reinforced by that of the people they represent. Despite the economic and social burdens

> involved, action to protect and assist refugees still enjoys widespread popular support throughout the world, support that is also expressed through vigorous and effective action by non-governmental organizations working alongside UNHCR in every region of the world.
>
> The international community's response to the problems of refugees must at the same time be viewed against the somber background of armed conflict and human rights abuses which force people to flee in ever-increasing numbers. Refugee flows are a symptom of failure to prevent, respond to or resolve crises at home, and the presence of well over eighteen million refugees in the world today is an indication of social disruption and personal tragedy on a massive scale. International protection as provided by countries of asylum in cooperation with the UNHCR is an effort to compensate for the protection that refugees should have received in their own countries, and its objective is not fulfilled until refugees once again enjoy protection as full-fledged members of a national community. (UN General Assembly, 1993: 2.1–2.3)

What is clear in this imagery is that refugees are seen as a problem existing prior to international regime activities, while the regime activities are represented as solutions to that difficult, morally demanding but not intractable problem of the refugee within the otherwise presumably unproblematic, stable, and secure territorial bounds of the sovereign state (Gallagher, 1989; Guest, 1991; Aleinikoff, 1991; Gordenker, 1987; Ferris, 1993a; Zolberg et al., 1986; Loescher, 1993). Theoretically, this view of the international refugee regime derives from a specifically functionalist conceptualization of international regimes. In conventional studies, international regimes are conceptualized as legal institutions around which the policy-oriented expectations of actors converge in specific issue areas (Kratochwil and Ruggie, 1994: 9). The instruments of such institutions or arrangements are issue-driven "principles, norms, rules, and decision-making procedures" that produce an intersubjectivity of knowledge among actors as to how to deal with what all the parties perceive as a common problem (Krasner, 1994: 99; E. Haas, 1994: 365). The efficiency and efficacy of international regimes derive precisely from this built-in regime quality—the generation, through norms, rules, and so on, of intersubjectivity among actors that in turn produces a "transparent" legal environment within which actors collaborate to tackle the common problems (Kratochwil and Ruggie, 1994: 10). In sum, in these studies the constellation of citizen/nation/state is regarded as primary; the refugee is accorded a secondary status, as an aberration of the prior norm; and international regimes, as a tertiary relation, are comprehended as mechanisms by which, in the face of a problem already there, an established, already effective territorial order might creatively orient and deploy its resources to resolve the aberration, close the circle, and affirm the hierarchy of citizen/nation/state once more.

REFUGEE SCENES, INTERPRETIVE REVERSALS: REFUGEES AS INTERNATIONAL ACTORS

Seen against the background of such a formulation of refugee issues, this study can be understood to start from a genealogical retheorization of the refugee problem based on a series of conceptual and practical departures. First, the study does not regard the sovereign state as an agent of global politics whose powers are unproblematically attributed to it by virtue of its representation of a bounded citizenry (domestic community) already in place and occupying an exclusionary territory (the space of sovereignty). Rather, it starts by posing the question of the state in terms of the problem of modern statecraft, a problem that goes to the heart of the practices of modern statecraft in local and global politics (Ashley, 1989b; 1993). It is a problem of how to inscribe, stabilize, and render effective a certain figure of the citizen that the modern state would represent and on the basis of which the modern state would claim to effect its sovereignty, its powers, and indeed its right to rule over a territorial inside—the domestic community of citizens. So the study starts with a question that the conventional studies on the question of the refugee do not pose: How is a certain figure of the citizen inscribed and institutionalized across the space, thus to speak of a domestic community of citizens whose will and desires the sovereign state then can represent? To answer this question, the study looks to refugee events and occurrences in global politics to suggest that they prove instrumental to this task of statecraft.

Second, not presupposing a prior, already fixed territoriality of political life, this study does not reduce the refugee to an aberration of the supposed proper subjectivity of the territorially bound citizen as represented in the conventional studies. Rather, it acknowledges the inherent difficulties in distinguishing and categorizing complex life experiences into those of the refugee and those of the citizen based on a prior presence of the context of state sovereignty as an already fixed and stable context, a finished project. As a corollary, it does not understand the refugee experience in terms of a loss of and/or exclusion from the protection that is presumed possible only within a national space and a national community represented and protected by the sovereign state.[5]

This study does not see refugees merely as problems, as represented in conventional studies. Rather, it contends that historically refugee presences have had paradoxical implications for the practices of state sovereignty in that they have been both disruptive (problematic) and recuperative (resourceful) of sovereignty practices. By the paradoxical implications of refugee presences, I refer to contingent moments of history when the presence of refugees has become both a "problem" to be addressed and a "resource" to be employed in the service of discursive yet converging social and political practices of representation that constitute the realities (the images, identities, subjectivities, and relations) of the sovereign territorial state.

On the one hand, refugees such as the Iliescu family in Germany or the Kurds in Denmark are fundamentally resistant to territorializing statist practices. As refugees, they transgress political, cultural, and socioeconomic borders and boundaries, often in the face of loud protests by those who claim control and mastery over those borders and boundaries. "Although they are unwanted," writes David Marsh, "they come from all directions" (1992). Adds Grzegorz Cydejko, "[T]hey come without documents and passports"(1993). The movements of "refugees," or their inertia, point to the unsettling of loyalties to familiar identities and localities. Perhaps unwittingly, refugees and the complexity of their experiences contest the seemingly axiomatic and atavistic "realities" of life, such as membership in a clan, tribe, or profession, or in a domestic community signifying a nation. As the German novelist Günter Grass points out, refugees become "irritants to the rigid orders of the self" (1993: 188), constantly reminding others of the arbitrariness and contingence of identity borders and boundaries. In this way, refugees help remake the conventional language in which the tales of the so-called citizenry, national community, and territorial state are told.

Paradoxically, it is at the very moments of undesirability that the presence of refugees and their images affords opportunities for participants in practices of statecraft. The practical force of their presence at the juncture of identity boundaries is negotiated, mediated, co-opted, and deployed as a referential resource useful in the production and empowerment of symbolic, metaphorical, formal, and institutional resources (along racial, social, cultural, and economic lines) to which states turn for anchor and for their own empowerment. Refugee images, represented in and through the vocabularies of "invasion," "flood," and "plague," serve as fertile grounds of reference. It is such a dynamic of representation that allows Vyacheslaw S. Srychev, the Moscow Interior Ministry's Department of Counterintelligence head in Russia, to inscribe the refugee as a threat to the "health of Russia": "Now we are speaking of refugees, more often than not, they are accommodated in our ecologically safe districts. . . . These people include a large number of persons threatening seriously the epidemiological situation" (Kremlin International News broadcast, 31 March 1993). The referentiality of refugees partakes in legal, economic, cultural, and political activities that attribute ontological antecedence to and privilege the citizen as the a priori proper agent adequate to the task of domestic community, the state as the facilitator of the conditions of community and their protector, and the sovereign territory of the state as the exclusive space where the domestic community becomes possible. Listen again to Srychev, who outlines to the public the state's efforts to control the foreigner situation: "So I can tell you that the other day, we jointly with the Ministry of the Interior, carried out the Operation Regime" to arrest the epidemiological danger—the refugee (Kremlin International News broadcast, 31 March 1993).

Third, exploring such junctures of complex referentiality and imagery, this book regards refugees not merely as problem-presences but as referential resources in the carrying out of what Michel Foucault calls "problematizations," which render refugees as affirmative resources for statist practices. "Problematization," writes Foucault,

> does not mean representation of a pre-existing object, nor the creation by discourse of an object that does not exist. It is the totality of discursive and non-discursive practices that introduces something into the play of true and false and constitutes it as an object for thought (whether in the form of moral reflection, scientific knowledge, political analysis, etc.). (1988a: 257)

Elsewhere, Foucault writes that problematization is the work of thought that

> transforms the difficulties and obstacles of a practice into a general problem for which one proposes diverse political solutions. It is problematization that responds to these difficulties, but by doing something quite other than expressing them or manifesting them: in connection with them it develops the conditions in which responsible responses can be given; it defines the elements that will constitute what the different solutions attempt to respond to. (1984: 389)

To the extent that refugees may be resistant, posing certain practical difficulties to the statist practices that work constantly to inscribe imaginary and/or physical boundaries of identity/difference that separate the inside from the outside, "us" from "them," and "the citizen" from "the refugee," they become objects of acts of problematization. The objective of problematization is to neutralize and accommodate the specific difficulties posed by refugee presences by reinscribing (and limiting) the meanings and identities of the difficulties themselves.[6] This is achieved best by reintroducing the refugee difficulties as a set of distinct questions or problems for which solutions could be formulated without drastically transforming the state-oriented logic that underpins practices of statecraft.

Refugee problematizations are, then, "knowledgeable" sets of orchestrated and coordinated activities that incorporate a specific figure of the refugee into the field of state practices in the form of a problematic body with peculiar characteristics, attributes, and experiences. This reintroduction is simultaneously an opening up of a specific refugee space of identity/difference and the conditioning of its content by imposing on it a distinct ontological and epistemological order that normalizes the refugee in congruence with the operative logic of practices of statecraft.

Refugee problematizations working in the task of statecraft occur in activities that (a) *incite* a popular and institutional discourse on refugees, (b) *statize,* that is, *inscribe* and *represent* the refugee event as a specific problem of and before the sovereign state, and (c) *regiment,* namely, *formulate* and *channel* imaginable statist solutions to the refugee problem in reply. Inasmuch as problematization is the constitution of discursive fields of identity, enabling and conditioning simultaneously, the crucial activity is not so much to produce and stabilize the identity and meanings of refugee experiences as to produce and stabilize the field of the refugee as a field wherein it becomes possible to engage in the politics of identity construction on an ongoing basis. It is through ongoing constitution and reproduction of the fields of identity and governance that the categories of agency—the citizen, the refugee, the beggar, the soldier—and the categories of identity—safety, stability, security, and freedom, as well as danger, instability, and insecurity—become viable and profitable in the nexuses of power relations. The processes by which a specific figure of the refugee is obtained and institutionalized become instrumental in the practices of statecraft, working to produce, transform, and stabilize the images and identities of specific hierarchies in statist terms, such as that of citizen and refugee and of inside and outside. Within the context of the sovereign territorial state, refugee problematizations affirm and privilege the postulated hierarchy of the citizen/nation/state constellation by conditioning and limiting the possibilities of actions and their meanings as to who is a citizen or who is a refugee or what the boundaries of sovereign statehood are or should be.

The privileging of the citizen/nation/state ensemble as the hierarchical imperative to life activities is not unsurprising, for the hierarchy of this triad of agents and identities is indispensable to any narrative of modern political life. What is important here is how refugees figure in relation to the hierarchy that is posited to be already in existence through prevailing relations and institutions of governance, participation, accountability, and representation. It is here that the refugee presence works as a useful referential resource, for the refugee's presence is so problematized as to privilege—to render as the most proper and most desirable—the hierarchy of citizen/nation/state.

What makes this privileging possible in the field of international refugee events are specific problematizations that articulate and circulate specific refugee figures in relation to specific essential tasks, such as the security, the stability, the welfare, and the self-governance of the community. Relative to these tasks, more often than not, the refugee subjectivity is inscribed negatively (particularly when coupled with that of an immigrant) as a lack or an aberrance, suspended indefinitely in a void, cut off from the land, the home, the homeland, the bounded community, and the nation. Problematized as such, refugees figure as lacking the citizen-subject's secure home, the citizen-subject's secure sociocultural affiliations, the citizen-subject's shared understandings with other citizen-subjects (which are indispensable to welfare and democracy), and the citizen-subject's secure ties to a community, of which the sovereign state is the representative and protector. Lacking proper ties to a community of citizens, refugees also lack proper ties to the state; they lack the state's protection and representation, thus further complicating the spatiotemporal arrangements that make democracy, welfare, and national security possible. In all, lacking those ties and qualities, they are seen as incapable of participating as effective, knowledgeable actors in the tasks essential to the efficient and orderly organization of the community—obtaining security, stability, welfare, and self-governance. It is here that refugee problematizations turn referentially resourceful, for at this moment it becomes possible to convincingly suggest that, let alone effectively participating in the process and projects of the community, refugees are or can be disruptive of those processes and projects, precisely because they lack in certain essential qualities and ties that constitute the community and allow for the establishment and stabilization of, for example, the institutions of democracy or welfare. Refugees do not properly belong to the nation, and as such they represent disruptions in the conditions of normality in life imagined in terms of the hierarchy of the citizen/nation/state ensemble (Huysmans, 1995; Den Boer, 1995). They must be regimented, even during those times when they deserve compassion and pity, lest the conditions of territorially bound life—the conditions of its welfare, of its ability for self-governance, of its security, or of its health, as the Russian colonel might say—irreversibly deteriorate into anarchy. In facing such a specter, for those who are imagined to properly belong to the nation, the operative motto might just become (as is the case nowadays), "The citizens of the nation unite against refugees, asylum seekers, and other displaced peoples under the state," that is, if those citizens want to protect their security, their welfare, and their democracy. So, for instance, as I show in chapter 5, refugees become targets of so-called humanitarian interventions in which the humanitarianism is generally subordinated to the exigencies of statism and in which intervention works to confine refugees in their "original" countries, in effect creating a new category of displaced humans: the "internally displaced." Or, as I show in chapter 6, in facing refugees and other displaced people, even exemplary democracies across Europe, universalist in their foundational rhetoric, nevertheless turn particularist, with their exclusivist particularisms articulated to the dynamics of the citizen/nation/state ensemble. So I am not surprised when I read in newspapers that "from Sweden to Spain, European governments fearing that a wave of asylum-seekers threatens prosperity and social cohesion have tightened access to and eligibility for asylum" (*Migration News,* June 1994).

In light of this, what I am suggesting is that the figure of the refugee is anything but the marginal problem-body it is conventionally seen to be. On the contrary, this figure appears at the intersections of power relations. The presence of groups of people marked as "refugees" becomes party to a specific problematization: the interplay of "connections, encounters, supports, blockages, plays of forces, strategies and so on which at a given moment establish what subsequently counts as being self-evident, universal and necessary" (Foucault, 1991: 76). Put more specifically, the site of the refugee, conceived in a variety of activities, becomes a site of modern statecraft.

Fourth, the book looks specifically to international refugee regime practices revolving around a number of intergovernmental instruments regarding the refugee. However, it understands regime practices not as tertiary responses to difficulties of the already present refugee bodies, but as modes of intergovernmental regimentations intimately involved in the active production and stabilization of what counts as the effective boundaries of sovereign statehood and citizenship in contemporary global life. In other words, the study does not relegate international regimes to the status of tertiary responses initiated by already empowered states in response to emergent problems and dangers that their citizens might regard as threatening. It sees regime activities as activities of statecraft that, to the extent they may succeed, reproduce and reaffirm contingent images, identities, subjectivities, relations, and institutions of sovereign statehood and citizenship amid circumstances of historical change.

REFUGEE PROBLEMATIZATIONS, INTERNATIONAL REGIMENTATIONS, AND STATECRAFT

Taking these four points, it may be said that this study reverses the familiar logical hierarchy of interpretation based on the posited constellation of citizen/nation/state. It does so by considering three puzzles on the question of the refugee. The first puzzle centers on the question of whether it is possible to retheorize the refugee discourse as one of the many boundary-producing discourses instrumental to the task of statecraft. Put differently, the first puzzle centers on the question of how the refugee problematizations might work in the constitutions and representations of the relations, institutions, and subjectivities of the sovereign state in local and global politics. The second puzzle revolves around the question of how these problematizations might be generated in a multilateral fashion, that is, through international regimes as activities of intergovernmental regimentation. And finally, the third puzzle is articulated around the question of how these activities of intergovernmental regimentation are imbricated and bound up with the articulations of a number of fundamental projects and practices in life, including human rights, humanitarianism, security, and democracy and democratic practices.

Responding to these puzzles, the study first looks to the ways in which the figure of the refugee has been historically problematized. It argues that the figure of the refugee in its historical articulations and transformations has been instrumental to the task of statecraft, that is, it has been instrumental to the enabling of a specific imagination of the world as a world organized in terms of the posited subjectivities, relations, and institutions of the modern territorial state. Second, it turns to international regime practices. It argues that international refugee regime practices, while purportedly concentrating on the problem of the refugee, might in fact be intimately involved in the active production and stabilization of what counts as the territorial being of the modern citizen, the very ground of the sovereign state—the citizen-man who, aware of the dangers and desirous of peace and security, constantly reproduces, in cooperation with other citizen-men, the covenant or social compact delegating power and authority to the state.

More specifically, in reversing the logic of interpretation, the study combines historical-archival research with interpretive strategies of genealogical research to pose the following question: How do activities of "international regimentation"—from the representation of the refugee problem, through the incitement of discourse in reply, to the channeling of imaginable responses—configure a space of the refugee, recognized as an idealized space of the refugee, as a point of reference for the rearticulations of state sovereignty in various fields of political conduct: security, human rights, democracy, humanitarian intervention? More simply, how do specific representations of the refugee become instrumental in the activities of statecraft that, in order for the state to exist, (must) constantly labor to produce the ground on which the sovereign territorial state can perform its representational function?"

The study poses these questions in the context of international regimes, since it argues that international regimes establish and foster an effective realm of statecraft in producing a repertoire of referential images that underlie the figure of the state. It contends that, in the face of a proliferation of challenges that undermine the long-dominant image of the global terrain as organized into a multiplicity of territorially bounded, sovereign spaces occupied by respective communities of citizens and represented by states, international regime practices work to incite, condition, and instruct the trajectories of viable actions, "defining the questions we need to respond to, the solutions we are compelled to search for and the ways in which we might just be able to solve or bring under control the problems and dangers of 'anarchy'"(Ashley, 1993). It further contends that, understood this way, the practices of international regimentation constitute what might be called a "conductorless orchestration of political activities"(Bourdieu, 1977: 73) by which, in spite of all sorts of challenges, the territorially grounded figures of the citizen and the state are recuperated and reaffirmed as yet primary and indispensable to the organization of global life.

The study suggests that a retheorization of the refugee elucidates the processes—the international regime activities as activities of regimentation—by which the "conductorless orchestration" of global political life produces the effects of citizenry and sovereign statehood, as it were, as the unquestionable practical realities of the day. It contends that the very presence of "refugee bodies" is incorporated as part of that orchestration into Foucauldian "true and false" plays within particular issue areas or fields of conduct, and is then transformed and regimented into specific refugee "problematizations" that play strategic roles in the rearticulations of state sovereignty and its principal agent, the state. From this perspective, it is plausible to theorize that the international and intergovernmental responses to refugee movements—from the *incitement* of formal or institutional discourse in reply, through *statization,* that is, the representation of the refugee problem as a specific problem of the sovereign state, to *regimenting*, namely, the channeling of imaginable concrete policy responses—are (or should be understood as) manifestations of the transformations of territorial governance.

For scholars and practitioners alike who are interested in the norms and processes of international governance, the study notes the possibility and the payoff of thinking about regimes in the active voice—in terms of the regimentation of subjective and objective positions (ways of interpreting problems and dangers and of conditioning possible responses) that are manifested in "rules, regulations, norms, [and] principles," and that work to stabilize the interpretation of the problems and dangers to which international regimes purportedly reply (Ashley, 1989a; 1993). The implications of such "internationalizing" or "intergovernmentalizing" stabilization for the viability and practical force of the state-oriented accounts of life—the citizen, nation, territory, community, democracy, human rights, and security—are vital.

THE BOOK IN BRIEF

Recognizing the significance of the "refugee" category for the practices of statecraft in international, national, and global relations, this study explores several aspects of multifaceted "refugee" issues. It commences by arguing that the history of the practices of statecraft, at least in European history, which is the primary historical focus of the study, has been bound up with, although surely not reducible to, the history of specific refugee problematizations.[7]

In chapter 1, the study establishes the theoretical linkages between the articulations of the refugee and refugeeness and the practices of statecraft. To show the ways in which the figure of the refugee becomes party to the task of statecraft, the study looks into conventional refugee representations to see how the refugee is ordinarily narrated and how its content—meanings, images, and identities—is negotiated, inscribed, and established in terms that bespeak a statist imagination of the world. The study maintains that the crafting of the state as a practical force in local and global politics takes place in multiple fields of statecraft constituted across times and places. Chapter 1 formulates a set of theoretical arguments on statecraft and refugees to establish that the refugee field, constituted in and through international regime practices as practices of intergovernmental regimentation, works as one of many fields of statecraft in which the contingent subjectivities, relations, and institutions of the state are produced, empowered, and circulated in history.

Chapter 2 is an analysis of the historical emergence and evolution of the category of the refugee in relation to the emergence and transformation of the identities and powers of the sovereign state and its counterparts, the citizen-subject and the domestic community of citizen-subjects. The chapter traces the relationship between, on the one hand, the refugee category in particular and the phenomenon of "human displacement" in general, and, on the other hand, practices and processes of statist governance from the late seventeenth century to the early twentieth century to argue that events of human displacement of which refugee events constitute one variety are intimately intertwined with the practices and processes of sovereign territorializing statecraft.

Chapters 3 and 4 examine the conceptual, organizational, and regimental development of the "international refugee regime" from the League of Nations in the 1920s and 1930s to the United Nations (from its inception to the present). This part of the study draws primarily on intergovernmental practices around the names of the League of Nations and the United Nations. The analyses in these chapters in large measure effect a radical rereading of the international refugee regime against a historical-archival and conventional, scholarly backdrop of refugee matters. A body of now voluminous theoretical work on international regimes by neoliberal institutionalists, which has formulated the conventional accounts of the international refugee regime based on a variant of the notion of the collective good, affords a point of critical departure for these chapters.

Chapter 3 is a retheorization of the refugee regime through a genealogical rereading of its history, particularly a rereading of the early history of regime activities from 1921 until 1930, by which refugee regimentations were thoroughly formalized and institutionalized under the auspices of the League of Nations. It is, in other words, a retheorization of the international refugee regime as contingent sets of refugee regimentation that have acquired a peculiar programmatic rationality of statist governmentality formulated in and through the League of Nations High Commissioner for Refugees (LNHCR) from 1921 until 1930.

Chapter 4 is an analysis of the practices of regimentation of the refugee from the 1930s until the present. The histories of a series of successive organizations established to deal with the refugee events and occurrences after 1930—from the Nansen International Office for Refugees, to the International Refugee Organization, to the United Nations High Commissioner for Refugees—are examined with a view to identifying ontological and programmatic continuities and shifts in refugee regimentations. This genealogical retheorization of the refugee regime, its supposed logic, its reasons and justifications, and its historical and contemporary difficulties serves also as a critical retheorization of the theories of international regimes.

The study maintains that as refugees' numbers increase, a wide range of regimentation activities work not so much to control the physical flow and mobility of peoples (for people flow in and out in the face of all kinds of barriers), but to problematize those movements as a way of effecting or imposing limits on contemporary political, social, and cultural trajectories of local and global life. It is in these sorts of problematizations that much-needed rearticulations of the state, sovereignty, security, stability, and order are obtained, however temporary and contingent they might be.

Around a variety of representations and problematizations of "refugees as reference points," chapters 5 and 6 examine how contemporary refugee representations as sovereignty practices constitute strategic discourses on and of security, human rights (humanitarian intervention), and democracy, all of which are linked epistemologically and ontologically to the discourse of sovereignty (as the informing logic of "normal" and "secure" lives). The following questions seem helpful here: How do refugee images enter into discussions in different issue areas and fields of activity, such as those of identity, security, and human rights? How do people speak of refugees? or, how are refugees talked about, written about, and referred to in the course of ordinary, everyday affairs? What vocabularies are deployed in speeches and stories on refugees? Put simply, what becomes possible by referring to refugee bodies as refugees?

In light of these questions, in chapter 5 the study looks into the linkages between the shifting discourse of humanitarianism, human rights, and humanitarian intervention and the administration of refugee bodies. In this chapter the study shows that in spite of the emergence of a more "interventionist" human rights posture in local and global interactions, regimentation of refugees as subjects or objects of human rights and humanitarian intervention is still informed by a statist imagination of the world and, in turn, works to recuperate the statist imagination in the face of changes and transformations that otherwise call into question the validity of just such an imagination. The study also observes that recent semantic adaptations in the discourse on human rights and humanitarian intervention manifest temporal and conceptual ties to the rearticulations of security discourse vis-à-vis refugee events. There is a manifest parallel between the reconceptualizations of security, humanitarian intervention, and humanitarianism around refugee events.

In chapter 6 the study examines the connections between refugee representations and the (re)conceptualization of the notion of democracy in Europe, with a specific focus on France, Germany, and England within the context of the European Community. The chief claim of this chapter is that refugees have increasingly become profitable subjects or objects in the (re)construction or (re)conceptualization of the practices of "democracy" in Western European spaces in ways that privilege the conventional territorial state-centric and citizen-oriented images of democracy. This chapter also claims that these (re)conceptualizations of "democracy" in Western Europe are moves toward more restrictive and exclusionary images of democracy and democratic practices. In a practical sense, they can be seen as movements away from a traditional liberal understanding of democracy as they herald further limitations on democratic practices and processes. More importantly, they can also be seen as moves that reinforce a "territorial incarceration" of democratic practices and ideals insomuch as they continue to turn to the inventories of democracy anchored in the state's territorial order.

1

Theorizing Refugee Problematizations as Practices of Statecraft

Narratives on Refugees

> One in every 130 people in the world has been forced to flee his or her home, and has become a refugee or a displaced person. More than 19 million refugees have been forced abroad, and a further 24 million have been driven from their homes and are "internally displaced" refugees within their own borders, the victims of "ethnic cleansing" and other forms of persecution. . . . The world is engulfed by refugees. The problem of victims in flight from conflicts and oppression blights rich and poor countries alike, and is rapidly spinning out of control.
>
> *Manchester Guardian Weekly*, 21 November 1993

REFUGEE REPRESENTATIONS AS INTIMATIONS OF THE NORMAL

Millions of people are moving across borders and boundaries around the globe. Once they are in circulation in larger contexts, movements of individual bodies have significant implications; they play an important part in the historically contingent practices and processes by which peculiar identities (of citizen and domestic community) are constructed, assigned, negotiated, resisted, and, most importantly, fixed in the image of the modern state. This is the thesis of this book.

Refugees are just such individual bodies. They move in the interstices of what Liisa Malkki (1992) calls the "national order of things," affecting its usual dispositions and configurations in countless ways.

Concomitantly, they are increasingly seen as sources as well as agents of change and transformation in local and global politics. Their subjectivity (agency) appears to be paradoxical. On the one hand, it is defined by their capacity to effect changes in sites of governance. On the other hand, it is construed by relations of inequality manifested in their vulnerability in the contemporary climate, which is adverse to their movements.

For some people, refugees constitute a disruptive presence in their host communities, disruptive of the processes of democracy, welfare, and security. The Political Committee of the North Atlantic Assembly, for example, refers to refugee movements as "a short- and medium-term security risk" requiring both prompt policy responses and long-term developmental solutions ("Convenient Cracks," 1993). Rudolf Seiters, the German interior minister in 1993, spoke of population movements, including refugee and asylum phenomena, as representing a threat to political stability in the whole of Western Europe (qtd. in "Germany, Poland," 1993). Echoing the same theme, Kenneth Clarke, then the British home secretary, intimated that "good race relations and a healthy sense of community depend on an effective system of strict immigration control" (qtd. in Robinson, 1992). Seeing refugees as part of an amorphous tide of immigrants inundating France, refugees "threaten the nation-state as a source of identity and cohesion," says Charles Pasqua, the former French interior minister (1994: 33). As Jacqueline Bhabha and Sue Shutter argue, in the cross-referencing mimicry of such ministerial pronouncements and popular reactions, "it is nearly as if the very word 'refugee' . . . become[s] something of an accusation" (1994: 256).

Others, however, see refugees in compassionate terms, as victims of events for which they cannot be held responsible, and because of this they deserve help and charity. "You see," reads one such plea, "refugees are just like you and me. Except for one thing. Everything they once had has been left behind. Home, family, possessions, all gone. They have nothing. And nothing is all they'll ever have unless we all extend a helping hand" (UNHCR, 1995). So people extend their helping hands to make refugees "have" something once again.

Whether effectual agents of change or vulnerable victims, refugees are transversal subjects whose movements bear on multiple processes of life, including those processes by which the boundaries of citizenship, ethnicity, political community, welfare, and democracy are defined and empowered. Their impact, real or perceived, in turn triggers an array of responses in different contexts and forms, creating a kaleidoscope of refugee vistas. These responses in their turn have real, practical impact on the possibilities of life for refugees, including the possibility of mere survival.

In Rwanda, for instance, soldiers desperately try to impose a specific identity on space, the difference of Rwanda from Zaire as a space of particular identities. Between Germany and Poland, border guards patrol, day and night, two hundred kilometers of the Lubiski region of the border to prevent Russians, Kurds, Romanians, Sri Lankans, and Gypsies from crossing into Germany. In southern Mexico, the response takes the form of refugee camps for Guatemalans established by the UNHCR, and in southern Turkey, there is yet another barbed-wire camp where refugees die either because of lack of food or because of bad food. In the United States, "rafter" refugees from Cuba and Haiti become the objects of indifferent laughter in late-night TV shows. In Bosnia, "safe havens" such as Srebrenica, Goražde, or Tuzla are established as a response to the refugee problem, where the warring parties kill safely and with impunity. In Kosovo, fleeing refugees are denied even this much, as ethnic cleansing à la Bosnia looms imminent. In the General Assembly or the Security Council of the United Nations, the response of governments to refugee events is a lip-service humanitarianism already subordinated to the interests of statism. In libraries of higher learning, the response to refugee events is to acquire mountains of "official documents" on refugees that necessarily "write" incomplete stories of the refugee. In Germany, the constitution is amended to limit the real possibilities of Germany as a refuge for those who seek it. In France, the moment of responsive practice turns out to be just a sentence or two uttered in a fleeting moment, as if uttering one's name: "Refugees smell non-French," says President Jacques Chirac in a newspaper interview; "Go, go and climb a tree," remarks a police officer to a refugee from the Maghreb. In Greece, government workers declare, "Refugees do not behave like the Greeks" (Marshall, 1993). They thus manage to forget that "Greece as a recognizable behavior" does not really exist (Herzfeld, 1988: 79–80).

It is through these responses and their representations in society at large that refugees figure into the political arenas both locally and globally and that a specific refugee discourse is produced. Inextricably linked to how refugees are regimented, refugee discourse in turn becomes party to a statist or, more properly, a "statized" imagination of the world as the presumed normal world in which people live.

How does this happen? How—by way of what practices and processes—is the figure of the refugee narrated, its content—meanings, images, and identities—negotiated, inscribed, established, internally ordered, and linked externally to other narratives of life, such as security, stability, peace, welfare, and democracy to affirm the state-oriented imagination of the world? The refugee discourse offers few clues.

What one notices immediately about refugee discourse is that it takes for granted, never questions, and starts by positing the paradigmatic hierarchy of the citizen/nation/state ensemble. There is an "already there" quality in the representations of this hierarchy, which is presumed to be already historically located, already articulated through prevailing forms and relations, and already empowered to speak and to be heard.

Consider, for example, the following representations of the refugee problem—from the inscription of the refugee problem to the incitement of discourse on the refugee problem, from the diagnoses of the refugee problem to the solutions of the refugee problem. To begin with, the universalized, ideal definition of the refugee enshrined in the UN Convention Relating to the Status of Refugees defines a refugee as

> any person who, owing to a well-founded fear of being persecuted for reasons of race, religion, nationality, membership in a particular social group or political opinion, is *outside the country of his nationality* and is unable or is unwilling to avail himself *of the protection of that country*; or who not having a nationality and being outside of the country of his former habitual residence, *is unable or unwilling to return to it*. (UN, 1988: 296; emphasis added)

A compassionate plea on behalf of refugees urges people to step forward to help refugees:

> Surely to help *victims* of our time in a spirit of humanitarian concern is part of a wider effort. When *we accept our neighbor* in need we have to *give him a basis on which to rebuild a new life. The refugee's greatest need is for a place among us, not only as a tolerated stranger, but as an active member of our society.* This is not only a matter for

> governments, but depends on all *citizens.* (UNHCR, 1971; emphasis added)

Sometimes, the compassionate gesture is genderized to suggest, as UNHCR officials regularly do, that "refugee women and children bear a disproportionate share of suffering" (UNHCR, 1995: 4). Against that uttering, a "hopeful" development in terms of gendered refugee experiences is noted to intimate progress in helping refugees: "Over the years, governments of countries admitting refugees have increasingly, though by no means uniformly, recognized that sexual violence can be used as an instrument of persecution, thereby providing valid grounds for claiming refugee status" (UNHCR, 1993b: 70).

Others see in refugees the harbinger of disruption, as does the Polish columnist Witold Pawloski, who wrote about refugees in the wake of an unprecedented rise in the number of refugees and asylum seekers in Europe in 1992 and 1993, of which Poland had its own share:

> Another blow has struck, confronting the troubled Poland with another major problem: of refugees. Prosperous European countries: Germany, France, Austria, Sweden, the Netherlands and the United Kingdom, have been using all legitimate means to close their doors to refugees. All over the world, the problem of refugees, or concern for the refugees, is a kind of *tax levied on democracy and prosperity.* Every state avoids the *refugees like the plague,* even if they travel in escorted carriages. (1993; emphasis added)

Michael Howard, then the British interior minister, echoed the same concern in 1995 when he said: "*We have a real problem in this country.* We are seen as a very attractive destination because of *the ease with which people can gain access to jobs and benefits. We must take firm action against bogus asylum seekers*" (qtd. in "Britain," 1995; emphasis added).

The UN High Commissioner for Refugees Sadako Ogata, to whose utterings scholars and policy makers turn as representing legitimate and/or desired responses to refugee events, diagnoses the refugee phenomenon when she states the "basic premise" of refugee relief work: "Displacement or uprootedness is a *transitory* condition: lack of national protection is an *aberration of the normal in which the state accepts the responsibility for its own citizens.* The objective must be to return to the *status ante*" (Norwegian Refugee Council, 1993:82).

While Ogata declares the "return to the *status ante*" to be the desirable objective, the UNHCR counsels states to create the conditions for such a return:

> The notion of prevention, therefore, is directly related to another key element of the emerging paradigm: *the concept of state responsibility.* Governments, in other words, must not only be held accountable for actions which force people to seek sanctuary in other countries, but must also be encouraged *to create the conditions which will allow refugees to return to their homelands.* (UN General Assembly, 1986; emphasis added)

These are characteristic representations of the refugee. Together, they reflect the refugee discourse at large in its multiple expressions, from defining the refugee to finding solutions to the plight of the refugee. They illustrate the specific vocabularies, significations, and classifications through which refugee stories are written, talked about, circulated, assigned contingent referentiality in wider fields of activity, and incorporated into peculiar sets of images of "normality" in life. It is through these vocabularies that refugees are attributed specific cultural, political, and legal meanings and identities that enable many to say effortlessly, "He is a refugee," or "She is a refugee," and continue to drive to their jobs, read the newspaper, sit through a lecture, or watch Bosnia, Rwanda, Kosovo, Haiti, or Cuba on television. In other words, these vocabularies are representative of the ways in which the name of the refugee unproblematically and axiomatically figures into the most ordinary daily conversations regarding community, security, culture, democracy, and so on.

Yet more importantly, these vocabularies point to the strategies of representation that work to create a crucial "normality effect" that underlies the symbolic political and cultural frameworks of life projects and processes that are considered important. Michel de Certeau calls this "the effect of awarding centrality to a specific category of signs, classifications, and subjects" while marginalizing others (1988: 120–21). Certeau argues that the act of awarding centrality simultaneously "establishes the possibility of classifying [other (marginalized) significations] as delays, aberrations or resistances and furnishes the base for a specific coherence, for a mentality, or for a system to which everything is referred" for meaning and legitimacy. It establishes what David Spurr, borrowing from Foucault, calls "a system of classification, arrangement and distribution in discourse which assigns positions, regulates groups, and enforces boundaries and which, through such discursive policing, can lay claim to truth" (1996: 62–63). As Richard Ashley puts it, this strategy "produces not only an ensemble of definite competent subjectivities—the recognized sovereign subjects whose voices are to be regarded as the authentic and unproblematic origins of meaning in that coherence or system—but also inscribes the borders and boundaries of the world of historical happenings and possibilities that these subjects mutually take to be necessary and natural conditions of their experience" (1988: 259). In short, the effect of awarding centrality establishes the base for privileging and promoting a specific imagination of the world as the "real" world out there.

This specific imagination is infused into the cardinal vocabularies by way of imposing a "direction" to the text. Practices that impose a direction to a text proceed by way of a series of practical and strategic questions formulated through historically contingent textual codes, signs, significations, and reference points—"hermeneutic, narrative, semantic, cultural, symbolic" (Fortin, 1989: 191). Hence, the direction of a text is managed or directed by way of certain questions asked, answered, or avoided, enigmas and binds posed, leads for solutions implied, core themes suggested, dominant images conjured up, meanings suggested, and relevant knowledge implied (191).

This representational dynamic, I argue, finds expression in the foregoing representations of the refugee problem. In them, the name of the modern territorial state is offered as the necessary coherence, mentality, and system around which a peculiar normality of life is presumed already to have been established. In them, the sovereign state—Poland, Germany, Russia—is cast as the exclusive site in which a multitude of life processes—community, democracy, prosperity, and compassion, as well as the "disruptive" and "problematic" moments of refugeeness—must find their origins, negotiate their presence, and work on the possibilities of their future. In fact, these representations commence with the name of a state, say, Poland or Germany, thus simply positing the state's centrality in the multiple landscapes of activities in which refugee events take place. "Another blow has struck," wrote Pawloski, "confronting the troubled Poland with another major problem: of refugees." Interestingly, the representations achieve this effect simply by invoking the centrality of the state—Poland, Germany, France, Austria, Sweden, the Netherlands, or the United Kingdom—in terms of a specific imagery of space, territory, and expressions of contemporary community and governance. Not surprisingly, a specific state-centric or statist imagination (direction) of time, space, identity, difference, security, community, and governance is built into the questions that are formulated to discuss refugee events.

Who is a refugee and who is not a refugee? What are the causes of refugee flows? How do refugee flows occur? What are the effects or impacts of refugee movements on the national community and the state sovereignty? Which actor(s) is (are) or must be in charge of dealing with refugee flows? What instruments might be effective in bringing these refugee situations under control? How might people be made to understand the need to do what must be done if the problem of the refugee is to be managed? Together, these "practical" questions presuppose and project a specific imagination of time, place, identity, subjects, relations, and institutions. They channel the energies and interrogations of the texts into a particular direction, awarding not only centrality but also legitimacy to a certain set of actors and their identities and meanings, in contradistinction to other actors, identities, and meanings. They implicate and are implicated in a definitive imagination of the world as a world of the modern state system. It is a world composed of a multiplicity of mutually exclusive, territorially bound spaces, such as Austria, Germany, and Hungary. Each of these spaces is occupied by a distinct, territorially bound community of citizen-subjects, such as the Austrian, Hungarian, or German community, and simultaneously represented and protected by the sovereign state within a clearly demarcated sovereign space (the Austrian, Hungarian, or German state). What makes this simultaneous representation and protection possible is the right as well as the presumed ability of each state to effect sovereign control over occurrences in its own territory (Ashley, 1988; 1989b; Luke, 1996). As Timothy Luke puts it:

> These states have hardened borders, inviolate territorial spaces and defensible centers in an international order of all other comparable states all of which are dedicated to maintaining territorial control over their sovereign spaces, resisting outside threats to their borders, containing internal challenges to their political autonomy. (1996)

Refugee events figure in such representations as occurring in this world of states presumed to be already fully and finally in existence. As Pierre Bourdieu would suggest, it is the kind of world where the centralized, privileged, and/or dominant images and relations are perceived as self-evident and natural. They go without saying because they come without saying (1986: 166). And, even in the midst of intense changes and transformations, subjects and objects, whether dominant or marginalized, seem ever familiar, and identities and meanings seem, as it were, stable and lasting. Hence, a refugee is understood to be just that, a refugee in search of a homeland; and a citizen, whether Polish or German, is simply that, a citizen, and not a refugee.

It is not surprising that all the imagery of the representations built around the name of the refugee as a problem strategically converges to point to the world of the definite, self-evident normality of states, of their clearly demarcated sovereign territories, and of the domestic communities of citizen-members. Meanings of words like *territory, sovereignty, country, homeland, democracy, citizen, refugee,* and *state* are constantly negotiated, differentiated, and hierarchized to affirm the state-centric imagination of the world. From the definition of the refugee to the solutions to the refugee problem, refugee representations reflect this orientation. The refugee problem, for example, is seen as "an aberration of the normal in which the state accepts the responsibility for its own citizens." The solution is then seen as the return to the *status ante*. This, the return to the country of origin protected and represented by the state, is the refugee's ultimate salvation. And it is the state alone that can facilitate salvation, as the UNHCR declares, by creating the conditions for refugees' return to their homeland. Even when attempts are made to appreciate the quotidian realities of refugee life, as in understanding gendered refugee experiences, these attempts are made possible through the affirmation of the state as the rightful authority capable of recognizing and validating those experiences. Recollect from an earlier reference that it is the state's recognition that finally "provid[es] valid grounds for claiming refugee status" on account of sexual violence directed at refugee women. That the recognition of gendered differences remains a rather empty gesture largely devoid of effective, concrete steps in policy and conduct is acknowledged only in whispers. What is significant is that in the representation and regimentation of refugee matters, the state is ascribed as central.

As suggested by Michel de Certeau, the ascribed centrality of the state results in the establishment of the name of the state as a distinctive coherence, a mentality, a system in and around which everything else is (imagined to be) positioned, and by reference to which all other things are (supposed to be) rendered meaningful. What is more important here is that not only is the state established as the beginning or origin of a specific kind of coherence, system, or whole way of living, but also it is represented as the sole facilitator of the historically contingent expressions of that coherence, that way of living. R. B. J. Walker calls this practicing "the politics of origin," wherein, "with the fixing of a temporal moment as a source of power, authority, and ambition, the sovereign state is established as the initial point from which all contemporary trajectories can be measured and controlled" (1991b: 448). It is as if there were no "outside" to the state.

The images of such a world are best described by Ernest Gellner in his study *Nations and Nationalism:*

> Consider the history of the national principle; or consider two ethnographic maps, one drawn up before the age of nationalism, and the other after the principle of nationalised centrality. The first map resembles a painting by Kokoschka. The riot of diverse points of colour is such that no clear pattern can be discerned in any detail. . . . A great diversity and plurality and complexity characterizes all distinct parts of the whole: the minute social groups have complex and ambiguous and multiple relations to many cultures. Look now at the ethnographic and political map of an era of the modern world. It resembles not Kokoschka, but, say, Modigliani. There is very little shading; neat, flat surfaces are clearly separated from each other, it is generally plain where one begins and another ends, and there is little ambiguity or overlap. . . . We see that an overwhelming part of political authority has been concentrated in the hands of one kind of institution, a reasonably large and well centralized state. In general, each such state presides over, maintains, and identifies with one kind of culture, one style of communication. (1993: 139–40)

I argue that it is the latter map, manifesting the hierarchy of the citizen/nation/state constellation, that the aforementioned refugee representations take for granted, never question, and start by positing.

In effect, they start by awarding a centrality to the sovereign state—the "given framework" of life within which all energies must be oriented to make the prevailing relationships and institutions work smoothly. Thus, refugee representations afford the rhetoric of statist affirmation.

Not surprisingly, taking the state in this fashion effectively short-circuits reflective action on the state itself. It employs a mode of response to the refugee that participates in the constitution of a reader-agent who, working through the texts, is made to be part of an intersubjective community, who will participate in the community effect, accept it as such, and move on. The reader-agent, in other words, is already put into action in the representations, in the rhetoric of affirmation. The mode of response shifts from reflective action to a sort of "mimetic" activity in which the community of Poles, for example, is simply posited, a community that is immersed in danger and that summons the reader to action without a question. Were we to stop and ask what Poland is, the Polish columnist Pawloski, for example, would be forced to reflect on this call to action on behalf of an already existing community and the state as the embodiment of its wills and desires. But such a question never figures, and the Pawloskis manage to move on. Critical reflections are short-circuited. The state remains affirmed, the refugee's ontology in relation to the state is fixed. But there is much more to be said about the state and the refugee, that is, much more about the contingencies of refugee stories narrated on the borders and boundaries of the state and about refugee matters regimented in practices and paradoxes of statecraft. We must do just that: say more first on statecraft, that is, how the state is awarded its centrality, and then on "refugeecraft," that is, how the refugee's body enables the borders and boundaries of the state.

THE PRAXIS AND PARADOX OF STATECRAFT

In refugee representations, what one notices is that the very activity of awarding centrality to the state requires that these representations of the refugee problem simply posit the sovereign state (and hence the modern state system as the given framework of life) as an axiomatic presence already in existence, its subjectivities already clearly and unambiguously articulated, the relationships among its subjectivities already fixed and put into circulation, and the institutions that inform and organize those relationships already empowered and at work. Once again, as Bourdieu would put it, it is "a self-evident and natural order which goes without saying" (1986: 166).

Although the positing permits the name of the state to be put at the center and says, "I just assume it to be self-evident," it does not resolve what is perhaps the most important problem of the sovereign state. For those who practice the state as a form of governance, it is the problem of knowing that the sovereign state is a historical effect, produced in and through practice, a historical artifact whose powers are manifested in a plethora of ways. It is the problem of knowing that the sovereign state is not a self-sufficient, pure, and objective presence, but a presence wholly dependent on the multitude of historically contingent and protean activities that engender or create, day in and day out, its presumed realities as the sovereign state. The most central among these practices is the claim that the sovereign state is an agent of representation, authored by and representing the territorially bound community of citizens presumed already to be in place.

According to Ashley (1995), this knowledge, this awareness, spells out a troubling paradox for those who practice the state: "The sovereign state secures its status—its social space, its claims to means of violence and rational administration of resources, its presumed right to govern over the bodies of men and women—by virtue of the claim that it is nothing but representation—something written by men, in the name of men, in the service of men, and in the answer to the fears and desires of men." The state secures its place as a site of reality only insofar as practices that underlie the state as a practical force can successfully produce and circulate the claim to the representation of a domestic community of men and women, citizens—subjects who, in constituting an organic community of citizens, are presumed simultaneously to author the state into existence and to submit themselves to it for representation and protection.

As Ashley suggests, what this claim necessitates is that "for the modern state to be empowered as a practically effective institution, there must be presumed to be a well-bounded domestic authority" (1993: 3–7), the community of citizen-subjects already there to author the state and in turn to be represented by the state. Short of such a practically effective presumption, the sovereign state would, in Ashley's fitting words, "carry utterly no practical weight." With this, Ashley argues, the fundamental problem of these activities—activities of statecraft—comes into full view. The problem is that this bounded presence of "representable citizen subjects" never simply exists in itself and that, "never more than an effect always in the process of being effected, it is an effect of practices of differentiation and institutionalization that work to produce it" (4–9).

This is the most fundamental problem of the state. It is a problem of how to inscribe, stabilize, and render effective a certain figure of the citizen that the modern state would represent and on the basis of which the modern state would claim to effect its sovereignty, its powers, and indeed its right to rule over a territorial inside—the domestic community of citizens. Arjun Appadurai calls this the "people production" necessary for the powers of the state, a task that is always carried out in uncertain grounds (1996: 43). Herein lies a paradox, the paradox of the state:

> If the sovereign state is to be an institution of material significance, this effect must be reliably and repeatedly produced in space and time, but the successful production of this effect requires that the problem itself never be explicitly posed, represented, or made visible in any other way. For the visibility of the problem is tantamount to the recognition that domestic authority, far from being a self-evident presence that might be represented in institutions of state, is itself a problematical institution that is produced through arbitrary practices. . . . Practices of statecraft, to be effective, must proceed as if this source of authority is always already there to be found and represented. (Ashley, 1993: 5)

It is precisely this paradox that Homi Bhabha highlights by pointing to the tension between the "pedagogical" and "performative" dimensions of the task of "narrating the nation":

> The ideological discourse that we are examining has no safety catch: it is rendered vulnerable by its attempts to make visible the place from which the social relation would be conceivable (both thinkable and creatable) by its inability to define this place without letting its contingency appear, . . . without hereby making apparent the instability of an order that it is intended to raise to the status of essence. (1993: 298)

It is here that one begins to glimpse the significance of this problem for the practices of statecraft. It is a fundamental problem, because it is concerned with the production of the foundational subject on whom the state's ontology—its very reason for being—rests. It is a problem, however, that is never to be explicitly posed, represented, or made visible in space or time. For the visibility of the problem would reveal that the citizen-subject's presence, its practical realities, identities, and powers, "far from being a self-evident and a natural presence that might be simply represented in the institutions of state," must be tirelessly and repeatedly produced in and through everyday practices of governance. Therefore, practices of statecraft must proceed in essential silence, as if the citizen-subject as the source of authority for the state is always already there to be found and represented (Ashley, 1993). They must simply commence by positing a specific hierarchical constellation of agents and identities—citizen/nation/state—to be always already there, while working tirelessly through *problematizations* in various fields of activity to effect the statist identities and images. They must *incite* popular and institutional discourses of problems and dangers; *statize* them, that is, inscribe them as problems and dangers before the state and community of citizens presumed already to be there; and *regiment* them in terms that privilege a statist imagination of the world.[1] They must engage in what Homi Bhabha elsewhere calls the "arrested representation," to carefully orchestrate the representation of difference to affirm the state (1983: 27).

Practices of statecraft must take these measures in order that a peculiar Cartesian spatiopolitical image of the world (Walker, 1991a; 1991b) is formulated and brought to bear upon a wide spectrum of life activities. At such historical moments of imagining, the world (space) is perceived to be discontinuous. It is understood to consist of multiple and mutually exclusive surfaces, as in the Modigliani painting. In it, "neat, flat, clearly separated surfaces"—sovereign territories called Poland, Germany, or Austria—represent or overlap with what Liisa Malkki aptly calls presumed, distinct "culture gardens" (1992: 28), which constitute the territorial ground within which the citizen-subject—the Polish or German citizen—the source of domestic authority for the state, is effected as a practical reality (Gupta and Ferguson, 1992). This effect is produced in multiple ways, as Foucault would suggest (1991: 75–77), operating in, resulting from, and resulting in a plurality of relations.

Michael Kearney, for instance, shows how the dynamics of the border landscape along the U.S.-Mexico border constitute just such a field of activity for statecraft. He lays bare the political economy of activities staged on and around the border as one of constructing a field of activity where the spectacle of the border serves as powerful reference for the projection of territorially bound citizenry and statehood (1991: 53–69).[2] Similarly, drawing upon the history of "the art of the state" in Italy, Donald Carter (1994) demonstrates that in the popular imagination in Italy, the constitution and mapping of the particular forms of otherness and marginalized subjectivity in the fields of work, criminality, and health have worked and continue to work in the construction of the definition of the "average" citizen upon which the "continuing project" of the state is dependent. Carter suggests that in the nineteenth century, vagrants, beggars, and gypsies were constituted to represent forms of otherness and marginality. In the twentieth century, he adds, refugees and immigrants were added to the list of otherness to serve the same function.[3]

In another context, the agricultural landscape of the 1913 Wheatland riots by immigrant laborers in the Sacramento Valley in California, Don Mitchell (1993) points to the forces of a transformative vortex of social interaction, yet another historical field of struggle that, according to Mitchell, afforded profitable opportunities for the practices of statecraft.[4] Moving into a more amorphous but no less instructive site in terms of the project of the state, Michael Herzfeld argues that the sites of cultural activities lend themselves to the task of statecraft. He shows the constitution of the boundaries of the sovereign state in the transformations of Greek culture and the concurrent role such transformations play in the construction of the notion of the Greek nation (1988: 79).[5]

These are a few perhaps successful instances of statecraft that have unfolded in a world where the complexities of life activities do not easily lend themselves to a project of the sovereign state as the sole spatial container of all good promises—security, prosperity, democracy, and so on. In fact, practices of statecraft must try to impose the logic of the sovereign state on a world of "a thousand and one" occurrences where there has never been and is not now any intrinsic, objective, self-evident structural "disposition" or "habitus" (Bourdieu, 1986) that patiently and incessantly guides people toward the sovereign state as the exclusive site for life courses.

Nowadays this task seems ever more difficult, considering the increasing volume, velocity, and intensity of transborder, transnational movements that pressure, challenge, and indeed metamorphose the conventional conceptualizations of what it means to live "within sovereign borders." In other words, a set of multidimensional historical changes that go under such diverse names as interdependence, globalization, supranationalism, and/or transnationalism (see Harvey, 1995; Basch, Scheller, and Blanc, 1995) make it ever more problematic to speak of the processes of local and global life exclusively in terms of a Cartesian spatial segmentation or territorialization organized solely around the image or name of the territorial state.

These challenges to the statist imagination of the world arise in multiple forms and multiple fields in the crucible of transversal, globalizing happenings throughout the world. William Connolly calls them "the powerful centrifugal, deterritorializing challenges [that emerge] in the acceleration of globalizing process" (1991: 463). Ashley speaks of them as "contemporary emergent uncertainties, ambiguities, and indeterminacies that put in doubt the identity of man [read citizen] in domestic society" in the internationalized life (1989b: 302). Appadurai identifies them in the global disjunctive politics that gives rise to "translocalities [that in turn] challenge the orderliness of the nation-state" (1996: 43). David Harvey locates them in "the power of capitalism to co-ordinate accumulation in the universal fragmented space where the place-bound politics faces many difficulties" (1995: 24). Jacques Derrida thinks similarly about what he calls "the new international." The concentration of global capital, the emergence of the "phantom states" of the Mafia and drug cartels, the increasing salience of exile, refugee, and immigration events, poverty, foreign debt, and connected mechanisms that starve or deprive to despair a large portion of humanity, Derrida suggests, amount to a reinscription or redeliniation of the state (1994: 77–94). Homi Bhabha thinks of them in terms of "crises of administrative and institutional representability" faced by states both in the North and in the South (1994: 269). Finally, Walker calls them "dislocations, accelerations, and contingencies of a world less and less able to recognize itself in the fractured mirror of Cartesian coordinates" (1991b: 445).

Amid these challenges, in short, the real lack of foundational telos for the state has become more pronounced and exposed. What is clear is that the modernist conceptions of the world, including the centrality of the state to life activities, now, their arbitrariness ever more visible, encounter counterformulations and counterconceptualizations of the possibilities of life.[6] The truth claims as to the permanence, naturalness, and self-evidence of the sovereign state (as the sole spatiopolitical site of life activities) and the citizen (as the sole proper subject of the state's political site) having been exposed, the task of statecraft seems now much more difficult and much more contingent than ever before. For the practitioners of the state, what is at hand here and now is nothing less than a crisis of representation of the relations and institutions of the state.

In the face of this crisis, while the practitioners of the state continue to hang on to the "permanence principle," (Walker, 1991b: 448; 1991a: 247) and loudly assert that the sovereign states may come and go without any question, they nevertheless simultaneously must work to project a statist image of the world and must do so across multiple localities. In other words, the task of statecraft in the crucible of globalization requires the coordination of activities across localities, lest activities of statecraft in one locale potentially disrupt the activities in other locales. As Arjun Appadurai suggests, "'People production' needs of one nation-state can mean ethnic and social unrest for its neighbors, creating open-ended cycles of ethnic cleansing, forced migration, xenophobia, state paranoia, and thus further ethnic cleansing" (1996: 43).

There is, in other words, a coordination problem across localities in producing the representable entities, images, and identities of the world as a world of sovereign states. It is a problem that goes to the heart of the anarchy problematic in international relations. It is the problem of a "conductorless orchestration of activities" in anarchy such that particular state-oriented images and identities are reliably effected and put into circulation across localities in the absence of a central, overarching sovereign power—a strategy empowered to produce just such an effect (Ashley, 1995). Nowadays, the fundamental problem of statecraft could be said to be the problematization, that is, the coregimentation, of the processes of life across localities so as to make it possible to imagine "national" and "international" spaces, even as countless transversal transformations across the globe constantly work to undermine such imaginations (Aleinikoff, 1995: 264).

In the face of all the difficulties that the contemporary processes of globalization pose for the activities of statecraft, how then is the task of statecraft carried out so that the contingent realities of citizen-subjects are produced and put into circulation? How, further, are these contingent realities made to underlie a specific hierarchy of territorially bound representable agents and identities, the citizen/nation/state, not only as the hierarchy that signifies a peculiar presumed normality to life but also as the hierarchy that is exigent, that must be maintained if that normality is to be preserved? How does the refugee relate to all these proliferations?

To answer these questions, I turn to the very sites in which the difficulties for statecraft are argued to emerge and proliferate. In other words, I turn to the sites of globalization and transversality, not, however, merely to affirm the emergent and extant difficulties, but to argue that historical happenings in these sites, while doubtless ushering in a certain "crisis of representation" for the state and threatening to undo the state's centrality in life, paradoxically also afford "new" resources for rearticulations of the sovereign state in multiple sites of policy and conduct. How can this be? How can it be that the state's centrality to life is being diffused on the one hand and recuperated on the other, all in the crucible of global and transversal occurrences?

It is here, at the junctures of paradoxical happenings where the modern territorial state is made, unmade, and remade, that the deterritorialized subject in global politics, that is, the subject who is cut off from the land, the home, the nation, the bounded community—in other words, the refugee—enters the scene. It is here that the refugee's presence goes to the heart of the paradoxes and predicaments of statecraft, and here that the refugee's voicelessness, his lack of agency, makes sense, offering a window into how the paradoxical dynamics of events and happenings in relation to the task of statecraft work or are made to work.

Before further elaboration on how this happens, two cautions against essentialization—essentialization of *history* and essentialization of the *state*—are imperative, since the notion of statecraft, historicized, is central to the analysis in this study. The first caution is to note that history is not a unidimensional or unidirectional experience without discontinuities, disruptions, breaks, confusions, recurrences, and ambiguities. Rather, history is the story of multiple fields of struggles or, as Michel Foucault (1991) puts it, multiple fields constituting a "polyhedron of intelligibilities," where occurrences have an endless number of elements, relations, and domains of reference (1991: 77). They entail no necessary, self-evident unity of elements, no particular direction, and no regime of relations across multiple domains of reference. All that might exist in terms of unity, direction, or a regime of relations and elements is brought about, and specific forces, entities, and subjects are constituted and empowered, only within the dynamics of history as multiple, intersecting, and overlapping fields of activity. History in this sense, as Richard Flores puts it, is the story of "actively engaging the social world" (1993: 178).

There are two significant elements to such a conceptualization of history. First, in terms of a polyhedron of fields of activity, one could not speak of an intrinsic essence to events that dictates their direction and naturally imposes their regime of relations. Directions and regimes are constantly imposed and reimposed by way of ongoing practices in various fields of activity. Fernand Braudel (1977) calls such a history "conjunctural." Second, from this view of history, one also could not speak of substantial essential entities (subjects, virtues, forces) that exist prior to history. Entities do not "first preexist and later enter into a combat or harmony. . . . Rather, they emerge on a field of battle and play their roles, there and there alone" (Dreyfus and Rabinow, 1983: 109).[7]

Conceptualized as such, history is understood as a totality of syncretic (dis)positions, identities, interests, maneuvers, tactics, techniques, and functionings (Dreyfus and Rabinow, 1983: 107) with potentially endless possible regimes of relations. There is among the entities, forces, and subjects a constant play of clash, contestation, accommodation, recuperation, cooperation, and collusion. There is not, however, any predetermined direction to their relations; they emerge and reemerge in constant activity. History is cast truly as a series of practices, events, and happenings.

The other caution is to take note that a conceptualization of history as contingent syncretic practices is instructive for the analysis of the sovereign state. Such a conceptualization makes it possible to see the sovereign state as what it really is: a convergent effect of both discourse and performance contingently produced and transformed in and through complex sets of practices across time and place. Conceptualized so, the sovereign state could not simply be understood to be present "out there" in the form of a particular stable discourse (content or meaning) or a set of unchanging or fixed performances (practices) subject neither to history nor to spatiality. The narrative and performative elements of the sovereign state are indispensably interdependent; practices or performances follow narratives, while narratives are generated by performances or practices (Miyoshi, 1993: 726; H. Bhabha, 1993), and they cannot remain unmediated by and impervious or insusceptible to changes across time and place. For the sovereign state to remain a viable force, practices of statecraft must consider the ongoing shifts and transformations in fields of political activities with a view to appropriating new narrative and performative resources with which to attempt to impose and reimpose a particular imagination on the changes and transformations.

Taking these two cautions seriously, it becomes possible to formulate inquiries on the status of the sovereign state through radically different vocabularies, locating the name of the sovereign state—as a force, subject, or entity—in the overlapping fields of history as fields of struggle. There, in these fields of struggle, the identities, meanings, and images of the sovereign state emerge and reemerge, as do the identities of the refugee, not so much as ineluctable but as discursively generated and imposed images and identities. Since they are the results of power struggles, they remain contested and therefore always necessarily in flux in order to maintain a certain viability.

The constructed identities and images or the fact of their constructedness as images and identities points to an important insight into the trajectories—past, present, and future—of the sovereign state as an agent of governance. These images and identities suggest the possibility that the contemporary patterns of changes and transformations, hence those of state sovereignty, are not necessarily configured as postulated in most of the contemporary discourses on the sovereign state and globalization; they do not necessarily manifest themselves in the form of inevitable unidirectional progressions, from particular to universal or from universal to particular (Walker, 1991a; Walker and Mendlowitz, 1990). They may, but do not have to, be solely in the direction of *either* a centripetal integration (under the preponderant exclusive power of the territorializing statist forces) *or* an increasing centrifugal fragmentation and deterritorialization of activities and forces (manifested in the birth of nonstate entities with global reach, replacing the territorial state). It might just be that a multitude of forces and agents—territorializing and deterritorializing; integrating, fragmenting, and reintegrating; localizing and globalizing; uprooting, rerooting, and transplanting—act simultaneously in interpenetrating and overlapping fields of identity and difference, negotiating and mediating a host of meanings, identities, and subjectivities, all of which converge to create the "real," "material" world we live in (Gupta and Ferguson, 1992; Appadurai, 1991; Walker 1990).[8]

I argue that such multiple currents or forces cohabit the fields of the sovereign state. In fact, the dynamics of relations among a number of subjects indicate that the arenas in which the activities of statecraft are formulated and undertaken are almost always cohabited with such forces and agents; they are, to borrow a metaphor from an old slave song, "like a restless sea, tossing and turning" those who are on it or in it.

Walker points precisely to such a development in the "restless" or "turbulent" (Rosenau, 1990) seas of contemporary globalization and/or transnationalization, where, he reminds us, the embattled sovereign state, as the flagship of a specifically modern articulation of political identity, both in space and time, manages not only to stay afloat but also to continually instill further confidence and trust in its current as well as its prospective passengers. A paraphrased Walker might ask: How, in spite of the fact that Cartesian coordinates are cracked, identities are leaking, and the familiar modern rituals of inclusion and exclusion sanctified by the dense textures of sovereign virtue have become transparent, do contemporary political identities and meanings remain largely constrained by ontological, political, and discursive options expressed most elegantly by claims about formal sovereignty of territorial states? Why do many still find it exceptionally difficult to renounce the security of Cartesian coordinates (Walker, 1991b: 446–47)?

Walker's answer is simple but instructive. Perhaps, he maintains, "the modern rituals of inclusion and exclusion," working to produce, project, and privilege the hierarchy of the citizen/nation/state, "still provide our most powerful sense of what it means to look over the horizon" and to feel we have security, stability, wealth, democracy, freedom, and order (1991b: 446). It seems that to theorize away the sovereign state does not automatically make it go away. Concomitantly, the issue of "how all this is possible" looms ever larger. Again, how, in spite of the increasingly intense and visible challenges, is the task of statecraft carried out?

The answers to these questions can and should be formulated within the framework of history as multiple fields of syncretic activities. By the same token, the sovereign state should be conceptualized as having been produced in such a "polyhedron" of fields of activity with multiple possible configurations of unity, direction, and regimes of relations. This orientation makes it possible to recognize that these sites are fields of challenges—difficulties as well as opportunities—for the practices of statecraft that attempt to impose a certain statist direction, mentality, or regime of relations on events by regenerating the culture of territorialization. Similarly, as I argued earlier, the sites in which globalization ushers in a "crisis of representation" also paradoxically afford "new" opportunities for rearticulations of the sovereign state. The shifting resources and technologies of self and community empower new ways of being and becoming, as well as "belonging."

REFUGEE PROBLEMATIZATIONS, INTERNATIONAL REGIMENTATION, AND STATECRAFT

It is at such junctures, where challenges and difficulties always generate opportunities, that refugee occurrences, conceptualized or "deciphered" (Spurr, 1996: 62) in a specific refugee discourse, work as one "transformative" field of policy and conduct useful for the activities of statecraft. How is this possible? In discussing the power of discourse, Stuart Hall offers a possible explanation. Reading Foucault on discourse and power, Hall argues that a discourse can never be "innocent," benignly expressing a given topic in life. Instead, a discourse always furnishes a specific description of the topic grounded in historical ideological formations. "A discourse," Hall writes, "is a group of statements which provide a language for talking about—i.e., a way of representing—a particular kind of knowledge about a topic. . . . The discourse makes it possible to construct the topic in a certain way, [and] it also limits the other ways in which the topic can be constructed" (1996: 201–2). Statements that constitute a discourse work together to create a "discursive formation" (Foucault, 1972: 31), a "discursive space" in which statements always imply or cross-refer to one another, always refer to the same subjects and objects, almost always establish the same hierarchy among subjects and objects, and "support a common institutional . . . or political drift or pattern." "Discourse is about production of knowledge through language . . . and language has real effects in practice: the description becomes" the source of what is true and what is false, and is thus instrumental in the articulation of the "normal" and "normality" in life, organized around specific subjects, relations, and institutions (Hall, 1996: 203). It is in this sense that refugee discourse, articulating and circulating a specific historical figure of the refugee (by way of concrete governmental and intergovernmental activities attendant upon refugee events), serves as one of many boundary-producing, normality-constructing discourses instrumental in the expression, empowerment, and institutionalization of a certain territorialized figure of the citizen-subject—the presumed foundational subject on the basis of which the sovereign state has historically been, and continues to be, articulated as an agent of representation.

Put differently, at any one time, refugee discourse reflects the processes and practices by which specific images, meanings, and identities of the refugee have historically been produced, differentiated from other subjectivities, institutionalized, and deployed as effective resources of and for practices of statecraft. The name of the refugee emerges as an open field of activity or, as Foucault (1984) suggests, as a battlefield where relevant identities and subjects are forged into effective forces of everyday affairs. The activities organized and the institutions established around the name of the refugee paradoxically help secure or affirm a specific version of the sovereign state, its raison d'être, and its technologies of governance that in effect allow the sovereign state to stay in the business of governance. In short, the field of the (representable) refugee becomes a boundless battlefield, a site, in which the name of the state is made to turn into reality, a thing, with practical effects for the lives of many (Wolf, 1982). This is my contention.

What happens here is significant in terms of the paradox of the state. The crucial element of the paradox is the task of creating the contingent "realities" of the state through practice—through discipline and punishment (Foucault, 1984) or through violence and rational efforts (Lefebvre, 1995)—while maintaining a silence about the nature and purpose of the task. The field of the refugee fulfills precisely such a need in that the activities of statecraft can proceed while never announcing the task as one of statecraft. Thus, the name of the state never figures as that which is under construction, for the name of the refugee—whose physical presence is written into a specific discourse with an economy of representation—serves as an alibi for the existence of the state. Vis-à-vis the name of the refugee, the state seems to exist always a priori.

The logic of the transformation of a mere name—the name of the refugee—into a practical field of activity, useful for the activities of statecraft, is the logic of problematization. It is through the activities of problematization that the deterritorializing dynamics of refugee events and occurrences—their capacity to disrupt the work of statecraft—are not only accommodated and neutralized but also capitalized upon and deployed as a series of contingent referential resources useful to the production of familiar statist images and identities—the citizen, national community, and state (Rose and Miller, 1992). It is around these identities and entities that a specific statist imagination of the world is built, not only as a world in which we live but also as a world that we must continue to produce if we aspire to live in peace, welfare, security, and democracy. How might problematization work to achieve all that?

Foucault, as I indicated earlier, understands problematization as the work of thought that "transforms the *difficulties* and *obstacles* of a practice into a general *problem* for which one proposes diverse political solutions" (1984: 389; emphasis added). According to Foucault, then, problematization is a response to the specific, concrete difficulties of a specific practice. It starts by recognizing the existence of peculiar difficulties. But the moment of recognition is not the crucial moment of problematization. Rather, the crucial moment is the moment of opening a specific space or a field of activity by "transforming" or articulating the *difficulties* into *specific problems* that could be given a response without calling into question the assumptions and postulations of the practice itself. In this sense, the act of problematization assimilates and absorbs the difficulties by recognizing (conceptualizing) them as specific problems in the ontological and epistemological terms of the practice itself. Problematization here, then, is a normalization—the conceptualization of difficulties as amenable and manageable problems (as in problem-solving theory) within a posited framework of practice.

Activities of problematization achieve such moments of assimilation not by "expressing" or "manifesting" the difficulties once and for all, but rather by controlling the very ground on which difficulties are cast into specific problems, elaborated, and interpreted, and on which solutions are formulated and implemented. Problematizations are thus oriented at the continuous construction and regimentation of the identities and powers of the subjects, who in turn can recognize or conceptualize a particular difficulty as a problem for a specific practice, and can act on it accordingly. The strategies of problematization proceed by introducing and reintroducing these subjects into a field of practice (by way of discourse) by inscribing on them certain meanings and identities as opposed to other possible meanings and identities. The crux of problematization, then, is the activity of reinscribing identities, meanings, and images that, for instance, project a "citizen" out of a peasant or worker at one historical moment while projecting a "refugee" or "illegal immigrant" out of the same peasant or worker at another moment.

It is in this sense that this study speaks of refugee problematizations as activities that constitute a specific field or space of the refugee that recuperates a host of statist images, identities, and meanings. It is in this field that the complex difficulties presented for the activities of statecraft by the movements and even the inertia of people are metamorphosed or reconceptualized as manageable problems within the logic of the sovereign state. It is also there that "problem bodies" are constituted as transformative sites in which the foundational subject of international relations, the citizen-subject, is produced, circulated, privileged, and, most importantly, statized, that is, "written" as something that is possible only within the sovereign territory of a state. Insomuch as the privileging of the citizen-subject as the foundational subject is indispensable for the state to exist, refugee discourse as a discourse of the marginalized and of otherness appears as a permanent fixture of statecraft. The refugee discourse, as Derrida (1976) might say, is a "necessary supplement" to the discourse of the citizen.

It is here that the previously mentioned need for cross-border coordination of efforts in dealing with refugees acquires urgency, for without the coordination of efforts across borders, as Appadurai (1996) suggests, one nation-state's activities to carry out the task of statecraft might disrupt another's, thus causing even more problems. The problematizations of refugee events in the service of statecraft therefore necessitate a regime of coordination and collaboration of relevant activities across territorial borders. In other words, they necessitate intergovernmental regimentation. Foucault suggests that, in problematization, it is through the coordinated activities of articulating dangers and elaborating problems and their interpretations that people are mobilized to action and, as an effect, participate in the constitution of knowing agent-subjects who will recognize the dangers and problems as such and act to solve or resolve them.

The modern international refugee regime affords a discursive and institutionalized space in which just such a regimentation across territorial borders becomes possible. The refugee regime, however, is not a manifestation of the powers of the already historically fixed states responding to the already manifest dangers and difficulties by formally representable rules of the regime. Rather, the regime itself is statecraft that actively produces the powers of states across borders precisely at those moments of intergovernmental regimentations in which dangers and problems get elaborated, their interpretations are mediated, and, as an effect, people are mobilized to recognize states as agents of problem solving and, in the moment of that recognition, are invested in and become party to the practices of statecraft. Regime practices, while purportedly concentrating on the problem of the refugee, thus work not so much to "solve" the "refugee problem" as to utilize those bodies marked as refugees in order to stabilize various territorialized relations, institutions, and identities that afford the state its reason for being.[9] Refugees come and go, but refugee regimentations remain constant, affording a precious field in which the state is awarded its proverbial centrality.

Who is a refugee? How and when do we know to call an event of displacement a refugee event to be thus registered and responded to? What are the characteristics of refugee events? What impact do they have on the ability of states to project and represent communities? What should be done with refugees? Taken together, these are the questions that channel the energies and guide the imaginations in the field of the refugee. It is instructive to recollect the spatial choreography of the landscape of images and identities as projected in refugee representations at the onset of this chapter, where "the citizen," "the refugee," "the state," and "the national community"—Poland, Germany, Iraq, Bolivia—are juxtaposed to constitute a convenient landscape of the present world in which we live. Even if one supposes that these are accurate representations of the landscape of relations, what Mitchell says of landscapes of life activities stands true: "Landscapes are like produced commodities, for while [c]ertain social processes make them, their [m]omentary final form often masks those processes . . . not directly telling the story of struggles that went into the development and provision [of landscapes]" (1993: 101).

It is precisely in this sense that I turn to the landscapes of relations in which the name of the refugee, juxtaposed to the name of the citizen, figures as the subject of lack, signifying its own aberrance and incompleteness vis-à-vis the citizen-subject. As is clearly reflected in the representations I have cited, in these landscapes the voice of the citizen is presupposed and projected as the voice of the ideal founding subject of the relations and institutions of the modern state system. It is the citizen-subject who would be at home within the territory of a modern sovereign state such as Poland, Austria, or Bosnia; who would be represented by the Polish or German state and afforded the protections of these states; and who, in recognition of all this, would freely accord to the modern state its legitimacy, its right to rule within the territorial bounds of the home, and its capacity to speak for the citizen-subject within and in the world beyond the territorial bounds of the home, that is, in the international arena (Ashley, 1993: 1–9).

Contrary to the presupposition of the citizen-subject as the proper, ideal subject of "natural" or normal orders of life, in the representations of these landscapes, the refugee figures negatively, as a lack, "suspended indefinitely in a void without a homeland" and clearly "unwanted," as possible new homelands close their doors on the refugee's face. The refugee lacks the citizen-subject's secure identity, the citizen-subject's secure home, and the citizen-subject's secure ties to a community. Lacking proper ties to a community of citizens, the refugee also lacks proper ties to the state; he lacks the state's protection and representation. Although an object of compassion and pity at times, in the final analysis she is truly "unwanted" or "undesirable," representing, "like the plague" (Pawloski, 1993), disruptions in the conditions of normality in life. She stands accused.

This problematization of the refugee has practical normative consequences for the refugee. As Edward Said might suggest, the act of defining the refugee in opposition to the national, rights-bearing citizen "delimits" the practical rights of the refugee (1979: 16). What this amounts to in terms of real possibilities in life is that the refugee is incorporated into (the discourse of) the national life only to be distanced from the possibilities in it, for the refugee's inclusion is a form of legal as well as popular marginalization in which the refugee figures as an aberrance (of the citizen-subject), incapable of participating in and contributing to the society (Silverman, 1992; Carter, 1994). The refugee is given a name only to be deprived of his ability to participate fully in the polity in which he finds himself. Thus, in refugee problematizations, the refugee's name spells out his voicelessness, his lack of agency, as the UNHCR depiction quoted in the introduction insists. "To exist again in more than name," to have "work," "home," and "decisions to take," the refugee must return "home," that is, he must have his territorial ties reestablished with the community of citizens represented and protected by the state. If the refugee is a woman or girl, she barely, and then mostly rhetorically, figures in the stories of recuperation of rights and privileges. And even then she is presumed simply to be seeking the statist ties for proverbial salvation.[10] Without these ties to the state, the refugee cannot properly enjoy the rights and privileges that the citizen-subject can by virtue of his or her proper rootedness in the territory of the state. The refugee stands at a loss outside the state.

When refugees insist upon their ability to make new homes out of any place (Soguk, 1995b), they are told that they exist only in name. The refugee knows this not to be true and moves on with the task of creating homes wherever and whenever she can. The "subaltern," contrary to Gayatri Spivak's lament, can indeed speak and be in spite of efforts to deny her the "space" to speak and be (1988; see also Arendt, 1958; Xenos, 1995). Refugees politicize the "space" by imploding the cartographic logic that engenders it. What the maps cut up, says Michel de Certeau, "stor[ies] cut across" (1984: 129). Refugees become those stories which cut across the cartographic logic of the territorial state and its privileged sites of identity and then start negotiating. In France, for instance, recognizing the power of naming, a Kurdish refugee renames his two daughters with French names in the hope that the task of creating a new home might become a bit easier for them. In Sweden, another refugee expresses his determination to begin that task anew when he declares his "rebirth" upon arrival in Sweden. Of course, that his declaration of rebirth may not be readily recognized is always a possibility. Still, refugees continue to claim their rebirth in the face of protests to the contrary. In Great Britain, yet another refugee goes on a hunger strike, risking death to show her determination to live, to speak, and to be. On the seventeenth day of her hunger strike, she is granted asylum in Britain—she is finally heard (Bhabha and Shutter, 1994: 237). Such are the struggles that have real impact on the lives of both refugees and nonrefugees; they determine one's life possibilities. Such also are the refugee problematizations.

In this study, I look into the history of refugee problematizations as a history of local and global regimentations in order to find out what "struggles" might have gone into the production, circulation, and empowerment of just such an imagination of that landscape. I thus undertake a genealogical study of the category of the refugee to see just how—by way of what organizational, bureaucratic, political, cultural, aesthetic, religious, and demographic practices; in David Spurr's terminology (1996), by what "teratology"—certain entities, identities, and images might have been marked as those of the refugee, signifying aberrances relative to the idealized subjectivities that are those of the citizen-subject. In the next chapter, I examine the emergence and evolution of the refugee category, which I contextualize in the genealogy of the wider phenomenon of human displacement from circa the Peace of Westphalia.

2

Refugees, Human Displacement, and Statecraft: The Ascent of the Territorial Nation-State

For you to whom one solitary spot is not appointed, but forbidden, the exclusion from one city is the freedom to choose from all.

—PLUTARCH

All national rootedness is rooted first of all in the memory or the anxiety of a displaced or displaceable population.

—JACQUES DERRIDA, *SPECTERS OF MARX*

The twentieth century has been called the century of the refugee (Loescher, 1993; Xenos, 1995; Said, 1994; Hope-Simpson, 1939). This characterization is well justified, considering the massive human displacements that have occurred in this century. The two world wars in the first half of the century and smaller but widespread conflicts in the second half produced vast populations of refugees (Loescher, 1993; Ferris, 1993b). Of all the developments that created refugees, those in the first quarter of the century contributed most to the dawning of the century of the refugee. Developments particularly circa the First World War led to massive human displacements hitherto unprecedented in both scope and intensity. These displacements were particularly intense in Europe and the Middle East, largely because of the unraveling of the imperial ancien régimes, the Ottoman and Austria-Hungarian Empires, under the disintegrating pressures of the war (Macartney, 1929; Hope-Simpson, 1939). The ensuing tumult, which radically unsettled the perennial ways of life, sent more than twenty million people on the road as refugees. There were the

Russians, for example, more than five million in number, either uprooted during World War I or escaped from revolutionary Russia after 1917. There were also the Poles, the Germans, the Armenians, the Greeks, the Turks, and the Hungarians, numbering in millions in each case, who constituted the human tide rolling across Europe and the Middle East. Never before in history had Europe and the Middle East seen such a sudden and massive uprooting of humanity. Refugees were everywhere, and the refugee condition seemed to be not so much an exception as the prevailing condition in the lives of millions. Something had to be done to deal with the massive populations of displaced people, and something was done. In 1921, under the auspices of the League of Nations, the League of Nations High Commissioner for Refugees (LNHCR) was established as the first international organization explicitly mandated to deal with refugee situations. The LNHCR started a tradition of intergovernmental refugee relief work that would come to constitute the bedrock of the modern refugee protection regime in the rest of the century. It was these developments—the massive displacements of humanity and the subsequent efforts to respond to them—that marked the beginnings of what has come to be called the century of the refugee.

Although the twentieth century came thus to be called the century of the refugee, it was not the first century in which refugees appeared. Historically, refugees existed prior to the twentieth century, although not in the fullest modern sense, as discussed in the introduction and chapter 1, in terms of their relation to the hierarchy of organization manifested in the citizen/nation/state ensemble. If formally defined exclusively in relation to this statist hierarchy, the refugee phenomenon would indeed be a phenomenon peculiar largely, though still not entirely, to the twentieth century, since the intergovernmental institutions that formally created the refugee category in relation to the statist hierarchy themselves emerged largely in the twentieth century. Refugees, however, have a history that extends far prior to the twentieth century, at least in terms of the emergence of the term *refugee* employed to refer to various populations of displaced people.

Etymologically, the English term *refugee* is the Anglicized derivation of the French term *réfugié,* which has been in use in France since the high medieval period. According to *Le Grand Robert de la langue française* (Robert, 1985: 156), the earliest known written reference to the term *réfugié* can be traced back to 1573, used in reference to persons fleeing religious persecution from the Low Countries under the anti-Reformation Spanish rulers. The French term itself derives from the Latin word *refugere,* meaning to flee (*fugere*) back (*re*), that is, to flee back to safety (155–56).[1] There is no clear evidence on the historical context within which the adoption from the Latin root words of the term *réfugié* might have occurred. The proverbial "origin stories" locate the emergence of the term *refugee* in the mass expulsions in Europe in the fifteenth and sixteenth centuries, including the expulsion of Jews and Muslims from Spain and the flight of Protestants from the lowlands in France (Zolberg, 1985; Baird, 1895; Loomie, 1963; Scouloudi, 1987; Vuilleumier, 1989).

Historically, the English term *refugee* emerged into the popular scene rather abruptly to refer to a specific event of displacement, the expulsion and flight of the Huguenots from France in 1685, which occurred after Louis XIV revoked the Edict of Nantes, thus shattering a fragile religious and political compromise between French Catholics and the Protestant French Huguenots. The revocation led to the expulsion and/or flight of two hundred thousand Huguenots from France into the neighboring countries of Germany, Switzerland, Italy, and the Netherlands, and across the English Channel into Britain. This event marked the date at which the term *refugee* was first introduced into the English language to describe large numbers of people escaping religious persecution into other countries. Historically, however, there is evidence that the term was known to some English speakers prior to 1685. For example, the French term *réfugié* had already appeared in one of the French-English dictionaries long before 1685. *A Dictionarie of the French and English Tongues,* published in 1611, included the term *refugié* or *refugée* and defined it as someone who has "fled, run, resorted unto for succor and assistance" (Cotgrave, 1611). In spite of this fact, the year 1685 is designated as the year of the adoption of the term *refugee* into English with the flight of the Huguenots as the first truly mass refugee event in Europe. In short, what differentiated the Huguenot case from earlier experiences of displacement, some of which were called refugee events as well, was that it came to be associated with the introduction of the term *refugee* into the English vernacular, a development that traditionally marks the beginning of the recorded history of the refugee phenomenon in European histories.[2]

So emerged the refugee onto the historical stage, but, according to many scholars, to have no drastic effect on the political and administrative landscapes for a long time to come. In fact, observers argue, between the Huguenot displacement and the refugee occurrences in the first quarter of the twentieth century, the refugee phenomenon remained limited in magnitude and saliency, not only in terms of the number of actual refugees (or those people who were called refugees) but also in terms of the significance of the refugee phenomenon for the host countries (Zolberg, 1985; Marrus, 1985). While the nineteenth century witnessed a rise in the number of refugees, especially in the second half of the century, observers suggest that the increase was too insubstantial to worry the hosts. It would be the twentieth century that would usher in alarming numbers of refugee populations, and, appropriately, it would be the twentieth century, not the eighteenth or nineteenth, that would come to be called the century of the refugee.

Historical developments after 1685 generally support this argument. In spite of the relative "internationalization" of the term *refugee* with the Huguenot displacement, the term did not find widespread and ontologically distinctive use either in the general public or in official discourses after 1685. For example, no consistent reference to the term *refugee* appears in acts or laws enacted within countries or in the agreements and treaties signed between governments until well into the nineteenth century. Moreover, the term seldom appears in the eighteenth century, except in a few popular resources and historical works by individual authors and in dictionaries and encyclopedias. A whole host of terms, including *suppliant, exile, asylee, émigré, fugitive, profugus,* and *banished,* as well as *refugee,* were employed to discuss human displacements and to relate them to the prevailing relations and institutions of specific times and places. Even the flight of the Huguenots, which took them to several countries, including England, Germany, Italy, Switzerland, Belgium, and the Netherlands, inevitably affecting the dynamics of those respective polities, is discussed generally, though not always, without the use of the term *refugee.* For instance, although a number of parliamentary or royal acts and decrees were intended to entice the Huguenots into various countries, there were in those acts only infrequent references to the term *refugee.* Instead, references were made to the "exile," "suppliant," "emigrant," or "stranger," or to the "religious brethren" or "the distressed Protestants."[3] In other words, the term *refugee,* insomuch as it figured in popular and official discourses of displacement, appeared simply as one of the many terms in use that constituted the political economy of the discussion on different forms of human displacement in those times. Interestingly enough, the practice of using multiple terms interchangeably to discuss the Huguenot displacement is employed in a reverse sense in discussing other displacement events as well. This relative "permissiveness" of vocabulary on human displacement is extremely important, and shortly I shall explain why that is so. For now, what is important to note is what this permissiveness might reflect in a historical, conjunctural sense about human displacement.

From a historical standpoint, some observers suggest, the permissiveness of the vocabulary (or the relative absence of the term *refugee*) perhaps indicates that from the Huguenot displacement to the late nineteenth and early twentieth centuries, there was no or little pressing need for clear-cut formal distinctions across various experiences of human displacement. Indeed, Aristide Zolberg writes that the defining characteristic of the period from the Huguenot incident to the middle of the nineteenth century was the relative absence of massive forced population movements (1985: 38).[4] Concomitantly, in such an absence, human displacement, including refugeehood (the degree to which the term *refugee* was in use), was not perceived as a compelling enough phenomenon to impel the host countries to act in a concerted and systematic fashion in order to control human displacement closely. Had there been a compelling need for such control, the argument goes, it might have necessitated the production of clear-cut formal parameters. Absent that need, especially until well into the nineteenth century, human displacement in general and refugeeism in particular had little clear-cut formal status vis-à-vis the institutions of the host countries. The reasons for this lack of "status" are episodic as well as contextual and manifest the dynamics of human displacement until the late nineteenth and early twentieth centuries.

First and foremost, until the twentieth century the numbers of displaced people were limited to a few thousand at a time. There were exceptions, but in most cases displaced people did not constitute large clusters in their displacement so as to attract any attention and be registered as such in the annals of history. Indeed, as many scholars contend, the Huguenot episode, which was the culmination of what could retrospectively be called the age of "religious cleansing" in the European era of absolutisms, produced the last mass displacement before the modern-day refugee flows of the late nineteenth and early twentieth centuries (Zolberg, 1985; Marrus, 1985; Macartney, 1929). Moreover, in times of mercantilism, which lingered well into the nineteenth century, human displacement (as well as voluntary movements of people from one place to another), under whatever name, was generally desirable, since the displaced brought with them knowledge and know-how, endowing host countries with many welcome factors of development (Dowty, 1987; Vuilleumier, 1989). Not the least important was the fact that the uprooted populations afforded rich pools of recruitment for the armies of competing European states. The Huguenot refugees, for example, filled the ranks of Dutch and English armies against France, while tens of thousands of Irish, uprooted between 1691 and 1791, joined the French armies to fight against the British (Tabori, 1972; Collinson, 1994). Prior to the twentieth century, in short, displaced people were often accepted into host countries, even if it was their skills, not so much their persecuted or exiled bodies and souls, that were being embraced.

In addition, the short duration of displacement rendered refugees noncompelling. As Michael R. Marrus highlights:

> Refugee situations . . . could scarcely endure for years at a time. Some refugees could support themselves one way or another, often indefinitely. Others found refuge thanks to the charity of the clergy, princes, or local notables. Still others merged with the poor of the host society and survived by begging, stealing, or occasional labor. . . . Premodern times knew no camps where masses of civilians could be interned for lengthy periods and needed no special category to suspend them outside the framework of the civilized community. Thrust unexpectedly on a society usually indifferent to outsiders of any sort, many refugees would quickly succumb to hunger, disease, or exposure. (1985: 5)

The life of a refugee, in other words, could be and often was not unlike life in a Hobbesian condition: "solitary, poor, nasty, brutish and short." Refugees could expect no regular support from the societies in which they were living, and it was precisely because of this lack of regular support that refugee life was generally difficult and, sometimes, very short: it was short because it was undesirable, and it was undesirable because, without any guaranteed help, it was nasty and brutish. Paradoxically, however, the refugee condition could also be empowering, for it was subject to no strict formal framework of exclusion that would otherwise "suspend [refugees] outside the framework of the civilized community." Refugee events in "premodern" times, in other words, did not necessarily remove people as dramatically from civil society in the host societies as did the modern refugee category formulated in the context of responses to refugee occurrences in the twentieth century. Upon displacement in premodern times, refugees certainly risked poverty and destitution, because of the absence of systematic interventions in their lives. Yet they also stood to benefit from nonintervention, for nonintervention afforded them a less encumbered access to life in host communities. The result of this dynamic was significant in refugee histories prior to the late nineteenth and the twentieth centuries. In these times, refugee status was largely, though not entirely, a nonstatus, particularly in terms of refugees' formal standing vis-à-vis institutions of the host societies. Refugees largely remained unimportant or were of little or no concern to the host countries, for they did not represent any drastic disruptions for the host countries. This was to last until the first quarter of the twentieth century, when, as was briefly portrayed at the onset of this chapter, refugees were catapulted to the fore of national and international agendas.

This understanding of refugees' status brings us to important questions. What role, if any, might refugees and other kinds of displaced people have had in their host societies before they became a source of immediate concern in the twentieth century? What was their relation to the forms of governance evolving, for example, since the emergence of the term *refugee* at the turn of the eighteenth century? How do we respond to these questions? Should we respond simply by saying that because refugees and other displaced people were relatively obscure, they did not have any impact on and/or did not play any role in the societies they came into contact with? I suggest that we should not, for while it is plausible to suggest that refugees were generally not disruptive to host societies and governments because of their small numbers and obscurity, this does not necessarily mean that they did not have any effect on the societies with which they came into contact. Nor does it mean that refugee effects needed to have been "disruptive" to be taken seriously and recorded as effects. Indeed, some effects, however small, I suggest, might perhaps have been constructive in a Foucauldian sense of power; that is, they might have been instrumental in certain developments in host societies. Given this possibility, the next question is this: What effects might refugees have had on the multiplicity of the processes to which they were exposed, either as fully integrated members of the host communities or as outsiders living marginal lives within the host communities?

In light of this reasoning, I want to propose that it is possible to offer a parallel reading of refugee histories that, while still rooted in the aforementioned argument on the relative marginality and obscurity of refugees prior to the twentieth century, complements that argument by seeing refugees' role in a constructive, productive light in the transformation of social and political landscapes. Specifically, this reading looks into the role that refugees might have played, actively or by virtue of their mere existence, in the emergence and transformation of the sovereign territorial state and its constitutive counterparts, the citizen and the nation. Let me begin by offering a heuristic to further clarify this line of inquiry.

In the twentieth century, the links, both conceptual and empirical, between the refugee category and the state, the citizen, and the nation are unambiguous, as has been discussed earlier in this book. By comparison, these links are not at all clear in the centuries preceding the twentieth century. Yet, one can argue, they are still there, not in a full-fledged, modern form, surely, but in an incipient fashion in terms of a general relationship between *human displacement* and state building or *statecraft*. These links become even clearer when examining refugee histories under the more inclusive conceptual tool of human displacement in relation to the practices and processes of statecraft, instead of examining refugee history prior to the twentieth century from a standpoint rooted in the modern categorical term *refugee* as defined in the twentieth century. There are several reasons for this orientation, but one is most compelling.

Historically, there is no question that, in spite of the existence of disparate terms describing various types of human displacement, the typology of human displacement until the late nineteenth and early twentieth centuries was not at all conceptually precise. Different terms such as *refugee* or *exile* did not necessarily represent mutually exclusive, ontologically distinct experiences, but rather represented conceptually and ontologically overlapping, if not convergent, meanings, particularly in terms of the practical relevance of human displacement to the processes of governance. The field of human displacement prior to the twentieth century was both conceptually and practically amorphous, and refugees, to the extent that the term *refugee* was employed to refer to displaced people, became part of this amorphous landscape. Refugees, be they Huguenots or others, went by many different names. They were called refugees, exiles, fugitives, and/or émigrés, in a practice of naming that, in effect, neither represented nor engendered or afforded any clear-cut, formal, institutionalized distinctions among these categories of displacement.[5] What made a more practical difference in the lives of these people was their predisplacement status. Certainly, the commonality among them was their displacement. But some were displaced intellectuals, others displaced artisans, and yet others displaced aristocrats. Each status enabled specific life opportunities in displacement. The artisans sometimes found jobs, albeit with some limitations on their labor; the aristocrats, such as the "joyous émigrés," found enough solidarity in the interstices of all-related European royalty to continue to have comfortable lives; and the intellectuals remained intellectuals while trying to stay alive. Some were luckier than others. In short, while refugee experiences appeared prior to the late nineteenth century, they did not always appear in a categorically distinct form. The vocabulary of and on human displacement was permissive, thus making it difficult to determine what groups of people were seen and labeled as distinctly refugees, distinctly exiles, or distinctly émigrés. While such distinctions were not always available, a more general yet practically significant phenomenon was often apparent: human displacement, a conceptualization with parameters broad enough to include those refugees and exiles whose displacement manifested a certain crisis, breakdown, or deterioration in relations of governance, but also narrow enough to limit displacement to those populations alone, that is, refugees and exiles (and not immigrant workers, diplomats, or travelers or tourists).

From the standpoint of this study, this conceptualization enables a specific argument, which is that, particularly since the first emergence of the absolutist states, human displacement, when manifesting a dysfunction in relations of governance, has historically been a symptom of governance in temporally and spatially contingent ways, its meanings, mechanics, and repercussions having certainly been complex and varied across different ages and places. Save the displacements that might have occurred because of natural catastrophes or epidemics (Moch, 1992: 28), displacements, whether under the name of the refugee or the exile, were a manifestation of statecraft, that is, something that happened in the course of statecraft or was a result of statecraft, something that manifested the difficulties of statecraft yet also was useful to the task of statecraft, something that escaped the control of statecraft but also was harnessed to the task of statecraft.

By the same token, it is possible to argue that, as unproblematic as they were, displaced peoples, whether the Huguenot refugees in 1685 or the royalist French émigrés in 1789 and the counterrevolutionary exiles in 1792–93 (Panayi, 1994; Tabori, 1972; Kohn, 1967), reflected the practices of statecraft. They reflected, for example, the government of the so-called reason of state of Louis XIV as the eighteenth century drew nearer, as well as the government of the revolutionary French state at work constructing the French nation as the eighteenth century came to a close (Brubaker, 1992). This argument amounts to stating that displaced people, of whom refugees constituted one loose category in a premodern sense, may not have been "disruptive" of the host communities, but they were certainly consequential to and implicated in the transformations of the host societies, even if only in epiphenomenal ways. Interestingly, history shows us that at times they were more than epiphenomenal, contributing substantially to the changes and transformations in the societies in which they found themselves.

Of the many events of displacement, in my opinion, three specific events—the Huguenot expulsion or flight in 1685, the French Revolution and the "joyous émigrés" from 1789 to 1815, and the Russian refugees circa the First World War—represent threshold developments. They are historical markers that illustrate materially as well as symbolically the relationship between statecraft and human displacement in European histories prior to the twentieth century (in the first two cases) and in the early twentieth century (in the Russian case). These events in human displacement, their dynamics, their force, and their practical consequences illustrate the practices and processes of a historical transformation of the political space in the image of the sovereign territorial state—the state defined less in ethereal or dynastic terms, more in modern territorial terms, and subsequently in national terms (Hobsbawm, 1990: 81; Hill, 1993: 104; Lefebvre, 1995; Noiriel, 1996: 212–15).

I argue that these three events of human displacement, manifesting a dysfunction in governance, represent significant turning points in the relation of human displacement to statecraft in European histories. They demonstrate the instrumentality of human displacement in the transformations of the state in history (a) from the absolutist state to the centralizing modern territorialized state in the Huguenot case, and (b) from the centralizing territorialized state to the centralizing nationalized state in the case of the French émigrés. Put in terms of statecraft, the Huguenot incident reflects a dimension of the territorialization of sovereign statecraft, while the French Revolution and the episode of "joyous émigrés" reflect a dimension of the nationalization of statecraft. Finally, the Russian refugee crisis reflects a dimension of the intergovernmentalization of statecraft. In all, in spite of temporal and spatial differences, sites of human displacement work as sites of statecraft in history. I shall proceed to examine the Huguenots and the French émigrés to demonstrate these links. The Russian refugee crisis will constitute the background for chapter 3.

THE HUGUENOTS, HUMAN DISPLACEMENT, AND STATECRAFT

Historically, the Huguenot displacement from France under Louis XIV represents one of the earlier attempts in Europe by the increasingly centralizing and bureaucratizing governments to intervene in the pastiche-like landscape of people to transform, shape, organize, and manage the relations of people in ways instrumental to the transformations of the government of the state. The interventions of governments, though materialized in multiple ways and forms, were underlain and facilitated by what Michel Foucault called a specific "political rationality linked to [a novel political] technology" of individuals (1988b: 160): the emergence of the "population" as a new form of collectivity. This rationality conceptualized the otherwise amorphous masses of people in a different light in terms of their relations to governments. Increasingly, its practitioners cast people not in theocratic terms, as subjects of a divine desire or heavenly purpose manifested, say, in the early feudal absolutist orders of the sixteenth and seventeenth centuries, but in anthropomorphic terms, as individual members of population communities of whose rational organization the state was to be in charge and on whose rational organization the state itself depended for its raison d'être and survival.[6] It was, one might say, the dawn of a novel rationality for regimentation of life activities. It is that momentous development that Foucault has in mind when he remarks:

> One of the great innovations in the techniques of power in the eighteenth century was the emergence of population as an economic and political problem: population as wealth, population as manpower or labor capacity, population balanced between its own growth and the resources it commanded. Governments perceived that they were not dealing simply with subjects, or even people, but with population with its specific phenomena and its peculiar variables: birth and death rates, life expectancy, fertility, state of health, frequency of illness, patterns of diet and habitation. (1978: 25)

Foucault calls the politics of this technology "biopolitics," where population—or more properly, individual men and women constituting a population, men and women as part of a population—became the object of the activities of the (emergent police) state, which had contemporaneous transformative effects both on the notions and realities of individuals, society, and community, and on the reasons and technologies of the state. The practical effect of biopolitics—simultaneously individualizing in its focus on individual men and women and totalizing in casting individual men and women as representative parts of a community—"was the increasing intervention of the state in the life of individuals, [and] the increasing importance of life problems for political power" (Foucault, 1988a: 160–61).

The "innovation" of population as the "object" of *statecraft* was undergirded by the emergence of a profoundly new approach in everyday life: "scientific" theory and method. The new approach effectively contested and supplanted the orthodox orientation predicated on the organizing role of "heavenly purposes" in nature as well as in society. Instead, the new approach, as articulated most prominently in the works of René Descartes, Isaac Newton, Francis Bacon, and Gottfried von Leibniz, imposed a mechanical and geometrical view on the universe of things (Knutsen, 1992: 94–97). Suddenly, human societies came to represent a specific (natural) matter in motion, a phenomenon of collectivity with observable relations of organization, change, and exchange. It was the ascent of "Cartesian reasoning" in the lives of men and women in a society as population.

The Cartesian reasoning intruded on the absolutist French state, perhaps earlier than any other state in Europe, to become the "reason of the state" (Bartelson, 1995: 154–56). The code word for the reason of the state, in turn, became "order" throughout the realm of the state (Moote, 1969: 235; Church, 1969: 373). As historian J. E. King suggests, the imperative of order throughout the realm necessitated a "complete knowledge of the facts of the realm" "or every possible detail of the state." "Louis XIV believed that he must know the realm to rule it well" (1967: 30–31). The methodical representations of the realities of the realm through reports, statistics, standardized tables, registers, memoirs, surveys, and periodic accounts became the means for knowledge (Hunt and Wickham, 1994: 26). Administrative archives were created for the collation, classification, and preservation of useful data. Vigorous accounting methods were applied to the finances of the state. The economy of the realm was coordinated as never before with laws regulating industries, commerce, and labor. The military was transformed into a disciplined force governed by *règlements* and exact administration (Anderson, 1984; Held, 1996). Furthermore, laws of the realm were systematized into a unified instrument for the control of individual conduct within the state (King, 1967: 43–45). What was being created in France, writes King, was a

> rational and mechanical state which operated according to set principles and in which the presiding intelligence of sovereign reasons could be made to control individual instincts. The reason was to supply security, certainty, and efficiency in the conduct of private life and subordinate this conduct to the interest of the state. (44)

"The policy of administrative reform and state-building," writes William Church, "was so extensive that it established the form of the French government until the [French] revolution"(1969: 372). A telling expression of this process, which also amply highlights the shift to biopolitics, is given in the memoirs of Jean-Baptiste Colbert, the chief minister of Louis XIV. Here is how Colbert instructs a regional magistrate in the affairs of the state: "I will say further, that if you wish individually to judge well and reasonably if there is misery in the province, consider whether cities depopulate, if commerce, if marriages diminish, if offices, lands and houses decrease in prices or not. These are sure means of judging the state of the province" ([1863] 1969: 38).

The importance of the emergence of the "rational and mechanical" state for the Huguenot displacement lies not in any immediate, direct link between the Huguenots and the state, but in the changing practices of statecraft, that is, in the changing relations of the state to the people within the realm. It is a question of how the reason of the state was conceptualized and articulated and how people within the realm of the state were related to this conceptualization and articulation (Shapiro, 1993: 9). Reading the relevant histories, in response it is possible to suggest that in the rational and mechanical state of Louis XIV, with biopolitics becoming increasingly the state's technology of government, people became the objects of interventions by the emergent impersonal and systematic apparatuses of the state, working, as it were, "for the reinforcement of the state's strength" (Foucault, 1988: 152).[7]

In more than one way, the Huguenot expulsion, as an event of forced human displacement, appears to be such a practice, an intervention devised to strengthen the state, as Foucault would say. It is instructive to remember that the revocation of the Edict of Nantes called for the expulsion of only a few thousand Calvinist priests, not the whole Huguenot population. The subsequent flight of about two hundred thousand Huguenots was neither fully expected nor at all desired by Louis XIV. Scholars offer various explanations for the revocation of the edict, ranging from the pressures from the Catholic establishment in France, to a desire to undercut Huguenot economic power (Church, 1969; Zolberg, 1985; Jacobson, 1996). However, even in their divergence, many of these explanations can be read in congruence with the argument on shifting practices of statecraft in France and on human displacement figures in relation to those practices.

Aristide Zolberg, a leading scholar of refugee histories in Europe, directly links the Huguenot expulsion as a refugee event to state building, in his words, to attempts "to perfect the most powerful state in Europe" (1985: 37). Zolberg sees the revocation as an instance of a "state-building project manifesting the pursuit of ideological unity—here indicated by public adherence to the official religion" (36). David Jacobson (1996) and Sarah Collinson (1994) offer parallel arguments. Jacobson suggests that "reformation placed a premium on identifying the loyalties of the populace and ensuring more homogenous populations. Consequently groups that carried the faith of opposing states were often expelled" (1996: 20). Collinson contends similarly:

> The rulers of this [mercantilist] period were concerned with questions of integration and sought to consolidate their power by promoting identification with their rule. Their power rested on religion, and so Christianity became the prime instrument of integration. . . . Just as authoritarian regimes of the twentieth century have resorted to expulsions of minority groups in the interests of national consolidation, so thousands of non-Christians and "heretics" were periodically expelled or forced to flee. (1994: 27–28)

Jacobson furthers the link when he proposes that "religious affiliation proved to be the basis of protonationalism, instilling an identification with embryonic French, Dutch, and English nationalities, among others" (1996: 20).[8]

The observation that the Huguenot episode represents an attempt at "the state's preservation, expansion and felicity" (Foucault, 1988: 148) is a matter of interpretation surely subject to contestation. What seems certain, however, is that the Huguenot displacement was a symptom of statecraft, as I have argued, something that happened in the course of statecraft. The expulsion of priests was a result of statecraft instantiated in the decision to revoke the Edict of Nantes. The episode was also a result of, as well as a response to, statecraft; the subsequent flight of Huguenots into neighboring countries occurred both as a result of and in response to the revocation. The episode was something that manifested the difficulties of statecraft, that is, something that escaped the control of statecraft. The inability of the powerful "mechanical and rational" French state to prevent the mass Huguenot flight from France attests to this fact. Yet the episode was also useful to the task of statecraft, as is evidenced in the symbolic "homogenization" of the polity in religious terms, which, according to Jacobson, might even have worked as the basis of a French "protonationalism." In all, the Huguenot displacement was part and parcel of a larger shift in practices of government by which the absolute state would begin to acquire the characteristics of a modern centralizing state.

An equally significant development represented by the Huguenot episode was the articulation of a specific concept of territory as a bounded, exclusionary space—a territory of particularity—within which the "realities" of the state and of the population were to become possible. This was an articulation of a marked territory as an uncontested and identifiable political location where power, place, and population were realigned to affirm the territorial(izing) state—a novel organization of polity that allowed the state to explore, display, and mobilize the resources of the territory in a more contained and controlled way. As with other inventories of resources harnessed to the powers of the territorial state, the Huguenot episode contains the signs and symbols of such a territorially bounding power (Mukerji, 1997: 1–3). This territorialization of life was reflected in the language of the new edict that revoked the Edict of Nantes. After "perpetually and irrevocably" suppressing the Edict of Nantes, the king declared: "We enjoin all ministers of the said Pretented Reform Religion who do not choose to become converts or embrace the Catholic, Apostolic and Roman religion, to leave our kingdom and the territories subject to us within fifteen days from the publication of the Edict" (qtd. in Golden, 1988: 136–37). The ensuing flight of the Huguenots from France claimed, posited, and projected in no uncertain terms the territorial boundedness of life for a definite population and the state. In that sense, the expulsion marked one of the earlier in a series of events that, from the seventeenth century to the twentieth century, firmly established, both in imagination and in practice, the notion of statist territoriality, or the territorial boundedness of life as the single most significant defining property in the existence of communities. In a historical sense, this was an extension of the logic of sovereign territoriality that was promoted to prominence in the Peace of Westphalia. The territorial character of the emergent form of governance was affirmed in the Treaties of Munster in 1648, which asserted:

> In order to prevent for the future all Differences in the Political State, all and every [one of] the Electors, Princes, and States of the Roman Empire shall be so established and confirmed in their ancient Rights, Prerogatives, Liberties, Privileges, free Exercise of their *Territorial Right,* as well in Spirituals and Temporals, . . . and in the possession of all these things, by virtue of the present Transaction, that they may not be molested at any time in any manner, under any pretext what-

> soever. ("A Treaty of Peace," [1648] 1969: 241; emphasis added; see also Donner, 1994: 6)

"The Peace of Westphalia . . . marked the beginning of the balance of power system. Most striking, however, was the enunciated principle of international relations following the Peace of Westphalia—*cuius regio, eius religio* ('to each region, its own religion')—which anticipated the principles of sovereignty and national self-determination" (Jacobson, 1996: 20; see also Knutsen, 1992: 77–79). This motto was clearly at work in the Huguenot episode, in that desired religious homogeneity was linked to the very identity of the state as a "political location" (Mukerji, 1997: 3); religion was a major resource in engendering an incipient, territorially bound French nationalism. In this sense the Huguenot expulsion could be seen as a crafting of the sovereign territorial state, an event by which the state was *projected* to be a territorially empowered, sovereign entity in its own right. The state occupied "a part of the earth's surface," a "circumscribed space" (Knutsen, 1992: 76; Lefebvre, 1995: 280), and was authorized to patrol it not only with a view to securing its external borders against enemies but also with a desire to shape its content—its population—to serve the felicity of the state.[9] This desire is characteristic of and essential to any territorial sovereign state. It is akin to what Michael Shapiro calls the "sovereignty impulse," which

> tends towards drawing boundaries around the self in order to unambiguously specify individual and collective identities, to privilege and rationalize aspects of a homogenous subjectivity that is eligible for membership and recognition and to constitute forms of non-identical and ineligible otherness, and to specify and bound the spaces in which subjects achieve eligibility and the space in which the collective has a dominion. (1993: 2)

The sovereignty impulse in a practical, historical sense produces a series of simultaneous effects by way of exclusionary identity practices based on dichotomizations in terms of space (inside versus outside), membership in a specific community (citizen versus non-citizen), and agency (state versus individual). It is an instrumental orientation that creates a "space" of eligibility and noneligibility and eligible and noneligible subjectivities constructed, as Henri Lefebvre puts it, through both violence and rational-political regimentation

(1995: 280–81). In the words of Jens Bartelson, it provides an "ordering principle" that produces "what is internal and what is external to states" (1995: 17)."[10] The sovereignty impulse as such was manifested in the Huguenot displacement in territorial and protonationalist ways and would be manifested in full force in the French Revolution, which was to produce its own share of human displacement.

THE FRENCH REVOLUTION, HUMAN DISPLACEMENT, AND STATECRAFT

If the Huguenot episode can be construed to be an early expression of the sovereignty impulse, the French Revolution should be seen as a climax of the work of the sovereignty impulse. By the same token, if the Huguenot episode represents a development in the formation of protonationalism, the French Revolution represents a development in the creation of nationalism as an ideology of the state, which, according to Rogers Brubaker, eventually resulted in "the invention of the nation-state" (1992: 46) and its counterpart, national citizenship—the most exclusive, unambiguous subjectivity of eligibility, which is membership in the nation-state.

Brubaker argues that "the revolution created both the nation-state (by abolishing jurisdictional boundaries within the nation) and nationalism (by constructing new boundaries and sharpening antagonisms between nations)" (1992: 44). Surely, the revolution did not create something out of nothing, but, instead, it reorganized the political space for the expression of a mélange of extant and evolving sentiments of collectivity through new power alignments and under new rubrics (see Finer, 1997: 1542–66). Affirming this view, Lucien Febvre writes that the "revolution [made] a group of subjects, vassals, and members of restricted communities into the body of citizens of one and the same state . . . [and] wield[ed] them into one powerful group which form[ed] a coherent mass within clearly defined borders." The invention of the nation-state and the national citizen, outlining new forms of eligibility, could not have been achieved without defining those forms of ineligibility against which the forms of eligibility were presumed, positively constituting what Febvre called "the coherent mass of citizen" (1973: 213–14). In fact, Brubaker suggests that such "paradigmatic" forms of eligibility were simultaneously created, predicating an ontological interdependence:

> By inventing the national citizen and the legally homogenous national citizenry, the revolution simultaneously invented the foreigner. Henceforth citizen and foreigner would be correlative, mutually exclusive, exhaustive categories. One would be either a citizen or a foreigner, there would be no third way. As a result of this stark simplification in the political geometry of membership, *l'étranger* could symbolize pure extraneity. . . . The revolutionary invention of the nation-state and national citizenship thus engendered the modern figure of the foreigner—not only as a legal category but as a political epithet, invested with a psychological charge it formerly lacked, and condensing around itself pure outsiderhood. (1992: 46–47)

What Brubaker suggests here is not simply that these categories coemerged by historical coincidence, but that they had to coemerge, for one would not have been possible without the other. Maxim Silverman concurs when he writes that "the construction of the national and the foreigner was part of the same historical process" (1992: 30). Gérard Noiriel (1996) agrees, arguing, for instance, that it was by making the foreigner visible in discursive political-administrative and popular-cultural ways that the nation was crystallized. Another way of stating this is to say that the construction of new forms of foreignness was indispensable to the historical process by which the notion of national citizen was crafted and empowered.

It is at this juncture where citizenship and foreignness implicate each other that human displacement becomes relevant to statecraft in the context of revolutionary France. Just as the production of the meanings and identities of the foreigner was integral to the construction of the national citizen as the proper subjectivity of the French nation-state (establishing the citizen/nation/state hierarchy), so the displacement of thousands that occurred as a result of the French Revolution was part and parcel of the processes by which the images and identities of the foreigner were produced, circulated, and made instrumental to the "invention of the nation-state." In *The Incidence of the Emigration during the French Revolution,* Donald Greer highlights this connection:

> During the last decade of the eighteenth century, France, convulsed by a great revolution, cast out victims of change, refugees from readjustment, fugitives from violence, disorder, and economic stress. These were the émigrés of the French Revolution. . . . Absent or present, in war or peace—for over forty years—during the revolution, the Empire,

> and the Restoration . . . the émigrés played an important, sometimes sinister, and often decisive part in the crucial events in the life of France. (1951: 1)

"The émigrés of the French Revolution": these displaced humans were indeed one of the compelling consequences of the Revolution and the developments that ensued. In the twenty-six years that stretched from the fall of the Bastille to Waterloo, there were several great waves of displacement from France (Tabori, 1972: 95). First came the exodus of aristocrats and those who were unalterably royalist. Thinking that their exile would be short and pleasant, these people called themselves the "joyous émigrés." Unfortunately for them, their exile was neither short nor pleasant; many spent long years in exile before they could return to France (Weiner, 1960: 8; Kohn, 1967: 43–49; Vuilleumier, 1989). The second exodus took place only a few months after the fall of the Bastille and involved the gentry, the squirearchy, *petite noblesse,* and ordinary people. Their flight came to be known as the "emigration of fear" or *émigration de surette* (Farquhar, 1967: 2; Weiner, 1960: 10). Another exodus occurred in late 1791, comprising the remnants of the aristocracy as well as the refractory priests. Yet another flight took place as a result of the counterrevolution in 1793. When the counterrevolution was defeated, thousands of its proponents went into exile in the neighboring countries of Switzerland and Spain, as well as Great Britain (Greer, 1951: 3; Lefebvre, 1964: 47). Paul Tabori tells us that "these waves of [flight from France] had tidal effects. . . . The French exiles carried their ideas into the distant corners of the world" (1972: 95).

This, indeed, was the case. However, equally significant was the impact these exiles had on France itself. As Greer somewhat dramatically states, "The émigrés played an important, sometimes sinister, and often decisive part in the crucial events in the life of France." Of all their activities, their presence as displaced people put into question the legitimacy of the new France (Kohn, 1967: 43–45). In a more practical sense, the émigrés led "émigré armies" against the revolutionary governments. When they could not form their own armies, they joined the armies of France's enemies (Tabori, 1972: 103–5; Greer, 1951). When, for example, England, Prussia, and Austria went to war against France in the War of the First Coalition, there were thousands of émigrés in their armies. Émigrés also fomented resistance from within France when they could and aided others whenever the opportunity arose. The counterrevolution, for example, included émigrés in its ranks (Vuilleumier, 1989: 12–14). Ironically, its failure swelled the ranks of émigrés (Kohn, 1967: 44). In short, the émigrés may not have been an overwhelming force to reckon with, but they were a force nevertheless in the political landscapes in France, England, Switzerland, Prussia, and other places in Europe.

Paradoxically, their images and identities were harnessed to the foreigner discourse that, as Brubaker and Silverman suggest, was a sine qua non to the emergence of the national citizen and the national state. Émigré images were appropriated to construct the paradigmatic foreigner not only legally but also in cultural and political senses. Émigrés became foreigners, as Brubaker makes clear, "not only as a legal category but as a political epithet, invested with a psychological charge [the foreigner] formerly lacked, and condensing around itself pure outsiderhood." Not surprisingly, to the question of who were foreigners, Brubaker replies: "in the political sense, émigrés, refractory priests, rebels, aristocrats, and other political enemies"(1992: 47). As a political epithet, the term *foreigner* thus could be and was attributed to the nationals who, in the words of Nicholas Xenos, were rendered "outside the nation" (1992: 79).[11] The displaced nationals, that is, émigrés, refractory priests, rebels, and aristocrats, became foreigners in that sense, perceived to be posing a certain threat to the processes of inventing the nation-state and the national citizen (Kohn, 1967: 47; Morrisey, 1993: 129–30; Xenos, 1992: 79; 1995: 238–39).

So, it was in the construction of these displaced bodies as foreigners that national citizenship was partially constructed and empowered. Displacements were a result of shifting practices of statecraft, but as such, they also constituted sites of statecraft instrumental to the nationalization of practices of statecraft. Émigré experiences and identities were problematized in a way that affirmed the logic of shifting practices of statecraft (from territorial state to territorial national state) while continuing the project of the centralizing state that had been started with Louis XIV. Pointing to this continuity in transformation, Roger Chartier, for example, writes: "Revolutionaries proclaimed an absolute rupture with the Old Regime, but they strengthened and completed its work of centralization" (1994: 178). The émigré experiences were helpful in this process, for in legal and popular representations, they became the embodiment of dangerous foreignness, treason, conspiracy, and criminality against which the proper subjectivity of the nation and of the national citizen was written juridically but also and more importantly, politically and culturally.

For example, starting in 1791 in France, a series of legal measures were introduced to deal with the émigrés (Farquhar, 1967; Soboul, 1974: 234; Kohn, 1967: 46–47, 61). Naturally, these political measures reverberated in the public at large, rendering émigrés more visible than their actual numbers would warrant. This "extra" visibility in turn enabled a resourceful politics around the name of émigrés, creating an antipathetic, if not a totally antagonistic, climate toward them. While many of these measures ostensibly targeted only émigré properties, almost all of them engaged in problematizing émigrés in a political sense, connoting their foreignness, their outsiderness to the body politic; émigrés, in other words, were "bad nationals," to be excluded from the body politic until they became enlightened enough to embrace the nation-state as the perfect representative body—simultaneously individualizing (in representing the national citizen) and universalizing (in representing the nation) (Baker, 1994: 191). The émigrés were cast as those who did not properly belong to this representative nexus of citizen, nation, and state and who were attempting to undermine, if not to destroy, that nexus (Baker, 1994: 191–92; Kohn, 1967: 61). They were "aberrant" subjects, "outside the sovereign," and as such they were an enemy, since, as Saint-Just had claimed, "whatever was outside the sovereign was an enemy" (qtd. in Kohn, 1967: 62). They were therefore "denounced" (Baker, 1994: 191). As a result, it came as no surprise when, reflecting this thinking, in November 1791 and March 1793, laws were enacted decreeing the death penalty for émigrés on mere verification of identity (Lefebvre, 1964: 47; Farquhar, 1967: 38).

The French émigrés were not the only ones made into "foreigners" in revolutionary France. Traditional foreigners, too, became objects of foreigner discourse. The traditional foreigners were diplomats, traders, laborers, and, in some cases, naturalized foreigners who were practically full participants in the society, thanks to the principle of jus soli, which governed citizenship laws in France before and immediately after the Revolution (Noiriel, 1996). There were also émigrés and exiles from other countries, such as the Irish who had escaped persecution in Great Britain from the early eighteenth century on. In general, these foreigners enjoyed as much freedom, if not more in certain situations, as any French subject not only prior to the Revolution but also during the early phases of the Revolution (Noiriel, 1996: 46–50). In fact, in 1790, during the universalist-cosmopolitan period of the Revolution, the revolutionaries abolished altogether the already vitiated, ineffectual foreigner law, contending that the law of the foreigner was against the principle of fraternity uniting all men and that France ought to open its bosom to all peoples of the world (Kristeva, 1991: 155–56; Brubaker, 1992: 39, 45). Foreigners, the revolutionaries stated, were equal with the French and should "be placed in a position of equality within the national community" (Noiriel, 1996: 46). However, when the Revolution turned more particularistic in 1792 at the climax of the émigré movement, the foreigners did not fare as well. They became targets of repressive measures, harassment, and outright persecution from 1793 onward (Brubaker, 1992; Tabori, 1972; Lefebvre, 1964; Hyslop, 1968: 35). Suddenly, "they became the ones who did not belong to the group," albeit in a different way than the French émigrés (Kristeva, 1991: 95, 156–67). Still, they came to signify an "outsiderness" dangerous to the Revolution. They became the "others" who might be the enemy within, perhaps in collusion with the enemies without. They were "outside the nation" once again. Their presence, too, was utilized as a source of foreigner discourse in a political sense. Under pressure, some of them left France—their first place of refuge—as "double exiles" in search of safety in third countries. Many, however, stayed and, as the Revolution started to lose its revolutionary zeal, became naturalized French citizens. While the foreignness was not always framed negatively thereafter, regardless, the foreigner presence became a permanent source of the foreigner discourse, fueling it in both the popular and legal arenas (Kristeva, 1992). Gérard Noiriel, for example, shows how throughout the nineteenth century that presence would lend itself to legal orchestrations of "the card and the code" on foreigners, by which foreignness would be materialized as a criterion to set the citizen apart (1996: 46, 213). In short, whether in a political-cultural sense or in a legal-institutional sense, from the Revolution onward, the problematized subjectivities of foreigners stood to affirm and further participate in the production of the national citizen as the proper subject of the

French nation-state. Significantly, the earlier legislation enacted to deal with foreigners would be the historical precursor of more systematic measures on foreigners that would come in the nineteenth century.

Taken together, these incitements, coupled with practices of statecraft in other fields of activity, such as education, cartographic innovation, the bureaucracy, and transportation (Braudel, 1988; Ford, 1993; Mukerji, 1997), were conducive of a politics of identity construction that, as Brubaker puts it, enabled the process of the "invention" and affirmation of the notion of national citizen and the national state. According to Brubaker, the process was also a process of "state-building," a claim by which Brubaker highlights the link between state building and the emergence of the notions of the national citizen and the national state (1992: 48). In agreement, it becomes possible to suggest that, in fact, the whole process was a process of state building or statecraft, but one that represented the transformation of the state from the territorial state to the territorial nation-state.

Historically, this transformation, namely, the invention of the national citizen and the national state, coincided with what I have called the nationalization of statecraft, a shift in strategies of statecraft that facilitated the clearest imagination and articulation of the citizen/nation/state hierarchy as the hierarchy of legitimate governance. Although employing a different vocabulary, Xenos highlights this transformation—the emergence of the nation as the site of statecraft—in his discussion of the notion of nation and the French Revolution: "In one stroke, the national assembly shifted the battle lines for the control of the state to the terrain of national identity: henceforward, those who were able to impose their version of who the nation was could claim to represent the national will and direct the state" (1995: 238). Concomitantly, the old slogan of the reason of state—"As the king wills, so wills the law"—yielded to a new slogan of statecraft: "As the nation wills, so wills the state." As Xenos intimates, that the nation's will was never simply in existence to be represented but had to be "willed" into existence in statecraft did not much matter. Nor did it matter that the nation itself was but a discursive phenomenon, a product of statecraft that needed to be reinvented day in and day out. What mattered was that the new hierarchy of governance had been successfully imagined and articulated.

The French Revolution became the primary catalyst, the vector of this imagination and articulation.

Significantly, while the Revolution was an essential catalyst, as I have already shown, human displacement became one of the sites of intervention that produced the resources of this imagination and articulation. In various problematizations of human displacement, whether under the name of exile, émigré, or refugee, many came to write what it meant to be properly rooted in the space of a national community, to properly belong in a national community, in other words, to be a national citizen constitutive of the national community and empowering the nation-state. Julia Kristeva (1991: 179) quotes Johann von Herder's revealing words to illustrate that kind of dynamic whereby a form of "non-identical and ineligible otherness" (in human displacement) is produced and circulated to define or inscribe the eligibility of self. "I observe foreign customs," Herder wrote, "in order to conform to the genius of my fatherland, like much fruit under an alien Sun." Herder's practical genius (in imagining the genius of his fatherland) lies in his grasp of the dynamics of creating and fostering the myths of fatherland; people need forms of otherness, forms of foreignness, real or imagined, to be able to "[invent] for themselves a 'we'" that could be claimed to be distinct from "they"—the foreigners (Kristeva, 1991: 24).

With the coming of the nation-state in the French Revolution, contends Kristeva, the modern form of foreignness was created: "The foreigner [became] the one who [did] not belong to the state" (1991: 96). According to this formulation of modernity, the displaced human beings—refugees, exiles, émigrés—were the foreigners. As foreigners, they did not belong to the state. But although they did not belong to the state in their *own* existence, they were made to point to those who presumably did belong to the state. Human displacement was intimately bound up with the broader processes of statist governance from the territorial state to the territorial nation-state.

How does the refugee figure in this equation? This question goes to the heart of this chapter. How can we understand the refugee's place in relation to statecraft in the exhilarations of the ages from the Huguenots to the French émigrés, from the French émigrés to the Russian refugees in the twentieth century? At the onset of this chapter, I argued that in studying the histories of refugees before the modern figure of the refugee was defined and institutionalized in the twentieth century, it is necessary to focus on general experiences of human displacement (within the parameters defined earlier in this chapter) instead of focusing solely on the proper category "refugee." This is so, once again, for the simple fact that the vocabularies through which human displacement was conceptualized prior to the twentieth century were permissive. I have already discussed this phenomenon at length. Still, a few examples might be further instructive. For example, although the people displaced because of the French Revolution were generally identified and referred to as "émigrés," there was a profusion of original historical references to them as "refugees" as well. Such references occur both in popular and legal arenas and should remind us that, perhaps, the peoples of the eighteenth and nineteenth centuries did not necessarily have clear-cut conceptual delineations across various experiences of displacement. Not surprisingly, when the French émigrés reached England after the Revolution, in the eyes of the English Parliament, at times they were "refugees" and at other times they were "émigrés." In February 1794, for example, they became "refugees" in "Supplies Granted by Parliament for the Year 1794." Yet they were named "émigrés" or "emigrants" in 1795, 1797, and 1799.[12] Similarly, the "joyous émigrés" may have decided to call themselves "émigrés," not "refugees" or some other name; but they were just that, "refugees," at least to an English lord, William Auckland, who in 1792, in a letter supportive of the displaced French émigrés, wrote: "The subscription in this country for the French refugees does us some credit" (qtd. in Weiner, 1960: 54). In fact, the term *refugee* would find increasingly wider use in public from the early nineteenth century on, though not in substitution of other terms, such as exile and émigré, but along with them (Porter, 1979). This development had already been heralded in the enlargement of the definition of the term in the 1797 edition of the *Encyclopedia Britannica,* which defined refugees as "all such as leave their country in times of distress." A number of authoritative studies, including those by Marrus (1985), Bernard Porter (1979), and Tabori (1972), point to this phenomenon of permissiveness and ambiguity.[13]

What it is important to note, then, is that terms pertaining to human displacement in and of themselves do not exhibit a precise cartography of the types and kinds of human displacement. Therefore, a scholar studying "refugee" histories since the Huguenot episode—the proverbial beginning of refugee history—must necessarily consider also the histories of "émigrés" and/or "exiles" (that is, within the previously defined parameters of human displacement in relation to the sovereign territorial state). This is not to suggest that refugees, exiles, and émigrés were all one and the same. Instead, once again, it is to suggest that histories of human displacement prior to the twentieth century are ambiguous histories, with complex experiential and conceptual imbrications. They must therefore be studied in their complex and ambiguous imbrications. Doing so, especially before the twentieth century, when conceptual distinctions become clear, enables us to see that, in their ambiguities in relation to the task of statecraft, various forms of human displacement, including refugeehood, converged to create a specific modern phenomenon in the nineteenth century that proved remarkably resourceful for statecraft (Silverman, 1992). From the mélange of imprecise, ambiguous terminology, a specific cartography of the foreigner (as a subjectivity of "non-identical and ineligible otherness" [Shapiro, 1993: 3]) was produced and simultaneously made instrumental in the construction of the national citizen as a definite subjectivity of eligibility, of membership in the nation-state. The foreigner, in short, emerged as a field of modern statecraft. The refugee also took a place in this field, along with the exile and the émigré, for each one was a foreigner who, in Brubaker's words, was made to be a "correlative other" of the national citizen (1992: 37).

THE FIELD OF FOREIGNER-ALIEN AS A FIELD OF STATECRAFT

In her study of the state and state sovereignty, Cynthia Weber (1995) argues that the modern state must control how its people are "written" and how their meaning is fixed. This is imperative for the state in order to be able to control its own destiny as a presumed representative agent. Of course, this imperative is nothing less than the fundamental task of statecraft, namely, the task of making and remaking, say, French citizens out of Gascon peasantry, or British citizens out of London proletarians or Ipswich silk weavers—a task that, as Richard Ashley (1989b, 1993) and Donald Carter (1994: 74) remind us, is permanent and must start anew every day.[14]

The foreigner emerged as a field of modern statecraft in precisely this juncture. As a modern category, the foreigner affords the state a space—the foreigner discourse in the legal as well as popular sense—

within which the state can control the "writing" of the people, at least the writing of some aspects of the people. To the making of the foreigner, in turn, human displacement contributes enormously. Presently, I will sketch out how this happens against the background of modern statecraft—how the foreigner category further emerged as a field of statecraft and how human displacement contributed to its making in specific ways until the twentieth century.

I look to France, again, against the historical background of which, I maintain, the nexus of statecraft, foreigner, and human displacement can further be illuminated. The nexus, I say, is revealed clearly against the historical background of France in the nineteenth century, for France, long after the French Revolution triumphantly declared its "already thereness" as a nation, still appeared in the making—a forever incomplete project, as Fernand Braudel (1988) intimates.

Reflecting on the evolution of the idea of a national France, in *The Identity of France* (1988) Braudel speaks of this "incomplete France," which, according to him, exhibits hardly any national unity in terms of culture, language, administration, or even religion. Braudel focuses on the diversity of dialects across the French regions, referring to "the thousand and one *patois* of the eighteenth century" in France (91). He offers a multitude of examples by which he demonstrates that as late as the early nineteenth century, there did not exist a linguistically "national France" and that a semblance of the "national France" had to be imagined and produced in and through practices of statist governance. Braudel calls this the practice of "Frenchification" (87–97), thus establishing the discursivity, that is, the constructed contingent qualities, of the Frenchness of French language and culture. Consider the following cases, which clearly demonstrate the absence of a national France, at least linguistically:

> In France, the language barrier could be comically impenetrable. Abbé Albert, a native of the southern Alps, describes an encounter: "Journeying a few years ago in the Limagne of Auvergne, I was never able to make myself understood by the peasants I met on the road. I spoke to them in French, I spoke to them in my native Patois, I even tried to speak to them in Latin, but all to no avail. When at last I was tired of talking to them without their understanding a word, they in turn spoke to me in a language of which I could make no more sense." (94)

> Lucien Febvre, born in Nancy in 1878, received a real shock [traveling through south-west France]—the shock of different civilization. [He wrote:] "A beautiful cross-section of France. But should one call it France? How exotic and remote these places are to us northern and eastern folk. . . . All this is so strangely disturbing and makes you feel far from home." (87)

These "French" vistas, according to Braudel, demonstrate that the "national France" was more a creature of imagination, a phantasm, than a reality, and that Frenchification—the birth of France—had to occur in a multitude of forms and fashions, not the least of which was the birth of a lingua franca with the spread of trade, the construction of major road networks (which completely transformed communications), and the centralizing interventions of government in education and religion that were facilitated by these transformations (1988: 95; see also Ford, 1993). Braudel hastens to remind us, however, that the national France is a continuing, problematic project that can never be finalized:

> What, then, do we mean by the identity of France—if not a kind of superlative, if not a *central problematic,* if not the *shaping* of France by its own hand. . . . It is a *process,* a self-inflicted conflict, destined to go on indefinitely. If it were to stop, everything would fall apart. A nation can have its *being* only at the price of *being forever in search of itself,* forever transforming itself in the direction of its logical development, *always measuring itself against others* and identifying itself with the best, the most essential part of its being; a nation will consequently recognize itself in certain stock *images,* in certain *passwords* known to the initiated (whether the latter are an elite or the mass of people); It will recognize itself in a thousand touchstones, in beliefs, ways of speech, excuses, in an unbounded subconscious, in the flowing together of many obscure currents in a shared ideology, shared myths, shared fantasies. (1988: 23; emphasis added)

This, the constitution of the images and identities, namely, the ways of speech, beliefs, passwords, and practical and practicable relations of the citizen-subjects as constituting the nation, is the cardinal task of statecraft, whether in France, England, Germany, or Italy. I contend, as do Brubaker (1992), Jacobson (1996), and Silverman (1992), that it is in the making of "a thousand touchstones, . . . beliefs, ways of speech" that the foreigner-other becomes productive and instrumental. The foreigner emerges as a form of otherness against which, as Braudel intimates, the notion of the self-cognizant nation can be imagined, produced, and circulated in both popular and legal-institutional senses. The nation "measures" and "recognizes" itself in part against the foreigner, in other words. It "crystallizes" itself in the orchestrated visibility and externality of the foreigner (Noiriel, 1996: 214–16).

Linda Colley shows this Manichaean dynamic to have been decisive in the emergence of the notion of "Britishness" as well (1992a: 311; 1992b). She contends that Britishness was formed largely in, among other things, the construction and/or recognition of practical "otherness" manifested in the religious (as well as imperial) rivalry between Protestant England and Catholic France from 1689 to 1815 (1992a: 321–22; 1992b: 11–43, 54–100).[15] The "British self," in other words, was at least partially constructed *externally,* against the "French other." Such a dynamic was also effected *internally,* in the presence of foreigners, such as the Huguenots or the French royalist émigrés, as well as in relation to other contending religio-nationalists in the British Isles, such as Irish nationalists (Colley, 1992a: 316; Weiner, 1960). For example, pointing to the construction of Britishness internally, Daniel Statt discusses how, in England, the production of popular stereotypical images of foreigners or aliens—refugees, exiles, émigrés—contributed to the "creation of images of national character" (1995: 187): "A rich repertoire of stereotypes of foreigners not only invited particular reactions to them when they set foot on English soil, but contributed to the coalescence of a strongly-felt sense of English—at times—British national identity in the eighteenth century" (186).[16] In his study of refugees in Victorian England, Porter highlights the same dynamics by which refugees become "outsiders" within:

> From a study of the ways in which Victorians reacted to the presence of the refugees among them, it is possible to learn far more than the Victorians' attitudes to the refugees and their causes. There is something to be learnt, for example, about how they regarded themselves and their own society; about their notions of "freedom" and their practices of it . . . about Victorian politics and the forces beneath it; about the tensions between governors and the governed. (1979: 9)

The Manichaean logic of identity construction that operated in England also operated in other places against the background of numerous populations of displaced people. In fact, nineteenth-century Europe experienced human displacement from Poland to Germany, from Italy to France, affording more than sufficient resources for such politics.

Among the first groups of displaced people, for example, were the Polish nationalists who sought refuge in other European countries in 1830 and 1831, after their quest for Polish independence from Russia was suppressed (Marrus, 1985: 15; Tabori, 1972: 118; Panayi, 1994: 32). A similar outflow of refugees had already taken place from Italy in the wake of the revolutions of 1820, 1821, and 1831. More would leave Italy as a result of the failed revolution of 1848 (Wicks, 1968: 6; Panayi, 1994: 33). The year 1848 also witnessed a flight of refugees from Germany, when their revolution of that year failed. As many as ten thousand people sought refuge in other countries, with most going to Switzerland, the United States, and England (Tabori, 1972: 115; Marrus, 1985: 17). Refugees from Germany, known as "Forty-eighters," and those from Italy were not alone in their displacement in 1848 (Zucker, 1967; Wittke, 1952). In fact, as Marrus writes, "the year 1848 saw an important new generation of refugees, now coming from all across Europe, as one uprising after another succumbed to counterrevolutionary repression" (1985: 17; see also Vuilleumier, 1989: 23-28). Defeated leaders of the June 1848 Paris uprising joined the ranks of the displaced as they sought asylum outside France. Decades later, about one hundred thousand French refugees would join their displaced brethren after the suppression of the Paris Commune in 1871 (Tabori, 1972: 113; Panayi, 1994: 33). As the nineteenth century continued to unfold, more people were displaced as a result of wars and uprisings and because of anti-Semitism, which would cause the displacement of 2.5 million Jews from Russia and Eastern Europe between the 1880s and World War I (Marrus, 1985). As displaced people spread throughout Europe, they became objects of the Manichaean logic of identity construction in popular and legal-institutional arenas.

Whether in London or Paris, refugees, exiles, and émigrés made quite a spectacle, signifying, as it were, an essential otherness by virtue of their folkloric and cultural differences relative to local folklore. These differences were appropriated into the realm of symbolic-representational resources to conjure specific images and identities of a self distinct from the others of the exile: an English-self, a French-self, a Dutch-self, namely, a citizen-self versus the exile-other, the refugee-other, the émigré-other, that is, the foreigner-other. The constant rendering of foreigners in this fashion made it possible to formulate the identities and subjectivities of a distinct "us," for there were, in the taste, appearance, and language of the exile or the refugee, the identities and subjectivities of ostensibly distinct "others." To many people like George Sala, an English writer, for example, refugees seemed strangely exotic creatures, for they

> had hooded, tasseled and braided garments of unheard fashion; hats of shapes to make you wonder to what a stage the art of sequeezability arrived; trousers with unnumbered plaits, boots made as boots were never made before; . . . marvelous gestures, Babel-like tongues; voices anything but (Englishly) human; the smoke as of a thousand brick-kilns. (Qtd. in Porter, 1979: 25)

In cases like these, foreigners were seen more as objects of curiosity and charity and less as agents of instability or anarchy. There were also cases in which foreigners were seen in less curious and more political terms, as elements disruptive of the "internal peace" and "abusive of the asylum" they were given (Green, 1987: 581). A note from the German Confederation in the aftermath of the 1848 revolution represents such sentiments:

> The serious attention of the Germanic Diet has been directed to the unheard of abuse which political refugees have made of asylum so generously granted to them in England. It is a notorious fact, that these enemies of public peace are increasingly employing all means at their disposal to rekindle in the different countries from whence they have come, the scarcely extinguished flame of disturbance which they themselves lighted. (Qtd. in Green, 1987: 581)

Regardless, foreigners' "strange" and/or "abusive" presence, reinscribed even more strangely in popular and legal discourses, was appropriated in the politico-cultural and politico-administrative processes of identity and difference to produce the markers of representational identities and entities—us/them, inside/outside, citizen/alien, community/anarchy. It could thus be argued that, in a paradoxical way, these foreigners within host societies symbolically participated in the constitution of the host communities as distinct communities to the extent that their look, language, taste, and even sense of style and aesthetics were harnessed to the generation of discourses of "otherness" as foreignness or alienness (Anderson, 1994; Tabori, 1972; Statt, 1995; Panayi, 1994). A reporter for the *Times* in London in the 1840s was contributing to such a discourse when he wrote: "Exiles wear hats such as no one wears, and hair where none should be—[they] are quite out of fashion and sometimes barely making ends meet" (qtd. in Marrus, 1985: 20).[17] This was the "constructive" role of the foreigner that afforded, in the words of Brubaker, the negative "correlative status" of the foreigner in relation to the national citizen (1992: 37). The foreigner became the indispensable "other" vis-à-vis the national citizen.

Kristeva suggests that the successful formulation and practice of this irreconcilable dichotomy between the foreigner and the national citizen is vital for enabling the very idea of the modern state, for it produces "the only modern, acceptable, and clear definition of foreignness" that implicates or even posits the modern state as the enveloping, exclusive site of life activities. "The foreigner is the one who does not belong to the state" or to the group that the state is there to represent. Rather, it is the citizen who belongs (1991: 96).

What makes this irreconcilable dichotomy of identities possible is, of course, statecraft, reworking power relations in their minutiae in discursive, contingent sites and moments at which human bodies are identified, marked, inscribed, and acted upon as alien bodies, not properly belonging to an imagined territoriality called France or Germany or England.[18] Article 4 of the French constitution of 1799, which declares that "the status of French citizenship is lost by naturalization in a foreign country," for instance, best illustrates the development of the mutually exclusive identity positions (qtd. in Arnold, 1994: 24). Thus conceptualized, one cannot be an alien and a citizen-subject simultaneously in one locality.

Against this background, I want to accentuate the general productive effect of the activities around the name foreigner; they are instrumental in at least two fundamental ways. First, they partake in the processes by which to effect what counts as the territorial source of authority for the sovereign state, that is, the citizen-subjects constituting a nation. Second, as activities constitutive of the boundaries of citizen-subjectivity, they are also simultaneously activities of statecraft by which the sovereign state is continually produced as an effective force in our lives and is "awarded an essential centrality," as Michel de Certeau would say.[19] How do the fields, sites, and moments of the "foreigner" get to be so profitable in reality? Insights are found in the formal development of the notion of the foreigner that appears generally under the legal term *alien.*

As early as the decades following the revocation of the Edict of Nantes, the notion of foreignness, as it applied to displaced people—foreigner as exile, foreigner as émigré, foreigner as refugee, foreigner as asylee, foreigner as suppliant—was invoked both in the discourses of governments and in popular discourses to point to the existence of politically distinct identities of people being defined in territorially bounded ways. While such identities (of subjecthood as opposed to citizenship) were certainly not modern, neither were they premodern, but perhaps they can be comprehended as "protomodern" in the context of the emergent state-driven biopolitics. This idea finds some evidence in the "governmental" responses to the flight of the Huguenots from France. For instance, in 1685, just four days after the revocation of the Edict of Nantes by Louis XIV, Frederick William of Brandenburg-Prussia, the Great Elector, issued the Edict of Potsdam, inviting Huguenots to Brandenburg. In the edict, he promised to treat "the persecuted French Protestants as the elector's natural subjects were treated."[20] Likewise, in 1709, the British Parliament passed an act for naturalizing the expelled Huguenots. The act alludes to

> many strangers of the Protestant or Reformed religion who out of a due consideration of the happy constitution of the government of this realm, would be induced to transport themselves and their estates into this kingdom, if they might be made partakers of the advantages and privileges which the natural-born subjects thereof do enjoy. (Qtd. in Grahl-Madsen, 1966: 10)[21]

An almost identical declaration offering naturalization to "unhappy and dispersed" Protestants—"all the privileges and prerogatives that our natural-born subjects enjoy"—was passed in 1709 by Holland and West Freiziland (Defoe, [1709] 1964: 6–8). Although the primary objective might have been to attract the wealth of the Huguenots,[22] these acts illustrated the position ascribed to perceived strangers or foreigners—whether they were called refugees, exiles, expellees, or suppliants—vis-à-vis the "subjects" of a monarchical state. Perhaps even more importantly, they illustrated the attempts by centralizing absolutist governments to situate the name and powers of the state in the center of life activities, including human migrations.

In fact, the proliferation of writings on foreigners along these lines parallels a gradual increase in similar statutes on aliens or foreigners across Europe. Although, with the advent of the absolutist states, European governments had inaugurated policies relating to foreigners or aliens through acts, decrees, and proclamations,[23] the Huguenot displacement seems to have marked a new beginning in terms of alien acts and municipal accords. In the beginning, however, these measures were usually ad hoc, in some cases undertaken to respond specifically to the dispersion of the Huguenots from France into neighboring countries. Two of the more prominent of these measures were the Edict of Potsdam, issued in 1685, and the British parliamentary Act of Naturalization, enacted in 1709 (Defoe, [1709] 1964: 6–7; Kiernan, 1978: 40; Green, 1987). These two proclamations notwithstanding, the measures of such intent mostly took the form of temporary arrangements within and among the countries, endeavoring not so much to find common grounds for action as to thwart open conflicts among them. An example of such a temporary measure is the exchange of letters between diplomats regarding the situation of an individual or individuals. Henry Baird reports one such exchange in 1704 regarding the question of asylum in Switzerland:

> Puisieux, his majesty's ambassador, hastily addressed an arrogant letter to the magistrates of Berne, complaining in bitter terms of the asylum found by the "traitor" Cavalier and his followers in Lausanne. The reply of the Bernese was a firm and dignified production, worthy of the best days of the republic, whose hospitable neutrality it vindicated with a fearlessness. (1895: 404)[24]

Beginning in the late eighteenth century and continuing through the nineteenth, these activities acquired a more institutional and systematic character, both within and across countries. Governments gradually instituted and regularized comprehensive responses to the problems of managing peoples (Hobsbawm, 1992; Hobsbawm and Ranger, 1992; Braudel, 1988). Individual governments devised similar foreigner or alien laws within their jurisdictions. In what might be regarded as the discursive elements of the emergence of the notion of the "international," many governments also signed numerous bilateral or multilateral treaties on extradition, treatment of "foreign nationals," the right of asylum, and so on. England and France led the way.

In England, there were several significant developments, each of which was motivated by displacements from France, though the entry of other displaced populations, such as the German Forty-eighters, surely contributed to these developments (Panayi, 1995: 201–51). Already, I have identified important legislation that offered naturalization to the Huguenots. A threshold development occurred with the passage in 1793 by the British Parliament of "An Act for Establishing Regulations respecting Arriving in This Kingdom, or Resident Therein in Certain Cases." This commonly known Aliens Act of 1793 came in the face of increasing immigration to England by the French monarchists displaced by the French Revolution. The act was designed to prevent an alien overflow into England. Indeed, accompanying a rise in xenophobia, the bill invested the government with the authority to prevent further entry into England and/or to expel any alien from England (Panayi, 1994: 21; Porter, 1979: 3). The act required that aliens "declare their names and previous residence and register with the magistrates whenever they changed their address. Passports were required" as well (Weiner, 1960: 80). Just as the French revolutionaries came to suspect foreigners living in France as the enemy within, so the British government feared that the displaced French were a fifth column. In 1796, the original act was "renewed," reflecting the fear that the émigrés were a threat from within. As a consequence of the renewal, the émigrés were subjected to more control, with many of them being moved inland from the coastal areas (Weiner, 1960: 121). While these acts surely served the immediate practical purposes, they also had a less visible yet still significant effect that attests to the claim as to the increasing state interventions in life. An argument could be made that the two acts, in addition to being practically useful, were also party to and further generative of the process of negotiating (or situating) the practical powers of the modern state into the heart of identity politics in England.[25] Indeed, they turned out to be the forerunners of a series of alien acts to come, which, in fashioning and maintaining a field of alien politics, would establish the state as the site of rightful agency and legitimacy in terms of arbitrating who can come in and who cannot or who belongs to the state and who does not.

One indeed wonders if the objective could simply have been to prevent immigration into England altogether, but if so, it was not for long, for immigration to England had been encouraged prior to, and would be encouraged again after, the enactment of the Alien Act (Cunningham, 1897; Loomie, 1963; Scouloudi, 1987; Cottret, 1991). Although the French émigrés had left a somewhat unfavorable legacy because of their political orientations, which risked continued British conflict with France, very few of those who had sought refuge in England "illegally" were expelled from Britain even between 1793 and 1823, a period of relative distrust toward refugees and exiles (Porter, 1979: 3, 68–70). Even as mercantilism withered away, many continued to believe that immigration, which comprised such categories of the displaced as refugees and exiles, was a positive contribution to the welfare of the country. In 1843, a select committee report on the laws affecting aliens summarized the feelings:

> It is desirable for every people to encourage the settlement of foreigners among them, since by such means they will be practically instructed in what it most concerns them to know, and enabled to avail themselves of whatever foreign sagacity, ingenuity, or experience may have produced in art and science which is most perfect. (Qtd. in Porter, 1979: 5)

An 1837 report of the Literary Association of Friends of Poland, headed by Lord Dudley Coutts Stuart, likewise asserted: "There are few branches of trade, art or profession in which there are not some refugees creditably occupied. Gentlemen by birth and occupation, officers of rank are established as Stationers, Tailors, Shoemakers, Tobacconists or working as apprentices of the humblest trades" (qtd. in Zubrzycki, 1956: 33–34).

In fact, attesting to this attitude, Porter reports that between 1823 and 1905, no alien was expelled from or denied entry into England. In 1844, another alien act came into effect, "authorizing for one year . . . the removal of aliens from the realm."[26] The act rearranged the status of alienage "favorably" for aliens (Jones, 1956: 67; Cottret, 1991: 51). Section 6 provided that, "upon obtaining a certificate of naturalization and taking the oath of allegiance, every alien now residing in, or who shall thereafter come to reside in, any part of Great Britain or Ireland, with intent to settle therein, shall enjoy all the rights and capacities which a natural-born subject of the United Kingdom can enjoy or transmit" (qtd. in Jones, 1956: 67). A new alien act was put into effect in 1847–48, to which some amendments were made in the 1870 Naturalization Act (Cottret, 1991: 51). The practical effect of the enactment of such laws was to further elaborate and regiment the field of alien politics and, by extension, to further establish and increase the legitimacy of the practitioners of the state as the ultimate arbiters.[27]

In France, the development of the field exhibited a trajectory parallel with that in England, albeit with greater political intensity and semantic clarity in terms of establishing the hierarchy of citizen/nation/state. In 1789, the revolutionary constitutional assembly produced a different notion of alienness or foreignness from that which had previously been expounded. It did so by writing an "active citizens'" decree (the Declaration of the Rights of Man and Citizen) in which the category of citizen was designated to be the rightful category enjoying the "natural and inalienable rights of man [such as] . . . liberty, property, security, and resistance to oppression." Yet, as stipulated in the third and fourth articles, for a man to enjoy these rights, he needed to be a citizen; he needed to belong to a nation and to a state:[28] "Only those organized into [belonging to] national residences are entitled to have rights" (Kristeva, 1991: 150). The declaration was followed by a passport law (*Loi relative aux passeports*) in 1797, specifying the rights of a French citizen to a passport;[29] a new constitution in 1799; and a new civil code in 1803.[30] Together, these laws marked the starting point for modern alien legislation, in that each document explicitly defines the alien category in relation to the citizen category. Finally, in 1832, a "Law Relating to Foreigners, Refugees Who Will Live in France"and, in 1848, "The Law of Naturalization for Foreigners Residing in France" established the field of alien politics as an indispensable element of the project of modern territorial governance in France.[31] These definitions and laws were not always practically effective, yet they were still instrumental in statecraft in that they afforded the space within which the state could continue to control how the nation was defined (Weber, 1995). To borrow Noiriel's terminology (1996), they allowed the state to "officialize" or, as I would put it, "statize" the issue, awarding the state more centrality and the powers of a legitimate arbiter.

The 1832 law was especially significant, for it became the earliest legislation to define the refugee by linking the identity of the refugee to a sovereign state as an already completed project. The law defined "foreigner refugees [as] those who are in France without a passport and without any kind of relationship with an ambassador." Charles

Dupin, commenting on this article in 1832, argued that "those who reside in France without the protection of their government are called refugees."[32] The statism in refugee status is clear here.

The 1832 law had come as a response to an influx into France of Polish, Spanish, German, Italian, and Portuguese refugees whose numbers were no more than twenty thousand until the mid-century (Marrus, 1985: 15). According to Marrus, not unlike the overall government attitude toward exiles and refugees in England around the same time, although the law imbued the French government with broad powers of expulsion, in practice the French were extremely lenient, expelling very few from French territory (16). In a sense, this attitude could be construed as the function of the assimilationist French doctrine on citizenship, jus soli, which emphasized one's relation to the sovereign territory instead of one's line of descent (Silverman, 1992; Brubaker, 1992). Still, the law strengthened the centralizing role of the French state further and affirmed the citizen/nation/state hierarchy that the French Revolution had articulated.[33] What the law did effect was a regime of control or a framework of regimentation comprising various legal and economic incentives and disincentives. For instance, it provided stipends for refugees, depending on their backgrounds. The richer and/or more prominent a refugee was prior to displacement, the higher the stipend was. In this curious fashion, the law also reflected the dominant bourgeois values of the times by reinscribing class differences on the refugee bodies. Yet it also invested the government with powers to intern refugees in certain cities, to issue identity papers, and to limit refugees' movements. In the interlocking web of relations and institutions related to refugee presence, which determined what should count as refugee identities and experiences, the state was reinscribed as the supreme agent in this aspect or experience of life. While many did not stop to contemplate actively the effects and implications of such practices, many others took heed or were forced to do so. They turned or were made to turn to "the state" for various reasons, thus partaking in the process of the crafting of the French state.

While the state could not (and in effect did not try to) prevent the movement of refugees, exiles, or other "moving" peoples in any substantial fashion by enacting and performing a prohibitive law, it was able to produce "symbolic capital" with which to speak at least of an inside and an outside to the state—a France with delineated borders and a French national community neatly overlapping with the borders of France. Finally, it was also able to speak of itself as a creature of this reality created and invested by the collective or "general will" of the French nation to have a national living space—France—with exclusionary borders. The cardinal effect of such activities was the statization of processes of displacement and replacement. The cartographic imagination of the nation found expression in the emergent rhetoric of the displaced human—the refugee or, perhaps, the exile.

The increasing state-centeredness of the politico-administrative and politico-cultural field of displacement was clearly manifested, for example, in the church's waning power in France to act as the arbiter in matters of displacement, whether in designating refugees or in actually intervening on their behalf. Tabori alludes to this shift and the concomitant shift in the meaning of displacement in terms predicated upon and affirming the statist relations and institutions:

> While the church still had the power to punish and exile (and to accept the exiled), this power was rapidly waning; the number of religious exiles declined while that of political exiles were swelling constantly. In any case it was the eighteenth century that created the idea of nation as contrasted to homeland, of citizen as opposed to subject, and thereby changed totally the very conception of exile. (1972: 87)

In other words, it was the state that increasingly defined what content to attribute to those who were called refugees. The state waxed while the church waned in significance, with the church being relegated to the role of a spectator.[34]

Another element of the alien politics found expression in the inauguration of formal extradition laws and treaties, of which the Belgian Law of Extraditions of 1833 was foundational, specifying various types of alien status, including that of the political offender and/or refugee. The law exempted political offenders from extradition by stating that "no foreigner may be prosecuted or punished for any political crime antecedent to the extradition, or for any act connected with such a crime, for any crime or misdemeanor not provided for by the present law; otherwise, all extraditions and all temporary arrests are prohibited."[35] The Belgian law triggered corresponding legislation in all of Europe, with this particular provision on political offense being widely adapted (Grahl-Madsen, 1966: 11;

Sinha, 1971: 172). The law of 1833, which was reenacted in the law of 1856, embedded this principle into future treaties by specifying in Article 6 that "it shall be expressly provided in the treaties that a foreigner may not be persecuted or punished for any political offense committed before extradition" (qtd. in Sinha, 1971: 172). Among the agreements or treaties that adopted this principle were the Convention on Extradition of 22 November 1834 between France and Belgium; the 1834 extradition treaty among Prussia, Austria, and Russia; the Franco-Italian Extradition Treaty and the British Extradition Treaty, both in 1870; the Extradition Convention of 14 August 1874 between France and Belgium; and the Swiss-German Extradition Treaty of 1874.[36]

Also significant in terms of the emergence of the "international" in the nineteenth century was the formulation of a number of "exemplary" nonbinding resolutions on the asylum, extradition, and expulsion of aliens by the Institute of International Law, which served as a common platform for the formalization of the control of people's movements and activities within and across borders (Plender, 1988: 2, 72-73). These resolutions were aimed at serving as the legal base for the facilitation of cooperation among governments. The institute adopted resolutions on asylum and extradition in Oxford in 1880, in Geneva in 1892, and in Paris in 1894. It also produced resolutions on the expulsion of aliens in Lausanne in 1888 and in Geneva in 1892 (Grahl-Madsen, 1966: 9–10; 1972: 10–11; Plender, 1988).[37]

In his seminal work *The Status of Refugees in International Law,* Atle Grahl-Madsen points out that this period also witnessed the birth of nationality laws in Europe, including the French Civil Code of 1804, the Prussian Law of 1842, the Netherlands Aliens Act of 1848, the nationality laws passed in Austria, Italy, and Russia in the 1860s, the Swiss Law of 1874, and the British Naturalization Act of 1870. These were contemporaneous with the alien laws identifying and regulating various manifestations of alienness or foreignness, as in refugeeness (1966: 11, 95, 319–20). Although Grahl-Madsen states that these were the first of the modern nationality laws, he does not attribute any extraordinary significance to this development in terms of their relevance to the crafting of the sovereign territorial state.

Contrary to Grahl-Madsen's fleeting interest, I believe this to be a historically unprecedented development in Europe with momentous implications for statecraft. More specifically, I contend that, occurring at the very juncture when alien legislation was being put into effect, nationality laws constituted yet another "face of the polyhedron" of the ascending project of statecraft. This was the constitution of yet another field of statist activity clearly linked to the name of the alien, whether a refugee-alien, an exile-alien, or an émigré-alien.

According to Michel Foucault, such instruments of power as laws, decrees, and acts serve a crucial function; by virtue of their presence, they work as sites or arenas for the articulation and rearticulation of a specific program of government that is expressed in the form of codes and norms of conduct in the face of practical difficulties, and that simultaneously specifies prescriptions to tackle those difficulties (1991: 79). Once enacted, the program is incorporated into the shifting morphology of power relations and institutions (Hunt and Wickham, 1994). These laws, decrees, and acts induce a whole set of effects "in the real," as Foucault puts it: "They crystallize into institutions, they inform individual behavior, and they act as grids for perception and evaluation of things"(1991: 79). They affect and reshape the field of possibilities, viabilities, feasibilities, and practicalities. They inform individual and collective trajectories as to what are possible life projects, which are viable subjects or agents, which are relevant knowledges, and what are practical strategies. Thus, taken together, the effects of these laws, acts, and decrees are significant especially in that they inscribe and further regiment the meanings and identities of the category of the alien in politics. In so doing, they constantly manage and conduct the ways in which the forms and content of alienness (foreignness) are defined and circulated in the popular scenes of everyday life (Kristeva, 1991: 96). They could be said to establish a field of alien politics as a field of statist problematizations, a field of statecraft, in which the refugee as a foreigner figures as an object of intervention and regimentation by the state. After all, as Kristeva puts it, "it is precisely with respect to laws that a foreigner exists" (1991: 96). Through the card and code, the identity of "foreigner" is materialized (Noiriel, 1996: 76).

It was through activities of problematization, that is, opening up, maintaining, and constantly reworking such fields of activity, that those who practiced the sovereign territorializing state could continue to invest life activities with a whole host of formalizing projects with such titles as "the Alien Act," "the Asylum Act," "the Franco-Belgian Extradition Treaty," "International Rules on the Admission and Expulsion of Aliens," and "the Act on the Naturalization of Aliens and Strangers." They could establish new bureaucracies; formulate and put into effect new rules and procedures; invite, entice, allure, coax, cajole, enchant, charm, court, or, if necessary, force people to organize and reorganize in the image of the treaties, laws, acts and declarations; open courts and appoint judges; sign treaties on the admission, naturalization, and expulsion of foreigners or aliens, including displaced people such as refugees, exiles, and asylum seekers, with their counterparts in places such as Paris, London, Bern, Hamburg, and Amsterdam; and sign more agreements as to how to achieve the declared objectives. And then they could turn to the people and cry out, *"Vive la France!"* or *"Deutschland über Alles!"* and the people could respond, *"Vive la France!"* or *"Deutschland über Alles!"* These were the regimentations of modern statecraft. As Kristeva (1991), Brubaker (1992), and others, like Hans Kohn (1967), remind us, in their convergent effects through the eighteenth and nineteenth centuries, such regimentations contributed to the ascent of the modern national state as the dominant form of governance.

Historically, the figure of the refugee relates to such regimentations in a specific way. Although in existence and increasingly more in use in both the popular and official discourses in the eighteenth and nineteenth centuries, the term *refugee* does not represent an indispensably critical category by itself, but it is still crucial in that it participates in making possible the production of a specific discourse of foreignness or alienness, a discourse of otherness and externality. Especially in the nineteenth century, the term *refugee* is employed in conjunction with other terms signifying human displacement, such as *exile,* to produce the contingent legal as well as popular images of the term *alien* (*foreigner*) as the correlative "other" of the national citizen. The alien or foreigner images, in turn, are so appropriated as to attest to the territorial boundedness of life activities organized around the hierarchy of citizen/nation/state (Silverman, 1992). The alien becomes a referential or, in the words of Michel de Certeau, a "re-citable" resource (1984: 185–89) by which this territorial quality is effected, privileged, and further legitimized—so much so that people are not only convinced of the declared truth of that kind of world but also ready and willing to participate in its remaking and even to die for it (Anderson, 1994). That, of course, is no less than the resolution, though temporary, of the fundamental problem of the modern state, which is to construct agents (people) who forget that their "peoplehood" or "nationhood" is only a series of historically contingent effects always in the process of being effected (Ashley, 1989a; 1993) through struggles in multiple fields of activities, including the field of the refugee.

It might be possible to see the refugee's role in all this in a historical light if we argue, as Eric Hobsbawm and Terence Ranger (1992) might, that the refugee category (in all its experiential and epistemological imbrications with other categories of displacement) is an "invented tradition" within an "invented tradition." Its meanings signifying territorial uprootedness are fashioned while fashioning the meanings of another invention, the territorially rooted, bounded citizen and, by extension, the territorially bounded community of citizenry and the corporate entity embodying their collective will, namely, the state. The practical construction of the refugee's meanings, images, and identities, in short, facilitates the "invention" of the "traditions" of the sovereign territorial state and subsequently the nation-state. The refugee represents a field of statist affirmations precisely in this sense—one of many fields of activity in which the powers and controls of the sovereign territorial nation-state and the citizen have been produced and expanded in history.

Historically, through the nineteenth century, the refugee regimentations were relatively successful in both conspicuous and unceremonious ways, largely because of the limited numbers of the regimented. These regimentations would be hard-pressed, however, with the displacement of millions immediately before, during, and after World War I, of which the Russian refugees became the historical embodiment. The displacement of Russian and other refugees was to amount to a rupture in all that seemed solid and was to catapult the name of the refugee into the heart of statecraft scenes. This rupture is explored in the following chapter, which aims to reread refugee histories as histories not simply of human displacement (histories that just happen to occur and then go away) but also of problematization and regimentation made to effect historical relations and institutions of territorial statist governance, even in the circumstances of a crisis in statecraft, as was the case in Europe in the early twentieth century.

3

Refugees, Intergovernmentalization, and Statecraft: The Birth of the Modern Refugee Regime

Population movements are indicative of a world in turmoil.

—Sadako Ogata
UN High Commissioner for Refugees, 1992

Narratives on Refugees

> It was in Astrakhan that I ran into some of the backwash of that flood of humanity which poured eastward across from Poland and Galicia during the great retreat of 1915. This particular stream had flowed across the Urals and down into Turkestan as far as Tashkend—almost to Bokhara. Typhus had taken half of them there and driven the rest back into Russia. . . . All along the road were crosses. And always they tried to put them in the most beautiful place. They put up a little fence or covered the grave with pine branches, or stuck a single branch in the earth, or tied on the cross embroidered belts. . . .
> *Others see:*
> *That is a nice place*
> *And lay their own dead with the others, side by side.*
> *And yet more come, and yet more.*
> *And the cemetery grows, stretching itself along the margin of the road. . . .*
> Under these dust clouds these streams pushed slowly eastward, consuming everything like locusts. They cut trees for fire, dug up peasants' potatoes; where they had passed there was not even grass left. Their carts were piled and hung with the strangest things—sometimes they

> would be carrying nothing but an iron roof, the most valuable thing they could bring away . . . down from above, from that impersonal, far-reaching power, whose very severity was thought necessary to hold this vast, loose, easy-going mass together, and had come an order. So-and-so . . . to such and such a place. . . . And they moved on—just as millions have gone on in Russia in the past and nobody knew.
>
> Arthur Ruhl
>
> *White Nights and Other Russian Impressions*

REFUGEE CONDITIONS AND THE CRISIS OF STATECRAFT IN THE EARLY TWENTIETH CENTURY

When one looked into the prevailing circumstances in Europe at the turn of the twentieth century, one looked into circumstances of monumental historical transitions in sovereign territorial governance, the trajectories of which were being negotiated more amid tumult and turbulence than amid peace and certainty. In fact, upon looking into the circumstances of governance at the turn of the century, what one clearly saw was a crisis of territorial governance manifested in the difficulties of imagining, effecting, stabilizing, and representing the ensemble of relations, institutions, and subjectivities that had come progressively but steadily to undergird a specific emergent statecentric imagination of the world.

What were some of the symptoms of this crisis? What were the mechanisms of disruption in statist territorial governance that created a crisis at the turn of the century? What were some of the ways in which the practitioners of statist territorial governance responded to forces of disruption? How did refugee events figure in this history?

At the onset of the twentieth century, this task of representation was made more difficult in the face of the hitherto unprecedented scope, intensity, and velocity of a set of peculiar transversal events, including wars, dissolution of empires, human migrations, and epidemics. The convergent effects of these and other events rapidly changed the countenance of European politics for the worse, engendering a crisis of statecraft and/or a crisis of representation.

Of all the transversal events and forces, massive human displacement was to prove most significant. Developments circa World War I had brought about the displacement of millions of people across Europe, Asia, the Middle East, and North Africa. The numbers in Europe were especially staggering, with virtually no group left untouched by the unfolding of events. Between the Balkan wars among Turkey, Greece, and Bulgaria in 1912–13 and the end of conflicts in Europe in the early 1920s, more than twenty million people were displaced (Macartney, 1929; Zolberg et al., 1989; Marrus, 1985; Loescher, 1993). Never before in European history had such a massive human displacement occurred. At hand this time around were not a mere two thousand or twenty thousand Polish, Italian, or Spanish exiles, but two million Poles, five million Russians, one million Germans, more than a million Armenians, Greeks, Turks, and Hungarians, and millions of others who formed the human tide rolling across European space in the hope of finding a place to live.

The displaced masses moved to save their lives, to be sure, but their movements also disrupted the perennial and not-so-perennial relations of territorial statist governance. Times were surely those of crisis for state-centric governance, which otherwise had been effected so meticulously and ceremoniously through a thousand ways and devices in the preceding centuries. The unprecedented displacement of vast numbers of people in the heart of Europe thus represented an epochal disruption in the processes of regimentation, with significant implications for territorial statecraft. In a general sense, the rapid and massive displacement of so many millions in a relatively short time drastically altered the environment of political activity, concomitantly forcing an alteration of the strategies and practices of regimentation by which territorially grounded traditions of the sovereign state were being effected.

In the course of these developments, the events of displacement also facilitated a concurrent radical metamorphosis in the strategic place of the refugee in the nexuses of regimentations. Suddenly, the name of the refugee turned omnipresent, employed as the master term to speak of human displacement. Terms like *exile* or *émigré*, which had been relatively more prominent in the constitution of the field of alien or foreigner politics, were relegated to oblivion, at least during and immediately after the First World War. The developments circa the war firmly conferred upon the refugee the central role in the field of human displacement, thus marking the beginning of what many have come to call the century or age of the refugee in modern state politics. The dawning of the age of the refugee was formalized in 1921 with the establishment of the first "international" refugee organization under the auspices of the League of Nations—the League of Nations High Commissioner for Refugees (LNHCR).

How did refugee events represent an implosion of the sense of territorial boundedness, a sine qua non that characterizes statist governance in history? What was the historical strategic significance of the first "international" refugee organization in terms of the practices and projects of statecraft? What did the notion of "international" represent in the context of massive human displacement—the age of the refugee? What did the LNHCR do?

THE EVENT: THE LEAGUE OF NATIONS HIGH COMMISSIONER FOR REFUGEES

The League of Nations High Commissioner for Refugees came into existence as a result of a correspondence from the International Red Cross Committee to the secretary-general of the League of Nations, Eric Drummond, and to the League of Nations. On 20 February 1921, the Red Cross Committee sent a letter and a memorandum to the secretary-general, drawing his attention to the situation of the Russian refugees which, it maintained, "urgently calls for solution, and which the League of Nations alone can handle with the necessary authority." In it, the Russian refugee situation was depicted in desperate terms:

> More than 800,000 Russian refugees are at present dispersed in all the countries of Europe, especially in the Baltic states, in Poland, in Turkey, in Bulgaria, and in Jugo-Slavia. These people are without legal protection and without any well-defined legal status. The majority of them are without means of subsistence, and one must particularly draw attention to the position of the children and the youths among them who are growing up in an ever-increasing misery, without adequate means of education, and who are in danger of becoming useless and harmful elements in the Europe of to-morrow. (League of Nations, 1921c: 228)

The memorandum declared that the participation of the League of Nations in the relief work was absolutely imperative. As the "only supernational political authority," the league was capable of solving the problem of the refugees, which had proved beyond the power of exclusively humanitarian organizations (227). The memorandum further stated that in spite of efforts by a host of organizations such as the International Red Cross, the Save the Children Fund, the International Union for Helping the Children, and various other Red Cross societies across Europe, many involved in relief work were "coming to see that their work does not suffice, that the problem should be dealt with in a more general manner, and that all efforts should be centralized"(228).

The proposal suggested that a successful centralization of efforts could best be achieved by the appointment of a General Commissioner for the Russian Refugees, designed after the Office of the General Commissioner of the League of Nations for Repatriation of Russian Prisoners of War. The task of the commissioner would consist, in the first place, of defining the legal position of the Russian refugees, organizing their employment as needed, and, above all, facilitating their repatriation to Russia. Additionally, it would be the responsibility of the commissioner to group together and coordinate the work of various private organizations. The memorandum ended with one last plea to the council of the league:

> If the former prisoners of war waiting to return to their motherland were worthy of the interest which the League of Nations displayed in them, surely also the Russian refugees, without protection, without country, likewise victims of scourge of war, will not be abandoned by the league of nations to their tragic fate. (229)

The council members, after consulting with member states and getting their approval on the matter, responded positively, in effect agreeing with the need to centralize and coordinate the efforts to deal with the various aspects of the Russian refugee problem. On 27 June 1921, the council adopted a series of resolutions recommending the appointment of a High Commissioner for Russian Refugees under the auspices of the League of Nations.

In one league resolution, the council recognized that the appointment of a commissioner would be "the best method of attaining a general settlement of the refugee question." The council also specified the commissioner's duties as "defining the legal status of refugees, organizing their repatriation or their allocation to various countries which might be able to receive them, finding them means of work, and, finally, with the aid of philanthropic associations, undertaking relief work among them." All of these duties, the council resolution stated, necessitated a "coordination of the actions taken in various countries, whether by the governments or by private organizations" (League of Nations, 1921i: 37). It was toward achieving this objective that the high commissioner's office was envisioned to work.[1]

The Norwegian explorer Fridtjof Nansen was appointed the first commissioner. Organizationally, the office had a very loose structure and a limited budget on which to operate. Furthermore, it had a limited mandate, as it was supposed to be a temporary organization to be dissolved upon the completion of its sole "duty," which was to coordinate international efforts to help resolve the Russian refugee problem (League of Nations, 1921i: 37).[2]

The legacy of the LNHCR as a specific event in the larger context of human displacement in the early twentieth century proved significant. It had broader historical implications for the transformation of the relations and institutions underlying the modern territorial state. One can ask a series of questions that might help bring to focus the significance of the LNHCR in the context of human displacement then and in the ensuing years: What were the implications of this particular event for the processes of the modern territorial state? What were some of the processes—relations and institutions—of modern statecraft with which the organization came to be bound, and the process that it in turn facilitated? How, by way of what practices, has the "refugee" (as signifying a peculiar subjectivity) been produced, put into circulation in the nexuses of power relations, and, finally, linked to the extant and emergent relations and institutions of the modern territorial state? How, in other words, might the activities around the name of the refugee have effected or worked as the practices of statecraft? How, finally, did the High Commissioner for Refugees figure in the practices and paradoxes of statecraft at the turn of the twentieth century in Europe?

It was amid uncertainty and flux in the conditions of statecraft that the LNHCR was born. Accordingly, it is in the context of that uncertainty and flux that its place in the history of statecraft must be discerned. I set out to undertake just such an inquiry in the following pages. I start my inquiry, however, against the background of how the LNHCR has been conceptualized in what I have loosely called the conventional studies on the refugee, many of which start their accounts of refugee histories with the LNHCR. They advance accounts of the LNHCR in which the crisis of statecraft never figures. Why?

THE LEAGUE OF NATIONS HIGH COMMISSIONER FOR REFUGEES: A RESPONSE TO A CRISIS OF HUMANITARIANISM?

CONVENTIONAL APPROACHES

Upon careful examination, what one notices immediately about the conventional approaches to the study of the LNHCR and to the question of the refugee is that these approaches assume the sovereign state and its counterparts, the citizen-subject and the domestic community of citizens, as self-evident. Starting from this postulate, these studies comprehend refugee events and the LNHCR in history in terms articulated to the modern notion of the sovereign territorial state. First, they regard as primary the territorially bounded national communities of citizens—the original national home—represented and protected by the state. Then, they accord a secondary status to the problem of the refugee, which presumably occurs as a result of disruptions in the original national home. Finally, they comprehend interventions in refugee events, such as those through the LNHCR, as tertiary responses by which, in the face of an extant problem, an established, already effective territorial order responds to resolve the crisis and to restore the normal hierarchy of citizen/nation/state. The citizen/nation/state constellation is unproblematic for the conventional studies.

Commencing thus, most conventional studies represent the founding of the High Commissioner for Refugees as a unique event insofar as the LNHCR emerges as the first interstate organization to deal specifically with refugee populations, starting with the Russian refugees. These studies see the objectives of the organization as both humanitarian and political. In their accounts, the LNHCR stands at the beginning of a distinct history of collusion between humanitarianism and practical political concerns in the early 1920s.

To begin, these studies contend that the organization came into existence out of widespread humanitarian concerns for the plight of millions of refugees, the magnitude of which had hitherto been unprecedented in human history. They refer to the historians writing on the conditions of the displaced people to offer insights into reasons for the call for humanitarian voices:

> A new burden was laid upon Nansen's shoulders. This was relief work among millions of political refugees whom the first world war and ensuing revolutions and civil disturbances had driven from their homes.

> These unfortunate people, uprooted and hunted, were dispersed throughout Europe and Asia and would not, or could not return to their own countries. Many of them were completely without the necessities of life and did not know where they might settle; without work, poverty-stricken, lonely and unwanted, they were shunted backward and forward from country to country. (Christiensen, 1966: 19)

Conventional studies suggest that a multitude of people working for nongovernmental organizations active in relief work shared similar humanitarian concerns. They point out that the appeal by the International Red Cross Committee to the league secretary as regards the establishment of the commissioner's office was itself driven and justified by humanitarian, not political, concerns. "The majority of refugees," the appeal states,

> are without means of subsistence, and one must particularly draw attention to the position of the children and the youth amongst them who are growing up in an ever-increasing misery. . . . It is impossible that there could be 800,000 men in Europe unprotected by any legal organization recognized by international law. . . . Russian Refugees, without protection, without country, likewise victims of the scourge of war, will not be abandoned by the League of Nations to their tragic fate. (League of Nations, 1921c: 228)

To this, these studies remind us, the reply of the league council was affirmative. It was here, they suggest, that the humanitarian concerns colluded with political ones. For example, they hold that the league's affirmative response was motivated also by a desire to tackle the political and economic difficulties that large refugee populations presented for the affected countries. Says one observer, "The influx of refugees was seen as a political and economic liability" (UNHCR, 1971). To make the same point, others cite a report prepared on the question of Russian refugees in 1921, which states that the refugees "constituted a very heavy charge upon several governments" (League of Nations, 1921f: 757). Or they refer to an observer who writes of the "substantial sums of money that were required to maintain refugees" (Christiensen, 1966: 19). Yet another publicist to whom many turn points to the "complaints of the poorer governments about the unfair economic burden to which they were subjected" (Macartney, 1929: 21). Similarly, they consult seminal works such as that by C. A. Macartney, in which he explains that the league understood very well that dealing with millions of refugees was beyond the capacity of not just the philanthropic organizations, but also "the harassed, impoverished and mutually suspicious post-war governments," which lacked the mutually agreed-upon mechanism to carry out the immense amount of negotiation necessary to address the problem of the refugee (1929: 19–20). The high commissioner's office would work to create such a mechanism and the tools needed for cooperation among those states.

With all their demonstrably rich and colorful, as well as insightful, analyses, the conventional studies share something in common: they see refugees as people who constitute a commonly recognized problem in the context of the sovereign territorial state, a problem beyond piecemeal, state-by-state solutions, one requiring interstate collaboration. It was the problem of refugees to which states responded by creating the LNHCR as the much-needed mechanism for cooperation among states.

The story of the high commissioner is narrated in terms of the emergence and evolution of what today's conventional studies refer to as the modern refugee regime. It is, however, a paradoxical story. On the one hand, the commissioner constitutes the proverbial starting point for the conventional studies in accounting the evolution of the modern international refugee regime. Conceiving international regimes as legal and institutional arrangements and mechanisms of collaboration—cooperation and coordination—among actors, the conventional studies see the tenure of the high commissioner's office as an inceptive stage in the eventual creation and subsequent refinement of a refugee regime (Grahl-Madsen, 1972; Gordenker, 1987: 17; Dacyl, 1990: 26; Rogers, 1992: 1114).

On the other hand, most of these studies hasten to add, the high commissioner's founding represents a relatively minor development in the history of the refugee regime, especially in terms of effective formalizations in the refugee field toward a full-fledged refugee regime.[3] In this sense, the LNHCR does not represent any effective, formal refugee regime. According to these studies, the effective formalization in the refugee field starts with the United Nations High Commissioner for Refugees and the adoption in 1951 of the binding Geneva Convention on the Status of Refugees. Although most conventional studies commence their accounts with the High Commissioner for the League of Nations and continue with a host of organizations that succeeded it between 1930 and 1951, they see the efforts in response to refugee occurrences in Europe prior to 1951 as ad hoc attempts at formalization, representing developments far short of effective formalization. They see them less as systematic attempts and more as a patchwork, lacking efficacy, temporal continuity, and spatial universality. It is the advent of the UNHCR in 1951, for these studies, that marks a turning point in the formalization of the refugee field. With the UNHCR begins the era of effective formalization in the field, the era of effective international regime activities with universally applicable arrangements devised to govern refugee phenomena and responses to refugee phenomena across time and place.

This paradox is accounted for in these studies by locating the high commissioner in the history of the evolution of the modern refugee protection regime. In terms of the modern refugee regime, the significance of the high commissioner, stress the conventional studies, lies not so much in its embodiment of effective regime tools on behalf of refugees as in the inception and promotion of the idea of international protection for refugees, for which the high commissioner stands in an embryonic fashion. They furthermore contend that a number of organizations that followed the high commissioner, from the Nansen International Office for Refugees, to the Intergovernmental Committee on Refugees, to the International Refugee Organization, all served the same purpose until 1951, when, finally, the *idea* of international refugee protection was fully institutionalized as the *ideal* in the form of a formal international refugee protection regime.

To repeat, however, in all this, the conventional studies never question the presence of the sovereign state and its constitutive parts, the citizen-subject and the domestic community of citizens. They attribute to the state a practical objective presence in life, subject neither to history nor to spatiality and in need of no affirmation or explanation. They commence, as it were, with a commandment of their own: "Thou shalt start with the name of the state." Most studies do just that and move on to speak of the LNHCR as an interstate organization founded by already given state-entities in history. While this orientation is certainly profitable in keeping the "open secret" of the state secret and its rhetoric of representation intact, it does not say much about the practices by which the state's otherwise presumed powers are produced and put into circulation. In a sense, it obscures the fact that the state's practical centrality in life, then and now, can be obtained only in and through "replicable knowledge practices of statecraft" (Ashley, 1988b: 262; see also Ashley, 1989a: 259).

Against the background of this conceptualization of statecraft, at this juncture I advance two interrelated arguments that differ from the conventional analyses. The first argument goes to the practices and paradoxes of statecraft. I contend that the LNHCR should not be understood simply as a tertiary response to the refugee problem by state-agents presumed to be already historically fixed. Rather, the LNHCR itself must be understood as a practice of statecraft of the first order, oriented to produce, stabilize, and empower contingent images, identities, subjectivities, relations, and institutions of sovereign statehood in local and global politics.[4]

The second argument offers a radically divergent reading of the history of international responses to refugee events starting with the League of Nations High Commissioner for Refugees. In this argument, contrary to the most conventional accounts, I contend that the LNHCR represents a significant development in dealing with refugee events and that it was during its tenure that the ontology of the refugee was fully determined and thoroughly formalized, thus enabling the subsequent regime activities. The period of regime activities prior to 1951, especially during the tenure of the LNHCR, as I read it, constitutes the most comprehensive and concentrated formative period of effective refugee regimentation in terms of opening and conditioning a specific refugee space and writing the refugee identity.

Theoretically, I begin with the first argument, maintaining that activities by and around the LNHCR must be seen as practices of statecraft. Historically, I begin in the early 1920s, with the circumstances and conditions into which the LNHCR was born. These were unmistakably conditions marking an unprecedented crisis of statecraft.

THE LEAGUE OF NATIONS HIGH COMMISSIONER FOR REFUGEES: A RESPONSE TO A CRISIS OF STATECRAFT

A GENEALOGICAL STUDY

Tumultuous historical conditions in Europe at the turn of the century testify that the posited or imagined orders defined in terms of the sovereign territorial state were not simply already in existence. Nor were the relations and institutions of the state affording a practicable, comfortable framework for life.

The events prior to, during, and immediately following the First World War led to the displacement of millions of people. By the early 1920s, the continent of Europe resembled one vast sea of moving peoples. There, everyone looked amazingly alike. As Daniel Warner (1992) observed, they looked like they were all refugees. In Russia, Poland, Armenia, Greece, Syria, Turkey, France, Hungary, Romania, or Algeria, they all looked the same—ordinary people who were on the move. One observer spoke of an emergent refugee "nation" consisting of diverse groups of people:

> A whole nation of people, although they come from many nations, wanders the world, homeless except for refuges which may any moment prove to be temporary. They are men and women who often have no passports. . . . This migration—unprecedented in modern times, set loose by the World War and the revolutions in its wake—includes people of every race and every social class, every trade and every profession: Russian aristocrats and, more lately, Russian technicians, Italian liberal professors and Austrian socialist workmen; German individualists of any and every stripe; Monarchists in Republics and Republicans in Monarchies; priests and radicals; artists and laborers; capitalists and anti-capitalists; the flower of the prosperous Jewish bourgeoisie and the inhabitants of East European half Ghettos; non-conformists of every race and every social, religious and political viewpoint. (Thompson, 1938: 5–6)

To others, Europe itself seemed without hope, beset by profound problems of the body as well as the soul. Fridtjof Nansen, in his Nobel Peace Prize acceptance speech in 1922, likened the Europe of the early 1920s to the "Dying Gaul, lying on the battlefield, mortally wounded":

> That is how I see the suffering people of Europe, bleeding to death on deserted battlefields after conflicts which to a great extent were not their own. This is the outcome of lust for power, the imperialism, and the militarism that have run amok across the earth. . . . The land [lies] in ruin everywhere, and the foundations of its communities are crumbling. People bow their heads in silent despair. . . . The soul of the world is mortally sick. . . . One is here reminded of the famous words of Oxenstjerna to his son when he complained about the negotiations in Westphalia: "If you only knew, my son, with how little wisdom the world is ruled." (Nansen, 1972: 361–62)

Although less dramatic than Nansen's rendering, consider the extraordinarily revealing portrayal by Count Tosti di Valminuta, the representative of Italy to the League of Nations, of the conditions in Europe in the early 1920s:

> The history of the last days of the Roman Empire is repeating itself, and we are witnessing today a vast nomadic movement, leading to the dawn of a new era in the old world of Europe. Urged on by the hardship of their lot, whole nations are leaving their homes in the war swept and devastated East and are seeking a roof and shelter in other lands. *New slips are being grafted on the old tree of Western Europe.* History will one day recount the effects of the influx of this new blood upon the advancement of the races and their vitality. The time-honored balance of our social classes is disturbed and the ancient order changed by millions of Russians, Greeks and Turks, and the hundreds of thousands of Armenians and Macedonians, who are sowing throughout the basin of the Danube and the Balkans the dangerous seeds of strife and unrest. (League of Nations, 1924: 148)

Indeed, the whole of Europe seemed without borders (real or imagined, separating the distinct postulated culture/nation gardens). Time-honored relations and institutions of life, which had once seemed eternal, were not timeless after all. Hannah Arendt observed the vulnerability of the ancien régime: "The explosion of 1914 and its severe consequences of instability had sufficiently shattered the facade of Europe's political system to lay bare its hidden frame. Such visible exposures were the sufferings of more and more groups of people to whom suddenly the rules of the world around them had ceased to apply" (1958: 267).

Undoubtedly, the primary cause of this crisis of representation was a succession of wars, from the Balkan wars, through the First World War, to the counterrevolutionary wars in Russia. The general state of social fluidity and insecurity engendered during these wars forced millions of people from their homelands. At the close of World War I, approximately ten million people in Europe had been uprooted from their prewar residences.

Ironically, a myriad of postwar attempts introduced presumably to deal with this and other disruptive effects of the wars caused the worsening of the conditions of life all over Europe. As the Ottoman, Austria-Hungarian, and Russian Empires rapidly disintegrated, the landscape of the empires gave way to a landscape in which the once seemingly perennial relations and institutions came crumbling down. A state of political and social fluidity, ushered in by the transversal effects of wars, empowered numerous forces and actors in postwar Europe intent on reshaping the countenance of European polities.[5]

Of all these forces, "nation-builders," the Hungarian historian Istvan Mocsy (1983) writes, came to the fore. E. M. Kulischer (1948), Hope-Simpson (1939), and Jacques Vernant (1953), too, single out the power of nation builders similarly. According to these observers, the nation builders scrambled to reorganize the ethnic, political, economic, and religious mélange of life in accordance with the sovereign territorial imagery that underpins the state system in local and global politics: the citizen/nation/state hierarchy (Jackson and Penrose, 1993).

The nation builders pointed to the imperative of embracing "national entities," such as the Hungarian, Romanian, and Czechoslovakian entities, as the constitutive, organizing entities of life. Ernest Gellner encapsulates the driving logic: "A man must have a nationality as he must have a nose and two ears" (1993: 6). Not only were the national entities to acquire an uncontested centrality in the organization of life, but also they were to correspond with the proposed territories of, in this example, the Hungarian, Romanian, and Czechoslovakian states (Mocsy, 1983: 9). Nation-statehood, envisioned in the destruction of polyglot imperial-dynastic systems, wrote Benedict Anderson, became central to the imagination of the future organization of the polities across Europe (1994: 319). In nearly all cases, the newly found alignment between nations and states in organizing the polity was less experienced and more imagined, through complex mediations and representations. More often, however, instruments of governance less complex than mediations and representations came into play. "Where national cohesion was absent," Mocsy writes, "direct physical force was to compensate" (1983: 9).[6]

The logical implication of trying to create a continent neatly divided into coherent territorial states, each inhabited by a separate ethnically and linguistically homogeneous population, was the mass expulsion or extermination of minorities and other unwanted populations (Hobsbawm, 1992: 135). The crisis of representation that had characterized the immediately postwar Europe was exacerbated and further intensified by the "nationalist revision" projects under way in numerous countries in Europe and Asia.

In their most extreme forms, these interventions (as practices of statecraft) took the form of population purification, or, as in the recently popularized terminology, population "cleansing" along ethnic, racial, or religious lines. The presence of "scripted others" in the space designated as national homelands was construed and represented as an obstacle to building nation-states as the representation of national communities. This logic was pervasive in Europe. Mocsy crystallizes it in the context of Hungary in the 1920s: "By the twentieth century Hungarian national identity was well defined and the nation's right to an independent existence, to form a nation-state, was universally recognized. But the social structure was in need of *revision*" (1983: 8; emphasis added).

Such a construal was common, a modus operandi across Europe and Asia, and subsequently led to the emergence of "revision" movements all across Europe and Asia under such names as Turkification, Russification, Hellenization, and Arabization. Historically, one of the most extraordinary episodes of revision practices was the forced relocation ("exchange") of millions of people between Turkey and Greece in the 1920s (Ladas, 1932; Tabori, 1972; Xenos, 1995). In a few months, about 2.5 million Greeks and Turks were forcibly "exchanged" to constitute the "nation" ingredient of the aforementioned hierarchy. Greece acquired a third of its postwar population as a result of the exchange. A paragon of forced population exchanges, this event attests to the historicity of the component parts of the modern state—"nation crafting" as "state crafting" and state crafting as nation crafting by regimenting people as populations, as objects of government.[7]

Other countries followed suit, "exchanging" or expelling those populations whom they considered "foreign" or "external" to the imagined national entities. Greece and Bulgaria, Bulgaria and Turkey, Hungary and Romania all exchanged populations. Austria, Poland, Romania, Finland, Turkey, and Czechoslovakia expelled large masses of people whom they considered "undesirables," generally with the acquiescence and even the help of international governmental and nongovernmental organizations (League of Nations 1921b; also see 1921d). The expulsions swelled the ranks of the already displaced. By 1924, displaced people were everywhere in Europe. It was in this historical context that Count di Valminuta lamented about "the vast nomadic movement" of refugees and other displaced people that, as he saw it, was grafting new realities on the old European tree and sowing "the dangerous seeds of strife and unrest." As transversal movements, they surely were.

It was this practical impact of the displaced people that the "nation and state builders," immersed in the task of "revising" social structures of their respective countries, failed to foresee. They failed to understand that their unilateral solutions to the problems associated with "the vast nomadic movement" of people would inevitably undermine and disrupt similar "revisions," in other places, attempts to articulate and practice a statist image of the world. This was so because the repertoire of solutions that the craftsmen of the early twentieth century—nation and state builders—had at their disposal grew rather small to emphasize expulsions and a few other tools for getting rid of the unwanted. The difficulty with expulsion was that it simply exported the problem of the unwanted into the next designated national territory, thus making it difficult for similar "revision" activities there to succeed.[8] As Rogers Brubaker explains, in the context of nation and state building in France and Germany in the nineteenth century, removing "unwanted migrants" from a state's territory meant their removal into another state's territory (1992: 27), where, in the words of Arjun Appadurai, the unwanted would complicate the "people-production process for the nation-state" (1996: 43). Practices of statecraft had gone terribly amiss precisely in this sense since the turn of the twentieth century, creating further difficulties for the task of statecraft.

The resulting difficulty, as described in Count di Valminuta's account, was that millions spilled over the designated borders and boundaries, thus, by virtue of their presence, calling into question the verity and viability of the organization of life in terms of the imagery of territorial boundedness. "The world as it is," one observer wrote, referring to those times, "is a place of unrest and agitation with desperate people taking desperate measures in the attempt to merely survive. And millions of people wandering more or less aimlessly, and battering at every conceivable door, being passed from frontier to frontier, will certainly do nothing to restore the world order" (Thompson, 1938: 11).

The presence of vast numbers of moving people outside the protection of internationally recognized authorities was a manifestation of the fact that the whole series of relations and institutions around which life's possibilities were imagined were simply not in existence as objective realities. Rather, they had to be actively produced amid a mélange of protean realities. These movements, while attesting to the historical (constructed) nature of such institutions and relations, also showed their precariousness in the face of temporal and spatial shifts. When Hannah Arendt wrote that "the explosion of 1914 . . . had sufficiently shattered the facade of Europe's political system," she was underlining the vulnerability of the status quo in the face of momentous changes and transformations in the aftermath of the First World War.

In short, the nomadic, transversal realities posed as concrete difficulties in the way of the state-oriented imagination of the world. The stark reality that there were millions of "people to whom suddenly the rules of the world around them [presumably the rules of the state system] had ceased to apply" clearly demonstrated that there was in fact a "beyond" or an "outside" to the otherwise presumably all-encompassing hierarchy of citizen/nation/state, the organizing hierarchy of life. In fact, many would question even the presence of any effective rules embodied in already established, already fixed governments of the state. In a report in 1927, Major Elliot, a rapporteur for the LNHCR, clearly pointed to and affirmed this phenomenon: "In the original stages, a very serious problem was presented by the influx of large numbers of disorganized and destitute refugees into countries where *the machinery of government was in process either of reconstruction or of creation*" (League of Nations, 1927a: 56; emphasis added). Not only was the "open secret" of the modern state system exposed, but also, and even more alarmingly, the very claim of the modern state to be the site of intelligible, organized, and secure life was in peril.[9]

Continuous efforts were thus called for to effect a statist organization of life within and across locales and to name it the "world of states." The displaced people, whether in their movements or in their inertia, whether in the process of crossing a designated border, resting in a campsite, or standing in a soup line, had to be regimented such that it could become viable and practicable to reinscribe the "need of the state"—to award centrality to the territorial state in the lives of individuals. This was the task of statecraft in the specific spatiotemporal juncture that was Europe in the 1920s.

Since the sovereign state is a historically produced artifact, a contingency and not a universal necessity (Gellner, 1993), the task of statecraft, Nikolas Rose and Peter Miller tell us, is one

> not so much of the accounting of power in terms of the power of the state, but of asserting how, and to what extent, the state is articulated into the activity of government; what relations are established between political and other authorities; what funds, forces, persons, knowledge or legitimacy are utilized; and by means of what devices and techniques are these different tactics made operable. (1992: 177)

I contend that it is in this sense that the task, and hence the problem, of statecraft in the face of mass displacements in the early twentieth century was one of "rearticulating" the sovereign state into the shifting sociopolitical terrain in which the displaced people were a powerful transversal, deterritorializing force (by virtue of their sheer numbers). More specifically, the problem of statecraft vis-à-vis the massive displacement of populations was to rearticulate the sovereign territorial state into the events of displacement in order strategically to position the state vis-à-vis the events of displacement so as to control their antithetical force and, if and when possible, even to render them a fund, force, technique, or knowledge useful for statecraft in the midst of a sea of changes.

It was at this historical juncture where the crisis of statecraft was most intense that the League of Nations High Commissioner for Refugees emerged. Its place (Europe) and time of emergence (the 1920s) were significant, surely signifying more than a historical coincidence.

Against this background, I argue that the LNHCR emerged as an instrument of statecraft; it was founded to open an intergovernmental, legal field of activity as a field of statist *problematizations,* thus to enable the regimentation of the transverse effects of the events of displacement. In an article entitled "Refugees—A Permanent Problem in International Organization," Lawford Childs refers precisely to this function of the LNHCR and successive League of Nations organizations dealing with refugee issues and events: "For over 18 years, the League has tortured the texts, confounded the jurists, baffled the adepts of unrestricted sovereignty, and maintained—in view of difficulties—a *quasi-permanent activity* in favor of the refugees" (1937: 204; emphasis added).

What Childs refers to as the "quasi-permanent [league] activity" is what I term the "opening" or the establishment (and the maintenance) of an intergovernmental refugee field as a field of statecraft. It was there, in and through this intergovernmental field of regimentation as a field of statecraft, that *events of human displacement were problematized* in state-oriented terms, that is, they were rearticulated (reinscribed) as a specific *refugee problem* characterized in terms of images, identities, and subjectivities that support the sovereign state. It was also there, in and through this intergovernmental field of statecraft, that the activities of problematization were subsequently institutionalized into a *formal* intergovernmental refugee regime.

The High Commissioner for Refugees stood at the crossroads of refugee problematizations, occasioning a plethora of governmental and intergovernmental, as well as popular, activities. A number of legal and institutional measures were generated. These measures would come to form the basis of a permanent intergovernmental legal discourse on refugees and would prove decisive in regimenting refugee movements. I shall examine these measures in more detail a little later. Before I do so, however, it is imperative to foreground them by pointing (in perhaps ponderous yet necessarily theoretical language) to two general effects of the multiple measures of refugee regimentations.

First, these measures facilitated the emergence and consolidation of an intergovernmental legal or formal refugee space as a field of statecraft. This meant an intergovernmentalization of the processes by which the refugee event was defined as a problem of sovereign statecraft. Second, while effecting a formalization of the refugee space, these activities also worked to "normalize" the refugee in statist terms: they appropriated the refugee vis-à-vis the posited relations and institutions of the state. They did this by articulating a specific program of governance through what Michel Foucault calls "procedures of exclusion" (cited in Procacci, 1994: 212), which in the course of governance worked as "procedures of inclusion," generating specific normality relations between objects and subjects and between subjects and subjects. Beyond the process of the formalization of the refugee, in other words, one could see a process of normalization. Through an emphasis on the need to help the poor refugees or to control the dangerous nomads, the inclusion of the refugee into the intergovernmental field of conduct and policy turned into a process of disciplinary action aimed at inscribing and continually restoring a specific "normal" relation between the refugee and the citizen, a hierarchy in which the refugee was always defined negatively vis-à-vis the citizen-subject, as someone who lacked the citizen's ties to the state (Procacci, 1994: 212).

The process of simultaneous formalization and normalization of the refugee through maintaining a field of policy and conduct under the name of the refugee was manifested, both conceptually and organizationally, in a number of organizational initiatives and legal conventions and protocols around the high commissioner's office, which operated from 1921 until 1930. After the dissolution of the LNHCR, such activities continued under the auspices of a host of other refugee organizations. The Nansen International Office for Refugees, the Intergovernmental Committee on Refugees, the International Refugee Organization, and, finally, the United Nations High Commissioner for Refugees, which is today the leading UN agency dealing with refugees, are among the most significant organizations that contributed to the formalization of the intergovernmental regimentation of human displacement under the sign of the refugee.

These organizations proved crucial in terms of refugee problematizations in that their existence induced two forms of continuities, *temporal* and *ontological,* that are essential to refugee regimentations as practices of statecraft. To begin with, they effected a temporal continuity in refugee regimentations by virtue of their continual presence. Each organization generally rose out of the ashes of another and withered into the one that followed. Whether they took the form of new instruments of regime relations or represented realignments of those instruments into new frameworks of policy and conduct, the organizations were linked to one another through historical events and overlapping mandates. Each was contingently situated along a continuum of intergovernmental refugee space as a field of statecraft, making possible a multitude of statecraft practices. Indeed, it is this constancy that Claudena Skran refers to when she writes that "the High Commissioner's office came to represent an outline of the current UNHCR" (1988: 280).

Furthermore, the activities of these organizations effected an ontological constancy in refugee regimentations or problematizations. More specifically, they effected the constancy of the figure of the refugee vis-à-vis the posited subjectivities and relations of the sovereign state. Each problematization, while it engendered historically unique effects, was still rooted in and enabled by previous problematizations in time and space. In spite of a whole host of alterations and changes in the course of history, an analysis of the "content" of the refugee shows (as I do in this and the following chapters) that the ontology of the refugee remained permanently linked to the postulated logic of the sovereign state. The significance of the organizations, then, lies in their productive presence, which, through the facilitation of the two continuities I have outlined, has afforded what I call the permanent field of refugee regimentations.

In light of this discussion, it could now be suggested that, in the history of the regimentation of human displacement, the emergence of the League of Nations High Commissioner for Refugees represented a historic shift in the strategies of statist governance. There were two dimensions to this shift. The first dimension represented a deepening or intensification in the problematization of human displacement under the sign of the refugee. This refers to the discursive activities by which a specific figure of the refugee was inscribed and brought to the fore as constituting the refugee problem in the twentieth century, and hence was designated as the proper object of intervention. The second dimension represented a deepening or intensification in the strategies of statecraft through intergovernmental projects dealing with the refugee problem. This refers to the discursive activities by which intergovernmentality emerged as a characteristic paradigmatic strategy of intervention in the refugee problem.[10] In summary, these two intensifications, occasioned by activities around the name of the LNHCR, facilitated a reconfiguration of the practical, legal, and institutional content of the field of human displacement to establish (a) the refugee, not the exile or the émigré, as the problem-figure of statecentric governance in the twentieth century, and hence the object of corrective intervention; and (b) intergovernmentality as the effective strategy of intervention.[11]

It is instructive, however, that neither the emergence of the high commissioner nor the evolution of the subsequent intergovernmental refugee regime was inevitable or necessary in the face of the events at the turn of the century. If anything, there is considerable historical evidence indicating otherwise, that is, that the high commissioner's office was born in the face of considerable reluctance by the League of Nations members to accept any responsibility for the displaced people (Hope-Simpson, 1939; Macartney, 1929). Furthermore, among the league members that founded the office, there was also a fear of "losing sovereignty" to a supranational organization such as the proposed High Commissioner for Refugees. Similarly, the activities around the commissioner that paved the way for the formalization and institutionalization of refugee regimentation were and continue to be in large measure contingent activities whose nature and scope were and still are mediated by the contingencies of the refugee events themselves. They were and still are, in a Foucauldian sense, activities whose nature, objective, and identities are shaped in the field of activity, not driven by a prior, ineluctable design to establish a particular refugee regime. The annals of the League of Nations demonstrate how even the league members failed to support the high commissioner consistently, in spite of the fact that the commissioner's office was their own creation. Many observers and practitioners, including Fridtjof Nansen himself, spoke of the ubiquitous efforts to undermine the work of the high commissioner throughout its tenure.

Although the high commissioner's office operated in an environment of ambivalence in terms of the support it received, its presence, however troubled, continued to afford a field of problematization as a field of statist regimentation of human displacement. That was crucial to the subsequent problematizations of human displacements in statist terms, for its activities prepared the ground on which succeeding organizations have built their problematizations.

It was precisely to this task, the continuous problematization of human displacement into refugee events ontologically congruent with the prevailing logic of sovereign statehood, that the LNHCR and its successor organizations were put. In what follows, I show how this happened by examining in great detail the specific historical organizational and legal developments that occurred under the tenure of the LNHCR.

REFUGEE PROBLEMATIZATIONS, THE LEAGUE OF NATIONS, AND THE FORMALIZATION OF A REFUGEE REGIME

The annals of the LNHCR are rich in refugee problematizations, from the recognition of refugee events as a problem for statecraft, to the formulation of responses that are in accord with the task of statecraft. In his lamentations on refugees as dangerous nomads, Count di Valminuta, for example, advocated a head-on, collaborative approach by governments to tackle refugee problems. For the count, the refugee event produced racial chaos, which gave birth to a new world crisis. "The League," he said, "should devote its whole attention to this racial chaos and the forces underlying the various racial currents, for only so can it help to tide over existing crises and prevent the present painful endeavor to stabilize the world from becoming a source of new crises" (League of Nations, 1924: 148).[12]

Many concurred with the count and were resolved to do something about refugees. Soon after the founding of the LNHCR, in different forums within and outside the structure of the League of Nations, a barrage of discourse surged on the "impact" of refugees on the imagined normal order of life. The content of the discourse is instructive in surmising how the refugee event was reinscribed into the sociopolitical and socioeconomic tableaux of governance. Consider the following articulations of the refugee presence, reinscribing the (content) of the refugee event from an object of curiosity and compassion to a subject of instability and insecurity. The Finnish minister M. Enckell suggested:

> One of the disadvantages of the presence of refugees is the demoralizing influence exercised on the Finnish population by these multitudes, composed, for the greater part, of persons unaccustomed to discipline and order and used to idleness. . . . Among the refugees belonging to the working classes there are many doubtful elements which require strict supervision and necessitate the employment of a large body of officials. . . . The presence of elements hostile to Finland has also been noticed; these, forgetful of the hospitality they are enjoying in Finland, have not hesitated to conspire against her. (League of Nations, 1921e: 1010)[13]

Consider also the remarks by M. Molloff, the Bulgarian representative to the assembly:

> In recent years, Bulgaria has made a great effort punctually to carry out the different stipulations of the Treaties of Peace. But the increasing influx of refugees, due mostly to the exchange of population brought about by the treaties, created a situation of indescribable distress for the families involved, a heartrending situation in itself, but one which also endangered the internal stability of the country and was liable to provoke serious disturbances that might have affected international relations. (League of Nations, 1926b: 113)

The words of Fridtjof Nansen, the first high commissioner, who advanced the true humanitarian effects of the organization, were equally alarmist:

> The refugee problem is a problem which affects the direct material interest of a great number of the governments of Europe, and which indirectly is of great importance to the reconstruction of Russia and through Russia to the reconstruction and prosperity of Europe and of the world. . . . The sufferings of the refugees have been very real and very great. It was inevitable that one and a half million people, taken partly from the most cultured and richest classes of a great country, scattered without sufficient resources, without adequate means of livelihood throughout the length and breadth of Europe, should suffer every hardship and privation. In Constantinople at one point, there was positive starvation. Refugees were found dead in the streets from hunger. . . . Throughout Europe there have been refugees suffering from poverty, hunger and destitution. I am continually receiving distressing accounts of the destitute condition of the hundreds of thousands of refugees in Poland, who also form a serious menace to the public health, not only in this country, but in states bordering on Russia. (League of Nations, 1922b: 113)

An Austrian government communiqué cast the problem of the refugee similarly: "The representative of Austria pleaded that it was the duty of Austria to repatriate all persons whose residence in the country was injurious to the Austrian people. . . . Her population lacked food and accused the refugees of intensifying the general distress" (League of Nations, 1921h: 101). Last, consider the observations of Gustave Ador in a report entitled "The Typhus Campaign in Eastern Europe," where he saw refugees as the unwitting carriers of epidemics such as typhus:

> Refugees are arriving from Russia in increasing numbers; matters such as the disaffection, clothing, provisioning, vaccination and placing in quarantine of the refugees claim to the fullest extent the activity and the resources of the authorities. At Baraniwitze, the most important of these quarantine stations, the installations were once quite insufficient, which had they been left as they were, would have constituted a serious menace to the health of Poland and of more western countries. (League of Nations, 1921g: 424)

No longer were the displaced people, whether called exiles, refugees, or émigrés, simply spectacles of curiosity, people with strange habits and clothes, the objects of giggles and laughter. No longer were they largely cast as objects of charity, people who needed help and got it because they were few in number and not seen as a threat. No longer were they generally seen as objects of desire in a mercantilist sense, people who were readily welcomed by rulers of countries because they were seen as likely to enrich the host countries with their wealth and knowledge, as the Huguenots had been seen. Although these sentiments—curiosity, compassion, charity, and desire—all played a significant role in the recasting of human displacement into a specific refugee problem, the imperatives of the governance of the territorial state dominated people's minds. Humanitarian sentiments did in fact drive many people who were active in refugee relief work, as was evidenced in the 1921 memorandum from the International Red Cross Committee to the League of Nations. However, for the practitioners of the state, humanitarian objectives were deeply invested with the perceived exigencies of statist governance. Massive human displacement, now identified as a refugee problem with certain characteristics, did not bode well for the fundamental task of statecraft. Instead, the massive nomadic movements of people were seen, in the words of Count di Valminuta, as planting "dangerous seeds of strife and unrest" and racial chaos throughout Europe. Such movements had to be regimented, and they were.

The LNHCR became the agent as well as the site of this regimentation. It became a locus of policy and conduct oriented to regimenting the disruptive powers of human displacement in the context of sovereign territorial governance. A historical examination of the organization's actual work clearly demonstrates this argument.

Having been authorized by the League of Nations, the organizational structuring of the commissioner's office under the leadership of Fridtjof Nansen reflected the enunciated objective of the organization, which was collaboration and cooperation among governments in dealing with the refugee problem. Accordingly, Nansen started off by establishing what he called "channels of communication and action with governments," which, in his opinion, were "evidently necessary" for "securing the full cooperation of the governmental and other authorities." To this end, Nansen asked "all the interested governments to appoint representatives to communicate directly with him and to whom he could make specific proposals for action" (League of Nations, 1922d: 386–87).[14] As also mandated by the founding resolutions, Nansen established representative offices in the interested countries to work on a more continuous basis with the governmental and nongovernmental organizations dealing with Russian refugees. Furthermore, he asked all nongovernmental organizations to form a "special joint committee" to advise him in all matters in connection with refugees in which they had special knowledge (387).[15]

While striving to put in place an organizational network, Nansen also worked to further internationalize and intergovernmentalize refugee issues on political fronts. The central theme to these early moves was the determination of the legal and juridical status of refugees. In late 1921, only months after he was appointed as the high commissioner, Nansen organized two international conferences on Russian refugees.

The first of the conferences convened on 22 August 1921 in Geneva, with the participation of eleven governments and a number of "philanthropic organizations" dealing with Russian refugees. The conference included delegates from Bulgaria, China, Czechoslovakia, Finland, France, Greece, Poland, Romania, the Serb-Croat-Slovene state, and Switzerland. The International Committee of the Red Cross, the League of Red Cross Societies, the International Save the Children Fund, and a number of other "philanthrophic" organizations sent representatives. As a Nansen report to the League of Nations on Russian refugees put it later, "This conference considered the problem of refugees as a whole, and adopted a series of resolutions which served as *guiding principles* for the work undertaken" (League of Nations, 1922e: 2–3).

The second conference was held the following month, in September 1921, in Paris. Sixteen governments and the same number of nongovernmental organizations sent delegates to this second conference. In the final resolutions of the conference, the participants instructed the high commissioner's office to undertake, in collaboration with the International Labor Organization (ILO), a comprehensive census of Russian refugees in all the countries to determine their professions, occupations, educational levels, family connections, and so on. Even more significantly, they urged the concerned countries to cooperate with the commissioner in dealing with Russian refugees in order to facilitate "burden-sharing schemes" that would benefit all the parties involved. Finally, the conference categorically stressed the necessity of coordinating and regulating the activities and practices in dealing with refugees by declaring that "the relief work was a matter for united international action and required the collaboration of all states" (League of Nations, 1922e: 2).

These conferences were significant events for at least two reasons. First, for the first time in the history of refugee events, the conferences brought together an impressive array of agents and entities, representatives both of governments and of nongovernmental organizations. Second, and more important, the conferences produced a number of elementary intergovernmental guidelines for conduct and cooperation among governments and nongovernmental organizations with respect to Russian refugees. "The first conference," Nansen wrote in his first report to the league, "considered the whole problem and adopted a series of resolutions on which the subsequent action of the High Commissioner has been based. [At the second conference] some of the matters dealt with in the resolutions of the first conference were further considered" (League of Nations, 1922d: 385).

When the conferences were over, the high commissioner's office stood at the center of activities regarding Russian refugee issues. Its centrality was due not to its power but to its function as a catalyst for the activities responding to refugee occurrences. In fact, its very presence facilitated a field of activity occasioning the practices of statecraft that worked, as I have shown, to recast *human displacement* as a specific *refugee problem* for the sovereign state. Its very presence, in other words, became instrumental in the repositioning of the practitioners of the state in the heart of the events of displacement. In the words of Rose and Miller (1992), the commissioner's presence afforded a strategic opportunity for "articulating" the state and its posited logic into the events of displacement, or for bringing the events of displacement "under state control." It is thus that the displaced people, or in Count di Valminuta's words "the nomadic people," were recast in the league conference as "refugees," constituting, in the language of the resolutions, a problem of interest to the entire world and involving all the states of the civilized world.

In the same fashion, the high commissioner's presence occasioned further practices that deepened refugee problematizations by intergovernmentalizing the regimentation of the refugee problem. The stage for this phase of problematization had already been set by the conference delegates, who declared:

> The conference is of the opinion that, *as the problem is of interest to the entire world,* it would not be just to leave the burden of relieving Russian refugees to the few nations which have hitherto borne along both for philanthropic reasons and by reason of their geographical situation, a course which might involve them in sacrifices beyond their power; and that not only all the states belonging to the League of Nations, but *all the states of the civilized world,* ought to be invited to contribute support in proportion to their resources for *this urgent and essential task* in the common interest of mankind. (League of Nations, 1921a: 902; emphasis added)

Notice here that the emergent institutional or formal intergovernmental discourse "diagnosing" the refugee problem as well as offering solutions to the problem exhibits a statist epistemology. It commences in statist terms, positing an a priori normal order to the world by simply declaring the refugee event as an event of "abnormality" in the otherwise normal conditions of governance.[16] This declaration amounts to an act of problematization that affirms a formal intergovernmental refugee field and simultaneously conditions its possibilities by linking its ontology to a postulation of the "civilized world of states," a world which, possessing specific intergovernmentally recognized subjectivities and institutions, is taken to represent the "normal" conditions of life on Earth. With this in mind, it could be said, and said convincingly, that the conferences held under the auspices of the high commissioner's office launched the process by which refugee regimentations were formalized in statist terms (in order to deal more effectively with the disruptive effects of human displacement for practices of statecraft).

This imposition of a statist ontology on the identity of the refugee was furthered and deepened through yet another event occasioned by activities around the high commissioner. It was the invention, in 1922, of a legal document, specifically, a certificate of identity that officially "documented" a displaced person as a "refugee." Identity certificates attributed certain qualities to refugees, linking them to a set of statist subjectivities and entities posited to be already historically well established. The devising of identity certificates for refugees, informally known as the Nansen passports, was significant in terms of refugee problematizations.

Recall from the earlier discussion that the creation of such a certificate was recommended in the resolutions adopted in the first international conference and further deliberated upon in the second conference. The delegates in both conferences had observed the importance of identity certificates for determining the juridical status of refugees. They had pointed out that most Russian refugees, possessing no recognized or legitimate identity papers issued by a government, lacked any sort of legal protection or representation by a state. Russian refugees either had been deprived of passports by the revolutionary government in Russia or had been unwilling to carry the passports issued by the revolutionary government. Lack of a passport proved to be a significant impediment for those refugees, especially in the face of ever stricter passport checks and other travel restrictions instituted during and immediately after the First World War throughout Europe (Skran, 1988: 281; Marrus, 1985: 92; Macartney, 1929: 20–21). Within a few months after starting his position as the high commissioner, Fridtjof Nansen quickly recognized the specific problem that the lack of passports presented for refugees. "This matter," he wrote in a report in early 1922, "to which we have given continuous attention . . . is of real—I might almost say of urgent—importance" (League of Nations, 1922c: 1137), for "a great many of the Russian refugees in Europe suffered considerably for the sole reason that they have been unprovided with any legal passports or paper of identity, without which they were unable to travel from the countries in which they found themselves" (League of Nations, 1922f: 396).

Consequently, in July 1922, Nansen organized an international conference exclusively to consider the legal status of Russian refugees. The conference, which was attended by sixteen governments, agreed to create a special identity certificate for refugees and stateless persons. Subsequently, more than fifty states, including all the European states, adopted the identity certificate as a substitute for a national passport (Skran, 1988: 281; Macartney, 1929: 26). In May 1924, Nansen passports were also secured for Armenian refugees displaced throughout the territories of the former Ottoman Empire (Hope-Simpson, 1939: 197). The certificates were later extended to Assyrians, Assyro-Chaldeans, and Turks in 1928, and to Saar refugees in 1935 as well.

The conventional interpretations stress that the objective in the institution of these certificates was merely to allow refugees some degree of freedom of movement and "the same measure of protection as is enjoyed by the nationals of a state" (Bentwich, 1935: 116). From a genealogical perspective, the institution of identity certificates for refugees represents objectives in addition to humanitarianism. In fact, it represents a move in the task of problematizing the refugee in terms instrumental to the practices of statecraft after the First World War. Its instrumentality, Donald Carter indicates, lies in the virtue of its emergence as an official document that constructs and conditions the representations of life, including the representations of the territorial state as an agent of governance. "The state," writes Carter,

> is a continuing project envisioned through official documents. From the cartographer's maps to the presentation of columns and graphs in daily reports, the state must create and re-create a vision, or visions of its own existence. . . . [As] a continuing project, the state's most important activity is the continual orchestration of its own existence. . . . The document, an artifact of the state, is a nexus of complex underlying cultural significations and classificatory practices that give life to [this] art of the state. (1994: 72, 77)

It is in this sense that the institution of the identity certificates, "documenting" "refugees," as distinct from, say, "citizens," must be seen as a practice of statecraft, one among an array of practices that craft the contingent powers and identities of the modern territorial state in time and space.[17] The logic here is simple. Carter calls it the "logic of incorporation and distancing" (1994: 93), which seeks to identify, document, and map specific forms of otherness (incorporation) constructed in the processes of producing specific forms of normalcy (distancing). To be sure, in the case of the high commissioner, the identity certificate, by virtue of its emergence, established and normalized a formal, intergovernmentally recognized refugee identity, that is, an identity reinscribed into congruence with the logic of statist governance at work across most of Europe. It inscribed and expressed a set of state-oriented politico-administrative significations and classifications under the rubric of the refugee.

Seen from this perspective, the identity certificate worked as an instrument of statecraft, enabling the practices that "invent" and "orchestrate" (the powers of) the state, in two interdependent senses.

First, the identity certificate enabled a set of practices that orchestrated the state into existence as a representative agent, representing and protecting what are seen as the a priori *normal* relations of governance manifested in the citizen/nation/state constellation. Second, it enabled a set of practices that orchestrated the state into existence as a corrective agent, intervening in what are seen as secondary to and an *aberrance* from the normal conditions of governance, namely, the conditions of the refugee, documented not in a national passport but in the identity certificate.

The identity certificate as a document embodies a specific vision of the state in the "documenting" of the refugee in opposition to the citizen. This vision is apparent in the discussions of a proposed change of the name "identity certificate" to "passport" in 1926. The task of envisioning and representing a specific vision of the state becomes amply clear in replies to a questionnaire on the issue. In response to the question "Would you agree to substitute the word 'passport' for the word 'identity certificate'?" replies by governments are revealing:

> AUSTRIA: Yes, provided that in order to avoid any misunderstanding, the words "for refugees" are added to the word "passport."
>
> BELGIUM: Yes, provided a distinction is made between national and refugee passports.
>
> ESTONIA: Inadvisable, for to describe refugee identity certificates as "passports" might give rise to a misunderstanding.
>
> FRANCE: The present denomination seems preferable, as it indicates the nature of the document and avoids confusion.
>
> ITALY: It would seem preferable to maintain the present denomination, to which might be added the words "in lieu of passport" in order to avoid confusion.
>
> LATVIA: Yes, provided that, in order to avoid confusion, the term "passport" is added to the word "refugees."
>
> SWEDEN: It would seem desirable to retain the term "identity certificate" in order to preserve a distinction between national passports and the identity documents for refugees. (League of Nations, 1926a: 11)

Why are these responses important? How do they punctuate statecraft? Instructive answers lie in the historical context in which a distinct identity certificate for refugees was necessitated, that is, was seen as imperative. It is interesting to note that the identity certificates emerged at a time when governments were also resurrecting their own national passport systems, issuing national passports to those whom they saw to be their citizens and requesting passports from those whom they considered to be noncitizens for entering the country. These new developments contrasted sharply with the period prior to the First World War.

Prior to the war, passports had fallen into disuse. Most officials never asked for them, except in some areas, such as the Ottoman and Russian Empires, where they were used for travel within the empires' borders (Marrus, 1985: 92). After the war, however (and with the advent of what Istvan Mocsy calls the "revisionist-nationalisms," which married exclusionary nationalism to the task of statecraft [1983: 9]), national passports emerged as yet another instrument of "envisioning" the state and its counterparts, the citizen and the nation. National passports became a normal part of the daily rhythm of statecraft, signifying a specific organization of life into territorial insides and outsides, of which passports in various shapes and colors were to be the symbolic demonstration. This imposition, however, was not without some resentment and resistance by those whose visions of self and community were still not in synchrony with the visions of territorial statehood and nationhood. Paul Fussell describes how passports were seen by the British literati traveling after the war:

> Affixed to this compulsory document was a photograph, a "most egregious little modernism" that shamed or humiliated those who loathed the idea of a banal likeness of themselves being on display; a reference to "Profession" that was an open invitation to self-casting and self-promotion, not to mention outright fraud, and a "Description of the Bearer" that presented unheard-of intimate details describing bodily features. (Qtd. in Marrus, 1985: 92–93)

The identity certificates, too, became part of the rhythm, not simply as documents that afforded a degree of freedom and legal or juridical recognition to otherwise statusless people, but perhaps more importantly, as instruments of statecraft useful in the representation or, in the words of Carter (1994), the envisioning of the sovereign territorial state in an intergovernmentally recognized document. So it was that, as Gérard Noiriel (1996: 46, 76) put it, "the card and the code" served statecraft once more. It was hardly a mere historical coincidence that the necessity for identity certificates was articulated contemporaneously with the articulation of the necessity for national passports for citizens.

This function of passports is in fact adumbrated, but not pursued with vigor, in a few works on refugees. Tommie Sjoberg, for instance, argues that with passports, "an instrument of cooperation was thus created when there were shared political interests among various participating governments in introducing an element of order into their dealings with a common problem" (1991: 27).[18] Similarly, Michael Marrus writes that, "however limited, the Nansen Passport was a significant achievement: for the first time it permitted determination of the juridical status of stateless persons through a specific international agreement" (1985: 95). Reflecting on the utility of identify certificates for the states, Felix Morley corroborates the point by suggesting that, while the certificate afforded refugees a degree of freedom of movement, it served an equally useful function for governments; it provided governments with a common "supernational" framework of policy and conduct as to the treatment of refugees within and across national borders (1932: 246).[19]

During the early years, the work of the Nansen office was by no means confined to "helping" the Russian refugees alone. Gil Loescher states that soon after Nansen started as the high commissioner, the initiatives he undertook on behalf of refugees mushroomed, and the functions of the high commissioner expanded (1993: 38). International refugee regimentation grew to encompass refugee settlement, employment opportunities, emigration, and linkage of refugee assistance with economic development.

In addition to handling the Russian refugees in Europe and Turkey, the high commissioner's office undertook various ad hoc tasks. The convergent effects of these tasks were considerable in fashioning possibilities for the field of statecraft. In 1922, for example, the commissioner was called upon by the league council to mediate the conflict between Turkey and Greece in regard to a population exchange. The commissioner's office worked as the principal agent "coordinating" the forced exchange of about two million Greeks and Turks between the two countries.

This involvement was remarkable in that it unequivocally exposed the imperatives of statecraft. The high commissioner became the instrument of the regimentation of populations that made it possible to speak of the ideals of citizen-subjects and their national communities, which would be represented by the sovereign state. As I have already discussed, the exchange of populations between Greece and Turkey was a crucial event in the production of national myths channeled into statist cultural, political, and economic institutions and relations (Hobsbawm, 1992; Kulischer, 1948; Ladas, 1932; Tabori, 1972; Hirschon, 1989). Interestingly, the transparent nature of the tensions of state-oriented regimentations of the lives of people found a curious and telling expression in the politico-cultural arena.

In a study on the role of culture in statecraft, Michael Herzfeld reflects on the patterns of adaptation among the carpet weavers of the Orthodox religious tradition who were forcibly transferred to Greece from Turkey (1988: 83–89). Herzfeld observes that initially there was considerable resistance to practices designed to cultivate a "Greek" identity among the weavers that were expressed through the institutions of statist governance.[20] The carpet weavers considered themselves not "Greeks" in secular, nationalist terms, but Orthodox Christians in religious terms. In spite of pressures from the government, for example, they refused to incorporate the designated "Greek" designs into their craft. Rather, they continued to weave their traditional designs, which they did not associate with a distinct Greek identity. They had to be subjected to further regimentation in order to forge a distinct sense of Greekness in their hearts—and they were, again with the help of the high commissioner as the embodiment of the intergovernmental regimentation of refugee movements.

Following the forced population exchange, the LNHCR undertook a massive scheme of resettlement in Greece, in effect facilitating the process that made it further possible to speak of a distinct Greek citizenry represented and protected by the Greek state. A Greek representative to the League of Nations expressed his government's gratitude to the high commissioner precisely for this reason:

> MR. CACLAMANOS: To the aid afforded by the League, I desire to pay yet another public tribute of gratitude. . . . According to the moving report recently communicated to the League by Mr. Howland, the distinguished chairman of the Refugee Commission, 750,000 refugees have already been settled by the Commission. Greek Macedonia has been completely transformed. In places where once there was uncultivated or waste land, field after field of rich crops can now be seen stretching farther than the eye can reach. Smiling villages are rising

> everywhere among the fields, and rugged and contented workers till the earth and make it rich and plentiful. Whole towns are rising around Athens as by wave of a magic wand. New industries are being founded and are developing all over the country. In a few years, the sacrifices made by our nation will bring their reward in the increased wealth of the country, thanks to the toil and labour of her newly acquired sons. (League of Nations, 1926b: 87)[21]

Also, during the attempts aimed at resolving the Armenian refugee problem in the Near East, the high commissioner's office functioned as the primary agent coordinating intergovernmental efforts (League of Nations, 1928; Bentwich, 1935: 119; Skran, 1988: 281). Moreover, in cooperation with "philanthropic organizations," it organized settlement projects for tens of thousands of European refugees in nearby countries such as France and in lands across the Atlantic Ocean such as the United States, Argentina, Paraguay, and Brazil (Bentwich, 1935: 119–20; McDonald, 1944: 212–13).[22]

While dealing with contingencies of this kind, the LNHCR continued its work in the legal and juridical field, facilitating the adoption of further legal instruments of coordination and cooperation among agents and entities. For instance, the office organized the Inter-governmental Conference on Refugee Questions in Geneva in May 1926. It was during this conference that for the first time Russian and Armenian refugees were formally defined and those definitions were duly incorporated into a number of legal instruments (see League of Nations, 1926). These definitions recognized refugees in groups rather than on the merits of individual cases. A Russian refugee, for example, was defined as "any person of Russian origin who does not enjoy or who no longer enjoys the protection of the government of the Union of Soviet Socialist Republics and who has not acquired another nationality" (Hope-Simpson, 1939: 227–28). This definition, along with that of Armenian refugees, was extremely important.[23] It was a historic marker in statist refugee regimentations, for it encoded the refugee unequivocally in state-centric terms, ontologically linking the refugee's identity to the state's posited territorial universe at a time when this universe was still in the making or, as Benedict Anderson puts it, was "less experienced and more imagined" (1994: 319). The refugee became one who was outside this universe, lacking ties to the national community and the state.

Lacking such ties, the refugee could not be represented by the state and was therefore deprived of the protections of the state.[24]

The problematization of the refugee as a figure of lack presented a dilemma. On the one hand, the solution to the refugee was formulated in state-centric terms, in terms of either repatriation into a community of origins or integration into a new community. To exist, the refugee had to enter some "territorial home" and had to have her or his territorial ties restored with a community of citizens and the state. On the other hand, the proposed state-centric measures to solve the refugee problem created an intermediary status of desire under the sign of the refugee, especially in the midst of a sea of desperate displaced people. Yes, the formal refugee status was to be a temporary status, but even as a status of lack it was still better than no status.

For those who were in dire need, a piece of bread or shelter was paramountly more desirable than a critical awareness of their relations to institutions of governance. In the league measures, for example, the Russians and Armenians who were officially designated as refugees were entitled to a number of recognized rights, none more desired and coveted than the identity certificate, which eventually gave refugees "the right of return" that had been missing in the original arrangement (Macartney, 1929: 28).

This paradoxical status—a figure of lack on the one hand and a figure of desire on the other—was productive to statist regimentation in that it rendered the displaced into a party willing to contribute to the constitution of territorializing, state-oriented refugee images and identities that in effect would affirm the primacy and normalcy of the citizen/nation/state hierarchy. For evidence, consider the following developments when the league was contemplating extending the refugee category to other groups.

In May 1926, the League of Nations Assembly moved to seek to extend to other refugee groups the juridical status that had been granted to Russian and Armenian refugees. The assembly adopted a resolution in which it instructed the high commissioner to "consider the possibility of extending measures at present taken on behalf of Russian and Armenian refugees to analogous categories of refugees" (League of Nations, 1927c: 1–2). As I have indicated, in the course of events, a number of refugee groups, such as Assyrians, Turks, Hungarians, Spaniards, and Saar and German refugees benefited from the extension of refugee status (Grahl-Madsen, 1966: 123–31). The extensions did not come without a challenge, however, from the Russian and Armenian refugees who had until then monopolized the status. The organizations representing these "refugee communities" moved swiftly to protect their refugee status as a "privilege." On 10 February 1927, the Central Committee for the Study of the Conditions of Russian Refugees wrote to Fridtjof Nansen, the High Commissioner for Refugees, as regards one of the measures, the identity certificates:

> The Central Committee fully appreciates the fact that Governments are at liberty to replace the system of Certificates in force by any other system convenient to them, but it wishes to state the refugees' point of view in order that a change which is absolutely contrary to their desire should not be attributed to any wish of their own. From the outset, the adoption of the "Nansen Certificates" met the wishes of the Russian refugees. They attach a capital importance to the certificate, which they consider and appreciate as a sign of legal recognition of their peculiar status. The "Nansen Certificate" is valuable in that it prevents a confusion which would be unjust as well as harmful. It is valuable as a proof of protection of the League of Nations, which might, if necessary, be strengthened. Without laying claim to an exclusive right to this *privilege*, the Russian refugees would consider the abolition of the "Nansen Passports" to be prejudicial to their interests.

On 25 February 1927, the Central Committee for Armenian Refugees sent a similar letter on the matter, in which it said:

> We learn that the services of the League of Nations are discussing a plan to replace the system of certificates by a single certificate for all those who are considered as "heimlatos" (without nationality). We hope that before taking any decision on the subject, an opportunity will be granted to the persons concerned, as especially to the Armenians, to express their opinion on a question which affects their interests so closely. We confine ourselves, however, at the moment to saying that the new measures would seriously affect the position of our compatriots, who have already suffered so much from the vicissitudes of international politics.[25]

This episode is instructive in demonstrating the positive, productive dimension of refugee problematizations as a play of power instrumental in statecraft. To be sure, the displaced people had been instrumental in refugee problematizations from the onset. They partook in the devising and implementation of the measures in various fashions. They founded advisory organizations and worked hand in hand with the LNHCR and individual governments. They joined in the "management" of refugee populations in camps and out of camps, participated in schemes of repatriation and resettlement, and even served as intermediaries between governments and other interested parties. Most never contested the regime of boundaries imposed on the movements of people. It was more true for the British or the French aristocracy and literati to be unsettled facing these measures than it was for most displaced people. For most of the displaced people, it was better to be a refugee than not to be at all. So they clung to the refugee status when they had it, or wanted to have this status when they did not possess it.[26] But it was at such moments of life and death that refugees were disciplined into action within the logic of statist hierarchy, with its paradigmatic normalities and abnormalities, and that their fears and desires were harnessed or appropriated for the construction of their own refugeeness as an abnormality, one that would affirm the correlative normality of citizenship and statehood. In displacement, in short, refugees bordered and bounded the citizen and the state.

This paradoxical role played by the displaced people themselves, either through their own organizations or through the LNHCR, was mirrored in the development of nongovernmental organizations in general (of which some were established by refugees themselves).[27] During the tenure of the LNHCR, nongovernmental organizations were the backbone of actual refugee relief work. Without them, it would have been impossible to carry out the relief work, and without the actual relief work, it would have been absurd to speak of an international refugee protection regime (Ferris, 1993b). Still, their activities were paradoxical and contributed significantly to the ascent of the refugee field as a well-regimented field of statecraft. On the one hand, these organizations acted as catalysts for the development of international measures of protection and relief. On the other hand, they worked as the functionaries of the intergovernmental regimentation, insofar as they partook in the extant and emergent measures regarding refugees without questioning the statist premises of those measures. They accepted the remedies for uprootedness in the statism, but they failed to see that, of all the remedies for uprootedness, the statism was one of the most totalizing and limiting, incarcerating all human bonds within the state exclusionary universal order.

Refugee problematizations continued throughout the decade. In June 1928, yet another conference of government representatives drew up an arrangement concerning the juridical status of the Russian and Armenian refugees (see League of Nations, 1928). It recommended that the high commissioner, through his representatives in different countries, should exercise a number of consular functions, including (a) certifying the identity and character of the refugees; (b) certifying their civil status on the strength of records in their country of origin; (c) giving certificates of good conduct, of former service, of university degrees, and so on, to refugees; and (d) recommending the refugees to the relevant authorities in matters of visas, admission to schools, and the like (Bentwich, 1935: 116; Hope-Simpson, 1939: 207; Grahl-Madsen, 1966: 127). The League Assembly approved these and other legal provisions regulating the economic, social, and legal status of Russian and Armenian refugees and invited states to adopt the provisions. The assembly, Norman Bentwich writes, also urged states not to expel a refugee from their countries until he or she was accepted by another state: "The tossing of the human victim from state to state was a standing injustice; the aim of the *voeu* of the Assembly was that the refugee should not be turned into an outlaw" (1935: 117). Although initially only a few states, such as France and Belgium, embraced these arrangements and acted upon them, they were eventually codified into international law in 1933 in the form of a binding convention, the Convention Relating to the International Status of Refugees (Marrus, 1985; Loescher, 1993; 1994; also Zolberg et al., 1989; Ferris, 1993b; Stoessinger, 1956).[28] Taken together, all these measures amounted to a further deepening of state-centric refugee regimentation.

At the onset of this chapter, I wrote that, in the conventional studies, the tenure of the League of Nations High Commissioner for Refugees, from 1921 to 1931, is assessed in qualified terms. The measures taken by and through the LNHCR are seen as measures with limited reach in terms of the historical evolution of the international refugee regime. They are seen not as measures that established an effective humanitarian refugee regime, but as those which, at best, established the refugee problem as a matter of international protection. In fact, most of the conventional studies assess the LNHCR by the successes and failures of the forceful personality of its first commissioner, Fridtjof Nansen, rather than by the ground-breaking nature and efficacy of the measures themselves.

To be sure, Nansen's charismatic and forceful personality did contribute to the foregoing developments. But this is of secondary importance. What is more central to the analysis here is the question of how the refugee field was opened and conditioned by the time of Nansen's death in 1930. In light of the analysis in this chapter, the answer to this question is crystal clear: by 1930 the field of human displacement had been thoroughly regimented and formalized through state-oriented problematizations in the form of conferences, conventions, arrangements, protocols, agreements, and resolutions.

The founding of the intergovernmental LNHCR in 1921 and the events that occurred as a consequence—the series of conferences in 1921 and 1922 that deepened the statist problematizations of the refugee category; the inventing of the so-called Nansen identity certificates that certified the sovereign authorship of the state, and the inventing of the techniques and accoutrements of "dealing" with the refugees, such as using refugee camps as sites of control; the writing of ever more comprehensive refugee definitions, first for the Russian and Armenian refugees in 1922 and 1926, and for other groups of refugees in the ensuing years; and, finally, the codification, on a voluntary basis, of a "civil" regime for refugees—were among the activities that effected a statist formalization of the field of human displacement under the sign of the refugee between 1921 and 1930. This history, I contend, is therefore to be read as much as a history of statecraft in crisis as a history of human tragedy in displacement. It might be instructive to repeat the words of Major Elliot, the league's rapporteur who in 1927 reminisced about the implications of the refugee occurrences in the first quarter of the century: "In the original stages, a very serious problem was presented by the influx of large numbers of disorganized and destitute refugees into countries where the machinery of government was in process either of *reconstruction* or of *creation*" (League of Nations, 1927a: 56). Seen against the post–World War I conditions in Europe in the early 1920s, Elliot's reminiscence undoubtedly grows in its revelations as to the realness of a crisis of statecraft in the 1920s and the significance of the LNHCR. Seen from the standpoint of such a crisis in governance, the LNHCR represented the emergence of a regime of control. In large measure, it was successful statecraft.

The developments that followed in the ensuing decades were variations and expansions on, rather than deviations from, the regime of control. They were further deepenings or intensifications of the problematizations of the refugee category, not revolutionary transformations in regimentation epistemologically and ontologically, as intimated in the conventional studies. Accordingly, from the 1930s until the present, in spite of drastic changes in the historico-political contexts in which refugee events have occurred, the ontology of the refugee category has remained unchanged, being firmly linked to and defined in terms of the ideal of the governance of the sovereign state. The faces and names of refugees have changed, but not the meanings of being and becoming a refugee. The names of the organizations that emerged to deal with refugees changed, but not the meanings of being and becoming a refugee. With the figure of the refugee as inscribed in the conventions and arrangements, a permanent field of state-centric discourse and action was opened wherein it became possible to negotiate and regiment the practical, disruptive effects of human displacement in local and global politics in terms affirmative of the state-centered organization of life.

It is here that refugee problematizations are intimately linked to international regimes and statecraft. In the modern world, no task of statecraft can be undertaken in isolation. Or I should say, the activities of statecraft undertaken in any one locality are potentially disruptive of ongoing activities of statecraft in other localities. There is, in other words, a coordination problem, a strategic problem of producing a world of multiple, mutually bounded representable spaces and communities. In the words of Richard Ashley, it is "a world in which activities [must be] regularly and reliably oriented amidst ambiguity and change to enable the constitution of domestic citizenries who can understand their fears and desire to be represented by the respective figures of state" (1993: 5). It is to this use that international regimes are put, and it was to this use that the LNHCR was put. Activities organized around or enabled by the LNHCR worked as activities of regimentation, manufacturing the realities and powers of the agents in the citizen/nation/state constellation as much as dealing with refugees as human beings under duress. Otherwise, without the practices of statecraft in other fields of policy and conduct, they—

the citizen, nation, and state—"would [have been] little more than contestable figures of speech" (5), rarefied abstractions existing only in names.

To quote Michel Foucault, the presence of groups of peoples marked as refugees became party to specific problematizations, to interplays of "connections, encounters, supports, blockages, plays of forces, and strategies which at [certain] moments establish[ed] what subsequently count[ed] as being self-evident, universal and necessary"—the state-centeredness of life (1991: 76). And the site of the refugee became one of many recuperative and transformative sites of modern statecraft.

4

Change and Continuity: Making, Unmaking, and Remaking the International Refugee Regime

And how am I to face the odds
Of man's bedevilment and God's?
I, a stranger and afraid
In a world I never made.
—AN ANONYMOUS REFUGEE

In the previous chapter, I argued that the history of intergovernmental responses to human displacement finds a peculiar expression in conventional studies. According to most of these studies, the "real," "effective" history of these responses starts in the early 1950s, with the advent of the UNHCR, which is seen to be the embodiment of a set of effective intergovernmental responses to human displacement. With few exceptions, including such scholars as Claudena Skran (1995) and Gil Loescher (1993), intergovernmental organizations that came before the UNHCR, including the LNHCR, figure in the conventional accounts largely as they constitute a historical backdrop against which the UNHCR may be designated the true marker of the modern international refugee regime.[1]

According to these studies, the achievements of intergovernmental responses prior to 1951 were acutely limited in terms of the kind of arrangements that could be understood as constitutive of a modern international refugee regime. Thus, if one were to speak of an intergovernmental refugee regime embodied in the activities of successive organizations prior to 1950–51, one would have to speak of a highly rudimentary regime formation, weak in its practical power temporally as well as spatially. There are several reasons for this phenomenon.

First, in spite of the original objective of the intergovernmental organizations, which was to facilitate collaboration among actors, the tenures of these organizations were characterized more as failures and less as successes in inducing coordination among governments; their activities were hostage to the power politics of the times, rather than driven in support of humanitarian purposes (Robinson, 1953; Stoessinger, 1956; Rogers, 1992; Loescher, 1993; Ferris, 1993b; Guest, 1991).

Second, whatever international instruments were devised, their mandates were limited exclusively to refugees from Europe or to a handful of European refugees stranded in other parts of the world, such as China (Robinson, 1953; Ferris, 1993b: 8; Suhrke, 1993: 2). Third, the number of states signatory to these arrangements was limited, which undermined the claim that there had evolved an international refugee regime in the interwar period, even if it governed only European refugees (Robinson, 1953, Ferris, 1993b; Zolberg et al., 1989).

Fourth, the practical power of the international arrangements on refugees was circumvented, because these arrangements dealt only with a select number of refugee groups even among the European refugees (Loescher, 1993: 40). A universal definition of the refugee was avoided. Furthermore, as the years passed, the climate turned considerably against refugees. Contributing to the unfavorable attitudes toward refugees was the advent of the Depression in the industrial world, which created masses of unemployed. Governments moved to curtail their commitment to refugee protection (which was defined largely as repatriation at the time). "There was," writes Loescher, "an absence of any consistent or coherent international commitment to resolving refugee problems" (1993: 41).

Furnished against the UNHCR's tenure since 1951, such observations, while certainly not inaccurate, run the risk of brushing aside as merely ad hoc and insignificant a host of intergovernmental activities prior to 1951 that are of monumental importance in regimenting refugee events in the first half of the twentieth century. They do so by presupposing that the intergovernmental regime(ntation) of responses to refugee events since 1951, of which the UNHCR has been the principal agent, has been dramatically different, more integrated, more effective (in spite of many failures and politicization), more comprehensive, and more advanced in protection and management than the responses before 1951.

Such, once again, are the claims of most conventional studies on the modern international refugee regime. However, such claims, held especially against their own premises, prove increasingly untenable. They fail to measure up to the historical-ontological premises they themselves set.

A careful comparative historical analysis, informed by concerns of statecraft, reveals that the UNHCR's efforts have not been more integrated, more effective, more comprehensive, or more advanced than the efforts that preceded them under other organizations. First, historically, the efforts by or through the UNHCR for dealing with refugees have been nothing more than variations or simple expansions linked ontologically and epistemologically to previous problematizations of the refugee, that is, to previous assumptions, postulations, and representations of the refugee. In other words, the refugee category had already been systematically "invented" and thoroughly regimented through the practices of regimentation prior to 1951, particularly during the tenure of the LNHCR, from 1921 until 1930. The activities of regimentation occasioned since the advent of the UNHCR represent strategic intensifications in refugee regimentation: their practical significance and power are effected through the production of a complex discursive cross-referentiality in discourse and action that constantly encodes, codifies, and catalogs human displacement into refugeehood. Second, as with the earlier activities of regimentation, the UNHCR's efforts have been orchestrated as much to regiment and render human displacement instrumental in the task of statecraft as to ameliorate the agonies of human displacement. Third, and contrary to the claims in the conventional accounts, the UNHCR's activities since 1951 have not inaugurated a more effective and more advanced refugee protection regime. Instead, like the organizations that preceded it, the UNHCR has reworked and maintained a representational refugee field of policy, action, and discourse as a field of statecraft.

These arguments become demonstrably clear when one looks into the scenes of intergovernmental efforts (or struggles; Mitchell, 1993) that have gone into the making of refugee histories before and after the UNHCR was established. Understanding the UNHCR necessitates a consideration, however brief, of the histories of the organizations that preceded it between 1930 and 1951. Against the background of these histories, it becomes possible to see the UNHCR in a different light, as a historical manifestation of intergovernmentalized refugee problematizations, working to accommodate and appropriate the practical force of human displacement in producing and privileging the boundaries of sovereign statehood and citizenship in local and global politics. The UNHCR thus appears as a manifestation of statecraft.

This chapter starts with analyses of the organizations that followed the dissolution of the LNHCR in 1930 yet preceded the UNHCR. Six organizations—the Nansen International Office for Refugees, the High Commissioner for Refugees Coming from Germany, the Office of the High Commissioner Responsible for All Refugees under the League of Nations' Protection, the Intergovernmental Committee on Refugees, the United Nations Relief and Rehabilitation Agency, and the International Refugee Organization—are discussed in the chapter. The purpose of this discussion is to show (a) how each organization represents spatiotemporal efforts at statist regimentations whose ontological and programmatic beginnings go back to the LNHCR in the 1920s; and (b) how the convergent effects of these regimentations work to produce a cross-referential, co-recognized refugee field as a field of statecraft. Then, against the backdrop of this discussion, the tenure of the UNHCR is examined by undertaking a comparative examination of the "grand" legal and institutional instruments, such as the 1933 and 1951 Conventions on Refugees, which oriented the practices of regimentation around previous organizations and the UNHCR respectively. The purpose of this examination is to demonstrate (a) why the UNHCR does not represent the beginning of effective refugee regimentations in history; and (b) how it should be seen as a practice of statecraft in time, oriented continuously to maintaining a representable refugee field of policy, action, and discourse so that the ideal of the sovereign state can be articulated and performed in local and global arenas.

INTERGOVERNMENTAL REFUGEE PROBLEMATIZATIONS AND THE INSTITUTIONALIZATION OF REFUGEE REGIMENTATIONS IN THE PRE-UNHCR ERA

After Fridtjof Nansen's death in 1930, the League of Nations decided, contrary to Nansen's advice, to reorganize the LNHCR in terms of its functions as well as its mandate and organizational structure. However, in honor of Nansen, the league named the new organization the Nansen International Office for Refugees (NIOFR). As had been the case with its predecessor organization, the NIOFR was envisioned as a temporary relief organization mandated to deal with the humanitarian and technical aspects of refugee problems. The political and legal protection of refugees was delegated to the league secretariat (Holborn, 1956: 7; Vernant, 1953: 24; Hansson, 1972: 283–85), and "it was scheduled for liquidation at the end of 1938" (Sjoberg, 1991: 28).

According to many observers, the tenure of the Nansen International Office was marred with failures, largely because of what Louise Holborn calls "unforeseen" challenges and difficulties. According to Holborn, four unforeseen problems arose during the NIOFR's period of activity, and these made it impossible to carry out its original plans:

> The first was the economic depression which drastically affected the employment of Nansen refugees. Labour permits became increasingly difficult to secure, and refugees were forced to relinquish their positions in favour of nationals. Refugees were expelled from countries for having no means of support and at the same time were refused entry into other states. . . . The second factor was the decline of the League's moral influence owing to setbacks which the system of collective security suffered after 1931. This inevitably reacted on the measure of protection which the League could give to refugees. Third, there had already been a tendency noticeable in the League . . . in favour of reducing League activities on behalf of refugees. . . . The last factor was the new refugee problem which arose in Germany . . . , an acute problem which made necessary a changed approach to the refugee problem as a whole. (1956: 7)

Acutely aware of the implications of these difficulties for refugee relief work, observers argue, the activities of the Nansen International Office concentrated more on the daily management of refugee affairs based on existing legal arrangements and less on trying to negotiate new arrangements or to expand the scope of the existing ones. An examination of this construing of the role of the Nansen International Office from a standpoint of the continuing management of refugee events, however, shows that it is somewhat misleading in at least two senses.

First, the organization's focus on daily refugee management was crucial in terms of orchestrating the intergovernmental efforts of the regimentation of human displacement. The continuation of efforts to produce representational resources useful to the task of statecraft was more essential than their actual success. Even then, the NIOFR labored to dispense with refugee populations in accordance with the already established principles of repatriation or resettlement. In a speech delivered during the Nobel Peace Prize acceptance ceremony in 1938, the president of the office, Michael Hansson, could register more than a few success stories along these lines (1972). The settlement of Saar refugees in Paraguay in 1935 and the construction of villages for forty thousand Armenians in Syria and Lebanon were just some of these efforts.

Second, and equally important, was the adoption of an international convention on refugees in 1933 that was binding on the contracting parties. This alone could be considered a dramatic step in terms of enlarging the legal scope of refugee regimentation, leading to further institutionalization and formalization in regimentation. The convention was based largely on the arrangements of 1926 and 1928 regulating the juridical and civil status of Russian, Armenian, Syrian, Chaldean, and assimilated refugees (Hope-Simpson, 1939: 210). The convention consolidated the arrangements on refugee status, regulating administrative measures, juridical conditions, labor conditions, welfare and relief, education, and the fiscal regime (Bentwich, 1936: 118). By 1938, nine states had acceded to the convention and a number of others had indicated their willingness to abide by its provisions without formally ratifying it.[2]

Another innovative aspect of the NIOFR was the formal incorporation of refugee representatives into the governing body. The first two members elected by the Advisory Committee of the Private Organizations were a Russian refugee and an Armenian refugee. This formal incorporation represents a significant step in the further intensification of refugee regimentation by enlisting the displaced people in the legitimation of the measures undertaken. It was a precedent-setting development and would be emulated by other organizations in various forms in the coming years.

In his Nobel Prize acceptance speech, President Hansson spoke of a new wave of refugees that, since the appearance of the NIOFR in the early 1930s, had overwhelmed the existing institutions and arrangements (1972: 283–84). He was referring to the new "flood" of refugees, largely of Jewish origin, escaping persecution from Nazi Germany and other fascist dictatorships in Europe (Loescher, 1993: 40). In response to the rise in numbers of refugees emigrating from Germany in 1933, the League of Nations had established yet another refugee organization, called the High Commissioner for Refugees Coming from Germany (HCRFG), which would last until 1938.

In the founding resolution in October 1933, the mandate of the new High Commissioner for Refugees Coming from Germany was defined as "to negotiate and direct international collaboration necessary to solve the economic, financial and social problems of the refugees" (League of Nations, 1933: 89–90). The office stood in contrast to other refugee organizations in terms of its formal relation to the League of Nations. The new commissioner's office would be separate from the league, and the commissioner would report to its own governing body, not to the council of the league, as other organizations had been doing (McDonald, 1944: 218).

The HCRFG exemplifies attempts at statist regimentation that have produced mixed results, both practically and strategically. On the one hand, the HCRFG's presence afforded many state-parties the excuse to assert that they were "doing something" to help refugees. To vociferous critics, they could show their "efforts" through the HCRFG. On the other hand, ironically, practically as well as strategically, the HCRFG was rendered by the same states too ineffectual to manage human displacement so as to release the pressure on statist governance in Europe.

According to scholars, the reasons for the practical and strategical ineffectiveness of the HCRFG lies in a general policy of appeasement toward Germany, then an influential member of the League of Nations. In fact, some scholars, including Loescher, argue that the political and organizational structure of the HCRFG had in fact been shaped to accommodate Germany. Loescher reports that "to avoid antagonizing Germany, the High Commissioner was instructed to avoid discussing causes stressing the political dimension of the refugee problem" (1993: 43).

The politically driven structure of the organization would prove enfeebling. James McDonald, the first commissioner, "immediately ran into problems as he desperately sought a solution for the growing number of Jewish and other refugees in the context of increasing anti-Semitism in Europe and the rise of Hitler" (Ferris, 1993b: 5; see also Loescher, 1993: 43–44; Holborn, 1956: 9; Hope-Simpson, 1939: 215–16). The organization did not receive any substantial financial or policy support to run programs for the massive outflow of people from Germany. Furthermore, as the practitioner McDonald himself later wrote, most governments refrained from lending much support to the HCRFG in pressuring Germany to cooperate on refugee matters (1944: 220). According to McDonald, policies of appeasement, coupled with exclusive sovereignty claims of states (pertaining to the entry into and exclusion from their territories of nationals of other countries), effectively truncated the ability of the HCRFG to implement any coherent policy on refugees coming from Germany. Nevertheless, the HCRFG was useful for statist regimentation in that it became a site of intergovernmental lip service, rendered more to political interests and less to the interests of refugees. Frustrated, McDonald resigned in 1935. In his letter of resignation to the League of Nations, he was scathingly critical of states' desire to maintain the niceties of the system of states even in the face of massive human suffering:

> When domestic politics threaten the demoralization and exile of hundreds of thousands of human beings, considerations of diplomatic correctness must yield to those of common humanity. I should be recreant if I did not call attention to the actual situation, and plead that world opinion, acting through the league and its Member-States and other countries, move to avert the existing and impending tragedies. (1935: 10)

The state of affairs in which the HCRFG found itself was similar to that circa the First World War. In the tumult and turbulence during and following that war, practices of statecraft in one locale had had disruptive transversal effects on similar practices in other locales, and it was these effects that had prompted people such as Count Tosti di Valminuta to call for intergovernmental intervention in the movements of the nomads of the century, the refugees. McDonald invoked similar imagery to muster support for his activities:

> The growing sufferings of the persecuted minority in Germany and the menace of the growing exodus call for friendly but firm intercession with the German Government, by all pacific means, on the part of the League of Nations, of its Member-States and other members of

> the community of nations. Pity and reason alike must inspire the hope that intercession will meet with response. Without such response, the problems caused by the persecution of the Jews and the "non-Aryans" will not be solved by philanthrophic action, but will continue to constitute a danger to international peace and a source of injury to the legitimate interests of other states. (1935: 9)

McDonald's audience was less receptive than the count's had been. After McDonald's resignation, the high commissioner's office focused on the legal protection of refugees who had already exited Germany and had been seeking refuge in other countries. Neil Malcolm, the commissioner from early 1938 to the middle of 1938, reported in his final statement to the league that about five thousand refugees had been helped by his office through various schemes of resettlement or through integration (Hope-Simpson, 1939: 217).

In 1938, the High Commissioner for Refugees Coming from Germany and the Nansen International Office for Refugees were consolidated into a single organization—the Office of the High Commissioner Responsible for All Refugees under the League of Nations' Protection (OHCAR) (Vernant, 1953: 25). On 1 January 1939, the new commissioner's office took over the protection of all groups of refugees who had been under the two former organizations. By a council decision of 17 January 1939, the Czechoslovak refugees coming from the Sudetenland were added to these refugees (Holborn, 1956: 9).

Observers suggest that the powers of the OHCAR were even more curtailed than they had been with the earlier organizations (Zolberg et al., 1989: 20; Ferris, 1993b: 5–6; Holborn, 1956; 1975): "The OHCAR's limitations were evident from the unwillingness of member states to assume greater responsibilities in dealing with the [r]efugee crisis" (Zolberg et al., 1989: 20). "It was denied the power to enter into any legal commitment whatsoever on behalf of the League, and the League assumed no responsibility, legal or financial, for [i]ts activities" (Loescher, 1993: 44). The OHCAR remained active until 1946 and was liquidated only months before a new refugee organization—the International Refugee Organization—came into existence in 1947 (Gordenker, 1987: 22–27; Gallagher, 1989: 579).

During the tenure of the fourth and last High Commissioner of the League of Nations, two other governmental organizations were founded to deal with refugees either exclusively or partially. The first of them, the Intergovernmental Committee on Refugees (IGCR), was founded in 1938 during a conference held in Évian, France, upon the invitation of the president of the United States, Franklin D. Roosevelt. The organization was established ostensibly in response to the failures of the successive league commissioners to deal effectively with the refugee problem. According to Aryeh Tartakower and Kurt Grossmann, it was "the realization that neither through the existing agencies of the League of Nations nor through private efforts could the steadily growing refugee problem be solved which prompted President Roosevelt to call the Intergovernmental meeting that convened in Evian" (1944: 412). According to others, however (Loescher, 1993: 45; Sjoberg, 1991: 48–52), the IGCR was set up to deal almost exclusively with Jewish refugees, although this was never officially, publicly authenticated. Yet a few others detected, as I argue, a larger strategic objective, considered in the context of the specific problem of refugees originating in Germany. Hear Dorothy Thompson, who wrote on the refugee problem in Europe in 1938:

> Too long the refugee problem has been largely regarded as one of international charity. It must be regarded now as a problem of international politics. Actually for the President of the United States to take a hand in it was, no doubt, a keen sense of self-preservation. The world, as it is, is a place of unrest and agitation with desperate people taking desperate measures in the attempt merely to survive. And *millions of people wandering* more or less aimlessly, battering at every conceivable door, being passed from *frontier to frontier,* will certainly do nothing to *restore world order.* (1938: 10–11; emphasis added)

Although written fourteen years after Count Valminuta's comments, Thompson's portrayal is similar to that of the count. Her reflections, perhaps unwittingly, point to the paradoxes and practices of statecraft in local and global politics. They point to the ongoing task of statecraft and to the exigency of the regimentation of the people on the "frontier" lines—the wanderers, the nomads, the refugees—in order to effect a particular imagination of order and hierarchy in the world. There was, in other words, more to the activities responding to refugees than the publicly declared objective of humanitarianism. "The appeal of President Roosevelt for international action to aid refugees," Thompson argues,

> is not only timely, generous and imaginative, but is extremely *necessary*—not for the sake of the refugees only, but for the sake of all countries that are *anxious* to prevent further unrest and economic and social *disequilibrium*. Obviously what this action *needs* is a *program* and efficient organization to deal with the whole matter. (10; emphasis added)

Thompson's laconic remarks are revealing in that they intimate the strategic concerns of statist governance beyond the bounds of a humanitarian call to duty. They also point to the disruptive implications of human displacement for the relations and institutions that underlie statist governance. Such sources of disruption, that is, sources of unrest and disequilibrium, had to be regimented, Thompson urges, not simply for the refugees' sake but for the sake of "restor[ing] world order." Accordingly, refugees were regimented. The results of regimentation in human terms were troubling, as millions of people were intercepted by states as objects of unrest and social and economic disequilibrium rather than as subjects deserving of refuge. The prevailing rhetoric in the political arena, however, remained one of grandiose compassion and charity.

Jacques Vernant suggests that "the IGCR's activities were severely handicapped by the war and were mainly confined to diplomatic representations in an effort to find opportunities for permanent settlement overseas" (1953: 27). Gil Loescher, however, argues that the reason for the IGCR's ineffectiveness had more to do with the governments' attitudes toward refugees in general and Jewish refugees in particular. The governments saw refugees as "disturbing to the general economy" and "posing severe strain on the administrative facilities and absorptive capacities of the receiving countries." Refugees increased international unrest and hindered the processes of appeasement in international relations (1993: 44–45). The IGCR, like the organizations that preceded it, was an intergovernmental instrument of such state policies, nothing much more.

Once World War II commenced, the activities on behalf of refugees by the IGCR were relegated to secondary importance vis-à-vis the war efforts. In 1943, the IGCR's mandate was expanded to cover "all persons who were displaced as a result of events in Europe" (Vernant, 1953: 27). After the war was over, the IGCR worked on various schemes facilitating relief work, repatriation, and overseas resettlement. In 1946, it also temporarily assumed the legal representation of the remaining Nansen refugees whose protection had been transferred to the fourth high commissioner of the League of Nations. In 1946, both the fourth high commissioner and the IGCR were eased out, to be replaced by the International Refugee Organization.

Before the IRO was founded, however, another organization came into existence in the context of the ongoing war. This was the United Nations Relief and Rehabilitation Agency (UNRRA), designed to provide relief and rehabilitation to displaced people in the areas liberated from German occupation. The UNRRA was to last four years, from 1943 to 1947:

> UNRRA was established in November 1943 by 44 governments. Its mandate was to provide: assistance in caring for, and maintaining records of persons found in any areas under the control of any of the United Nations who by reasons of war have been displaced from their homes, and, in agreement with appropriate governments, military authorities or other agencies, in securing their repatriation or return. (Vernant, 1953: 30)

Unlike previous organizations, from the onset the UNRRA was well financed. From its inception in 1943 until 1947, when it was disbanded, the UNRRA received $3.6 billion to finance its projects. But in spite of its strong financial standing, the UNRRA's activities were quite politicized, first, because it had to accommodate the exigencies of the war as determined by the military leaders in the early part of its tenure, and, second, because it had to operate in the crucible of the emergent cold war in the latter part of its existence. In the beginning, for example, organizationally, the UNRRA was subordinated to the Allied armies (Salomon, 1991: 50–51).[3] Its field operations were largely under the control of military administrators who saw refugees more as obstacles in the way of the war efforts than as people in need of help (Dinnerstein, 1982: 16). As Marrus puts it, in private, refugees and displaced peoples were commonly viewed by military administrators as "a bother to be overcome" (1985: 321), a view that, some historians argue, paved the way for widespread "maltreatment" of refugees in military-controlled camps (Dinnerstein, 1982: 17; Marrus, 1985: 322).[4]

This view of refugees and displaced people did not, of course, figure in official public documents, which would continue to express a sense of optimism, progress, and commitment to helping refugees and displaced people. For example, a memorandum put forth by the headquarters of the Supreme Allied Expeditionary Force on the very same question of "displaced people and refugees in Germany" would read as follows:

> GENERAL POLICY.
> (a) The liberation, care and repatriation of United Nations displaced persons is a major allied objective. All available resources at the disposal of military commanders will be employed to accomplish it as a direct military responsibility. As soon as military conditions permit, UNRRA may be requested to undertake this responsibility.
> POLICY OF THE SUPREME COMMANDER, AEF.
> (a) To relieve conditions of want among United Nations displaced persons, and to protect them against interference and ill-treatment on the part of German authorities or population.[5]

Reading this memorandum in light of the wary military view of refugees and displaced people, one realizes that public enunciations on saving refugees did not necessarily match and/or reflect the practical concerns of the military administrators in charge. From the standpoint of refugee relief work, it is difficult to judge what the problems experienced while the military was in control of refugee relief work meant or represented at the time. Surely, they were not representative of all relief efforts, yet, to the degree to which they existed, they also highlighted the great potential for humanitarianism to be subordinated to practical exigencies of the day, sometimes under the very name of a humanitarian organization. The UNRRA had such unfortunate beginnings.

The UNRRA's management suffered from political limitations and administrative shortcomings. Because the UNRRA funds were not to be used for housing, food, or clothing, and because the UNRRA was never intended to provide law and order, security, or transport, the organization remained throughout its existence subordinate to the military men (Marrus, 1985: 321). Worsening the UNRRA's position in the field was its less-than-perfect image with the military men. In the words of the British general Sir Frederick Morgan, who headed the UNRRA's German field operations, the soldiers saw the UNRRA as "that adventitious assembly of silver-tongued ineffectuals, professional do-gooders, crooks and crackpots" (qtd. in Marrus, 1985: 322).

In spite of such practical impediments, which practically paralyzed the UNRRA, as Marrus suggests (1985: 320), the UNRRA's work still looked good on paper, because its name reached people as the Allied armies defeated the German armies across Europe. After the war, the principal mission of the UNRRA emerged as the speedy repatriation of displaced people, a task carried out in coordination with the Allied military authorities. According to one estimate, the UNRRA assisted in the repatriation of six million displaced persons (Vernant, 1953: 30).[6] Repatriation, though initially the desirable form of solving the problem of displacement, became a source of conflict between the emergent Eastern and Western blocs, as millions of people originally from Eastern European countries and the Soviet Union refused repatriation. At the end of 1945, approximately 2 million people had refused repatriation and sought refuge in camps (Gordenker, 1987: 23–24). These people were called "the non-repatriables," the politics around whose lives heralded and expedited the emergence of the cold war between the East and the West. On the one hand, the Soviet Union interpreted the UNRRA's reluctance to repatriate people forcibly as an anti-Soviet position and accused the UNRRA of being an instrument of the West. On the other hand, the United States, which had been providing about 70 percent of the UNRRA's budget, saw the UNRRA's activities of relief and rehabilitation in the East as activities that helped to consolidate Soviet control over the region (Loescher, 1993; Marrus, 1985; Gordenker, 1987).

In sum, the UNRRA's name was too contaminated in the minds of policy makers to be allowed to continue its operations. From late 1946 well into 1947, the Truman administration began blocking grants to the UNRRA, a policy that, in effect, brought about the eventual demise of the organization in 1947. On the part of the Truman administration, the overwhelming feeling was that "it would be easier to create a new organization than to resolve the existing problems with UNRRA" (Ferris, 1993b: 7). The United States pushed to fruition the emergence of yet another refugee organization—the International Refugee Organization (IRO), which had been in the making within the context of the United Nations since December 1946.

Interestingly, the controversies surrounding the UNRRA demonstrate how a refugee organization can be made to work as a political field of policy, conduct, and discourse. They show how refugee bodies in their most corporeal form turn into contested corporeal as well as symbolic sites of power articulated through the idioms of ideology, ethnicity, culture, and economy, in turn articulating and empowering the identities and subjectivities of those ideologies, cultures, ethnicities, and economies. That refugees from the Soviet Union and other Eastern European countries were "voting with their feet" shows how refugee bodies could be harnessed to symbolic representational practices articulating specific projects, in this case the ideological project of the "communist East" versus the "capitalist West."

In December 1946, a draft constitution for a specialized agency charged with repatriation, protection, and resettlement or reestablishment of the remaining refugees and displaced persons in Europe was approved by the United Nations General Assembly. As with the preceding organizations, the International Refugee Organization was conceived to be a temporary agency, with a three-year mandate. Specifically, the IRO was termed a nonpermanent specialized agency of the UN, permitted to operate outside UN supervision with its own budget and membership. Of the thirty governments that supported the IRO agreement, only eighteen ratified its constitution in the end (Marrus, 1985: 342). None of the Eastern European states formally became members of the agency, though they remained rooted in the refugee field and continued actively to engage the agency in various channels, a reality that immersed the IRO in a constant stream of controversies centering on the question of repatriation or resettlement.[7]

In most conventional accounts of the history of the IRO, these controversies predominate, while little attention is paid to the question of the intensification of the strategies of refugee regimentations. There are a few scholars (Zolberg, 1989; Zolberg et al., 1986) who address the issue. Nevertheless, they address it only tangentially, still operating within the paradigm of statist governance. Statecraft as a project of governance investing in refugee occurrences never figures in their narratives.

Beyond this, there are also those who see in the IRO's activities the seeds of a truly effective international regime in refugee relief work. Holborn, who is acclaimed to have written the "authoritative" history of the IRO, argues that "the creation of IRO was an outstanding landmark in the history of international action on behalf of refugees and displaced persons and in the development of the international organization itself." (1956: 45). Citing a speech by the French representative, Raymond Bousquet, Holborn suggests that the International Refugee Organization

> was heralded as the first real effort by a world-wide organization of fifty member nations to gain a clear picture of a problem painful in its human aspect, delicate in its technical side, and politically extremely difficult, and to find a solution for one of the most heart-breaking problems . . . which . . . has confronted the conscience of mankind. (Holborn, 1956: 45)

Such humanitarian announcements prevail in formal as well as popular accounts of the IRO. Curiously, the sensitive, "difficult" political issues, which provoke a deluge of controversy behind closed doors in formative meetings and conferences, hardly become visible in the public discourse of the institutional or popular variety. "Politically extremely difficult" aspects, in other words, find only fleeting references in the discourse, and even then from the standpoint of predicating the primacy and normalcy of the relations and institutions of statist governance under duress. Eleanor Roosevelt, then the U.S. representative to the United Nations, speaking while the draft constitution of the IRO was being devised in December 1946, remarkably illustrated this point:

> Each member *government* of the United Nations has a direct selfish interest in the early *disposal of this problem.* As long as a million persons remain with refugee status, they *delay* the *restoration of peace and order in the world. . . .* They *represent* in themselves political, economic and national *conflicts* which are *symbolic of the work which lies before nations if peace is to be restored.* While they remain a solid mass in assembly centres, they deteriorate individually, and collectively they represent a *sore on the body of mankind* which it is not safe for us to ignore. (UN General Assembly, 1946; emphasis added)

As with Thompson's remarks on the "objectives" of the IGCR in 1938, Mrs. Roosevelt seemed preoccupied as much with "order in the world" as with humanitarian concerns for refugees. The order of which she spoke was to be accordingly reflected in the constitution of the IRO, particularly in terms of the objectives of the IRO. Articles I(a)–I(c) of the general principles of the IRO constitution stated:

> (a) The main object of the Organization will be to bring about rapid and positive solution of the problem of *bona fide* refugees and displaced people, which shall be just and equitable to all concerned. (b) The main task concerning refugees and displaced persons is to encourage and assist in every way possible their early return to their countries of origin having regard to the principles laid down in paragraph (c) (ii) of the resolution adopted by the General Assembly of the United Nations on 12 February 1946 regarding the problem of refugees. (c) The organization shall endeavor to carry out its functions in such a way as to avoid disturbing friendly relations between nations. (Qtd. in Holborn, 1956: 583)[8]

These objectives were to facilitate order in the world, and that clearly meant the "reestablishment" of the refugee with a space of particularity, a territorial inside, a country of origin, represented and protected by a state. The reestablishment of the refugee's ties with a state was "written" as the condition of "normality" and order in life. Holborn interprets the quoted paragraphs thus: "The broad function of the Organization was to care for, and protect, and reestablish the refugees in a normal life" (1956: 50). "The fate which refugees had experienced," she continues, "made them feel physically and morally uprooted. They were isolated in a strange world, separated from their own culture by all the things around them" (190). Having so characterized the world of the refugee as the world of loss, lack, and "abnormality" (191), Holborn then moves to *statize* the refugee's condition in terms of both its reasons and its solutions: "[The refugee's] sense of not belonging is the common lot of the *stateless*" (192; emphasis added). The ideal of the state postulate, in short, continued to define the imaginations of "order in the world."

It must be stressed that the significance of the IRO in terms of statist governance lies not in the great controversies signifying either the divisions of the cold war or the remarkable IRO achievements on behalf of refugees, thus instantiating the ability of "member nations" to cooperate. Rather, the significance of the IRO lies in the inauguration of a creative new strategy of problematization, or regimentation, of the refugee while ontologically remaining linked to earlier problematizations of the refugee in statist terms.[9] Let me explain.

The IRO's constitution underscored a seeming expansion in the definition of the term *refugee* to include a more generalized understanding based on the merits of individual cases. To be sure, it retained the definition of refugee based on group affiliations. For instance, the constitution referred to the "victims of the Nazi and Fascist regimes, Spanish Republicans or other victims of the Falangist regime," and "persons who were considered refugees before the outbreak of the second world war," which, in effect, meant the so-called Nansen refugees transferred over to the IGCR after the dissolution of the fourth high commissioner of the League of Nations in 1938. However, in addition, the constitution of the IRO also included a generalized definition of the refugee as a person "who has left, or who is outside of his country of nationality or of former habitual residence, and who as a result of events subsequent to the outbreak of the second world war, is unable or unwilling to avail himself of the protection of the government of his country of nationality or former nationality."[10]

Aristide Zolberg calls this definitional expansion a "major institutional innovation" in dealing with refugees, which foretold the possibility, in a theoretical and institutional sense, of the universalization of an individual-oriented refugee protection regime (1989: 23). This "innovation" was surely not one of ontology (redefining a refugee's relation to the statist hierarchy of organizing life) but one of strategy, affording governments yet one more level of control and regimentation—the individual level. The innovation did not necessarily make it easier to claim refugee status. If anything, for many refugees, it made it more challenging, as it proved difficult to certify, document by document, the history of one's persecution. The International Refugee Organization formally ceased operation in December 1951, though informally it had been crippled before that date, not only because of the typical politicking among its member countries but also because another refugee organization—the UNHCR—was in the making. Regardless, the IRO's legacy, both organizationally and in its affirmation of the earlier state-centric conceptualizations of the refugee, continued to bear on the ensuing efforts in refugee protection. In December 1950, those efforts produced the UNHCR, the last of the major intergovernmental organizations dealing with refugees.

The IRO was the last of the formal intergovernmental organizations before the UNHCR came into existence. As with the histories of organizations such as the LNHCR, the NIOFR, and the IGCR, all of which preceded the IRO, it is plausible to speak of the history of the IRO in terms that focus on its "humanitarian legacy." Undoubtedly, it is true that millions of displaced people benefited from the activities of the IRO, just as millions of displaced people had benefited from the services of the previous organizations. The work of Fridtjof Nansen with the LNHCR, for example, attests to such a humanitarian legacy of organizations like the IRO.

While it is important to acknowledge this role of intergovernmental efforts in general in dealing with refugees, it is equally important to point to intergovernmental regimentations of refugee events from the LNHCR to the IRO, which generated a field of activity whereby refugee events could be harnessed to the task of statecraft. From the standpoint of refugee problematizations, the establishment and maintenance of a refugee field as a field of statecraft was in fact the most consequential, cardinal effect of intergovernmental efforts of regimenting the refugee and refugee events. It was in and through this intergovernmental field of regimentation as a field of statecraft that *events of human displacement were problematized* continuously in state-oriented terms, thus affirming the primacy of state-oriented relations and institutions in time and place. This was so to the extent that regimentations privileged the citizen/nation/state hierarchy as being both normal and essential to security, safety, and welfare in life. At one level, this privileging came effortlessly, for the refugee life, with "severest restrictions" on where a refugee could go and what a refugee could do (Arendt, 1958: 292) and without the protection of the state itself, attested to the dangerous conditions of life outside the nexus of the citizen/nation/state hierarchy. To be a refugee, as Elfan Rees somewhat overdramatically says, indeed might have meant to live "isolated in anarchy, overwhelmed by a sense of not belonging. It was to deteriorate in the frustration of camp life—reduced to the privacy of a strung blanket. It was to live in despair and in a moral vacuum" as a "marginal man" (1959: 19). Who would want to remain a refugee under such conditions? However, as Hannah Arendt intimated, the "refugee conditions" that made refugees desire to "re-integrate into a national community" (1958: 292) were themselves partially the products of governmental and intergovernmental regimentations. Refugees were languishing in camps not because they wanted to, but because they were denied free movement in a world organized around the citizen/nation/state hierarchy. "Suddenly," Arendt wrote, "there was no place to where migrants could go without the severest restrictions, no country where they would be assimilated, no territory where they could found a new community of their own" (293). "Moreover," she continued, "this had next to nothing to do with overpopulation; it was a problem not of space but of political organization" (294). This political organization, of course, was the system of nation-states that encoded life's possibilities in exclusively state-oriented terms. For the refugee, then, the only practically viable salvation was to be reintegrated into the system on terms that the system set—terms that discursively, by force and patient guidance, enabled the construction of a refugee agency, a limited agency that would recognize the refugee's own aberrance vis-à-vis the citizen/nation/state hierarchy and would express his or her desire for reintegration into the statist universe and out of liminality. This method of privileging was, in effect, nothing less than statecraft performed at intergovernmental junctures. The activities occasioned through the IRO and the organizations before the IRO between 1921 and 1951 opened, intensively conditioned, and maintained precisely such a refugee field as a field of statist discourse and action. The UNHCR was born against that background.

THE INSTITUTIONALIZATION OF REFUGEE REGIMENTATIONS IN THE UNHCR ERA

By 1951, thirty years of organizational growth and intergovernmental activities had firmly established the refugee field as a field of statist problematizations. The series of intergovernmental organizations became the vehicle that enabled contingent strategies of regimentation as part of a political regime of statecraft. Strategies of regimentation effected through one organization provided the ontological and epistemic foundations on which successor organizations were built, and the requisite reformulations of approaches to refugee problems were enabled in the context of temporal and spatial changes. The tenure of the League of Nations High Commissioner for Refugees, from 1921 until 1930, was the most crucial period in this respect, for the commissioner came to represent the processes of regimentation through which a categorical, statist definition of the refugee was formulated and institutionalized, a definition that eventually came to undergird the definitions of the refugee in the constitutions of the succeeding organizations, from the Nansen International Office to the Intergovernmental Committee and from the International Refugee Organization to the United Nations High Commissioner for Refugees.

The practical effect of the institutionalization of the category of the refugee that assigned the bounds of identity and action in the refugee events was the institutionalization of a permanent refugee field as a field of statecraft. The tenure of the LNHCR thus stood at the onset of a distinct history of practices of statecraft by which a specific, idealized refugee field was refashioned and institutionalized, that is, rendered permanent, as one of the many fields of statecraft.

As I have already suggested, at any one historical point, a multitude of discursive and nondiscursive practices went into the fashioning and refashioning of the refugee field as a field of statecraft. Of all these practices, however, the generation of intergovernmental arrangements, agreements, conventions, and protocols was the most effective. These intergovernmental instruments worked to condition the politico-administrative and socioeconomic environment of human displacement by defining the "true" refugee and by infusing into the refugee category a program of rights and privileges, as well as duties and responsibilities, through the play of inclusion and exclusion. Although these legal instruments and their disciplinary accessories could not engender a total control over the processes and practices of displacement, they were nonetheless able to effect a practicable regime invested with signs and symbols of power that were anchored in the state, thus conditioning the field of life possibilities.

Between 1921 and 1951, a series of bedrock measures of regimentation—measures of formalization and institutionalization—were inaugurated. The Arrangement with Regard to the Issue of Identity to Russian Refugees (1922), the Arrangement Relating to the Issue of Identity Certificates to Russian and Armenian Refugees (1926), the Arrangement concerning the Extension to Other Categories of Refugees of Certain Measures Taken in Favour of Russian and Armenian Refugees (1928), the Agreement concerning the Functions of the Representatives of the League of Nations High Commissioner for Refugees (1928), and the Arrangement Relating to the Status of Refugees (1928) were some of the measures passed between 1921 and 1930 under the auspices of the LNHCR. Between 1930 and 1951, more such measures were adopted, among which were the 1933 Convention Relating to the International Status of Refugees, the 1936 Convention concerning the Status of Refugees Coming from

Germany, the 1938 Convention Relating to the Status of Refugees Coming from Germany, and the 1939 Additional Protocol to the Convention concerning the Status of Refugees Coming from Germany, not to mention the institution of a number of organizational constitutions, such as that of the International Refugee Organization.

In addition to these intergovernmental grand conventions and arrangements, there were virtually hundreds of agreements obtained between these organizations and individual governments or nongovernmental organizations. In her seminal study of the International Refugee Organization, Holborn, for example, refers to 39 agreements between the IRO and individual governments, 4 agreements between the IRO and the military authorities, 21 agreements between the IRO and the resettlement countries, 43 agreements between the IRO and voluntary agencies, and 110 resolutions relating to refugees, all generated from April 1948 to June 1953 (1956: 575–775).

The practical cross-referential, convergent effects of these measures were significant in terms of a statist regimentation of human displacement under the productive sign, the refugee. The measures were cross-referential in three senses: temporally, programmatically, and ontologically. Temporally, they were cross-referential in deriving their authority from earlier measures. Consider, for example, the 1933 Convention Relating to the International Status of Refugees, in which chapter 1, article 1, reads: "The present Convention is applicable to Russian, Armenian, and Assimilated refugees as defined by the Arrangements of May 12, 1926, and June 30, 1928."[11] Consider also the constitution of the IRO in part 1, section A, "Definition of Refugees," in which the term *refugee* applies to "persons who were considered refugees before the outbreak of the second world war" (qtd. in Holborn, 1956: 584). This, of course, as I have already discussed, refers to the so-called statutory Nansen refugees, transferred over to IGCR after the dissolution of the fourth high commissioner of the League of Nations in 1938. Finally consider the temporal cross-referentiality of the 1951 Geneva Convention:

> For the purposes of the present Convention, the term refugee shall apply to any person who: (1) Has been considered a refugee under the arrangements of 12 May 1926 and 30 June 1928 or under the Conventions of 28 October 1933 and 10 February 1938, the Protocol of 14 September 1939 or the Constitution of the International Refugee Organization." (UNHCR, 1951)

In addition to their temporal cross-referentiality, these measures were also cross-referential programmatically, that is, in determining the regime of solutions stipulated to deal with refugee events. Repatriation, integration, and resettlement as specific alternative solutions to the refugee problem, for example, were first formulated under the League of Nations High Commissioner for Refugees. So was the identity certificate, which, as a watershed innovation, formally charted a specific refugee identity as distinct from the identity of a citizen in the statist terrain of governance. Similarly, many specific mechanisms by which refugee events were managed were invented and normalized in the course of regimentation history prior to the birth of the UNHCR.[12]

Finally, these instruments were cross-referential ontologically, in terms of inscribing and reinscribing the defining conditions and qualities of refugeeness. In all the instruments, the refugee was defined based on his or her territorial ties to the "country of origin," and the state was defined as the sovereign authority over the country. Taken together, the foregoing measures were significant in that they articulated the statist program of governance in the category of the refugee and, as instruments of productive power in the Foucauldian sense, they transformed the conditions of the refugee's existence, that is, his relations, his links, his imbrications with wealth, resources, rights, duties, means of subsistence, territory, community, and the state, and his singular emergence and programmatic treatment as a refugee (Foucault, 1991: 93).

By 1951, these practices of statist governance had already thoroughly regimented the meanings and identities of the category of the refugee and refugeeness and had established the refugee as an object of statist intervention. It was into this already intensively regimented field of the refugee that the UNHCR was born. Contrary to the claims of most conventional studies, the UNHCR was neither an innovation superior to nor a significant expansion of the regime of statist practices already at work. It simply was a continuation of the statist problematization or regimentation of human displacement under the formal sign of the refugee that had begun with the League of Nations High Commissioner for Refugees in 1921. A simple reading of the history of the UNHCR illustrates this point.

The United Nations High Commissioner for Refugees was established through a statute adopted by the United Nations General

Assembly on 14 December 1950. Its mandate was promulgated in the first paragraph of the statute:

> The United Nations High Commissioner for Refugees acting under the authority of the General assembly shall assume the function of providing international protection . . . to refugees who fall within the scope of the present statute and of seeking permanent solutions for the problem of refugees by assisting governments and, subject to the approval of governments concerned, private organizations.[13]

The second paragraph announced the "nature" of the new organization: "The work of the High Commissioner shall be of entirely non-political character; it shall be humanitarian and social and shall relate as a rule to groups and categories of refugees."[14] Not unlike the preceding refugee organizations, the high commissioner's office was conceived as a temporary agency (Holborn, 1975: 89–92). Its mandate was for three years, with an annual budget of $300,000.

In many ways, the UNHCR resembled the organizations that preceded it. As with others, for instance, it was conceived as a temporary humanitarian organization with limited powers. Such similarities notwithstanding, there was one significant difference regarding its scope: the UNHCR's scope was defined more broadly than that of the previous organizations. It extended not only to peoples who were considered refugees under the arrangements of 1926, 1928, 1933, 1938, or 1939, or under the constitution of the International Refugee Organization, but also to "any other person who is outside the country of his nationality, or if he has no nationality, the country of his former habitual residence" to which the refugee was unwilling to return because of a well-founded fear of persecution by reason of race, religion, nationality, or political opinion (UNHCR, 1951).

Armed with this broader definition of its scope, the UNHCR was poised to effect two important expansions in the refugee field. First, it was poised to establish formally an individual-oriented refugee definition, shifting away from exclusively group-oriented definitions that had characterized the mandates of previous organizations, such as the mandate of the LNHCR dealing with the Russian and Armenian refugees (Zolberg et al., 1989: 25). Second, and more importantly, it was poised to establish a refugee definition without temporal and geographical limitations. The new organization would have been able to effect these expansions were it not for the 1951 Geneva

Convention Relating to the Status of Refugees, which articulated the legal framework circumscribing the practical authority of the UNHCR.

The Geneva Convention established the parameters of action for the UNHCR that would "be acceptable to the governments" (Holborn, 1975: 93). These operational limits were to prove incapacitating for the UNHCR, at least for the first few years of its tenure. Of all the limits, however, the most important was in regard to the geographical and temporal limits imposed by the 1951 Geneva Convention. The Geneva Convention defined the issue of scope more narrowly in the definition of the refugee, covering only those individuals displaced because of events occurring before January 1951 in Europe (Gallagher, 1989: 580; Loescher, 1993: 57; Zolberg et al., 1989: 25; Guest, 1991: 590). It was then left to the discretion of the governments to apply the definition to other refugees in other parts of the world. According to article 1(2) of the convention, the term *refugee* applied to

> any person who as a result of events occurring before January 1951 [in Europe] and owing to a well founded fear of being persecuted for reasons of race, religion, nationality, membership of a particular social group or political opinion, is outside the country of his nationality and is unable, or owing to such fear, is unwilling to avail himself of the protection of that country; or who not having a nationality and being outside the country of his former habitual residence as a result of such events, is unable or, owing to such fear, is unwilling to return to it. (UNHCR, 1951)

In a commentary on the convention, while recognizing its geographical and temporal limitations, Nehemiah Robinson points to its achievements with a view to highlighting its historical significance in terms of the specific rights and privileges accorded to refugee status:

> First, the Convention was an attempt to establish an international code of rights for refugees on a general basis. [S]econd, although many of the provisions of the present convention have been modeled upon those of previous arrangements, the scope of rights included in this Convention exceeds that of any earlier agreement. It is the first agreement which covers every aspect of life and guarantees to refugees—as a minimum—the same treatment as to foreigners enjoying special favors. [T]hird, the Convention is the first to have enlisted the participation of such a number of states in its drafting. . . . The

> fact that the conference of plenipotentiaries that drafted this convention was attended . . . by 26 states and two observers, must make it more acceptable to the governments. [F]inally, all preceding conventions referred to European refugees only. . . . The present Convention can be applied to refugees from any part of the world. (1953: 6–8)

Representative of much of the literature on refugee issues, Robinson's claims edify on the politics of origins and authenticity—the authentic origins of the international refugee regime. However, these claims do not hold against a careful historical scrutiny. Even when the critical questions on the general effects of intergovernmental responses to human displacement are put aside, a cursory look into the 1951 Geneva Convention reveals comparative temporal, ontological, and programmatic parallels, if not uniformities, between the Geneva Convention and previous measures such as the conventions of 1933 and 1938 and the constitution of the IRO. This observation is confirmed in the annals of the United Nations. In January 1950, a memorandum from the secretary-general to the Ad Hoc Committee on Statelessness and Related Problems on the "status of refugees and stateless persons" states: "The idea of an international juridical status of refugees is not new. Effect has been given to this idea in various international agreements (Conventions of 1933 and 1938, and so forth). The present preliminary draft is, of course, to a large extent derived from these precedents."[15]

When the preliminary draft was concluded, it still read like its precedents to a large extent, except with the stricter temporal restrictions I have noted. A comparison of the 1933 and 1951 conventions on refugees produces convincing evidence in support of this argument, both from the standpoint of the range and nature of rights and from the standpoint of the ontology that underlies the refugee definitons. Before I address the ontological uniformities, allow me to identify adminstrative, juridical, and civil similarities and uniformities between the two conventions.

Perhaps the cardinal principle of the 1951 convention is the principle of *nonrefoulement,* which is hailed as the "most tangible element of the incipient international refugee regime governing refugee flows" (Desbarats, 1992: 284). This principle hardly ever figures in the discussions of regimentation prior to 1952 in spite of the fact that it was instituted as a binding rule in the 1933 convention, from which it was subsequently adopted into the 1951 convention:

> [1933 convention, article 3(1):] Each of the Contracting parties undertakes not to remove or keep from its territory by application of police measures, such as expulsions or non-admittance (refoulement), refugees who have been authorized to reside there regularly, unless the said measures are dictated by reasons for national security or public order. (Qtd. in Hope-Simpson, 1939: 574)

> [1951 convention, article 32(1):] The contracting States shall not expel a refugee lawfully in their territory save on the grounds of national security or public order. . . . No contracting State shall expel or return (refouler) a refugee in any manner whatsoever to the frontiers of territories where his life or freedom would be threatened on account of his race, religion, nationality, membership of a particular social group or political opinion. . . . The benefit of the present provision may not, however, be claimed by a refugee whom there are reasonable grounds for regarding as a danger to the security of the country in which he is. (UNHCR, 1951)

Furthermore, a number of other items, under juridical status,[16] administrative status,[17] employment,[18] and education,[19] are either very similar or identical between the two conventions in terms of the extent of rights and obligations for refugees and states.

With scrutiny, it becomes clear that the regime of "rights" that Robinson identifies as original to the Geneva Convention had already been encoded in the previous measures, and that the "new" regime had not advanced the "cause" of the refugee any more than the previous measures had. With scrutiny, too, it becomes clear that an increase in the number of states becoming signatories to the "binding" convention was not tantamount to the full application of the provisions of the convention to displaced people. This had already been well demonstrated by the governmental indifference to the plight of millions of displaced people before, during, and after the Second World War. Such measures, when clashing, say, with war objectives, were quickly relegated to secondary importance, if not to practical oblivion.

But perhaps the pivotal, most consequential uniformity was the underlying ontological uniformity that made possible the continuous problematization of the images, identities, and boundaries of the refugee and refugeeness in terms positing the state and its counterparts, the citizen and the domestic community of citizens. The refugee, inscribed in the successive conventions as a figure of aberration and lack, stood to assign and attribute axiomatic primacy and normality to the hierarchy of the citizen/community-of-citizens/state, which, in terms of concrete historical happenings, has always been more imagined than real or practiced.

The uniform casting of the refugee in exclusively state-centric terms characterized the earliest intergovernmental practices of representing the refugee from the LNHCR to the NIOFR, and from the IGCR to the IRO. The refugee came to be defined not in terms of any quality or experience, but in terms of his or her relation to (that is, separation from and/or return to) a space of original national community—the community of citizens—represented and protected by the state. For example, the earliest definition, adopted in 1926 and 1928 by the League of Nations, defined a refugee as a "person who, for one reason or another, is not protected by the government of the state of which he has been, or still is, a national" (qtd. in Hope-Simpson, 1939: 3–4). The following definitions of Russian, Armenian, and German refugees, adopted in 1926, 1926, and 1938 respectively, should then come as no surprise:

> Any person of Russian origin who does not enjoy or who no longer enjoys the protection of the government of the Union of Soviet Socialist Republics and who has not acquired another nationality
>
> Any person of Armenian origin, formerly a subject of the Ottoman Empire, who does not enjoy or who no longer enjoys the protection of the government of the Turkish Republic and has not acquired another nationality
>
> Any person who has settled in [Germany], who does not possess any nationality other than German nationality and in respect of whom it is established that in law or in fact he or she does not enjoy the protection of the Reich (Qtd. in Hope-Simpson, 1939: 227–28; see also League of Nations, 1927c)

The phrases "no longer enjoys the protection of the government of" and "has not acquired another nationality" continued to be the bedrock of subsequent attempts to define the refugee, thus placing the sovereign state at the center of refugee practices. In fact, as I have noted, the 1951 Geneva Convention Relating to the Status of Refugees simply reiterated the principle of the state-centeredness of refugee issues, in chapter 1, article 1.

Ontologically, as with the antecedent definitions obtained through the activities of successive intergovernmental organizations, the refugee definition in the 1951 convention posits an a priori presence of a territorially bounded *national community* with a specific form of membership and governance. The modern *citizen,* occupying a bounded territorial community of citizens, is cast as the proper subject of political life, while the modern *state* is cast as the representative agent mobilizing law, force, and rational administrative resources in order to guarantee certain protections for the citizens. From these premises, a refugee is defined negatively as one who *lacks* the citizen's unproblematic grounding within a territorial space and so lacks the effective representation and protection of a state.

To Robinson and many others, these arguments on the ontology of the institutional discourse as productive of the state-effect make little sense. For them, the state—the citizen and the domestic community of citizens—is always already there, in existence as practical forces in life, in no need of production. Presuming the self-evidence of these entities, Robinson instead suggests that the significance of the 1951 Geneva Convention lies as much in the legal and institutional framework that it stipulates as in its initial tangible improvements in the refugee relief field. To bolster this belief, she enlists the support of the president of the conference of the plenipotentiaries, who viewed the convention with similar thoughts: "While the convention did not fulfill all the desires either of governments or those responsible for the care of refugees, it did establish a satisfactory legal status which would be of material assistance in promoting international collaboration in the refugee field" (qtd. in Robinson, 1953: 8). According to conventional studies, it is precisely this potential of the Geneva Convention as a facilitator of international collaboration that marks a turning point in the history of refugee relief and protection, that is, the establishment of a legal and institutional system understood as an international refugee regime. The convention served as the pivot of the international community's response to refugees (Ferris, 1993b: 7), and the UNHCR became its acting agent in the international arena.

"The Convention regulate[d] in a detailed manner the status of refugees, thereby providing Contracting States with a uniform basis for the treatment of persons or groups eligible for protection" (UNHCR, 1993b: 7). It also required that the contracting states cooperate with the UNHCR in the exercise of its functions, thus reinforcing the UNHCR's role as a lead agency in charge of refugee work on behalf of the UN. However, the way to cooperation was paved with obstacles. The UNHCR faced significant difficulties from its inception. The most formidable was the context of cold war politics, which produced an aura of distrust among the states. In this environment, the parties to the cold war considered the UNHCR to be a political agent of their adversaries. The Eastern-bloc countries, led by the Soviet Union, saw as suspect the whole regime of relations established within the context of the United Nations, and did not partake in its affairs at all. In the Western bloc, there was an inconsistency in the attitude toward the UN system and the UNHCR. The United States in particular assumed a critical posture vis-à-vis the UNHCR. Not only did the United States not sign the UN convention, thus refusing to be part of the new regime of relations pertaining to refugees, but, more importantly, it undermined the practical power and legitimacy of the UNHCR by depriving it of funds.[20] Lacking needed financial support and equipped with an operating budget of just $300,000, the UNHCR made only a minimal impact on the situation of refugees in the immediate postwar era (Loescher, 1993; Loescher and Monahan, 1990; Ferris, 1993b).

A $2. 9 million Ford Foundation grant in 1952 infused lifesaving capital into the UNHCR, thus practically saving it from demise (Gallagher, 1989: 582; Read, 1962: 10; Loescher, 1993: 66). While the grant did not transform the agency into a powerful force in refugee protection, it enabled it to develop an operational network consisting largely of nongovernmental organizations of which it stood as the coordinating entity, a link between governments and the nongovernmental operational organizations. Its usefulness as a coordinating entity was proven during the Berlin crisis of 1953, when a sudden threefold increase in the number of refugees entering West Germany threatened to swarm facilities. The UNHCR responded to the crisis successfully by coordinating various efforts in dealing with refugees (Read, 1962: 14).[21]

The year 1956 marked a turning point in the history of the UNHCR. It was the year of the Hungarian Uprising, which prompted the invasion of Hungary by the Soviet Union on 4 November. The events produced a mass exodus of people from Hungary into Austria and Yugoslavia. At the request of the Austrian government on 4 November, the UNHCR launched an emergency operation while also appealing to governments for help.[22] The operations were very successful, especially in coordinating the efforts of a number of organizations, including the Intergovernmental Committee for European Migration (ICEM) and the United States Escapees Program (USEP), that had hitherto shunned or competed against the UNHCR.

Observers of the UNHCR readily agree that the international response to the Hungarian refugees represents a conceptual expansion of the refugee regime of the 1951 convention, to the extent that the response went beyond the specific temporal mandate of the convention, which defined as refugees only those people displaced before January 1951 (Gordenker, 1987: 36; Gallagher, 1989: 582; Holborn, 1975: 394). The Hungarian episode, they suggest, convinced many states, including the United States, that refugee crises in the form of mass human displacements were not phenomena of the past (Guest, 1991: 590) and that they had to be dealt with regardless of the temporal and spatial limitations of the convention.[23] Contributing to this thinking were the developments in postcolonial Africa, where an uneasy symbiosis of wars of independence and the process of decolonization produced vast numbers of refugees (Dacyl, 1990: 30). By 1967, the number of refugees in Africa was close to one million (Zarjevski, 1988: 19). By 1972, the numbers were well above one million, with refugee movements also emerging in other parts of the developing world, such as India and Pakistan in 1972 (Rystad, 1992; League of Nations, 1921g; Zolberg, 1989; Ferris, 1993b; Gordenker, 1987).

The widespread emergence of refugee problems in Africa and in other continents resulted not only in the reconfirmation of the earlier belief that the refugee phenomenon was not a thing of the past, but also in the recognition that it was a phenomenon occurring throughout the world. The refugee phenomenon called for effective responses. One such response came in 1967 in the form of a supplementary UN protocol on refugees. The Protocol Relating to the Status of Refugees amended the 1951 convention, dropping from the text the phrase "as a result of events occurring in Europe before January 1951," thus ending the formal distinction between the convention's determination of refugee status and the scope of the refugee definition in the UNHCR's daily activities. At last, the Eurocentric refugee regime had shed its temporal and geographical bounds, thus becoming truly universal in its formal consideration of refugees.

Since 1967, the 1951 Geneva Convention and the 1967 protocol have provided the universal legal basis for the determination of refugee status and have specified the procedures for the treatment of refugees. However, numerous other regional instruments also emerged to further supplement the UN instruments, which otherwise continued to constitute the bedrock of the refugee regime. Two of the most significant of those regional instruments are the 1969 Organization of African Unity (OAU) Convention Governing the Specific Aspects of Refugee Problems in Africa, and the Cartagena Declaration adopted by the Latin American states in 1984. The OAU convention had a significant impact on the scope of refugee definitions in a larger sense. It expanded the definition of the refugee to be one

> who, owing to external aggression, occupation, foreign domination, or events seriously disturbing public order in either part or the whole of his country of origin of nationality, is compelled to leave his place of habitual residence in order to seek refuge in another place outside his country of origin or nationality.[24]

The significance of the OAU definition was that it meant not a formal but a practical expansion in the scope of UNHCR activities. As a result, the UNHCR was involved in situations well beyond its formal mandate, a quality not unfamiliar to the practitioners and observers of the UNHCR, considering that the initial conceptual and functional expansions in dealing with refugees had been realized in the same fashion. The Cartagena Declaration, too, expanded the scope of access to refugee status, by defining refugees as "people who have fled their country because their lives, safety or freedom have been threatened by generalized violence, foreign aggression, internal conflicts, massive violation of human rights or other circumstances which have seriously disturbed public order."[25] The result of these instruments was to broaden the category of displaced or uprooted peoples eligible for refugee status, at least theoretically. Although such regional initiatives have broadened the scope of refugee status to deal with regional and global political and economic exigencies, the 1951 UN convention and the 1967 UN protocol continue to underlie the legal and institutional framework of refugee protection that is the modern international refugee regime.

Taken together, however, the implications of these two instruments for the refugee field are extraordinarily significant, in a way that radically diverges from the conventional interpretations. First and foremost, these measures maintain the statist refugee field by providing a definitive "legal" discourse. Although presented as an objective, true discourse, this legal discourse works to establish canons of theory and praxis as regards refugee issues. It establishes not only the institutions and instruments of the theory and its praxis but also the taste, aesthetics, morality, and values that inform the theory and praxis. By virtue of their cross-referentiality, taken together, the instruments acquire an independent authority, an authorship that regiments the recognizable images and identities of what it means to be a refugee, thus effectively determining the boundaries of legitimacy with respect to refugee happenings. To the extent that the cross-referentiality of the instruments frames the debate on refugees, it creates for these instruments what Edward Said might call a superior positionality vis-à-vis all other possible contesting accounts of what it means to be displaced, to be a refugee (1979: 20–21). In the interface of these measures, the specific accounts of the refugee in circulation acquire a mass density and referential power not only among themselves but also in the mass culture at large.

Thus, the measures constitute the ground or field in which most of the studies on refugees are undertaken and to which refugee accounts are referred for legitimacy and authenticity. This ground could be called the common ground of positioning, where grand measures with a uniformly statist definition of the refugee articulate a specific regime of control, with its economy of objects and subjects as well as of codification, that is, "norms, rules, regulations and decision-making processes" (Said, 1979: 20–21). As Said reminds us in *Orientalism,* to the extent to which the majority of the discourse is located in relation to the measures as the source of authenticity and the author of refugees, the superior discursive positionality of these grand measures continues to reproduce a particular kind of refugee field (regime) as a field of statist regimentation (1979: 20–21). In other words, multiple accountings of refugee events since the turn of the century, interacting with institutional and symbolic practices of power, help fashion and refashion the field of the refugee into one of the many fields of statecraft, enabling as well as reflecting certain politico-administrative, politico-cultural, and socioeconomic practices invested by the statist imagery of life (Foucault, 1988; Laclau and Mouffe, 1985).

Of the practices used in the linking of these measures as practices of statecraft—that is, of the practices used in the establishment of a cross-referentiality among these measures—the play of exclusion and inclusion in terms of reasons, causes, manifestations, and identities of the refugee looms historically most effective. The play of "You are a refugee, but she is not" becomes a powerful instrument of power. Such differentiations, and more that are achieved through a play of exclusion and inclusion immersed in the language of origins and authenticity, prevail in all measures.

Embedded in the cross-referential interface, these measures facilitate the fashioning of a field of activity in which a specific economy of regimentation—a determination of the range of reasons and causes presumably producing refugees, of the scope of analysis needed to account for them, and of the range of responses to address them—is continually imposed on the fluidity of a thousand faces. In other words, the proliferation of the institutional and pertinent popular discourse in the refugee field, while claiming to open refugee events to novel approaches, works instead to discipline and regiment the multiplicity of refugee identities, voices, and experiences. It appropriates these multiple refugee identities, voices, and experiences in the preservation of a refugee field with a peculiar ontology. The strategy of inclusion and exclusion thus works to condition practices in the refugee field.

The parallels and uniformities in intergovernmental regime practices and discourses across the decades point not so much to the poverty of the field in regimentative terms, as to the wealth, efficacy, and historicity of the productive practices of refugee regimentations as practices of statecraft. These ontological as well as programmatic parallels and uniformities attest to the ubiquity of the practices of statecraft. The ubiquity of such practices, however, does not mean that they have been simply arbitrarily and freely all-powerful; they have had to operate in socially constructed fields that have not offered unlimited possibilities for intervention and that have included practices resistant to the state's interventions (Foucault, 1991: 68). Historically, state-oriented practices imagined and empowered the state's universal knowledgeable order through "the card and the code" (Noiriel, 1996: 45), but refugees were always capable of subverting the card and the code and dislocating the knowledgeable processes of the state's order in their primary daily desire to survive.

The UNHCR's history is a story of regimentations informed by such struggles, some of which have been more successful than others. The last two decades attest to this observation. Starting from the late 1970s and early 1980s, millions fled their countries largely because of wars of various kinds, such as foreign invasions, civil wars, and abrupt changes of governmental regimes. Conflicts in Iran, Afghanistan, Cambodia, Nicaragua, El Salvador, Angola, Ethiopia, and Kurdistan represent the sort of conflicts that led to the formation of large refugee movements in the 1980s. In 1985, the number of refugees worldwide was more than fourteen million, with no indication that the increase would subside any time soon. By 1985, the UNHCR was under formidable pressure. According to some observers (Harder, 1993; Guest, 1991), some administrative problems notwithstanding, the major problem of the UNHCR derived from its desire to maintain an effective refugee protection regime that had increasingly come under challenge by governments apprehensive about refugee movements for various social, political, and/or economic reasons. For many governments, whether sending or receiving refugees, the refugee phenomenon had become hopelessly permanent. Neither of the traditional solutions embodied in the international refugee system—repatriation or resettlement—seemed to have been working (Dacyl, 1990: 29). Repatriation had become largely impossible, as the conditions in the sending countries remained precarious. Resettlement, too, had fast become a nonsolution, as it proved virtually impossible to find any country willing to receive tens of thousands of refugees permanently. A trickle of refugees was allowed in for resettlement, yet millions were condemned to live in dilapidated refugee camps throughout the Third World.

Reminiscent of the restrictionist mood in the 1930s, in the 1990s the objective in refugee regimentation shifted more forcefully to the containment of the problem in the place of origin or to unabashed obstructionism, which became the most widely employed strategy as the receiving states, one after another, instituted extremely restrictive policies regarding refugee acceptance (Fernhout, 1993; Arboleda and Hoy, 1993; Suhrke, 1993; Guest, 1991). In all these developments, the UN instruments on refugees, and the UNHCR as the UN agency designed to carry out the policy objectives stated in those instruments, have afforded and continue to afford an intergovernmental field of regimentations.

Today, these regimentations inform, mediate, and guide the trajectories of the practices and projects of democracy, human rights, and humanitarianism, including humanitarian interventions. They work in our culture. They are imbricated in all aspects of our lives; they become instrumental to the articulation and rearticulation of a number of state-oriented notions and projects around which we organize our lives. These notions and practices range from democratic projects, to issues of national and international security, to human rights—the stability and welfare of the society in which we live. In all of them, refugee regimentations filter refugee images and identities. Refugees may enter our personal and collective field of vision day in and day out, but we hardly ever see them other than through spectacles paradigmatically productive of statist ends and beginnings.

It is possible to see further how the figure of the refugee works as a powerful referential resource employed in the production and stabilization of a variety of familiar images and identities around which our understanding of normality and legitimacy continues to be formulated and practiced. In the rest of this book, in chapters that derive mostly from Euro-Mediterranean histories, I examine how this happens in various fields of policy and conduct, including security, humanitarianism and intervention, and democratic processes and practices. In other words, I look at how the state's universal order is articulated, empowered, and stabilized and how refugees figure in this project, not only as its productive objects but also as subjects subversive of it.

5

Humanitarian Interventions as Practices of Statecraft: Recrafting State Sovereignty in Refugee Crises

The subject of refugees and displaced persons is at the cutting edge of international concern today not only because of its humanitarian significance, but also because of its impact on peace, security, and stability.

—Sadako Ogata
UN High Commissioner for Refugees, 1994

Narratives on Refugees

> The drama which struck northern Iraq in early April will always mark refugee history. The unforeseen consequences of the [Gulf War], the violent events which broke out in the provinces of Iraqi Kurdistan, followed by the desperate flight of hundreds of thousands of people, deeply shocked public opinion. A succession of bewildering figures flashed over the teletexts: 10,000 displaced persons, then 30,000, 50,000, 500,000, one million, perhaps more, moving in hordes toward neighboring countries.
>
> *Refugees*, 12 June 1991

On April 5, 1991, the UN Security Council, in an unprecedented fashion, overrode the Iraqi government's assertion of sovereignty, which had been used to deny humanitarian access to Kurdish refugees. Viewing mass upheaval as a threat to international security, the Security Council in Resolution 688 insisted "that Iraq allow immediate access by international humanitarian organizations to all those in need of assistance in all parts of Iraq. The subsequent creation by American, British, French, and Dutch Marines of safe havens for the

> Iraqi Kurds within northern Iraq may prove to have been a turning point in the evolution of global humanitarian ethics. Certainly, it suggests what an aroused global community can do when denied access to civilians imperiled within a country.
>
> Thomas G. Weiss and Larry Minear
> "Groping and Coping in the Gulf Crisis:
> Discerning the Shape of a Humanitarian Order"

In recent years, the study of humanitarian interventions has proliferated.[1] This proliferation has come on the heels of a number of catastrophic developments that, in response, triggered "humanitarian interventions" purportedly undertaken to stop or alleviate massive human sufferings resulting from these catastrophic developments. Intervention in Iraqi Kurdistan, the former Yugoslavia, Somalia, and Rwanda are the most conspicuous, precedent-setting examples of humanitarian interventions.

While the recent catastrophic developments have thrust the issue of humanitarian interventions to the fore, the study of humanitarian intervention has been a perennial preoccupation of scholars in history, particularly in the past two centuries, starting with the advent of absolutist states and continuing through the formation and consolidation of modern territorial states. Classical scholars of international relations such as Hugo Grotius, Emmerich Vattel, and Christian Wolf[2] and more contemporary publicists such as W. A. Dunning, Lassa Oppenheim, and Ellery C. Stowell[3] have all dwelled on the issue of humanitarian intervention.

Even a marginal reading of both the classical and the more contemporary work on humanitarian interventions indicates that historically, the preoccupation with the issue revolves around a wide range of other issues, some of which are more pronounced in the contemporary studies. They include human rights, national and international peace, security, democracy, and, most important, state sovereignty both as a principle and as a practice. Furthermore, among the contemporary works, the interest in the issue pertains to an array of normative themes arising in the context of humanitarian interventions. The nature, efficacy, ethics, and legality of humanitarian interventions are but some of the normative themes explored in these works.

These works represent a highly diverse area of study; perceptions, conceptualizations, and assessments as to what humanitarian interventions mean vary across scholarly disciplines and organizational fields. For instance, while a number of actual intervention events go under the name of humanitarian intervention in popular as well as governmental discourses, there is no particularly firm consensus on a politico-legal definition of humanitarian intervention. Instead, many scholars and policy makers offer commentaries on humanitarian interventions in terms that outline the circumstances and conditions under which humanitarian interventions should take place. There is, in short, no paradigm of humanitarian intervention around which views converge. Disagreements over the legality, efficacy, and ethics of humanitarian intervention continue to prevail.[4]

These are surely significant issues that merit further study. What interests me here, however, is not the examination of these issues per se. It is not my objective to focus, for example, on the examination of the effectiveness, legality (say, from the standpoint of customary international law), and/or morality of humanitarian interventions. Nor is it my purpose to arrive at a definition of humanitarian intervention that would lay the foundation for a paradigm in humanitarian interventions. As I say, these are significant questions that must be addressed, inasmuch as interventions, humanitarian or not, are real events affecting human lives in a tangible fashion.[5] Nevertheless, what interests me more here is the way in which all these studies, while having diverse orientations on various substantive and normative issues, converge on an issue that is of crucial importance to national and global governance—state sovereignty. It is fair to say that, of all the issues under consideration, the majority of studies on humanitarian interventions concentrate most on the issue of state sovereignty, regarding sovereignty as the generative and operative principle underlying the organization of global politics in the contemporary world. Specifically, they focus on and examine the implications of humanitarian interventions for the principle and practices of state sovereignty.

The examination of state sovereignty is singularly important, for the question of state sovereignty goes to the very heart of national and international relations: it is around the principle of state sovereignty that a specific imagination of the world as a world of sovereign states is obtained, empowered, and privileged, and that practical realities of "living within sovereign borders" and having security, peace, stability, welfare, and human rights are historically effected and practiced.[6] This—the exploration of the implications of humanitarian interventions on state sovereignty—is also the focus, the substantive interest, of this chapter. The question, in other words, is not whether humanitarian interventions are truly humanitarian, but how they could be reconceptualized in their relations to state sovereignty as the operative principle of national and international governance. However, my approach differs somewhat from most contemporary studies. Let me explain.

HUMANITARIAN INTERVENTIONS AND CONVENTIONAL DISCOURSES

When one looks into contemporary studies on humanitarian intervention, one immediately notices that most of these studies perpetuate a certain dichotomy of interpretation in analyzing the implications of humanitarian interventions for state sovereignty and, indeed, the sovereign state as a form of governance in local and global politics. On the one end of the interpretive spectrum are instances of theorizing that construe humanitarian interventions as markers of a historic erosion of state sovereignty as a principle and a practice of political organization in life across the globe. These construals are positioned in the larger globalizing and transnationalizing landscape of life where historically peculiar relations and institutions of state sovereignty, under pressure from globalizing developments, are seen to melt into a "transnational air." "A number of developments," writes Nancy Arnison, for instance,

> are chipping away at sovereignty. National borders have become increasingly porous as trade, mass communications, and environmental degradation hasten global interdependence. The growth of international human rights law during the last four decades has made important inroads into sovereignty. . . . The citadel of sovereignty is beginning to crack. (1993: 199–203)

"The world community," Paul Lewis adds, "has broken new ground in international law, slowly laying the foundations of a new right of outside intervention in the formerly sacrosanct internal affairs of sovereign states" (1992). Concurring with this general observation, Thomas Weiss and Larry Minear state that

> as the world moves from the Cold War to the post–Cold War era, sovereignty as traditionally understood is no longer sacrosanct. The age-old balance between state assertions of sovereignty and inter-

> national expressions of solidarity with those who suffer has begun to shift perceptibly in favor of those who are in need. (1993: 60; also see Minear and Weiss, 1993: 38–39)

In much the same vein, others, such as Robert Jackson (1993), Guenter Lewy (1993), and John Dunn (1994), line up to articulate the negative implications of humanitarian interventions for state sovereignty. Jackson, for instance, writes that "humanitarian intervention thus seems to repudiate the norm of non-intervention itself and the international foundation of state sovereignty upon which that norm rests" (1993: 584). The philosopher Dunn, meanwhile, writes of the necessity of intervention in the face of massive human loss in spite of the hazards of intervening in the internal affairs of other countries. "What exactly is the alternative?" he asks emphatically. His answer is poignantly clear in its implications for the status of state sovereignty in global politics: "To stand by deliberately while murder or genocide are being done is not to commit them yourself. But it certainly is to make a deeply implicating choice" (1994: 259–60). Patrick O'Halloran encapsulates the possible response when he argues that

> there is a notable shift in the fundamental notion of the inviolability of the sovereignty of each nation-state. A new rule is emerging: There are circumstances in which the world community can, in defense of our common humanity, interfere in the national affairs of a sovereign nation state. (1995: 1)

Meanwhile, former secretary-general of the United Nations Javier Pérez de Cuéllar hints at the presumably deterritorializing implications of such an activist response on state sovereignty. He declares that what "we are clearly witnessing is probably an irresistible shift in public attitudes towards the belief that the defense of the oppressed in the name of morality should prevail over frontiers and legal documents" (qtd. in Lewy, 1993: 626). In sum, in the larger global landscape, to many observers, humanitarian interventions signify yet another dimension of the "erosion" in state sovereignty.

There are, however, other observers who, while acknowledging the shifts and transformations in the landscape of global politics, see humanitarian interventions differently as regards their implications for state sovereignty. These observers find themselves positioned on the other end of the interpretive spectrum (Nanda, 1992; Garigue,

1993; Boutros-Ghali, 1994; Donnelly, 1993). For these observers, humanitarian interventions represent no fundamental erosion in state sovereignty. The proponents of this view argue that the interventions in Iraq, Somalia, and Bosnia and Herzegovina can be explained and justified within the provisions of the UN system as a framework for international governance. Specifically, they argue that the interventions in these places can be accounted for within the logic of the collective security arrangements of the UN system embodied in the UN charter, and thus they translate into no violation of state sovereignty above and beyond the provisions specified in that charter. Provisions governing such activities, they remind us, have been part of the UN system since its inception and have been reaffirmed on numerous occasions.[7] While these studies representing humanitarian issues are no doubt richly varied, exhibiting all contesting viewpoints, it is nevertheless fair to say that they honor a statist hierarchy of interpretation and analysis.

In these studies, humanitarian intervention involves already constituted, already given state-centric identities and entities. From the premise that the modern citizen is the a priori proper subject of political life to the understanding that the modern state is an agent of representation and protection, deriving its powers from the citizens it represents, the statist hierarchy informs the conventional studies. In them, it is construed that the citizens, occupying a bounded territorial community, author the state by way of a covenant that accords legitimate powers to the state. In return, the state mobilizes resources at its disposal to guarantee certain protections for the citizens and to facilitate the enjoyment of the natural rights of the citizens. As Fernando Teson notes, this protection and representation of the natural rights of the citizens is the ultimate justification of the existence of the state (1988: 15).

The social covenant or compact defines the rights and duties of the entities that are party to the hierarchical arrangement among citizens, domestic community, and state. In the hierarchy, the state is endowed with sovereign powers, but such powers are predicated upon its proper representation of the will and desires of the domestic community of citizens. For it is only on the basis of a domestic community that the sovereign state could claim to effect its sovereignty, its powers, and indeed its exclusive right to rule over a territorial space free from outside intervention.

These studies see a humanitarian crisis occurring when a state, breaching its contractual duty of protecting and representing the domestic community, turns predatory against a section or the whole of the domestic community, exceeding the bounds of legitimate violence. The actions of the Iraqi state against its own citizens after the Gulf War constitute such a crisis. A humanitarian crisis is also seen to occur when a state fails or disintegrates and is no longer able to effect its protective as well as representative sovereign power over the domestic community. The cases of Somalia, the former Yugoslavia, and Rwanda illustrate this kind of humanitarian crisis. In both scenarios, the very existence of a domestic community is endangered, resulting in the practical nullification of the social compact, including the nullification of the provision of freedom from outside intervention. In the face of a state gone aberrant or a state that has failed, the international community, representing the collective will of the community, moves into what would otherwise be the sovereign domain (territory) of a state to save the people (Charvet, 1997).

A state that thus violates the original compact, Jackson maintains, "must expect to have its sovereignty invaded by the international community" (1993: 593). Further justifying the "invasion of sovereignty," we are told, is the emergent international human rights regime composed of regional and universal human rights instruments. Building on the Universal Declaration of Human Rights, there has been a steady stream of multilateral human rights treaties. The most comprehensive are the International Covenant on Economic, Social, and Cultural Rights (1976) and the International Covenant on Civil and Political Rights (1976), which were ratified by 117 and 114 states respectively. A number of other instruments—on refugees (1951, 1967), racial discrimination (1964), women's rights (1979), torture (1984), and children's rights (1990)—have entered into effect, becoming part of the tapestry of related human rights instruments (Donnelly, 1993: 623). At the regional level, the European Convention on Human Rights (1953) has emerged as a comprehensive regional human rights regime (Donnelly, 1993: 622–25; Jacobson, 1995: 9).

In spite of a degree of resistance to the mandates articulated in these instruments, Donnelly contends that they nonetheless "have created a strong and comprehensive set of international human rights norms to which most states publicly subscribe" and which states need to uphold to maintain their legitimacy in the international arena (1993: 623). Likewise, David Jacobson argues that states must increasingly take account of international human rights laws in their dealings (1996: 9–10). States that violate the spirit as well as the letter of the covenant as manifested in these and other laws open themselves to a potential invasion of their sovereignty in the form of humanitarian interventions.

This is how the tale of humanitarian interventions is narrated in most contemporary studies, regardless of their views on the impact of intervention on the sovereign state. This tale, however, is not a "neutral" one. It does not merely narrate occurrences that must be understood as humanitarian interventions under specific circumstances. Rather, it is an orchestrated narration that has a "centering effect," regimenting our perceptions of the world in terms of prevalent statist relations and institutions (Huysmans, 1995: 55). The tale of humanitarian intervention as told in these studies begins, in the words of Michel de Certeau, by "awarding" an axiomatic "centrality" to the state and its sovereignty (1988: 120).[8] It regards the state and its sovereignty as primary, assigning a secondary status to the problem of humanitarian crisis, and comprehends humanitarian interventions as tertiary responses by which resources of the territorial order of states are marshaled to respond to the crisis and to restore the peaceful order of the state. These studies so begin in order to speak of either an erosion or an affirmation of state sovereignty vis-à-vis humanitarian interventions. In all this, a paradigmatic territorial statism remains central to the discussion; it is, as Ernest Gellner (1993) might suggest, almost instinctual.

In discussing the emergence of the notion of nation, Gellner refers to the curiously powerful dominance of the idea of nation in the lives of people, as if the nation is an inherent, timeless attribute of humanity, here to stay as long as humanity exists: "A man without a nation defies the recognized categories and provokes revulsion. . . . A man must have a nationality as he must have a nose and two ears." It is in the same sense that the state figures in the lives of people, according to these studies on humanitarian interventions: "Just as a man must have a nation, a nation must have a state to represent and protect it, for to be without a state is to stand alone 'outside' in a dangerous world of anarchy" (1993: 6). This essentialized link between the nation and the state is imagined to be simultaneously territorial, achieved through a politics of "place-making" (Gupta and Ferguson, 1992) that spatially bounds the manifestation of the link between the nation and the state. The state, the nation, and the place are seen as layered and imbricated, creating the discursive spatiopolitical landscape that is the sovereign territorial national state. The motto of the statist protections and assurances in life is thus furthered to its territorialized logical end: "Just as a man must have a nation, a nation must have a state to represent and protect it," and the state must possess a bounded space within which it can afford certain protections. This is the most elemental imagery that the basic practices of statecraft work to produce, and this is the imagery that most studies on humanitarian interventions conjure up in their analyses, even as they speak of disruptions in this hierarchy in the form of interventions. After all, a humanitarian intervention can take place only after locating its bounded operative site.

Starting with the state and its territorial trappings, these studies go on to say that humanitarian interventions are either activities chipping away at the citadel of sovereignty or mere manifestations of state sovereignty in the face of specific problems. Their tale, however, remains just that, a tale in constant need of narration; it offers no convincing explanations as to how such processes of erosion or affirmation are effected, if in fact these processes constitute the central *problematique* in humanitarian interventions.

The problem here, as I see it, is that such an essentialist conceptualization of the sovereign state inevitably leads to a reifying conceptualization of state sovereignty as an either/or binary—either an eternal presence or an increasing absence (withering away) of state sovereignty. In the words of R. B. J. Walker (1991a), in these studies, state sovereignty is seen either as a permanent reality of the international order or as simply an ephemera, as if it were here today and gone tomorrow. State sovereignty and indeed the sovereign state, Walker (1991a; 1991b), Richard Ashley (1988; 1989a; 1993), Cynthia Weber (1995), and Michael Shapiro (1993) urge, are neither permanent nor ephemeral. The appearance of permanence is simply an effect of a complex set of practices—practices of statecraft—"working to affirm continuities and to shift disruptions and dangers to the margins, while the appearance of being passé is a result of the failure to affirm the hierarchy of identities and meanings that underlie the sovereign state" (Walker, 1991a: 48). Both the state and its sovereignty are historical artifacts of governance crafted in and through practices of statecraft. To paraphrase Alexander Wendt (1994), sovereign states are what their crafters make of them, but always through complex sets of narrative and performative practices of statecraft, practices that "simulate" the state, as Cynthia Weber (1995) says, by considering the ongoing shifts and transformations in the fields of political activities and appropriating new narrative and performative resources with which to attempt to impose and reimpose a particular order on local and global alterations, changes, and transformations. This, once again, is the fundamental task of statecraft.

HUMANITARIAN INTERVENTIONS, PROBLEMATIZATION, AND STATECRAFT

I want to suggest that so-called humanitarian interventions might be instrumental to this task of statecraft in that they constitute a specific field in which activities of governance are orchestrated vis-à-vis the challenge or the difficulty—the humanitarian crisis—to rearticulate state sovereignty and the statist hierarchy it signifies not only as natural but also as necessary to the peaceful, stable, and secure organization of local and global politics. In this sense, humanitarian interventions are not simply activities of a tertiary order, undertaken to resolve a problem, but also practices of active regimentation, oriented to produce, stabilize, and empower the specific territorially bound and territorially activated hierarchy of citizen/nation/state on which the very ontology of the state system continues to rest. Humanitarian interventions make possible the imagination of the state system and its attendant hierarchies and are ontologically guided and delimited by them. Active determination or bounding of the space in which intervention can take place is nothing less than an affirmation of territorial statism, even in moments of violence and force from without. Liisa Malkki puts this most succinctly when she argues that humanitarian interventions constitute a privileged site within which the international community of states creates itself (1996: 378).

The internationality of interventions (that is, interventions by the so-called international community) is crucial, for humanitarian interventions are internationally or, to state it better, intergovernmentally orchestrated sets of practices. At a basic level they do more than attend to the problem of humanitarian crises. They are, to use the Foucauldian terminology, intergovernmental activities of *problematization* that work principally to recuperate state sovereignty in the face of specific historical challenges that call into question the very viability of statist hierarchies and state sovereignty as the operative principle in international governance.

Among the historical challenges to the system of sovereign states are overwhelming human catastrophes defined as humanitarian crises which, whether due to genocidal warfare, widespread famine, or environmental disasters, typically engender massive refugee events. To comprehend humanitarian interventions as being recuperative of statist relations, institutions, and subjectivities, it is necessary to look into how humanitarian interventions are problematized, especially in terms of security concerns in local and global politics. The problematizations encoded with security concerns are particularly instructive in refugee crises in demonstrating the productive, recuperative import of humanitarian interventions. So, it might be possible that refugee crises, particularly those that have elicited interventions, afford instructive insights into the dynamics of humanitarian interventions as practices of statecraft.

How are specific refugee crises problematized (reinscribed) as humanitarian crises demanding response from the international community, thus to enable the undertaking of humanitarian interventions that then work, as I claim, to recuperate state sovereignty in the very act of seemingly violating it? The recuperative logic of problematization, I suggest, is at work in the conceptualization of humanitarian interventions in security terms during refugee events. It is at work from (a) the incitement of popular and institutional discourse on specific refugee crises as humanitarian crises, to (b) their statization as humanitarian crises, that is, their representation as a specific problem of the sovereign state, to (c) the formulation and channeling of imaginable statist solutions in the form of humanitarian interventions.

The field of humanitarian interventions as a field of statecraft is opened by a problematic event or a series of events—a humanitarian crisis—that disrupt the relationship of the constitutive agents of the citizen/nation/state hierarchy. A humanitarian crisis is seen to be the result of a breakdown in the proper norms or forms of governance of the sovereign territorial state. This is the moment of recognizing an event, such as the Kurdish refugee flight or the refugee crisis in Bosnia, as a specific problem for the practice and project of sovereign statehood. The moment of recognition is a deliberate moment in problematization. How the event is represented as a problem is significant for subsequent activities undertaken to respond to it.

In the conventional studies, we are left with the impression that, in the face of an event of humanitarian crisis manifested in excessive human suffering, such as refugee crises, the object of humanitarian intervention is human-beings-as-victims to whom help must be extended even, if necessary, without the consent of the sovereign (Helton, 1992: 374–75). Thus, we are told, humanitarian interventions take place in order to put an end to human suffering when, in the words of the French ambassador to the UN Jean-Bernard Merimee, "a state [kills], without any limitation, its citizens" (qtd. in Chadwick, 1992). At least, as J. N. Pieterse (1997) argues, this is so in the "pathos of humanitarian interventions." The "actual engagement" might tell a different story.

I am not about to suggest that "humanitarian interventions" are not humanitarian at all. It is true, for example, that the intervention—"Operation Provide Comfort"—in northern Iraq in the waning hours of the Gulf War in 1991 was humanitarian in the sense that it provided much comfort to millions and helped save hundreds of thousands of human lives. It is also true that the intervention in Bosnia has saved and continues to save hundreds of thousands of lives.[9] Similarly, the intervention in Somalia eased the conditions of massive starvation that, were it not for the intervention, would probably have killed masses of people. However, while the "humanitarian" aspects of the interventions should be recognized and lauded, it is also possible to argue that humanitarian interventions are not simply activities of international solidarity in response to massive human suffering. In fact, it is possible to suggest that in the so-called humanitarian interventions, humanitarianism is generally subordinated to the exigencies of statism. Beyond humanitarianism, in other words, are intergovernmentally orchestrated practices of statecraft that, while purportedly oriented primarily to alleviating human suffering in maverick states, also rearticulate and reaffirm the peculiar images, identities, relations, and institutions that signify the citizen/nation/state hierarchy as the foundational hierarchy underlying the modern territorial state system (Huysmans, 1995: 55–57; Hoffman, 1993: 202).

Admittedly, it is rare that one would encounter an account of humanitarian interventions in precisely these terms. However, it might be possible to glimpse such recuperative, state-oriented dynamics of humanitarian interventions by looking into intergovernmental discourse and conduct on humanitarian interventions, particularly in those instances of interventions triggered in response to massive refugee events. The interventions in northern Iraq, Somalia, and Bosnia are such instances, coming on the heels of massive internal and international human displacement. I argue that examination of the discourse of interventionist humanitarianism in such massive refugee events evinces the practical underpinnings that link humanitarian intervention, state sovereignty, and statecraft. Such an examination is guided by a number of questions: How, in those instances, was the problem of crisis *articulated* in terms of a refugee event? What was posited and included and what was questioned and excluded in the articulation of the problem? What was pronounced and what was obscured? How were the refugee events problematized as events of humanitarian crisis demanding response, thus enabling the undertaking of humanitarian interventions? How, in other words, does the refugee get constituted as an *object* of humanitarian interventions? And what does the *object,* once problematized, represent or signify relative to the posited relations, institutions, and meanings of the citizen/nation/state hierarchy?

I believe that, together, these questions help point to the linkages between humanitarian interventions in refugee crises and the artifice of statecraft in the late twentieth century. To illustrate, I turn to a specific intervention that has fueled the humanitarian intervention discourse in an unprecedented fashion: the intervention in Iraq in April 1991 in the aftermath of the Gulf War.[10]

HUMANITARIAN INTERVENTIONS AS MEANS OF CRAFTING STATE SOVEREIGNTY: THE KURDISH REFUGEE CRISIS

Narratives on Refugees

> Early April 1991, shortly after the Gulf War had ended, armed conflict between the Iraqi government and disaffected groups within the country provoked one of the largest and fastest refugee movements in recent history.
>
> UNHCR
> *The State of the World's Refugees, 1993: The Challenge of Protection*

> The flight soon turned into a human tragedy on a massive scale. The crisis generated tremendous pressure on Western governments to intervene. . . . They sought to deal with the crisis as a standard relief operation but for a variety of practical and political reasons this proved to be inadequate. After a degree of transatlantic debate, they therefore decided to establish protected areas within Iraq to enable Kurds to return in safety to their homes. . . . In so doing they created an important precedent for humanitarian intervention.
>
> Lawrence Freedman and David Boren
> "'Safe Havens' for Kurds in Post-war Iraq"

It is generally accepted that UN Security Council Resolution 688 of 5 April 1991 paved the way for and justified the allied intervention in Iraq to save the Kurds, for it was oriented to provide humanitarian assistance to Kurdish refugees in the face of Iraqi defiance. Many in policy-making and academic circles as well as in the popular media argued that the intervention was indeed a humanitarian intervention (Minear, 1992; Adelman, 1992; Nanda, 1992).

The president of the United States, George Bush, echoed a similar logic, arguing that in the face of a humanitarian crisis manifested in excessive human suffering as in northern Iraq, victims must be helped even, if necessary, without the consent of the sovereign. "Some" he said, "might argue that this is an intervention into the internal affairs of Iraq, but I think the humanitarian concern, the refugee concern is so overwhelming that there will be a lot of understanding about this"(qtd. in Freedman and Boren, 1992: 55). In the U.S. Congress, the chairman of the House Foreign Affairs Committee said, "We are intervening in the sovereignty of Iraq, I think for good reason here, to help these Kurdish people"(qtd. in Freedman and Boren, 1992: 82). The French ambassador to the UN, Jean-Bernard Merimee, offered a concurring reason for the humanitarian intervention in Iraq: "Definitely, the idea is beginning to prevail that sovereignty is not a sufficient reason for a sovereign state to kill, without any limitation, its citizens, and that the international community has a sort of moral right to intervene" (qtd. in Chadwick, 1992).

Security Council Resolution 688 is worth quoting at length, because it is representative of the specific vocabularies, significations, and classifications through which humanitarian interventions are written, talked about, circulated, and assigned contingent referentiality in wider fields of activity. It is through similar vocabularies that humanitarian interventions are attributed specific cultural, political, and legal meanings and identities that enable many naturally and effortlessly to say, "What took place was a humanitarian intervention."

> THE SECURITY COUNCIL,
> MINDFUL of its duties and its responsibilities under the charter of the United Nations for the maintenance of international peace and security . . .
> GRAVELY CONCERNED by the repression of the Iraqi civilian population in many parts of Iraq, including most recently in Kurdish populated areas which led to a massive flow of refugees towards and across international frontiers and to cross border incursions, which threaten international peace and security in the region,
> DEEPLY disturbed by the magnitude of human suffering involved, . . .
> REAFFIRMING the commitment of all member states to the sovereign, territorial integrity and political independence of Iraq and of all states in the area . . .
> CONDEMNS the repression of the Iraqi civilian population in many parts of Iraq, including most recently in Kurdish populated areas, the consequences of which threaten international peace and security in the region;
> DEMANDS that Iraq, as a contribution to removing the threat to international peace and security in the region, immediately end this repression and expressing the hope in the same context that an open dialogue will take place to ensure that the human and political rights of all Iraqi citizens are respected;
> INSIST that Iraq allow immediate access by international humanitarian organizations to all those in need of assistance in all parts of Iraq, and to make available all necessary facilities for their operations. (UN Security Council, 1992)

While in most political and popular accounts we are encouraged to believe in a humanitarian ethos maintaining that interventions take place in order to put an end to human suffering, the opening paragraph of the resolution articulates a different reason for intervention. This is significant, for this paragraph frames the normative policy context, pointing to the larger issue at stake—"the maintenance of international peace and security." The maintenance of international peace and security, not human suffering, we are thus instructed, is the prevailing concern in the minds of the council members.

Clearly, the opening paragraph of the resolution betrays more frequent efforts to frame the intervention primarily, if not exclusively, in terms of human rights. It betrays the political and popular ethical stylization of intervention as primarily humanitarian. Although we are repeatedly and patiently instructed, say, by George Bush or the French ambassador, to believe that intervention is driven merely by a desire to save lives, the official justificatory discourse suggests that a different concern animates intervention efforts.

The object of the intervention, in this discourse, is not human beings as *victims* of a *state* gone *aberrant*. Rather, the object of intervention, the resolution instructs us, is human beings as *refugees*, namely, *citizens* gone *aberrant* to become *refugees*. The object is not refugees as human beings, but human beings as refugees, in the words of the resolution, flowing "towards and across international frontiers and [effecting] cross border incursions, which threaten international peace and security in the region." The object of intervention is, in the most simple terms, *refugees* problematized as a threat to international peace and security. It is the threat of refugee movements to international peace and security that the council is "gravely concerned" about, especially considering the transborder, transversal implications of refugee movements in the region.

The problem—the humanitarian crisis—is defined not so much in terms of human beings in need of relief and comfort as in terms of refugees who constitute a problematic category of people—people who lack the qualities of the proper subjects of the state, the citizen-subjects. Similarly, one could suggest, the problem is defined not in terms of a state gone aberrant but in terms of the product of state activities, namely, refugees as an aberrant category of people that must be dealt with.

Bill Frelick (1992a, 1993) offers a corroborating interpretation. His analysis is instructive, as is intimated in the title of his article "The False Promise of Operation Provide Comfort." "The resolution," Frelick writes, referring to Resolution 688,

> is important both for what it says and for what it does not say. It frames its condemnation of Saddam Hussein's repression not in terms of human rights violations committed against Iraqi citizens inside Iraq, but rather in terms of the massive flow of refugees toward and across international frontiers caused by the repression. (1992a: 4)[11]

The influential Turkish columnist Ali Sirmen also zeroes in on the Kurdish refugee bodies, suggesting that they constitute a security problem for the whole region:

> There is another issue to which more attention needs to be given. The problem of the refugees, who were uprooted and driven to the borders by the pressures from the government of Saddam, is no more the internal affair of Iraq exclusively, but has become an international problem that bears on the internal stability of many regional countries and, by implication, on the stability of the whole region. Turkey has successfully defended this position in the United Nations and, with support from France, facilitated the adoption of Resolution 688. (1991; my translation)

Clearly, it is the citizens, not the state, that go aberrant, becoming refugees as a result of events beyond their control. Although the state violates the compact, it still remains a state, already there, as it were, already established with and through prevailing relations and institutions, and already empowered to speak and be heard. This construction of agency is demonstrable in the language of Resolution 688. What the resolution calls for or, in this case, asks from Iraq, "as a contribution to removing the threat to international peace and security," is simply to end the repression, open dialogue, and recognize that its activities of statecraft to effect its sovereign power in the territorial locale of Iraq have to be carefully regimented lest they endanger, as they do now, the activities of statecraft in other locales and threaten international peace and security.

In fact, Iraq was an integral part of the regimentation of the problem pragmatically, symbolically, and rhetorically in terms of the conventional territorializing discourse of international relations. The United Nations and individual governments, including the permanent members of the UN Security Council as well as Turkey, went to great lengths to incorporate Iraq into the process of dealing with refugees. While the parties expressed outrage toward one another publicly through diplomatic and military channels, they collaborated extensively to smooth out the refugee problem. On 18 April 1991, for example, the UN, with the explicit support of and even prodding from the allied powers, signed a twenty-one-point "memorandum of understanding" with the Iraqi government ("United Nations," 1992), which affirmed Iraqi sovereignty over all humanitarian activities in all of Iraq (these activities included the allied operations in the "safe haven" in northern Iraq, without making any specific reference to them). In a minimal sense, the memorandum had a symbolic as well as a rhetorical utility for projecting (imagining) Iraqi sovereignty as the principle regulating life activities in the country (when, materially, that was clearly not the case) and for projecting Iraq as a territorially bound, exclusive sovereign space for the habitation of Iraqi citizens—a sovereign space separate from Turkey and Iran.[12] The memorandum simulated Iraq's sovereignty at a moment of its material absence.

In essence, the problem of humanitarian crisis in the Kurdish episode is defined in terms of a figure of aberrance, namely, the refugee, not the state, who stood as the problematic body to be treated and whose body became a material and symbolic site of recovery of the state's imagery and reality of its powers, capacities, bounded territory, and people. In the resolution, as in other instances of dealing with the refugee problem, the prescribed solutions lie in recovering the potential citizen in the refugee by reentering the refugee into the citizen/nation/state hierarchy. In real terms, that means the reestablishment of not just the refugee's territorial ties with the national community or the country of origin from which the refugee comes, but, more importantly the refugee's ties with the state, which is the legal representative and protector of the national community. Accordingly, writing in the Turkish daily *Cumhuriyet*, Kemal Kirisci, an academic with close ties to the Turkish foreign ministry, identified "repatriation" as the best solution to the Kurdish refugee problem:

> The best solution to the problem is to create the environment which would be conducive to returning the refugees to Iraq on their own cognizance, an objective for which Turkey needs urgently to work through diplomatic channels. This objective may yet necessitate a pragmatic approach toward the Iraqi government. If a political solution that will facilitate the refugees' return to their homes is not found soon, Kurdish refugees may find themselves in the same circumstances as the Palestinians who have been living in refugee camps for the last 43 years. (1991; my translation)

The USSR ambassador to Turkey, Albert Cernisev, argued similarly in an interview with a *Cumhuriyet* reporter: "There is no alternative for the Kurdish refugees but to return to their homes. What is of crucial importance is the question of confidence and trust between those who left their homes and Baghdad. This confidence could be rebuilt in time" (Congar, 1991; my translation).

To exist again, the ambassador asserted, the refugees must return "home"; they must have their territorial ties reestablished with the community of citizens represented and protected by the Iraqi state. What is clear here is that specific problematizations of the refugee in humanitarian crises affirm not just the primacy and normalcy of the subjectivity of the citizen but also its absolute necessity for the possibility of living "at home" in peace. It is only the citizen-subject who can exist properly, in a community of citizens made possible only within the spatial borders of the sovereign state. As Ambassador Cernisev intimated, one must not even think that there could be an alternative to territorially bound homes and citizenship that is anchored in the state and that affords rights and privileges still denied to refugees. Located outside the state's order, refugeeness represents homelessness, and homelessness represents a lack of agency, a voicelessness, or, as Malkki puts it, a "speechlessness" (1996: 378). "Persons who find themselves in the classificatory space of 'refugee,'" writes Malkki, "suffer from a peculiar kind of speechlessness. . . . Their accounts are disqualified almost *a priori,* while the languages of refugee relief, policy science, and development claim the production of authoritative narratives about the refugees" (386). Refugees may speak, but they are not heard. "People often ask what it was like," says a Bosnian woman refugee, "but most people do not listen when you tell them how bad it really was" (Amnesty International, 1997: 3). Beyond losing their voices, refugees also lose their faces and names, coming to project an "anonymous corporeality" (Malkki, 1996) on a canvas of a mass of humanity without faces, without names, and without personal histories to reckon with.

In this sense, and not surprisingly, the discourse of intervention regarding the refugee mirrors the wider discourse on the refugee, which denies the refugee any proper individual subjectivity through mutually referencing, co-recognizing, standard representations and managerial practices. But humanitarian intervention discourse regarding the refugee does more than simply efface the refugee by rhetorically emptying the content of the refugee's otherwise complex experiences. The humanitarian intervention discourse actively reinscribes the refugee, refilling the content of the refugee's experiences through languages of securitization. Rewritten through the signs, tropes, and codes of national and international security, refugees in humanitarian intervention discourse appear not simply as a mass of humanity in need of the international community's help, but as a potentially dangerous mass of humanity, "flowing," "flooding," and posing difficulties to the international community's logic and praxis.

The Kurdish refugee crisis uniquely enables one to focus on the linkages between refugees and security issues in constructing humanitarian interventions. Other humanitarian crises, such as that in Bosnia, exhibit similar dynamics of problematization historically and in a contemporary sense, centering on the saliency of the problem of the refugee.

It is indisputable that interventions in Somalia, the former Yugoslavia (particularly Bosnia and Herzegovina), and Rwanda came in the face of massive human displacement. In all these situations, the refugee problem was identified as a source of insecurity and instability, especially for the neighboring countries. The case of Somalia, where, according to many observers, the intervention was purely humanitarian owing to a disintegration of the Somali state, attests to the significance of human displacement in humanitarian interventions in general and as regards security constructions in particular. The leading UN refugee agency, the UNHCR, pointed to the security implications of the refugee situation in Somalia for the neighboring countries:

> In the turmoil that had befallen Somalia, the refugees were fleeing a combination of violence, anarchy and drought. The obvious dangers of a continuing exodus of epic proportions, and the difficulties of providing assistance in the midst of the insecurity that plagues Northern Kenya, were compelling arguments for looking beyond the traditional approach of delivering assistance only to the country of asylum. At the request of the UN Secretary General, UNHCR therefore launched a cross-border operation in September 1992 with the aim of stabilizing population movements inside Somalia itself and stemming the momentum of refugee flows into neighboring countries. The cross-border programme was given a new lease with the deployment of a US-led multi-national force in December 1992. (1993b: 93–95)

The construction of the refugee in security terms is unequivocal in a UN report appropriately entitled *International Co-operation to Avert New Flows of Refugees*:

> Massive flows of refugees could impose great political, economic, and social burdens upon the international community as a whole with dire effects on developing countries, particularly those with limited resources of their own. It is stressed that massive flows of refugees may not only affect the domestic order and stability of receiving states but also jeopardize the political and social and economic developments of entire regions and thus endanger international peace and security. (UN General Assembly, 1986)

Similarly, in Bosnia, the humanitarian intervention came on the heels of what the UNHCR called the "upheaval in the Balkans," manifested most impressively in the displacement, both internal and cross-border, of 3.6 million people by July 1993. Not unlike the safe havens that had been established in Iraq in 1991 to keep the Kurds in Iraq, thus placating Turkey's fears and projecting multiple national "homes" under the signs of Turkey, Iraq, and Iran, dozens of so-called safe havens (which, as we now know, were not so safe) were established in Bosnia by way of humanitarian intervention under the auspices of the United Nations. Shortly after the policy went into effect, Amnesty International produced a report in which it criticized the European governments for closing their doors to refugees from Bosnia by using safe havens as an excuse. "European governments," the report stated, "led by member states of the European Community (EC), have taken the position that people fleeing Bosnia-Herzegovina should remain in safe areas as close to their homes as possible. As a means of implementing this policy most European governments have imposed visa requirements for people from the former Yugoslavia" (1993).

The European governments steadfastly declared, just as Turkey had claimed in denying the Kurds refuge in April 1991, that all their policies were devised based on their commitment to international refugee regime instruments, particularly the 1951 UN Geneva Convention and the 1967 UN protocol on the status of refugees, to which all now turn for anchor in speaking on the subject of the refugee.[13] In effect, the very instruments that were put in place to "help" refugees find refuge were appropriated actually to deny them the refuge they so badly needed.[14] The Amnesty International report disputed the enunciated commitment and futilely went on to protest the restrictions by arguing that "people at risk of serious human rights violations have an internationally-recognized right to seek asylum in other countries" (1993). Not many governments listened when the UNHCR, the appointed guardian of the internationally recognized refugee rights, agreed with the Amnesty report and appealed to the European governments not to limit the right of refugees to apply for asylum. The appeal fell on deaf ears, as particularly the European Union (EU) member countries proceeded to institute some of the most draconian measures under the guise of harmonizing EU immigration policies (J. Bhabha, 1993a; 1993b). On 6 June 1993, the *Manchester Guardian Weekly* heralded the coming of these policies, which had been formulated by the newly formed Expulsion Sub-group of the Ad Hoc Group on Immigration (Carvel and Webster, 1993).

Instead of accepting refugees, European governments opted for a "safety zones" policy that would supposedly facilitate the provision of assistance to the needy (Frelick, 1993: 443). However, far from being a breakthrough for assistance to the needy, the policy, argues Frelick, "instead affirmed power politics as usual. . . . The rhetoric was humanitarian. . . . But there was something else going on: the prevention of a refugee flow" (441–42). After all, the French foreign ministry spokesman, Daniel Bernard, had said, "We have to try to keep them in [the former] Yugoslavia" (qtd. in Frelick, 1993: 443). But why, and at what cost to refugees themselves? The real cost to refugees was diffused and obscured in what Stjepan Mestrovic called "the simulation of concern, the fiction of humanitarianism" in a "postmodern response to human suffering" in which "arrested," that is, manipulated, representations (Bhabha, 1983: 37) created a sterilized industry of "suffering-watching" from a safe distance.[15] A Bosnian refugee, however, knew better of the realness of the suffering: "Everybody slaughters whom he chooses and where he chooses. Total freedom of slaughter and harassment . . . nobody is responsible for anything" (Amnesty International, 1997: 16).

Europe's determination not to allow massive refugee movements out of the former Yugoslavia finds its roots in the ever-intensifying strategy of "writing" the refugee through the semiotics of security images and identities. Jef Huysmans (1995) calls this the "securitization" of the refugee, whereby refugee images and identities are encoded and recoded through the extant lexicon of security notions and concerns and the recoded refugee images and identities in turn are appropriated to conceptualize the security images, identities, and subjectivities centering on the sovereign state.

There has been a proliferation of institutional, scholarly, and popular discourse in this direction since 1990. Consider the following examples:

> With a growth in unwanted and often uncontrolled population movements, refugees are increasingly perceived as a challenge to the integrity and security of both sending and receiving states. . . . What is clear is that it no longer suffices to discuss the subject of refugees within the narrow national context or as a strictly humanitarian problem requiring humanitarian solutions. . . . Refugee problems are in fact intensely political: mass migrations create domestic instability, generate interstate tension and threaten international security. (Loescher, 1992a: 4–5)

> Unwanted migration, such as refugee movements, can also frequently threaten inter-communal harmony and undermine major societal values by altering the ethnic, cultural, religious and linguistic composition of the host populations. (Loescher, 1992a: 41)

> At local levels throughout Europe, grass-roots organizations and politicians are having to cope with increasing numbers of incomers. The authorities' concern is heightened by their realization that at the heart of the problem is the question of how far immigrants threaten the internal security of Europe. (Stewart, 1992: 1)

> Europe sees immigration as inextricably bound up with its political, economic, and social well-being, as well as its future security interests. (Meissner et al., 1993: 53)

> II. THREAT—8. To illustrate . . . , included are the maps describing the areas of political conflict, missile technological capacity and potential for massive migratory movements . . . as well as a table of ballistic missile technology along the southern Tier [of Europe]. Many of these threats have either been dealt with in other NAA reports or because of their characteristics, can not be discussed here at length, i.e., immigration or proliferation of military technologies. Nevertheless it is important to underline their interconnection. For instance, in the case of massive flow of migration, it may represent a serious threat to the stability of immigrant receiving countries. Proof of such an assertion can be found in the Albanian case with relation to Italy. . . . A main object of co-operation should thus be the promotion of the strength of the nation-state system in the southern region to obtain permanent and stable partners of co-operation. (Herrero, 1993: ii)

> Borders are becoming increasingly permeable which, combined with instability or lack of economic perspectives in the poor countries, leads to the intensified immigration and refugee processes, fueling fears of other states and serving as a source of hostility. (Pastusiak, 1994)

The crucial effect here is not just that the refugee images are encoded through the locutions of security concerns but that these images, once encoded with specific statist security images and identities, are lent to the reconstitution of statist images and identities. They are lent to the task of statecraft in precisely those times, as Longin Pastusiak notes, when the perennial projects of statecraft—borders, citizens, domestic community, sovereign territory, and so on—are called increasingly into question in the crucible of transversal political and economic occurrences (see also Ashley, 1993: 5–10; Huysmans, 1995: 63; Hoffman, 1993: 202).

Huysmans writes instructively, speaking of "securitization of migration" in general as a "stabilizing strategy" of the state: "In contemporary Europe, the nation-state is no longer taken for granted. In the struggle for the nation-state, a highly securitized migration could well be a strategy for re-affirming the identity of the state" (1995: 63). Hoffman concurs, while also introducing the notion of intervention into the debate. It might be possible, he suggests, "to see acts of intervention (or nonintervention) as the affirmation of existing boundaries and their constitution" (1993: 202). Ashley argues that all these activities have to be subsumed under the sign of modern statecraft, by which the identities and subjectivities of the modern state are produced and stabilized at any particular time in history, including times of uncertainty and crisis. "Modern statecraft," he writes,

> works to fabricate and institutionalize a new problematization that incites and conditions people's attention to those emergent uncertainties, ambiguities and indeterminacies that put in doubt the identity of "man in domestic society." In the same stroke, it fashions, exemplifies, and offers patient instruction in an aesthetics of existence whose values and criteria dispose people both (a) to understand these uncertainties as problems and dangers that occupy some region of "anarchy" external to the domestic time and place of the sovereign "man" and (b) to willingly support a state, its law, its technologies of violence, its administrative resources and its international regimentation

> of economic, environmental [and political] policies as means by which the problems and dangers of "anarchy" might be solved or brought under control in the name of "man." (1993: 9)

Refugees, securitized in and through humanitarian interventions, stand, in this sense of statecraft, as objects of interventions that are paradigmatically statist, because "the intervening parties operate within a statist paradigm and demonstrate a fundamental incapacity to imagine anything but a state-centered solution" (Pieterse, 1997: 86). The humanitarianism of humanitarian interventions is paradigmatically delimited by its statism. True to their statist ontology, humanitarian interventions are oriented, as if by "habitus," less to care for the needy, the displaced, the one in crisis, the refugee, and more to manage the "people-producing" activities (Appadurai, 1996) across borders that are so essential for the state's practical and representational claim to rule over a bounded territory and a territorially bound people.[16] Refugees become instrumental in this effort, if only in a paradoxical way; they are both disruptive (problematic) and recuperative (resourceful).

They are disruptive, for, doubtless, mass refugee flights call into question the value and effectiveness of the citizen/nation/state hierarchy as the normal organizing hierarchy of life. The event of displacement, the refugee event as constituting humanitarian crises, attests to the fact that even under the all-powerful Leviathan, the state, a "continual fear and danger of violent death" might prevail, and "the life of man" might be "solitary, poor, nasty, brutish, and short" (Hobbes, [1651] 1962).

Characterized by such conditions, refugee crises as humanitarian crises do not bode well for a successful articulation and empowerment of the organizing hierarchy as imperative for order, stability, peace, and security in life and for hope for the future. If left unregimented, refugees undermine the efforts to effect this hierarchy. This danger, and thus the contingency of the hierarchy itself, was clearly recognized in the UN report *International Co-operation to Avert New Flows of Refugees,* which stated that "massive flows of refugees may not only affect the domestic order and stability of receiving states but also . . . endanger international peace and security" (UN General Assembly, 1986: 9).

In this sense, refugees manifest the difficulties of the sovereign state, or state sovereignty. Paradoxically, however, through humanitarian interventions, refugee bodies also work as resources for statecraft. Earlier in the book, I wrote that refugees politicize space by imploding the cartographic logic that claims to engender rootedness. Building on Michel de Certeau (1988), I wrote that refugees become the stories that cut across such logic. It is now important to add that as refugees cut across space, they themselves—their bodies, their stories, their real and constructed images—become "spaces" just as political and open to reinscription and redrawing as the maps they renegotiate and shift. It is in this sense that actual refugee bodies, such as the Kurdish refugees who straddled the borders of Turkey, Iran, and Iraq in April 1991, work as concrete, material, and indeed, corporeal links between the principle—the claim—of state sovereignty articulated to the citizen/nation/state hierarchy and practices of statecraft that strive to effect the contingent realities of the hierarchy in time and space and to present them as normal and necessary to peace and security in life. It is to this use that humanitarian interventions are put as mechanisms of intergovernmental regimentations of the fears and desires of people, orienting activities regularly, repeatedly, and reliably enough amid incessant transversal challenges and difficulties to secure the state's universal order, both imagined and real."

WORDS OF EMPHASIS

Humanitarian interventions make it possible to craft historically contingent relations and institutions of the sovereign territorial state intergovernmentally. Curiously, the general argument about intergovernmental statecraft finds supportive evidence in the shifting context of an institutionalized site of intergovernmentality—the United Nations. In a 1994 speech on the role of the UN in a changing world, then secretary-general of the United Nations Boutros Boutros-Ghali spoke of "enlightened multilateralism as the guarantor, not the enemy, of state sovereignty and the integrity of state" and identified the United Nations, "an instrument of its member states," as the agent of "enlightened multilateralism." "Member states," he further maintained, "must take on a new responsibility. They should see the United Nations as the protection of their will, not as something separate and apart." To do otherwise, Boutros-Ghali cautioned, "would mean a descent into ever-deepening troubles and ultimately, chaos" at a time of unprecedented global interactions.[17]

I suggest that humanitarian interventions do in fact represent activities of statist multilateralism; however, they are oriented more to regiment difficulties of statecraft in power politics in an age of transnationalization and less to serve the needs of those who are under duress. They surely do not represent an enlightenment or a qualitative shift in ethics of governance in terms of human rights in the so-called international community, if it is understood as consisting of states. J. N. Pieterse's words are fitting: "Does this seem cynical? What is cynical, and what is disturbing about humanitarian interventions, is the stark discrepancy between moral pathos and actual engagement" (1997: 88).

Let me emphasize that I am not trying to negate the "humanitarian" dimension in interventions. To claim this without any qualification would be essentializing and unsyncretic, denying to (what go under the name of) humanitarian interventions the syncretic possibilities of human-oriented moments and impulses. As with other projects of power and governance, humanitarian interventions may and do escape the control of their protagonists in what Fredric Jameson (1981) calls "politically unconscious" ways and enable human-oriented moments even when they are principally oriented by governmental concerns. In other words, humanitarianism in humanitarian interventions is possible, but not in the epistemology it is predicated on, conceptualized in congruence with the logic of territorial statism and its trappings of exclusionary ethnicized, nationalized, and racialized identities. Rather, humanitarianism becomes possible precisely when it frees itself from the statist logic, however tentatively and temporarily. Otherwise, humanitarianism in humanitarian interventions—at least, historically—remains thoroughly marginalized to the needs of statism.

From a normative standpoint, the situation certainly could be better. There are those who are saying just that and more, embracing the emergent genealogical attitude toward the refugee and attempting to historicize the refugee with a view to listening to and hearing the refugee. Liisa Malkki emphatically argues: "It is necessary to state that these forms and practices of humanitarian interventions do not represent the best of all possible worlds, and that it is politically and intellectually possible to try to come up with something better"

(1996: 389). This may indeed be possible, but, more often than not, it is not even attempted, not because it is not desired but because its possibility is imagined only within the paradigmatic bounds of the statist array of identities, institutions, and relations.

To paraphrase Michel Foucault, humanitarian interventions represent a dimension of a statist regime of governmentality by which men govern men (1991: 79). Two intimately interconnected paradoxes, as I have described, effect a humanitarian intervention dimension of the regime. The paradox of the refugee enables a myriad of practices of statecraft, of which humanitarian interventions constitute a strategic manifestation. Such interventions are practices of statecraft, but they themselves are paradoxical in that they recuperate the statist images, identities, and subjectivities in the very events of violation that are presumed to undermine statist relations and institutions. Inasmuch as humanitarian interventions target refugees as objects of intervention, they appropriate refugees to the task of statecraft; refugees become not only a manifestation of the difficulties for the sovereign state but also the site of statist practices that, attendant upon refugees, endeavor continuously to rearticulate the state-centric imagination of life possibilities in local and global interactions. The site of the refugee reconceived in humanitarian interventions becomes a transformative site of modern statecraft. As Jan Jindy Pettman puts it, "Bodies, boundaries, violence, and power come together in devastating combinations" (qtd. in Eleonori, 1997: 37).

6

Refugees, Predicaments of Territorial Democracy, and Statecraft in Europe

The world we live in is one in which human motion is more often definitive of social life than it is exceptional.

—Arjun Appadurai
"Sovereignty without Territoriality:
Notes for a Postnational Geography"

Once viewed as minor irritants, asylum seekers, refugees, and immigrants are increasingly seen as sources of change and transformation for the places they affect.[1] Scholars and policy makers alike seem to concur on this point, though they arrive at different interpretive conclusions as to the nature of changes spurred by refugees and immigrants.

European governments generally share in this view, though mostly they construe refugees, asylum seekers, and immigrants more as people posing various forms of risks and threats and less as people under duress. Consequently, as a commentator observes, in recent years, "from Sweden to Spain, European governments fearing that a wave of asylum seekers threatens prosperity and a social cohesion [are] tightening access and eligibility for asylum" (*Migration News*, June 1994). "Britain," said the British home secretary Michael Howard, "should be a haven for refugees, not a honey pot," as he simultaneously introduced a draconian asylum bill that effectively negated the possibility of access to that haven (qtd. in *Migration News*, December 1995). Not many qualified for the "haven," a reality that is increasingly prevalent as countries close their doors to "socially and politically unsustainable" elements (qtd. in *Migration News,* May 1994).

In the academic realm, an increasing number of scholars (Loescher, 1992b; 1993; Ferris, 1993a; Stewart, 1993; Suhrke, 1993; Rogers, 1992) now agree on the significance of international migration in its varying forms for the rethinking of a wide range of issues central to the dynamics of the post–cold war world. Gil Loescher (1993), Elizabeth Ferris (1993a), Rachel Brett and Elaine Eddison (1993), and Jürgen Habermas (1992) remind us, echoing the voices of the policy makers, that issues of asylum and refugeeism exceed the bounds of humanitarian concerns, for they touch directly on debates over national and international security, nationalism, ethnicity, development, citizenship, and democracy. Academic commentaries on human migrations are more varied than their governmental counterparts. They produce as many critically optimistic accounts as diagnoses that corroborate the pessimistic or alarmist governmental appeals on the subject.

In a special issue of *Praxis International* on citizenship, democracy, and national identity, Habermas brings to the fore one of the immigration-related subjects that has spurred popular, institutional, and academic concern. Habermas situates the immigration debate in the heart of questions of citizenship, democracy, and national identity in the contemporary currents of history in European spaces:

> The tremendous influx of immigration from the poor regions of the East and South with which Europe will be increasingly confronted in the coming years lends the problem of asylum seekers a new significance and urgency. This process exacerbates the conflict between the universalistic principles of constitutional democracies on the one hand and the particularistic claims of communities to preserve the integrity of their *habitual ways* of life on the other. (1992: 1)

Habermas, of course, is not alone in linking immigration, refugeeism, and asylum with the notions of citizenship, nationality, and democracy in Europe. In fact, a literature precisely on these themes has proliferated since the dissolution of the East-West conflict. Nowadays, to study immigration or refugeeism is inescapably to study issues of democracy, citizenship, and nationality. Conversely, to study notions of democracy and democratic practices, citizenship, and political community and its transformations in Europe means also to examine questions pertaining to immigration and refugeeism in Europe.

The titles of recent studies alone reveal the theoretical and thematic interfaces of immigration and refugeeism with citizenship and democracy: "Citizenship for Some but Not for Others: Spaces of Citizenship in Contemporary Europe" (Kofman, 1995); "International Migration and the Politics of Admission and Exclusion in Postwar Europe" (Leitner, 1995); "Migration and European Nationalism" (Walsh, 1993); "Citizenship and Exclusion: Radical Democracy, Community, and Justice" (Bader, 1995); "Democracy and Demography" (Greenhouse, 1994); "European Citizenship, European Identity, and Migrants" (Martiniello, 1995); "Political Asylum, Immigration, and Citizenship in the Federal Republic of Germany" (Steger and Wagner, 1993); "Immigration and Republicanism in France: The Hidden Consensus" (Hollifield, 1994); "A Host Country of Immigrants That Does Not Know Itself" (Schnapper, 1991); "Refugees in Sweden: Inclusion and Exclusion in the Welfare State" (Ring, 1995); and "Exclusion, Injustice, and the Democratic State" (Walzer, 1993). In all of these and other studies, the theoretical premise is that moving people, whether called refugees or immigrants, or economic or political refugees, or voluntary or forced migrants, affect either directly or indirectly the relations and institutions of participatory politics and democracy in Europe. In most of these and other studies, however, the effects of moving people are construed generally as being negative, defined only by a capacity to disrupt the inveterate processes and practices of democracy by placing "extra" burdens on them.

Against this prevalent conceptualization, I, too, explore the effects of refugee, asylum, and immigrant movements on democracy, democratic projects and practices, and subjectivities, particularly in Western European spaces. However, reading the refugee and asylum scenes differently from the prevailing conceptualization, I see refugees, asylum seekers, and immigrants not simply in negative terms, that is, in terms of their capacities to effect disruptive changes in sites of governance, including in sites of what William E. Connolly (1991) calls "territorial democracies" in Europe. Rather, I see the refugee and immigrant subjectivities in their paradoxicalness, manifested simultaneously in their capacity to force radical changes in various sites of territorial governance and in their vulnerability, both literally and metaphorically, which is rhetorically harnessed through the vocabularies of race, ethnicity, religion, and culture to various politico-administrative projects useful for the very sites of governance in which refugees, asylum seekers, and immigrants find themselves. I argue that refugee and immigrant subjectivities are similarly paradoxical in their effects on various practices that go under the name of territorial democracy in Europe; they are not only resistant and disruptive but also accommodative of and instrumental to certain processes and projects of territorial democracy organized around the modern, territorial nation-state. Refugees and immigrants, for example, are resistant insofar as they transgress political and cultural borders and boundaries and undermine familiar meanings of democratic life and its institutions as the domain of the "citizen." Their movements partake in activities that construct and negotiate new identities for the subject of democracy in Western spaces. However, they also accommodate or recuperate some of the conventional practices of democracy inasmuch as they participate in the exclusionary legal, cultural, political, and economic practices of a specific kind of democracy, which privilege the citizen as the proper entity adequate to the task of democracy and the sovereign territorial state as the facilitator of the conditions of democracy.

I contend that this paradox finds expression in contemporary Western European spaces in the midst of an unprecedented and ever increasing agitation and incitement around the names of refugees, asylum seekers, and immigrants. These incitements render the refugees, asylum seekers, and immigrants *visible* beyond their real, corporeal presence. This extravisibility is of crucial importance to the issue of democracy in Europe, both theoretically and substantively. Therefore, I begin here, locating my interests in the issue, both theoretically and normatively, at the juncture of these incitements. I do so not because I think these incitements are simple, uninterested representations of refugees, asylum seekers, and immigrants in their relation to European democracies, but because I think these incitements make possible the specific convergent representations of refugees and immigrants that then paradoxically become instrumental in the conventional practices of territorial democracies. These representations, in other words, are discursively orchestrated practices that work to reaffirm the relations, institutions, and identities of the territorial, citizen-oriented democracy. More importantly, however, to the extent that territorial democracy is a specific manifestation of the sovereign territorial state, I argue that representations instrumental to the conventional practices of democracy are also enabling representations of the state that afford the state its raison d'être and that enable its relative centrality in life precisely when that centrality is being diffused in the crucible of extrastatist developments in the world. In this sense, these representations of refugees and immigrants, produced in and through proliferating convergent incitements, are also nothing less than practices of statecraft.

Contextualized in light of these arguments in Western European spaces of democracy, particularly in France, Germany, and Great Britain, in this chapter I have two overlapping objectives. The first objective is to explore how refugee and immigrant movements affect, that is, challenge as well as become the subjects of, the practices and processes by which the conventional citizen-oriented, territorializing conceptions of democracy are rearticulated in Western European spaces. The second objective is to explore how these rearticulations and reconceptualizations could be comprehended as practices of statecraft, practices that afford the state its "reasons for being" in a world where its practical relevance to the lives of people is being attenuated day in and day out.

I start with a brief outline of the statist territorial democracy, also referred to as the citizen-oriented democracy, through the works of Connolly (1989; 1991) and R. B. J. Walker (1991a; 1991b).[2] I start with these scholars, for their work on the connections between the notion of territorial democracy and the sovereign territorial state most effectively enables me to introduce the notion of the deterritorialized, migrant subject into the discussion of the topic. Their work facilitates my contribution to the theoretical discussion and helps clarify my normative orientations, that is, my concerns as an immigrant, a refugee, with regard to the practical consequences of the politics around the issue. In what follows, I hope to articulate these concerns with a view to exploring openings for more tolerant and more compassionate conversations on an issue otherwise ripe for manipulation.

DEMOCRACY, TERRITORIALITY, AND THE SOVEREIGN STATE

Connolly (1991) and Walker (1991a; 1993) contend that, in late modernity or postmodernity in Europe, when one thinks of democracy, one necessarily thinks of the relations and institutions of a territorial democracy defined in terms of the sovereign territorial state and its counterparts, the citizen and the nation (Connolly, 1991: 463). The statist, territorial democracy is rooted in a political imagination that is based on

> (1) the grounding of an internal politics upon a contiguous territory; (2) the recognition of a people (or nation) on that territory, bound together by a web of shared understandings, identities, debates, and traditions, which, it is said, makes a common moral life possible and provides the basis upon which distinctions between citizen/alien and member/stranger are constituted; (3) the organization of institutions of electoral accountability and constitutional restraint that enable people on the territory with shared understandings to maintain legitimate rule over themselves while protecting fundamental freedoms and interests; . . . (5) the elaboration of a series of internal differentiation that enables a plurality of styles of life to coexist within the territory of the state; and (6) the recognition, as sovereign, of external entities that cross a minimal threshold with respect to the preceding elements . . . making it possible for the internal politics of legitimate rule to be ratified by recognition of the sovereignty of each state by others. (Connolly, 1991: 463–64)

According to Connolly, this imagination fosters a unique sense of territorialized democracy construed in terms of a desired alignment between accountability in the search for legitimate standards of collective action and the ability to identify them in one territorially bounded place. According to Walker (1991a: 252), the territorialized democracy so construed is an imagined "Hobbesian" move away from anarchy in a moment of contract into a territorially delineated community where the precise limits within which claims to citizenship and community are formulated can be articulated and practiced vis-à-vis other such communities through practices of inclusion and exclusion. Both Connolly and Walker maintain that the notion of statist territorial democracy derives from the invoking of the peculiar statist hierarchy of the citizen/nation/state. Imagined as a corollary to this hierarchy of agents and identities, in the contemporary notion of territorialized democracy, the citizen occupies the central place as the constitutive element of community in the territory or space of the state. It is within this territory of the state that democracy—that is, participation, representation, accountability, dissent, creativity, and change—becomes possible. The territorial state is accorded its significance because it becomes the sole provider and protector of that space, which presumably is the only place enabling both citizenship and democracy. As Walker stresses, "The legitimacy of the state depends in the final instance on the claim that it, and it alone, is able to allow the citizens of particular states to participate in broader humanity" by making possible the presence of the particularity of the inside (1991a: 252).

While Walker points to the contingency of the statist claim over democracy and democratic projects, others move to canonize the statist claim. Michael Walzer, for example, argues that "statelessness is a condition of infinite danger" (qtd. in Connolly, 1991: 471). For him, territorial exclusion and closure, of which states are the agents as well as the embodiments, are the source of democracy insofar as they facilitate the formation of particular shared understandings among people, which in turn facilitate a viable (democratic) political community: "The distinctiveness of cultures and groups depends upon closure and without it, cannot be conceived as a stable feature of human life. If distinctiveness is value then closure must be permitted somewhere" (Walzer, 1983: 38–39). According to Walzer, territorial states afford this closure, which makes possible the determination of particular shared meanings around which a distributive democracy can be established and practiced: "A stateless world would be a world without particular meanings inhabited by radically deracinated men and women," hence without democracy (34; also see Walzer, 1993).

Although he does not subscribe to the exclusivist view propounded by Walzer, Jürgen Habermas nonetheless suggests that "democratic processes have hitherto only functioned within national [read territorial] borders" (1992: 9):

> The nation state provided both the infrastructure for rational administration and the legal frame for free individual and collective action. . . . The nation state laid the foundations for cultural and ethnic homogeneity on the basis of which it then proved possible to push ahead with the democratization of government since the late eighteenth century although this was achieved at the cost of excluding ethnic minorities. (2)

"To date," he continues, "genuine civil rights do not reach beyond borders" (9). The state, then, necessarily stands at the heart of democratic imaginations and possibilities.

Paraphrasing John Herz, Connolly unfolds the otherwise confounding, circular logic of territorial democracy:

> A nation is at home with itself only if it governs itself; nation states need internal legitimacy to promote stability, external security and economic efficiency; the most legitimate mode of self-governance today is democracy; and modern democracy must be organized within the bounded territory if it is to be. (1991: 475)

This statist claim on the nature and possibilities of community and democracy has been the dominant claim both historically and contemporarily. While in fact this might have been the case, as Walker too notes, this dominance has never been free of challenge; it has always been contingent. The statist claim on the democratic project has had to be continually produced in the face of disparate challenges. Its perceived permanence is more a contingent historical effect always in the process of being effected through practices of statecraft (Ashley 1993: 28).

Historically, for example, Veit Bader reminds us that the production of the dominant history of the "nation, hence the dominant meanings and practices of participation in the nation, namely, the meanings of democracy, required the erasure of rival memories and histories" (1995: 219). Even Habermas readily accedes to the point when he writes that the production of the nation-state meant the "exclusion" of what were constructed to be the "ethnic minorities" (1992: 2).

Arjun Appadurai also takes note of a permanent exclusivist quality in this history, in that statist claims on democratic projects, though universalist in rhetoric, usually demanded "homogenous people with standardized packages of rights." This, of course, generally resulted in a politics of inclusion and exclusion orchestrated in terms of the logic of a territorializing nation-state (1996: 45). For many people engaged in this modus operandi, such a politics was construed as ineluctable for the realization and maintenance of order and stability as well as democracy, that is, self-governance through the state. The territorially bound, citizen-oriented democracy, as the artifice of statecraft, came thus to be seen as the most rational and most efficient manifestation of national self-expression and governance.

However, as is noted by Habermas, resistances to such politics, far from withering away in time, have proliferated from within and without, as minorities, stateless people, the racially oppressed, refugees, and immigrants have pressed for their rights in various contexts spanning territorial borders and boundaries. Their resistance, coupled with developments in other fields of activity, has challenged the centrality of the modern territorial nation-state as never before.

Nowadays, these challenges to territorializing statist practices arise in multiple forms and multiple fields in the crucible of transversal, globalizing happenings throughout the world. Jef Huysmans, for instance, finds them in the interstices of globalizing economic and political processes that make the distinctions, real or imagined, between local and global and national and international "disappear" (1995: 63). Homi Bhabha thinks of them in terms of "crises of administrative and institutional representability" faced by states in both the North and the South (1994: 269). Ash Amin construes them as those forces which "replace the territorial idea of the local, national and the global spheres of social organization and action by a relational idea that results in global interconnectedness, multiplexity and hybridization of social life at every level" (1997: 129). Guillermo Gómez-Peña calls them pressures that effect a borderization in the world where vast sectors of humanity are deterritorialized in acts that either expand borders or shoot holes through them. We become border-crossers all in the polysemantic geographies of border areas (1996: 102–4).

The challenges are multiple economic, political, cultural, financial, and technological happenings that threaten to undo the time-honored cultural practices by which the state's centrality to the lives of human beings is affected and continually reproduced. Clearly, contemporary developments in the junctures of global or transversal happenings put in question not merely this or that aspect of the modern state as a form of governance, but the state as a whole, as a distinctive coherence, a mentality, a system of governance in and around which everything else is (imagined to be) positioned and by reference to which all things are (supposed to be) rendered meaningful. Such developments, I argue, spell out nothing less than a crisis for modern statecraft.

Of all the challenges that are now threatening to undo the practices of statecraft, the most radically unsettling and most elusive are the deterritorialized and deterritorializing transversal subjects, that is, refugees. However, as I have established, the impact of refugees on the practices of statecraft in general and on the practices by which the citizen-oriented democracy is privileged in particular is paradoxical.

REFUGEES, TERRITORIAL DEMOCRACY, AND STATECRAFT: CHALLENGES AND RESOURCES

The mapping of particular forms of others in popular imagination including vagrants, beggars, and gypsies in the nineteenth century [in Europe] resonates with contemporary state projects which seek to document and identify new alien newcomer groups. . . . The marginal became for the state a permanent feature of its structure, in part the apparatus of the state is constructed on the basis of the existence of this other reality.

—DONALD CARTER
"THE ART OF THE STATE:
DIFFERENCE AND OTHER ABSTRACTIONS"

Ask them about the state, they don't even know what the state is, they only know God.

—SENEGALESE MIGRANT IN ITALY
SPEAKING OF OTHER SENEGALESE MIGRANTS

In reality, the state must be conceived as an Educator. . . .

—ANTONIO GRAMSCI
SELECTIONS FROM THE PRISON NOTEBOOKS

Refugees challenge the time-honored practices of democracy insofar as they call into question the legitimacy of exclusionary political and cultural practices that center on the citizen. By moving into the space of the citizen, they expose the exclusionary limits of conventional narratives of democratic life as the domain of citizens in a domestic community only in spite of their rhetorical universalist justifications. All people might be born equal, but only those who "belong to the nation" (Kristeva, 1991), dictates the logic of the statist territorial democracy, can partake in democracy and enjoy its fruits, such as suffrage. Refugee bodies disrupt that logic and the societal peace and tranquillity it postulates by virtue of presumed "shared understandings" among the members. By their mere presence, refugees force those who hold once-comfortable descriptive and explanatory positions and postures to recognize drastically unfamiliar (hence unaccommodated) forms of otherness and subjectivity, be they in terms of language, skin color, mores, or, as the president of France Jacques Chirac once put it, unfamiliar "smell and noise" (qtd. in Rapaport, 1992: 96). As the novelist Günter Grass points out, they become "irritants" to the phantasm, the chimera of "Germanness," for example, highlighting "the inveterate foreignness that exists between Germans" (1993: 186–88). Referring to the historical paragons of nomadism, the Sinto and the Roma, who face unprecedented levels of hostility in most of Europe, Grass writes: "They could teach us how meaningless the borders are; the Roma and the Sinto do not recognize borders. The Gypsies are at home everywhere in Europe. They truly are what we claim to be: born Europeans" (188). Thus, refugee movements help construct and negotiate new identities for the consideration of democratic programs and projects in Western spaces, though they may not be the most powerful mediators of the new directions of democracy.

Paradoxically, however, by their mere presence in the supposed space of the citizen, refugees also prove to accommodate some of the conventional practices and understandings of democracy. As I have noted, the practical meaning and force of their presence are mediated, co-opted, and deployed as a referential resource for the conventional democratic practices that privilege the citizen as the most proper agent adequate to the task of democracy, the sovereign state as the facilitator of the conditions of democracy, and the sovereign territoriality as the sine qua non for a coherent domestic community in which, as Michael Walzer would have it, democracy becomes possible (1995: 24). As I wrote earlier, the privileging of the citizen/nation/state ensemble as the hierarchy imperative to democracy is quintessentially modernist and not surprising as such. What is more important to note in refugee representations is how refugees figure in relation to this posited hierarchy and how a certain desire for or "will to" this hierarchy is produced and circulated widely, including among refugees who come to construe the hierarchy as indispensable to effective participation in society and who move to affirm it in ways expected of them. If nothing else, given the opportunity, refugees do not remain aloof to the enticements of citizenship. Historically they have shown a willingness to integrate into the citizenship category, to fulfill its demands dutifully and to help stabilize its privileged, but never finalized, content.

Consider, for instance, the case of a man, once a "refugee" but now a "legal immigrant," whom I met in 1993 in El Centro, California, the regional headquarters of the U.S. Immigration and Naturalization Service. The bumper sticker on his car read: "My child is the proud recipient of the good citizenship award." If nothing else, it seems, the stamp of the state afforded this refugee a unique "legitimacy" to enjoy a hot California afternoon in a conspicuous manner.[3]

In fact, the name of the citizen stands at the heart of identity politics organized around the modern notion of the sovereign territorial state, for it is by constructing and reaffirming the voice and content of the citizen that various manifestations of the notion of community—us/them, inside/outside, democracy/nondemocracy—are imagined and questions of membership within the perceived community are resolved (Connolly, 1991: 472). It is here, in the moments and events of constructing the citizen as constitutive of a domestic community of men and women as citizens, that the name of the refugee turns resourceful. Activities that construct an image of the citizen with peculiar characteristics and content are also activities of constructing the noncitizen, who supposedly lacks those essential characteristics. As Ruth Lister puts it, activities of constructing the noncitizen, the foreigner, the refugee, are also constructing the citizen around whose name a community of men and women is organized into a community of citizens with its peculiar hierarchies (1995: 2). As Connolly and Walker intimate, such identity activities construct the identity "walls" that separate "us" from "them," safety from danger, and citizen from noncitizen, stranger, or refugee.

In these moments of identity construction as boundary construction, refugees situated against the postulated normality of the lives of citizens as the agents of democracy appear to be paradoxical supplements (Derrida, 1976). On the one hand, their presence testifies to the imagined completeness of the category of the citizen. On the other hand, that presence signifies its own aberrance and ineffectuality vis-à-vis the posited qualities of citizens. Such moments of supplementarity are also moments of problematization no less important in their total convergent effects on the transformation of the meanings of the category of the citizen and the notion of democracy than the effects of the French Revolution on the emergence of citizenship and democracy. How does this supplementarity work? In answer, the politics of the refugee category (which includes asylum seekers and, in some instances, immigrants) proves helpful.

In its broadest form, as I have shown in earlier chapters, the refugee problem is comprehended in statist terms. Refugee bodies become resources for new problematizations of the contemporary notion of democracy that are intimately bound up with the image of the sovereign territorial state as the sovereign, democratic, national state (Connolly, 1991: 464). The links between the new problematizations of democracy discourse and the problematizations of the sovereign territorial state are clear, since, in the modernist conceptions of democracy, the very possibility of democracy has always been linked to the supposed presence of a well-bounded territory patrolled by the forces of the sovereign state. Therefore, neither the problematizations of state nor the problematizations of democracy are secondary, or tertiary, to one another; rather, they are enabled simultaneously through the same practices. It is the "writing" of the notion of the territorially bounded space that allows for, or makes possible, the "writing" of a community of citizens as forming the perceptual infrastructure—"Frenchness," "Germanness," or "Englishness"—of the modern state. The community of citizens constitutes the sovereign space for the realization of democracy and empowers the state forces for the organization and protection of democratic forces and practices. In other words, such notions as stability, security, community, and democracy are linked to one another through continuing and necessary rearticulations of the notion of sovereignty through a pastiche of territorializing practices of statecraft.

The argument here is basic and derives from the general hypothesis on statecraft that undergirds the central inquiry of this study. As a corollary of this general hypothesis, in this chapter I contend that the ongoing problematizations of the discourse on democracy are not solely attempts to clarify or refine the concept of democracy in the face of transversal happenings, such as the movements of refugees,[4] but also practices of statecraft engaged in statist problematizations of such happenings.[5] Those problematizations work to incite, statize, and regiment transversal happenings, albeit not without resistance and counterproblematizations, as we shall presently see. Consider the following instances of incitement by which the refugee presence is linked conceptually and practically to the prevailing relations and institutions, including those understood to undergird democracy in the West.

In 1993, writing on the increasing visibility of immigrants, refugees, and asylum seekers in Europe, Edward Mortimer, a reporter for the British newspaper the *Financial Times*, took note of an attendant proliferation and intensification of discourse on the issue. "Few subjects," he wrote, "are more intensely discussed between European governments than asylum and refugees with at least 10 intergovernmental bodies holding between them over 100 meetings at ministerial or official levels in the course of 1993." Similarly, Myron Weiner observed that "heads of states, cabinets, and key ministers involved in defense, internal security, and external relations focus their attention more and more on migration and refugee issues, convening more conferences, issuing more reports, writing more regulations and laws" (1993: 91).

Increasing incitement in the governmental and intergovernmental arenas was paralleled by an intensification of incitement in popular European media on precisely this subject. Media reports reflected the complexity and multiplicity of activities that go into problematizations, both of democracy and state sovereignty vis-à-vis the movements of refugees, asylum seekers, and immigrants. Here is a representative sample: "Europe Slams Doors on Immigrants"; "CSCE Leaders Paint a Dark Future of Refugee Wave from East"; "Invisible Barriers Are Going Up as European Borders Open"; "New Wall of Despair in Europe: Even as the Iron Curtain Has Been Lifted, the West Is Erecting Its Own Barrier—This One to Bar Migrating Poor from Rumania, Hungary, and Other Nations"; "Looking Increasingly like Fortress Europe"; "E.C. Gears for Meeting on Immigration Policy"; "Protests Erupt over Vote to Limit Refugees"; "Europe Moves to Keep Out Refugees"; "French Confirm Trains May Be Used to Expel Immigrants"; "E.C. Ministers Agree on Moves to Reinforce Fortress Europe"; "E.C. Gets Tough with Unwelcome Immigration"; "West Discards Welcome Mat for Refugees: Hopes Dashed for Many Fleeing East Bloc"; "Targeting Foreigners—Searching for Germany's Soul"; "Germany: Racism Brings Refugee Rights and Democracy into Focus"; "European Parliament Debates Rise of Racism, Xenophobia, and Extreme Right"; "At the Gates"; "Refugees Challenge a Continent's Stability"; "France Curbs Immigrants under New Law"; "Them"; "Germany, Poland Sign Agreement to Curb Refugee Flow"; "Six Central European Countries to Sign Migration Pacts"; "Germany to Help Czechs to Control Refugees"; "Romanians Become Stateless in Germany to Avoid Expulsion"; "European Walls of Prejudice Unlikely to Halt the Flow of Refugees"; and

"Influx of North Africans Arouses Doubts for France's Melting Pot: Wrenching Questions about Xenophobia, Racism, Citizenship, Assimilation, and National Identity Come to Surface."[6]

These reports surely reflect the complexities of the problematizations of refugee, asylum, and immigrant events vis-à-vis the prevailing democratic relations, institutions, and sentiments, including those in Europe. More importantly, however, coupled with the intensification of activities at the governmental and intergovernmental levels, they constitute a crucial step in problematization: an incitement of popular and institutional discourse on refugees, asylum seekers, and immigrants that, attaining a certain level of hegemonic uniformity through contextual and textual cross-referentiality, works to reinscribe refugee and immigrant identities in a specific way and anticipates, even urges, a certain kind of response in return. Although always facing resistance and not always successful, the discourse works to authorize (make possible) conversations on refugees and immigrants, but ones that are already conditioned. It works to frame the conversations and, more often than not, encourages, for example, a retired woman in Paris to say, "There is not enough wine in the glass, and my benefits are in danger because the government is spending so much to help the immigrants." The extent to which the cross-referentiality of the incitements at various levels and forms frames the debate on refugees and immigrants creates what Edward Said calls a "strategic location" for the discourse, which renders the discourse authoritative and superior vis-à-vis all other possible contesting accounts of what it means to live with refugees and immigrants in the polity. The discourse in circulation then "acquires a mass density and referential power [not only with respect to its constituent parts], but also in the mass culture at large" (1979: 21). It acquires "the power to narrate or to block other narratives from forming or emerging" (Said, 1993: xiii). It becomes hegemonic, doubtlessly, with significant practical-participatory and normative effects and consequences.

I argue that such a development has been under way in European spaces in discussions on refugees and immigrants. The specific vocabulary used in the discussions produces a general convergent effect throughout Europe. As the representative sample of headlines demonstrates, the terms used most are those that certainly connote an underlying economy of desire. Words and phrases like *wealth, poverty,*

Europe, the Third World, the South countries, refugees, illegal immigrants, tide, rush, flood, frontier, border, territory, barrier, wall, fortress, foreigner, citizen, right of blood, right of birth, security, lack of security, stability, destabilization, burden, welfare, warfare, plague, invasion, smell, noise, and many more all converge to produce images of two unassimilable desire-worlds that stand in contradistinction to one another. One is the prosperous, secure, and democratic world of the West European; the other is an amorphous tide, a flow that is besieging Europe from all directions and forcing it to become a fortress in self-defense.

Also constructed in contradistinction to one another are the postulated desiring subjects of these conflicting worlds. On the one hand is the citizen—Pierre, Hans, or Cecile—the proper subject of the democratic European space. She or he is equipped with historical knowledge and cultural experience, "creative energy" and "healthy skepticism," sine qua nons that presumably cultivate the conditions of democracy within community. On the other hand is the stranger, refugee, or immigrant, who is just a part of the tide without any mentionable individuality. He or she appears to have only a collective content and voice: a refugee or an immigrant, not Ravi, Hasan, or Josefina with a memorable individual history. Her or his vocabulary is cast as too strange to be decipherable, and her or his hopes, fears, and desires as too alien and threatening to be embraced into a version of the European aesthetic of life. Here, the problematization of the encounters between citizen and noncitizen places the citizen self against the amorphous flood, the other, in defense of the borders and boundaries of democracy.

The stories of this flood of people that the West now faces are told as the stories of political, economic, and moral "warfare" and "damage" in the heart of the host communities (Rudge, 1988: 11). Faced with this "tidal wave" of the unfamiliar other, the once generous West is now forced to consider its own survival. Thus, questions of citizenship, community, national identity, and democracy gradually become the high issues of the day. "Europeans are worried," writes one author, speaking to the larger issue of immigration, which is emblematic of refugee issues:

> The source of their worry is the increasingly ominous evidence of a new migration of peoples from the east and from the south. There is

> more to this Xenophobia. As the Modern Age began five hundred years ago, the danger of invasions of Europe (a recurrent danger that had existed for more than a thousand years) began to vanish. At the end of the Modern Age that prospect, though in different forms, appears again. (de Lusignan, 1994: 1)

The metaphor of tidal wave takes on a specific millennial meaning—barbarian invasion—that is widely adumbrated, but never publicly enunciated, in the rhetoric of many in Europe, including politicians and journalists. Instead, the phrase "cultural incompatibility" is employed as an encoded signifier for the barbarian-immigrants, "the voracious monster 'Homo migrans,' heading from the South and the East towards the North and the West" (Leitner, 1995: 271, quoting K. J. Bade). The questions as to the survival of community, national identity, and democracy become the prevalent questions of the day. Under siege, Europe is forced to take measures to secure its survival. The headline "Europe Agonizes over Halting Immigrant Rush" attests to this imperative. To those who might question the legality or the ethics of such moves, individual governments respond by arguing that immigration control in the broadest sense is a matter not of racism, xenophobia, or economic apartheid but of rational policy making "dependent upon a nation's capacity to absorb immigrants" (Pasqua, 1994: 33). Host countries, they are told, must take into consideration the economic, sociocultural, and political implications of immigration that might be quite negative, such as rising unemployment among the citizens, increasing pressure on the social and welfare institutions of the host country, and criminality among immigrant populations (Pasqua, 1994).

Official prose invoking the limits of the "nation's capacity" generally assumes a spectral tone in public. As Helga Leitner (1995) points out, it does not matter whether the descriptions of immigrational phenomena are accurate or not. What matters is that such "spectral politics" affords convenient devices for the territorial state dependent for its legitimacy upon the successful production and circulation of territorially bound images and realities of the citizen/nation/state hierarchy.

There are surely counterincitements in Europe as well, activities of incitement that foster cross-cultural solidarities, thus working to diffuse the Manichaean politics of identity that constructs and pits a

"Europe-under-siege" against a "barbarian-immigrant/refugee." In other words, counterincitements in the form of resistance to the intense hostility against the stranger, the refugee, and the immigrant throughout Europe, both by refugees and by the "citizens" of Europe, infuse new meaning into the polity. The very presence of refugees and immigrants in the supposed space of the citizen becomes an act of renegotiating familiar juxtapositionings of identities and their images and meanings. In other words, refugees and immigrants partake unceremoniously and resiliently in the forging of new possibilities for living in the routines of everyday affairs.[7] Undoubtedly, their routines are fraught with all kinds of difficulties, as they usually constitute the underclass of their new homelands. Still, they inject new meaning into the streams of community, perhaps managing to remind some "natives" of their own foreignness, as in the case of a sixteen-year-old French boy, Bertrand, in the company of his immigrant friends from Senegal, Tunisia, and Morocco. He adamantly asks a reporter to note that "his grandfather had come originally from Sicily" (New York Times News Service, 15 June 1995). Naturally, Bertrand represents a larger universe of "natives" whose views of "the foreigner within" are not spectral, exclusivist, or condemnatory. Some of them understand very well that in addition to their primary selves—their citizenship—they have "other" selves—refugee or migrant selves informed by either their present experiences or their lingering memories. Many human-rights or solidarity groups representing millions of people across Europe promote more inclusionary, cross-cultural, and accommodative perceptions of immigrants and refugees. France's SOS Racism and MRAP (Movement against Racism, Anti-semitism and for Peace), Britain's Anti-racist Alliance, Germany's Bundes Deustchland SOS Racism, Belgium's antiracist group MRAX, Spain's APDHE (Spanish Human Rights Association), the Netherlands' NICH (Netherlands International Center for Human Rights), and a number of church-sponsored sanctuaries are among that spectrum of organizations.

In short, as refugees, asylum seekers, and immigrants become or are made to become more visible, incitements on the implications of their presence proliferate. These incitements enable various problematizations, both statizing and destatizing, in their regimentations of refugees or asylum seekers and in the ways in which refugees' presence is linked to the practices and projects of territorial democracy.

REFUGEE PROBLEMATIZATIONS AS TERRITORIALIZING PRACTICES

German Chancellor Kohl's reaction to the prevailing climate of tension in the country in the face of the refugee problem illustrates the statizing of the refugee issues. On 10 December 1992, he declared that "the Federal Republic is a democracy that knows how to defend itself and will prove it" (qtd. in Klusmeyer, 1993: 104). The refugees' presence is thus inscribed as an event that the state must deal with for the sake of the "Republic" and its "democracy." Accordingly, as Weiner suggests, practitioners of the state focus their attention on refugee issues (1993: 91).[8] Furthermore, think tanks, policy groups, international governmental and nongovernmental organizations, and journalists turn to refugees as intriguing objects of contemporary local and global conditions. Ordinary individuals are invited to partake in the process of statizing, by organizing press conferences, town hall meetings, referenda, and elections. Multiple voices and events of incitement proliferate.

In France, the Nationality Act of 1993 (for all practical purposes, an asylum and immigration act) proposed identity spot checks for anybody who did not "look French." In Austria, an official of the Interior Ministry rewrote the security discourse by referring to refugees as "submarines" working under the imagined open seas of Vienna (Reuters, 14 May 1991). In a similar tone, Timothy Garton Ash remarked in the *New York Times Book Review*: "Yesterday the experts were counting warheads; tomorrow they will be counting refugees" (qtd. in Vita, 1991). Meanwhile, in Russia, the strategist for the Interior Ministry's Refugee Department, Col. Zbigniew Skoczylas, spoke of "his" "refugee wars." "I treat it like a war," he said, referring to his strategy for dealing with refugees (qtd. in Vita, 1991). Under a rather telling headline, "Them," Carla Rapaport (1992) wrote of "many Europeans" who, in the face of European unification, feared that the rights of immigrants and refugees and their children would be further extended to include voting and citizenship. In the same report, "many experts and academics," such as Jean-Claude Chesnia, head of the National Institute for Demographic Studies in Paris, warned about the "start of a long period of chaos . . . in the wake of the wave of political and economic refugees who are expected to crowd into Western Europe in the few years to come" (qtd. in Rapaport, 1992: 96). Erwin Faul, a retired German academic, writing in *German Comments*, an English-language daily linked to the ruling Christian Democrats, expressed his fear of the rise of "multiculturalism" in the following fashion: "If the right to participate in politics is granted, ethnic groups will attempt to gain decisive influence on immigration policy and open floodgates, thus withdrawing sovereignty from the traditional leading group" (qtd. in Marshall, 1992).

Consider also the case of Hautmont, a small town in France's depressed northern industrial region, where the residents decided to organize a referendum on asylum and immigration to show their utter displeasure with what they considered to be their government's loose policies on immigrants and refugees (Agence France Presse, 28 June 1992). In the German town of Rostock, as neo-Nazi youth attacked a refugee hostel, reports contended that ordinary people in the neighborhood stood by and applauded the ravaging youth. Reportedly, some were also heard to have been yelling, "Foreigners out. They are not people, they are pigs" (Inter Press Service, 28 August 1992).

The consequences of such practices are instructive: while they place the state in the center of the "refugee" problem as they revolve around the state's laws and institutions, they also affect the process of territorial democracy understood, most simply in terms of political participation in the polity. Historically, in most cases, this process has produced increasingly restrictionist and exclusionary policy responses to refugees and immigrants throughout Europe in the 1990s. Most European countries, including Germany, France, England, Switzerland, Austria, Belgium, and Italy, took dramatic legal measures to curb immigration in any form. The first target of these legal measures was the right of asylum embodied in two United Nations instruments on refugees: the 1951 Geneva Convention and the 1967 Protocol on the Status of Refugees. Arguing that most asylum seekers in Europe were bogus claimants, European countries moved to narrow the scope of right of asylum in practice while publicly expressing their undiminished compliance with the UN instruments. Germany, for example, rolled back the right of asylum in May 1993 by changing the German Basic Law. Although the right to asylum remained in the Basic Law, its scope was drastically curtailed with the introduction of a "third safe country" clause. According to this clause, asylum seekers are expected to apply for asylum in the first safe country they enter. Subsequent legislation by the German government declared all of Germany's neighbors to be safe countries, thus effectively truncating the right of asylum in Germany for all but a few who might manage to fly into Germany. Not surprisingly, the stiffening of the German system intensified responses in neighboring countries such as Poland, the Czech Republic, and Austria. Imitating Germany, Germany's now "safe" neighbors declared their own neighbors to be "safe," signing more bilateral and regional agreements with one another to stem the tide. Not surprisingly, "a 1994 compilation prepared by the Secretariat of Inter-governmental Consultations on Asylum, Refugee and Migration Policies in Europe, North America and Australia, lists 30 separate bilateral agreements involving Western and Central European states."[9] The impossibility of seeking refuge in that environment was amply reflected in a tragicomic newspaper report:

> If you think about it there is really only one ideal asylum-seeker as far as German authorities are concerned. . . . His name is E.T. E.T. has two things going for him. He wants to go home, and is not interested in becoming a permanent burden on the German taxpayer or of taking away a job. Further he arrived not by land but from outer space where there are no safe third countries. . . . Judges in Berlin have just reaffirmed the bizarre clause on "safe third states." . . . That clause was a great idea. So great that the countries bordering Germany have in turn announced that they are surrounded by a ring of safe buffer states. Asylum seekers can now find themselves being passed on from one state to another traveling farther and farther east where human rights count less and less. At some point, the refugee will end up in North Korea, secure third state bordering on the Russian Federation. (Koydi, 1995)

In France, such responses went far beyond asylum to cover immigration in the broadest sense. In November 1993, the conservative French government enacted what are called Pasqua Laws, designed to control the spiraling immigration problem under the motto "zero immigration." First came the nationality law, which eliminated the "automatic and involuntary way in which citizenship was attributed to second-generation immigrants." It required that children born of foreigners (legal immigrants) in France file a formal request for naturalization between the ages of sixteen and twenty-one (Hollifield, 1994: 169). While the nationality law legally marginalized second-generation immigrants, the second law, an immigration bill, was designed to restrict the civil and political rights of immigrants across the board (Hollifield, 1994: 16–17; de Lusignan, 1994). Yet a third law, writes Sami Nair,

> did away with the right of immigrants to obtain a residency permit after fifteen years in the country. . . . Moreover, a broader chill has accompanied these measures: Mixed marriages (between a French citizen and a foreigner) are regarded by officials with suspicion and those who "look" like "foreigners" are increasingly liable to be checked for identity papers. Exclusion, not integration, is now the heart of the agenda. (1996: 78)

On April 1996, a parliamentary commission in France called for further tightening of the country's immigration laws to discourage "unauthorized immigration" to France. Among the forty-six recommendations put forth by the commission were

> restricting the access of illegal aliens to free health care and education, fingerprinting visa applications from some countries, holding suspected illegal immigrants for up to 45 days in order to facilitate their deportation should their illegality be proven, denial of long-term (ten year) residency permits to anyone who has committed petty offenses, including "disturbing the peace" no matter how long ago, and computerized registry of anyone offering lodging or hospitality to foreigners. (*Migration News,* May 1996)[10]

Nair argues that the proposed legislation and recommendations are targeting not unauthorized immigrants, as would be claimed, but legal immigrants and asylum seekers in France (1996: 78).

Not surprisingly, licensed with restrictive immigration and asylum laws, successive French governments, like their counterparts in Europe, have primarily operated with the assumption that the vast majority of those who seek refuge or asylum in France are "economic migrants," not refugees, even if they claim otherwise. At best, we are told by French authorities, these people can be called bogus refugees or bogus asylum seekers, and, as bogus claimants, they must be turned away.

France and Germany have not been alone in promulgating ever more restrictive measures against immigration, whether under the name of reforming asylum procedures, preventing illegal immigration, or controlling legal immigration or refugee movements. In February

1996, for example, the British government passed an "asylum and immigration bill" in the House of Commons, which promised a spate of new restrictions to asylum procedures. Increasing the number of countries on the "white list" of "safe countries" was one promise in the bill. Restricting asylum seekers' eligibility for welfare benefits was another promise. On 21 June, a British court of appeal struck down the welfare ineligibility rule as "uncompromisingly draconian," making it "impossible for asylum-seekers to pursue their claims" (*Migration News,* July 1996; August 1996). As of this writing, even under the new Labour government of Tony Blair, the restrictive mood prevails; refugee lives continue to hang in a precarious balance.

The rising austere mood at the national level has also been reflected in intergovernmental contexts, particularly in the evolution of Europe from an economic community to an economic as well as a political union. European Union members relentlessly, though not always smoothly, have pursued a common European regime on migration and asylum. Several foundational agreements, such as the Schengen Agreements of 1985 and 1990 and the Dublin Convention of 1990, were signed to harmonize immigration policies of the member countries. This European supranational regime curtails in a draconian fashion the right of asylum and the movements of would-be refugees in the community countries.[11] In addition to such supranational arrangements, a wide variety of measures for immigration control were introduced at the intergovernmental level. The result of these moves has been a deepening of intergovernmental regimentations at the community level (see Leitner, 1995; Collinson, 1994; Den Boer, 1995; J. Bhabha, 1993a).[12]

Monica Den Boer argues that all such measures were "control-inspired" and were made possible by rearticulating (problematizing) immigration and refugeeism in terms of internal and external security concerns, that is, by criminalizing the refugee, the immigrant, or the asylum seeker.[13] This ideological reinscription, she writes, "transforms the image of the government into a sacroscant image: . . . the role of the State is pictured as that of the Guardian Angel of national security, and of the 'national' (i.e., non-immigrant population)" (1995: 97). What Den Boer is trying to foreground is that the reconceptualizations of the possibilities and parameters of democracy vis-à-vis migratory pressures amount to much more than is proclaimed in the spectral politics that calls for limits on the participatory rights of refugees and immigrants. To be sure, the effects of producing anxious populations could be and in fact are devastating enough, since they generally curtail the autonomous participation of refugees, asylum seekers, and others in the community (more legally than practically, but with real consequences). Still, the reconceptualizations of democracy are not oriented simply to streamline democratic institutions vis-à-vis the specific difficulty of refugee, asylum, or immigrant movements. They are also practices of statecraft orchestrated to reconstruct and empower territorial democracy continuously as a manifestation of sovereign statist governance. As Den Boer suggests, they are the affirmations of the state in the lives of people precisely when globalizing circumstances seem to be attenuating the state's practical relevance and power in life.

REFUGEE PROBLEMATIZATIONS AS DETERRITORIALIZING PRACTICES

While some practices situate the name of the state centrally as the arbiter of life experiences, there are also practices that produce alternative problematization of the refugee in relation to a host of territorially oriented, exclusionary practices and processes that presumably assign the meanings and boundaries of the normal in the world. These practices work in the extraterritorial field of activity. They exhibit extraterritorial or transborder awareness of and sensibilities toward life. Even when they work in and through the "system," their activities are intensely deterritorializing, as they negotiate new openings within the politico-administrative and cultural space of community. As Julia Kristeva suggests, they infuse ever so radicalizing meanings into even such bedrock concepts as the nation (1992: 50–58). For instance, as a response to the proposed changes in the French nationality law, Harlem Désir, the founder of SOS Racism, launched a new political group in 1992, appropriately named the Movement. The Movement's participation in the processes of new problematizations of democracy was different from that of SOS Racism in that the Movement attempted to open up a space within the official space (parliament) to promote noncitizen voices. It fielded candidates in French national elections as well as in elections for the European Parliament in 1994 to bring to focus, among other things, the rise of racism and xenophobia.[14]

Many such formal and informal groupings are becoming more

active in the political terrain in Western spaces, constantly injecting new meanings and nuances into the discourse of the theory and praxis of democracy. For instance, on 19 June 1993 in France, thousands of people demonstrated against the controversial nationality law, bringing together about one hundred organizations across the spectrum—"anti-racist groups, immigrant support groups, trade unions, foreigner's associations and left-wing parties" (Agence France Presse, 19 June 1993). In France again, in April 1995, people came out in solidarity to protest the death of a Moroccan refugee who reportedly had been thrown into the Seine River by the French fascists. In early 1997, in response to a new effort by the conservative French government to restrict the rights of immigrants and asylum seekers in France, French masses, spearheaded by a group of French artists and writers, came out in support of immigrants. They held placards that intimated the historical migrant or the refugee in the citizen: "1st, 2nd, 3rd generation: we are all children of immigrants" ("Protesters Spotlight Discussion," 1997). Similar demonstrations took place in Germany after a November 1992 arson attack that killed five Turkish citizens, three of whom were children born and raised in Germany. Interesting acts of solidarity were staged throughout Germany. More than three hundred thousand people took to the streets in Bonn to demonstrate their solidarity with the "foreigners." Taxi drivers put signs on their cars declaring, "My friend is a foreigner." Soccer teams played friendship matches with "foreigner" teams. Curiously, even some Turkish and German youth gangs have started collaborating to exact revenge on neo-Nazis. Celebrities, academics, and intellectuals have produced shows, papers, and articles stressing the dangers of the anti-immigrant direction. In one such article, Günter Grass warned of a certain imminent danger in targeting immigrants, refugees, and asylum seekers in the instructive heading "On Loss: The Condition of Germany" (1993). The loss of immigrants, refugees, and other so-called foreigners would be the loss of Germany, Grass was suggesting.

Pierre Bourdieu (1986) points out that similar life positionings or similarities of the mediating experiences of life create contingent alliances out of seemingly disparate and distant lives. In Italy in 1992, the long-standing Jewish community marched along with Arabs, Palestinians, and others in condemning racism. Many Italians, including friends of mine, either joined or supported similar marches.

Meanwhile, Romanian Gypsies in Germany started relinquishing their citizenship to avoid expulsion from Germany. Facing a government crackdown on these and other refugees, in response, some German churches started providing sanctuary to the refugees (Hockenos, 1994: 9; Tactaquin, 1994: 4–6; Reuters, 16 March 1993). In short, many people working with and within these groups and organizations have attempted to inject accommodative meanings into the debate on refugees and immigrants. To this effort, Denny Mendez, a Dominican immigrant living in Italy, contributed by becoming Ms. Italy in 1996. Many protested by arguing, in reifying vocabulary, that a Dominican could not represent "Italian beauty," but many others supported her, thus testifying to the historicity, that is, socially produced nature, of Italy as gendered beauty. The prime minister, Romano Prodi, commented on the selection in language that seemed, on the one hand, inclusive and expansive of Italy as a project and, on the other hand, racializing: "Italy is changing. We also have black soccer players, and this too is a sign." An Italian commentator captured the significance of the event for Italy as a set of historical experiences when he argued, "Italy became a land of immigrants without ever deciding to, and, in some cases, without ever wanting to" (qtd. in Bohlen, 1996).

REFUGEE PROBLEMATIZATIONS AND DEMOCRACY

What are the effects of these refugee events on the relations and institutions around which European peoples claim to have organized their polity and to have shaped their territorial democracies? Proponents of statist moves maintain that the measures taken are not, and thus must not be understood as, nativist antirefugee or anti-immigrant measures. They are instead imperatives forced upon overwhelmed host countries by practical historical realities: the increasing volume, velocity, and disruptive political and economic effects of immigrants, refugees, and asylum seekers. Hear Charles Pasqua, the former French interior minister, on this point: "Immigration policy is neither a 'fortress' nor a 'sieve.' Its policy prescriptions depend upon the nation's capacity to absorb immigrants. It is not a theory, but a political instrument used to address a practical problem" (1994: 33). Even if Pasqua is taken on his word that practical problems deriving from mass immigrant and refugee movements have to be faced, the pivotal question of the effects of the policies in larger societal contexts remains to be addressed (Soysal, 1994; Silverman, 1992). In other words, addressing a "problem" necessarily produces or effects certain changes.

What I contend here could be formulated as follows: Responses to the problem of refugees cannot simply be seen as practical transitory measures, designed merely to handle "the challenges of the day" emanating from migratory movements. These responses—whatever form and content they assume—should be seen as measures that shape and reshape the relations and institutions that make possible and simultaneously condition the scope and properties of peace, security, and democracy in life—whether in France, in Germany, or in the European Community. From the incitement of formal or institutional and popular discourse on refugees through statization, that is, through representation of refugee events as "problems" before the state, to the regimentation of imaginable concrete statist policy responses and resistances to them, responses to refugee movements are measures with significant powers that may or may not reproduce statist images and identities in their societal ramifications.[15]

Clearly, the way in which refugees, asylum seekers, and immigrants are treated, that is, managed and regimented, will have direct effects on specific processes—political, cultural, and economic—by which particular qualities in life, such as democracy, security, stability, and peace, and identities and subjectivities, such as citizenship, are articulated and practiced as qualities and/or subjectivities of desire and privilege. Subjectivities of privilege may at the end of the day truly privilege: "Citizenship in Western liberal democracies," writes Bader, "is the modern equivalent of feudal privilege—an inherited status that greatly enhances one's life chances" (1995: 214). In much the same way, "citizenship," writes Walzer, "has a certain practical preeminence among all our actual and possible memberships," for it allows for an exclusivist membership in the democratic state which is essential for a democratic civil society" (1995: 24). Insomuch as privileged subjectivities afford practical enhancements—say, a passport or a welfare check—they work as instruments of statecraft in projecting the postulated alignment between the ideal of the state and practices that go under the name of the state. If nothing else, responses to immigrants, refugees, and others shape the environment and influence the climate in which people live.

These kinds of identity practices are finding an increasingly more fertile and more profitable ground in refugee problematizations. In this ground, the difficulties and challenges of "being" (German or French, secure and democratic) or "becoming" (German or French, secure and democratic) are being problematized, that is, attended to and renegotiated by way of a multitude of discursive and nondiscursive activities that do not necessarily announce themselves as pure activities of security or democracy but are interlocked and bound up with one another. Even when an activity announces itself as a specific security measure or a democratic measure, it certainly has implications on a variety of other issues and phenomena. For instance, it would be rather naive to suggest that the latest change in the German Constitution with a view to "regulating" asylum has no significant implications for perceptions of security and/or community. Consider what the German interior minister said in the aftermath of signing a treaty with Poland to curb the refugee influx from Poland into Germany: "Illegal population movements represent a threat to political stability in Western Europe" (Reuters, 7 May 1993). The British Foreign Office minister of state, Tristan Garel-Jones, in concurring, said that "maintaining firm immigration controls helps to keep fascism at bay" (qtd. in Den Boer, 1995: 97). In 1997, Alain Juppé, then the French prime minister, criticizing the opponents of the restrictive immigration bill his government had proposed, applied the same logic when he suggested that lack of control over immigration and asylum would amount to "making the bed of extremism" in France ("Protesters Spotlight Discussion," 1997).

Could we then negate the proposition that "a healthy sense of community," "good race relations," or the declared objective of "keeping fascism at bay" inevitably implicate and are in turn implicated in the projects of democracy and their relations to issues of international migration, including refugeeism and asylum? Perhaps that was the question in mind when Ulrike Klose, a German Social Democratic leader, suggested that "unregulated immigration endangers the stability of democracy and only serves right-wing rabble-rousers" (*Manchester Guardian Weekly*, 6 June 1993), or when Habermas wrote that "the right-wing xenophobic reaction against the estrangement (*überfremdung*) caused by foreigners has increased throughout Europe"(1992: 13). Aware of the multiple sites and multiple effects of identity or boundary activities, specific problematizations of democracy, that is, historically contingent rearticulations of democracy, have to be interrogated at the intersections of meanings and identities where the effects of many practical activities in a variety of fields—security, human rights, humanitarian intervention, community, and citizenship—converge to point to, and even exemplify, the shifts as well as recurrences and recuperations in the idea of the state as a form of governance.

INTIMATIONS ON THE PRESENT, INTIMATIONS FOR THE FUTURE

What, then, is one to make of all this agitation and incitement around the name of the refugee in terms of its implications, if any, on the conventional notions of territorial democracy? It is instructive to go back for a moment to two points in this chapter. The first is about "intersections." I have indicated that the effects of many discursive and nondiscursive activities converge to fashion the possibilities and trajectories of living. The second point has to do with problematization. I have interpreted problematization to be a thought process rooted in praxis that constructs a field of activity, its objects and subjects, in terms of problems and difficulties, and then produces responses to those difficulties. I have also argued that the differentiating and hierarchizing contingencies of the present are crucial to problematization in that their focus and intensity condition and mediate the effects of the responses produced.

These two aspects of the chapter are suggestive of the most insightful interpretive direction that this discussion can take in lieu of conclusions. They suggest that in problematization we look for the intersections where the activities of differentiating and hierarchizing among objects and subjects of a field of activity produce specific identity effects. It is those identity effects which stabilize, destabilize, and stabilize again what it means to be that momentary self—citizen, refugee, immigrant, democrat—that has to keep reconsidering itself in view of the availabilities and expectations of resources. When seen from this angle, the previously mentioned activities around the issues of refugeeism, migration, and democracy lend themselves to several possible readings.

First and foremost, it could be argued that convergent effects of the differentiating and hierarchizing activities increasingly speak of a more restrictive and exclusionary democracy. What makes that direction possible is the continuous stabilization through ongoing problematizations of the exclusionary domain or field of identity where the hierarchy between the categories of citizen and refugee is maintained. The citizen represents the qualities of the inside (of a national space)—intelligence, stability, security, cooperation, and democracy—while the refugee represents the "loss" or "lack" of all these qualities, since she or he is not properly rooted on the "inside" even if she or he lives there. Once they move into the space of the citizen uninvited, refugees and immigrants are cast as subjects undermining and even truncating the capacities of the "national inside" so that the state can maintain a viable community, cooperation, solidarity among the citizens and a democratic organization of the polity. In addition to emitting "bad odors" and "unpleasant noise," they become economic burdens by being either "lazy bums on welfare" or by "stealing jobs." The convergent effect of a variety of activities around that hierarchy is to prod many toward embracing more exclusions, thereby differentiating and hierarchizing further. Hence the unceasing hostility toward refugees, immigrants, and "strangers," open or subtle racism, discrimination, exclusion, marginalization, and new restrictive laws and practices. Above all, those convergent effects feed into the birth of a new normative European identity, a mixture of Europeanism and citizen-orientedness of democracy that recognizes itself as the rational, moral, and universal hegemony capable of "adjudicating" the values and labels of humanity (Said, 1993: 45–46).

In the final analysis, this reading argues that the presence of "foreign" bodies, which are marked and so recognized as refugees and immigrants, is thus exploited in Western spaces in order to rewrite limited versions of conventional democracy as a convenient instrument of maintaining Europe's relative economic, political, and cultural privilege. Between the images of the besieged "Fortress Europe" is a projection of a normatively hegemonic Europe (an imagined European self) that wants to see itself as hegemonic in all senses.[16] It wants to colonize (literally and figuratively) but does not want to be colonized; it wants to import or impose voices, identities, and meanings but refuses to consider the legitimacy of other voices and identities. It sees itself as the tourist with an inherent right to go anywhere in the world and to play at ethnography and anthropology but insists that each and every non-European must be either a "fake" refugee or an illegal immigrant trying to sneak in. For that self-imagined and self-projected Europe, there seem to be just two meaningful categories of moving people: the European tourist "self" and the non-Western refugee "other." The reformulations of its democracies reflect this mentality in their construction and treatment of the refugee and the immigrant other.

A second reading starts from the same premise of increased agitation and incitement but derives more optimistic intimations. It is a reading that recognizes the agitation and incitement as a manifestation of disturbances in the once supposedly secure and stable categories of identity in Western spaces now penetrated by refugees and immigrants. Connolly suggests that

> democracy needs common points of reference through which issues can be defined and pressures for action can be organized. . . . It is an egalitarian constitution of cultural life that encourages people to participate in defining their own troubles and possibilities. . . . It is moreover, an ethos through which newly emerging constellations might reconstitute identities previously impressed upon them, thereby disturbing the established priorities of identity/difference through which social relations are organized. (1991: 476–77)

Hence the possibility of enlarging the meaning and scope of democracy as a variety of groups—refugees, immigrants, and citizens—participate in the construction of "adjusted" identities that recognize themselves as contingent and necessary responses to the drastically different difficulties of living. Such are the radical problematizations in which participants are willing, and in fact are forced, to reconsider the familiarity of the strategies and perceptions of selfhood and otherness, belonging and strangeness, possession and loss (of identity), community and outside in the face of changes and transformations. All this takes place in spite of the territorializing moves of the modern state and its claims on the identities of territories called France, England, Germany, Poland, Austria, or Europe. As Connolly suggests, it might just be possible that a common point of reference, the bodies of refugees and immigrants, serves as the instrument for the "disaggregation of democracy in order to escape the confines of the territorial state. . . . Today, a decent democrat must sometimes be disloyal to the state that seeks to own her morally and politically" (1991: 478–79). The examples in Western spaces of resistance to exclusionary and restrictive projects of democracy (such as the resistance of SOS Racism in France, which is able to make extraterritorial connections and establish cross-cultural solidarity, as well as that of refugees and immigrants themselves) are ample demonstration of the possibilities of problematization that will create new openings and possibilities of democracy across spaces and cultures. This might mean a renewal of democracy, albeit in different forms and meanings.

A third, but not the last possible, reading tends to study the new problematizations of democracy as constituting yet one more field of problematization where the activities are geared to fulfill a double function: to reproduce the image of the state while rethinking democracy. In theory, this reading shares with the second one the understanding that, across the globe, novel conditions unleash forces that challenge, undermine, and in fact escape the exclusive claims of territorial states over the images and possibilities of living. However, such challenges do not necessarily herald the demise of statist sovereignty practices. Indeed, as is explained in the paradox of Refugeeism, the practical force of some of these true challenges is co-opted or appropriated by those who practice the territorial state as a form of governance, to stabilize a specific aspect of the state: the community of citizen in which democracy is realized. In other words, the very challenges advanced vis-à-vis the claims of the territorial state always run the risk of lending themselves to political maneuvers working to recuperate the state as a significant and necessary element of intelligent, secure, and democratic living. Nowadays, for instance, it is partially by reference to refugee and immigrant bodies that the rearticulations of democracy in the Western spaces work to reaffirm the inevitability of the territorial state to the normality of life. The epistemic logic and ontology of democratic projects remain rooted in the premise of the world as consisting of discontinuous, separate "culture/[nation] gardens" (Malkki, 1992: 28) such as France, Germany, or Austria, which posit already finished cultural, social, political, and aesthetic projects of identity.

Consider, for instance, the case of a Kurdish refugee in Germany, appealing to the German Federal Constitutional Court in an effort to reverse an earlier decision by an administrative court rejecting application for asylum. What is interesting in this case is the illustration of the statizing language with which refuge or asylum events are encoded and made intelligible at large. In reversing the decision, the Federal Constitutional Court concluded: "A persecution is of political character if it causes purposive violations of the rights of an individual, based on characteristics relevant for asylum, which are of such intensity that *he is excluded from the state's universal peaceful order.*"[17] Clearly, the court started by according an a priori centrality as well as a normality to the state-centric imagination of the world. The premise that the world consists of discontinuous, separate "culture/nation gardens" takes a final, almost sacred form in that the state's order represents the "universal peaceful order," exclusion from which is tantamount to the loss of security and of democratic identities and possibilities. The case of the Kurdish refugee attests to this practical reality.[18]

On the basis of this premise is presumed the presence and primacy of the territorialized order of sovereign states. The difficulty of mounting the kind of challenges to such a territorialization of the possibilities of democracy and democratic practices is indirectly but skillfully implicated by Edward Said:

> When we ask ourselves, "Whose human rights are we trying to protect?" we need to acknowledge that individual freedoms and rights are set irrevocably in a national context. To discuss human freedom today therefore is to speak about the freedom of persons of a particular nationality or ethnic identity whose lives are subsumed within a national territory ruled by a sovereign power. It is also true that withholders of freedom, its abusers so to speak, also belong to a nation, most often also a state, that practices its politics in the name of that nation's best, or most expedient interests. (1993: 46–47)

In an article curiously entitled "A Host Country of Immigrants That Does Not Know Itself" (1991), Dominique Schnapper affirms this territorializing nation-statist logic in an affirmation that, beyond its avowal of statism, has far-reaching practical effects in terms of life possibilities for immigrants, refugees, and others. It is those effects, say, on a refugee's or an immigrant's capacity to participate effectively in the polity, with which I am most immediately concerned. Let me clarify this concern. Schnapper argues that the best possible solution to the questions of immigration is integration into the national communities, for example, integration into France defined by the Jacobin tradition. For her, France is a more or less finished project, a peculiar culture garden with particular sociocultural qualities into which immigrants enter. Once in France, she contends, immigrants must dispense with their particularism, for if their particularisms maintain a bifocality, that is, if they insist on clinging to a culture of another territoriality, thus undermining the culture or tradition that defines France, their particularisms become unacceptable: "France cannot call into question this tradition without calling into question its very existence as a state. No nation can have suicide as a vocation" (59–60).

While seeming to be integrationist, Schnapper's discourse, I argue, participates in spectral politics. It comprehends immigration as a phenomenon of essential otherness defined in the context of France as a finished product, which immigrants are asked to embrace and in terms of which immigrants would remake themselves. Schnapper, however, would be hard-pressed if she were asked, What is this France that immigrants must embrace? Is France not, as Fernand Braudel says, a "forever incomplete project" to which immigrants contribute by virtue of simply being, not by virtue of embracing or dismissing a paradigmatic political, cultural, and/or aesthetic ideal (1988: 23)? Is France not what its participants make of it, a process that is destined to go on indefinitely—always open-ended, "always mobile and processual, partly self-construction, partly categorization by others, partly a condition, a status, a label, a weapon, a shield, a fund of memories . . . a creolized aggregate" (Daniel and Knudsen, 1995: 6)? Braudel, at least, would answer yes, and so do I. This recognition is crucial for questions on democracy and immigrational processes, for it amounts to a recognition of immigrants or refugees not as essential outsiders but as practical insiders to the process that is France, contributing to it in a thousand obscure ways. This is the reality, whether Pasqua or Schnapper likes it or not. Immigrants say, "We are here, we work, we are happy, and we are here to stay." What is at stake, then, is how this reality, the agency of the immigrant, is recognized and accommodated without fueling spectral politics, which surely makes impossible compassionate and tolerant encounters between, in effect, the old-timers and the newcomers in the indefinite task of constructing France. The recognition of the "already insiderness" of refugees and immigrants might just engender further democratic participatory capacities for refugees and immigrants. In this way, the statist territorializing democracy may or may not stand, but, at least in the short run, a certain immigrant named Dilek—my niece living in Germany—stands a better chance of being, becoming, and participating.

Conclusion

No nation is an Island,
Nor a containment even
A wall cannot divide.
The human spirit
Like weeds in concrete
Breaks through.

—CARMEN H. ANDERSON

OUTLINE OF THE HISTORY OF THIS WORK

In the early 1990s, a number of catastrophic events in Iraqi Kurdistan, the former Yugoslavia, and Rwanda sent millions of people on the move. Others, too, across the world left their homes or were forced out of them for various reasons, becoming refugees or displaced people. As the number of refugees and displaced people steadily rose, so did interest in refugeeness and displacement, spurring a proliferation of activities regarding the refugee—a proliferation that in turn rendered the refugee even more visible. It was against that background that I first came to the question of the refugee.

At first, I was tempted to do what many do when speaking or writing about refugees: cover several issues generally taken to be essential to any discussion of the subject of the refugee. One might call these the nuts and bolts of refugee issues, ranging from the recent proliferation of the number of refugees to a proliferation of activities undertaken in response to refugee events, including analyses of refugee events and contributions to their possible solutions. After taking note of the increasing visibility of refugees and the proliferation of activities on refugees, I located myself in this burgeoning field of study and action, seeking to identify the issues, sharpen the analyses of the problem, and offer possible solutions by producing authoritative narratives regarding the refugee and for the refugee. These were surely important issues needing to be dealt with, and indeed they have been dealt with by many able scholars concerned with refugee issues. While I necessarily was attracted to these issues, at the same time I was very much puzzled with the discourse on refugees, a puzzlement that directed my inquiries further.

The discourse on the refugee, on human displacement, it seemed to me, had no place for its very subject: refugees. In fact, the discourse on the refugee was not only largely blind to refugees in denying them a place in the discourse, but also strangely estranging for refugees in that it denied them any meaningful agency for acting on life's circumstances and for initiating and leading productive lives. When the refugee seemed to exhibit any sign of agency in the discourse, either as some kind of threat or as someone whose agency was manifested in her will to drag her body between distances, she hardly ever figured as a person but was part of an amorphous mass, faceless and speechless. A reporter wrote on the Cambodian refugees in precisely this sense: "Wasted by malnutrition, they kept coming. With bodies shedding life as nonchalantly as feathers falling off a bird, they kept coming" (qtd. in Spurr, 1996: 24). Refugee discourse, even in its most compassionate moments, seemed either to erase the refugee as an agent in life or to represent her as "placeless," properly belonging nowhere as a refugee. "The fact is," a UNHCR poster exclaimed, "refugees are just like you and me, except that they have nothing. And that is exactly what they'll always have unless we help." Another poster remarked, commenting on a picture of a baby sleeping in a hammock that seems to be anchored in a vast white emptiness, connoting a "placelessness" that typically defines the refugee in discourse, "Every year, thousands of babies are born with a serious handicap. She looks pretty normal. But she was born a refugee—and that is serious." Represented as a "serious" void with no personal, family, or communal ties, belonging nowhere but in the vast emptiness against which she was figured, the refugee, like that baby refugee, in discourse became, in the words of Michael Dillon (forthcoming), a "worldless being . . . amongst the worldliness of others"—at best a marginal figure.

It is not that I had ever thought that refugees did not need any help or that they were full agents of their lives. But, taking seriously the faces and words of refugees themselves, I also knew that refugees were capable authors of their lives, even in displacement and even under circumstances not of their full choosing. Taking a clue from Stuart Hall's reminder that "no discourse is innocent" but that all discourses serve certain interests (1996: 205), and working within this field of discourse, I wanted to know how the refugee discourse works to effect the refugees' powerlessness. But more importantly, I asked, what purpose does the discourse serve? So, the cardinal question I have posed in this study is not merely how the discourse is produced and how the refugee is rendered voiceless in the discourse, but what the discourse does, how the discourse itself perhaps produces certain practical effects that become instrumental in specific projects.

In search of responses, I looked to the definition of the refugee, or more specifically, to the representational hierarchy of agents and identities in relation to which a person is defined as a refugee, a figure of lack or abnormality or aberration. This relational hierarchy is the hierarchy of the citizen/nation/state constellation, the hierarchy that the refugee discourse takes as given, the normal hierarchy, in which the refugee discourse defines the refugee as a figure of aberration, a figure of lack, lacking proper agency, proper voice, proper face.

Rejecting the givenness of this hierarchy of agents, arguing that all such agents are social artifacts whose powers and realities get produced through contingent practices in history, and, finally, seeing discourse as a specialized field of articulation and empowerment for such practices, I theorized that perhaps the refugee discourse is instrumental in the constitution of the very hierarchy in relation to which it appears as secondary and that the refugee, in much the same way, is productive or constitutive of the citizen from which he is inscribed to be an aberration. More specifically, I theorized that the refugee discourse, articulating and circulating a specific historical figure of the refugee (by way of concrete governmental and intergovernmental regime activities attendant upon refugee events), serves as one of many boundary-producing discourses instrumental in the expression, empowerment, and institutionalization of a certain territorialized figure of the citizen-subject, the presumed foundational subject on the basis of which the sovereign state itself has historically been, and continues to be, articulated.

Against this theoretical orientation, in the broadest sense, my objective in this book has been to explore the historical ontological and epistemological linkages among the citizen, the nation, the state, and the refugee to see how they may have implicated and been implicated in one another's historical making. More specifically, my objective has been to examine how the historical processes of creating refugees—"refugeeing"—may have been imbricated with and may have supported the knowledgeable processes of governance through which the relations and powers of the modern territorial state have been produced and circulated in history, particularly in European histories since the late seventeenth century. In short, in this book, I have tried to examine how, historically, "refugeeing" may have figured in the processes of "statecrafting."

Through an examination in European histories of the ways in which the figure of the refugee has been historically problematized as a specific problem before states, I have shown that the histories of statecraft and refugeeing have been intimately bound up with each other and that the figure of the refugee has been integral to statecraft, the art of imagining and socially producing the state's territorial universal order. Most instructively, however, I have demonstrated that although construed as a marginal figure of aberration in the statist refugee discourse, in effect, the figure of the refugee is much more than just a marginal body. On the contrary, it is essential to statecraft, particularly at the intergovernmental level, because inasmuch as its meanings and identities are constructed contrapuntally, that is, in connection with the production of the identities and meanings of the citizen/nation/state hierarchy, the refugee figure is functionally central to statecraft even in his socially produced, discourse-bound marginality, a marginality that is vitally productive of the normative centrality of the citizen/nation/state hierarchy in life. This is the paramount argument of this book. As for "real" refugees and displaced people—humans in displacement—I have tried to say that their canvases of life are shaped by the simple imperative of struggle for survival regardless of how they are represented, talked about, and referred to in discourses of state legitimation.

WHAT IS MISSING? THOUGHTS FOR FUTURE STUDIES ON THE REFUGEE

Although in this study I have focused on the historical regimentation of the refugee through governmental and intergovernmental practices, those practices should not be taken to constitute the most significant aspect of the refugee in history. Rather, in line with the heuristics of a genealogical attitude, it might be suggested that such regimentations should be seen as one of many possible beginnings useful to understanding the refugee event in terms of the "polymorphism of [refugee] elements, relations and domains of reference" (Foucault, 1991: 77). With this understanding, it becomes possible to see, for example, that the focus on the practices of statecraft through regimentation is tantamount to the study of a limited face of complex refugee events and that the incorporation of other dimensions or, in the words of Foucault, other "external relations of intelligibilities" that concurrently make possible the effecting of the refugee event in history is always possible (1991: 77). There are, in fact, several such dimensions that do not systematically figure in this study, dimensions whose explorations are necessary in future work on the refugee if we are to comprehend the refugee event as a "polyhedron of intelligibilities" in history (Foucault, 1991: 77). I will describe four of these dimensions here.

First, it is instructive to note that practices of statist regimentation do not take place in a context of historical forces already predisposed to the imagined directions of regimentations. Rather, there are always multiple forms of resistance and accompanying dissonant voices that counterproblematize regimentations. Resistant practices take place in a thousand ways and forms. They are encountered in the movements of a Kurd or a Bosnian who sees the possibilities of life not in a world imagined through an interpretive hierarchy of the citizen/nation/state constellation but in a world imagined as continuous space with opportunities for living. They are found in literature, in novels, satire, and poetry in which the identities imagined and imposed on human bodies (the identities of a refugee, for example) are effectively reimagined, opening the way for reconsideration of otherwise seemingly self-evident, inveterate subjectivities and positionalities. In the poem "The Border," David Chorlton is engaged in just such a reimagining:

A refugee has crossed
so many borders, he becomes
invisible where countries change
their names. When he stops
in the shadows to catch
his breath, pieces
of a border lace his shoes. (1994: 30)

Similar counterproblematizations in Günter Grass (1993), Julia Kristeva (1991), and Daniel Warner (1992) are effected in a challenge to the practices of statist regimentations. It is true that for statist regimentations to be effective, resistant practices have to be managed, if not stifled. How then, by way of what strategic practices of regimentation, are the practices of resistance managed or stifled, and to what effect? How does the field of resistance configure and refigure in response to regimentations? How, through what practical ways, do the practices of resistance render ambiguous what is otherwise offered as categorical and self-evident in order to point to ongoing transformative happenings and to intimate future possibilities? How, if at all, for instance, do these practices render ambiguous the imagined distinctions between the citizen and the refugee in order to create conversational possibilities between them? And how can we theorize such conversations without privileging, as the conventional discourse on the refugee does, the citizen-subject as the proper subject of life? These are a few of the questions that come to mind under the theme of resistance, constituting yet another dimension or face of the multifaceted refugee event. Much more research and study are to be done in reply to these questions.

Second, while the study focuses on the problematizations of the refugee as useful to the problematizations of the citizen-subject, its treatment of the citizen has been more stylistic than its examination of the problematizations of the figure of the refugee in history. I have treated the citizen more in a shell-like form, exploring less the changes and stabilizations of the content of the figure of the citizen than the regimentations of the content of the refugee. What in particular has changed in the strategies by which the content of the citizen-subject has been historically produced and stabilized? How does the figure of the refugee appear in the context of changes and continuities? The incorporation into future studies of the historical transformations and stabilizations of the content—the identities and images—of the citizen points to another face of the refugee event as a subject of study in the genealogical sense. More research remains to be done in this direction as well.

Third, this study has not incorporated in a systematic, sustained fashion the role of international nongovernmental organizations (INGOs) in the problematizations of the refugee, both historically and in a contemporary sense. Historically, INGOs have been indispensable to the practices of regimentation, particularly because they have been the traditional frontline agencies applying the policies to concrete occurrences. Recall that it was a letter from an INGO, the International Red Cross Committee, that set the stage for the birth of the League of Nations High Commissioner for Refugees. Today, there are hundreds of INGOs representing various worldwide groups, from religious organizations, such as the World Council of Churches, to secular and/or professional organizations, such as Doctors without Borders, Amnesty International, Lawyers for Human Rights, and many more. These organizations operate in the same fields of regimentation and statist territorialization explored in this book. However, their effects on statist, territorializing practices of regimentation are not explored at all. Are INGOs in the refugee field agents of deterritorialization or reterritorialization or both? Future research along these lines stands to increase the power of genealogical studies on the refugee. Interestingly, governments seem curious to explore and regiment the effect of INGOs in the refugee field. In late 1994, for example, a number of governments in Asia and Europe commissioned the Refugee Studies Program at Oxford University to develop intergovernmentally acceptable guidelines of engagement for INGOs in host countries. Could this be seen as a practice of statist regimentation?

Fourth, as I indicated at the outset, this study has not systematically explored the question of how non-Western histories in refugeeing and statecraft figure with respect to the theoretical arguments presented here. Can we theorize these histories from the standpoint of arguments and hypotheses on statecraft? There has not been any study engaging non-Western histories of displacement in this sense. The available body of literature on human displacement in non-Western spaces consists largely of descriptive studies. This area, too, merits further study.

Finally, and perhaps most importantly in the practical realities of refugee lives, this study has not foregrounded the role of gender in human displacement. This is so not because of an intrinsic indifference to gender, nor because of an attempt to marginalize gender in refugee histories, nor because of an orientation in refugee studies that posits a gender-neutral history; in fact, I have been cognizant that refugee histories are gendered histories just as much as they are histories invested with a mélange of cultural, ethnic, racial, and politico-economic processes and projects. Rather, the reasons for this lack of foregrounding have to do with the primary substantive interests and orientations of the study. Let me offer some thoughts on this issue that should help not only to reiterate the primary orientations and objectives of this study but also, and more importantly, to intimate how the relative presence or absence of gendered thinking can be understood in relation to those orientations and objectives.

Gender in refugee issues is all about difference, the difference in the experiences of refugee men and women. Both women and men become refugees, but not in quite the same way. They both live refugee lives, but generally in substantially different ways. In other words, there are considerable differences in how men and women experience refugee life and in how those differences are perceived and incorporated into policy and conduct. What is important here is that differences are not inconsequential in terms of the circumstances of refugee life; they condition the countenance of life in displacement, which, reflecting broad patterns and processes of a still largely patriarchal organization of life, affords more fortunes to refugee men than refugee women. These fortunes represent not simply the relative privileges of refugee men in relation to refugee women, but also, and more urgently, the recovery or recuperation of a priori gendered hierarchies that, in the first place, make possible, inform, and sustain gendered refugee experiences.

Both women and men are displaced, but displaced female bodies are made to become specific sites of power where gendered, hierarchizing power relations privileging men over women (and male agency over female agency) are recuperated and stabilized precisely at a time (displacement) when those power relations are disrupted and most vulnerable to shifts and transformations. Refugee women, to put it succinctly, are instrumentalized even in displacement, becoming useful in the recovery or recuperation of agency of the men, of agency as masculine.

Sometimes the recuperation takes place in brutal ways, through rape and other forms of sexual assault, which are a constant threat for refugee women. Refugee women are victimized before and during flight, as well as in refugee camps. Stories of sexual assault are countless and, in their plethora, speak of the relentless sexual siege that refugee women endure:

> At age 18, she arrived from the two-week track through the Danakil desert, physically exhausted, badly dehydrated, and with blistering sores from exposure on her feet and body. But the most terrible part of her ordeal, she points out, was the three days she was held at the border jail and raped repeatedly. (Martin, 1991: 17)

> Two of the young and pretty girls were taken to the front of the boat and raped. Everyone heard everything, all of the screams. That is what I remember, the screams. After a while the screams stopped, the crying stopped and there was silence. (Martin, 1991: 17)

These compelling anecdotes surely say much about the vulnerability of refugee women and are instructive in pointing to the difficulties of life for refugee women. Because of this, they are finally, though painstakingly slowly, gaining recognition as grounds for refugee status. But they are also important in their silences as to how refugee women still manage to survive and even resist in the face of adversities. Still more importantly, such anecdotes are telling as to how, without broader contextualization, they support certain representations of refugee women that help sustain broad patterns and processes of patriarchy. As Helene Moussa argues, depicting women refugees exclusively as victims gives rise to their portrayal as passive subjects, dependent on their male counterparts for survival and salvation (1993: 18–19). Typically, refugee women's displacement is presented in alarmist terms, intimating a general paralysis, a loss of their agency. This treatment in turn normalizes a general disenfranchisement of refugee women, so much so that women are denied the simplest opportunities to participate in the shaping of their refugee lives. They are even denied opportunities to secure their minimum needs, ranging from food to clothing to basic means of sanitary protection (UNHCR, 1995: 4). Not surprisingly, refugee women are cognizant that their vulnerability is obtained and maintained through daily power relations. A Rwandese refugee, Esther, captures it well: "When men are in charge of giving out plastic sheeting, they often forget the weakest people" (qtd. in UNHCR, 1995: 4)

Refugee women, in short, run tremendous risks—their displacement may be not simply from the physical geographies of familiar lives but also from geographies of social and political agency within which, against all odds, they develop their practical powers, however discursive and tentative. As I said at the outset, if refugee men suffer from the reality of single displacement—the physical displacement—refugee women suffer from a double displacement—a physical displacement from the so-called home community and a symbolic and at times violent displacement from agency. Surely, such a displacement is never total and final, for refugee women continue to make and remake their lives unceremoniously, but it makes life immensely more difficult, if not deadly.

Here, what I am trying to highlight is the gender-specific contingency of refugeeness for women and men, which future studies must explore more urgently. The experiences of more than fifty thousand Bosnian women who were raped in a war that was particularly brutal powerfully attest to the gendered refugeeness for women and highlight the need for further interrogations of gendered refugee lives. Of course, a gender-specific approach is not simply about the specificities of the lives of refugee women, but must be "contrapuntal" (Said, 1993), simultaneously showing the intimate linkages between the subordination of women and the privileges of men even in displacement. After all, the specificities of the experiences of refugee men are largely about refugee men's relative privileges vis-à-vis refugee women. Still, this approach must be taken carefully, for while it is generally, though surely not always, true that refugee men have more control over their lives than do women, it is also true that there could be many instances during which refugee men experience violence equal to the general subordination of refugee women in most situations. Think, for example, of the three thousand Muslim refugee men who in 1996 were taken away by Serbs from the so-called safe haven of Srebrenica in Bosnia, never to be seen or heard of again. They were most likely murdered—a fate that befell tens of thousands of Muslim refugee men in Bosnia. Refugee men, too, are instrumentalized in power networks, but in different ways—today murdered, tomorrow taken to concentration camps, and yet another day put to work to build more camps to concentrate refugees, both men and women.

These are all specific gendered experiences on which future studies ought to focus in analyzing refugee experiences. While it is important to do a genealogy of the refugee along these terms—in terms of the question "What happens to whom?"—it is also important to do a genealogy of the refugee in more general terms, in terms of displaced human bodies, men and women, the commonalties of whose displacement, both extant and politically manufactured, are then appropriated to various projects. I have argued that the commonalties are harnessed to the project of producing and reproducing the quintessential modern statist hierarchy of identities and entities, that is, the hierarchy of citizen/nation/state that today still undergirds the idea as well as the ideal of international relations. This study is largely an attempt to understand how the commonalties are harnessed to this task. This is not to argue that the task is gender-neutral (or race- or class-neutral) but to suggest that it is gender-neutralized (as it is race-, class-, and ethnicity-neutralized). Let me try to explain.

When a man and a woman flee, they surely face distinctly gendered experiences. Still, at a political level, they become the subjects of institutional practices that, on the one hand, reproduce or recuperate gendered (or for that matter, racialized or ethnonationalized) power relations between men and women and, on the other hand, "define" them in a universalizing definition (such as that in the 1951 convention and the 1967 protocol on refugees) that is then employed to regiment refugees, both men and women, more as refugees, that is, as noncitizens lacking proper subjectivity, and less as men and women. From the standpoint of statecraft, in other words, the production of citizenship is the primary, most fundamental task to which the "universalized" image and identity of the refugee is harnessed. This study focuses largely, though not exclusively, on this level of refugee events and occurrences, for it is here that the gendered as well as racialized or ethnonationalized specificities of refugee experiences are conditioned and controlled to affirm a universalizing and ideal discourse of statecraft. It is here that the task of statecraft—the production of the citizen/nation/state hierarchy as the normal hierarchy in life—is gender-neutralized or race-neutralized in and through representation and regimentation.[1]

What seems important for statecraft is for the refugee, either man or woman, to go before an asylum officer (a state agent) and ask for recognition from the state as a refugee (thus affording an axiomatic normality and centrality to the state), not so much to describe how the refugee has arrived there, unless highlighting the journey serves political and popular ends for statecraft. The 1993 British evacuation before the mass media of Irma Hadzimuratovic, a wounded five-year-old Bosnian girl from Sarajevo is the kind of journey that serves statecraft (Bhabha and Shutter, 1994: 230). For the state, whether a refugee woman is raped (or whether a refugee man is murdered) may not, in the words of Spike Peterson and Anne Runyan (1993: 25), be "all that important to warrant being spotlighted." It may even be something to be silently swept into the dustbin of history.[2] Historically, the effect of such selective representation has been a steady but constant institutionalization of responses to refugee events at governmental and intergovernmental levels which in this century came to be manifested most consequentially in the modern international refugee regime.

I suggest that it is possible to study such practices of institutionalization as practices of statecraft and also to highlight or spotlight in an interventionist mode the gendered background of the institutionalization—in other words, to tell the story of rape and murder as well as to expose less violent but still repressive practices that produce refugee women's subordination, practices which, if not told and retold, even if only tentatively and in fleeting moments, may never get spotlighted. This is an ever more pressing issue for future studies on refugees.

I have described some of the other faces of the refugee event as a "polyhedron of intelligibility." Undoubtedly, further studies in these and other areas would enrich our understanding of the refugee event as a process (Foucault, 1991), as "refugeeing" in multiple fashions and for a myriad of objectives. The focus in this study on a specific dimension of statecraft, the intergovernmental institutionalization of refugee regimentations, is equally important, particularly because this focus enables us to see how, since the seventeenth century, refugeeing has historically taken place in concrete popular and institutional settings of statist governance to become useful to the task of statecraft. It might be instructive here to recollect some of the important points of the study.

RECOLLECTIONS OF REFUGEE REGIMENTATIONS IN HISTORY

Of all the claims in this study, the claim of "refugeeing" is cardinal. It is cardinal because it disallows thoughts of the refugee as an already given, historically self-evident figure of human displacement and shows how the refugee as a figure of human displacement is a politically produced effect, always contingent, always subject to history. A refugee, this claim reminds readers, never simply is, but is made to be in all aspects of displacement. And in all aspects of displacement, the refugee's regimented or unmolested experiences—the processes of "being" or "being made" a refugee—are linked to and imbricated with the process by which people govern themselves and others.

In the book, I have argued that European histories since the late seventeenth century bear witness to this general claim in specific ways. In other words, they support the argument that since the emergence of the figure of the refugee in Europe, both in name and body, there has never been a perennial refugee figure and/or refugee identity to be at once recognized and represented regardless of time and place. Rather, refugee images and identities have shifted and have been altered in the historical encounters of protagonists and antagonists. They have been neither innate nor inherited, but always inscribed in process, in the historical making and unmaking of things, relations, and institutions in the hands of human agents. And it is in that process of inscription that the figure of the refugee—its contingent identities, images, and meanings—has historically come to be implicated in the practices of governance—in this case, in the practices of statist governance in ascent in Europe. The refugee figure, shaped incessantly within the historical institutional settings of statist governance, has signified or even expressed, in symbolic and material ways, the exigencies of such governance, as statist governance has evolved from absolutist to sovereign territorial governance and from sovereign territorial to sovereign national governance. It has appeared in fields of such governance and was problematized there to be inscribed with specific spatiotemporal meanings centering on the statist governance. Historically, then, refugee problematizations have been oriented and indeed have worked, to the extent they have succeeded, to attribute to the refugee specific identities and subjectivities congruent with the always emergent, but never finally stabilized, form of statist governance in Europe. In this study, I have tried to show that "refugeeing" has been instrumental in this sense, particularly since the late seventeenth century.

In European histories prior to the twentieth century, although the figure of the refugee did not appear prominently, the refugee being but one figure that signified human displacement, along with the exile, the émigré, and the suppliant, it nevertheless proved instrumental to the task of statecraft: its practical presence and its inscripted images and identities, emerging and converging with those of the exile, the suppliant, the immigrant, and the émigré, were appropriated over time to effect a specific institutional field of statecraft under the sign of the foreigner-alien. It was in the contra identity or image of the figure of the foreigner-alien that the identities of the nonalien, namely, the citizen, were articulated, empowered, and institutionalized in and through constitutions, nationality and extradition laws, and alien acts.

I have shown, for example, how the constitution (inscription) of the foreigner or the alien other, of which the refugee constituted a category, was linked to the articulation and effecting of territorial statist governance in Europe in multiple discursive ways—in alien acts, in nationality, asylum, and extradition laws, in participatory and welfare regulations, in the marginal sectors of industry, and in travel documents or passports as well as popular cultural constructions. In Richard Ashley's conceptualization (1989b; 1993), the discursive ways that constituted the identities of the foreigner or alien as the one who did not belong to the state's territorial order were practices of statecraft also, constituting simultaneously the identities of the citizen as one who did belong to the state's territorial order, upon which the state drew in real and symbolic ways to legitimize its powers and privileges. Many observers (Statt, 1995; Porter, 1979; Panayi, 1994; Tabori, 1972; Braudel, 1988; Brubaker, 1992) have pointed to this relation. In the words of Fernand Braudel, alien images—images of refugeeness, exile, and emigration—as images of territorial displacement were instrumental in the identification of "a thousand touchstones" on which the "nation" was inscripted and territorialized in the image of the state (1988: 23). The refugee figure, problematized in various contexts, contributed to the processes of making and remaking the world of the state in the eighteenth and nineteenth centuries.

The examination of the historical linkages between refugeeism and the practices and processes of statecraft in the twentieth century has evinced a similar relationship, but in a more intense and regimented fashion. It has shown that circa the First World War, the refugee figure attained unprecedented primacy relative to other figures of human displacement. One of the reasons for this was the sudden surge in the numbers of people displaced because of the dissolution of ancient empires and wars in the first quarter of the century. Another reason, however, was a shift in the practices of statecraft, which married the notion of "state building" with a politically and culturally exclusionary notion of "nation building." In most cases throughout Europe, this shift led to the "racialization" of these processes, such as Hellenization, Hungarianization, Germanization, and Turkification, resulting in the displacement of millions of people in addition to those who were already "out of place." The practical impact on sovereign territorial governance was crippling, not simply in terms of "managing" the movement of millions of the displaced but more importantly in terms of the increasing difficulty in effecting more or less stable, normative articulations of the sovereign state as an agent that would represent the territorial reality of its own people—articulations that then had to be put to work effectively in the governance of a multiplicity of diverse locales to produce the "nation" effect. The displaced people themselves, by virtue of their existence, attested to the failure to effect such articulations. Something had to be done to reintegrate the state's territorial and nationalizing order into the political landscape, now so porous. This, in Ashley's terminology, represented a "collaboration problem of the first order" (1989b; 1993). The question was the perennial one of producing and stabilizing and territorially bounding practical boundaries of the state across otherwise vast and territorially continuous space.

The answer to this quandary came in the form of a shift in the strategies of governance in dealing with massive human displacement in general and the so-called refugee problem in particular. The shift was an intergovernmentalization of activities of statecraft and took the form of the first intergovernmental refugee organization—the League of Nations High Commissioner for Refugees.

Coming at a historical juncture when the crisis of statecraft was more intense and more complicated than ever, the LNHCR proved to be a productive instrument of intergovernmental statecraft. It emerged to open or fashion an intergovernmental field of activity as a field of problematization whereby it became possible to regiment the effects of mass human displacements by "writing" a specific state-oriented refugee subjectivity out of the transversal indeterminacies and ambiguities of human displacement. By means of activities through the high commissioner, the massive human displacement was normalized, that is, rearticulated into a manageable "temporary refugee problem" in terms that posited the primacy, normalcy, and permanence of statist relations and institutions. The commissioner's office facilitated this intergovernmental regimentation of the refugee in a variety of cross-referential settings, from official arrangements, conventions, and protocols to popular and scholarly commentaries. In the period between 1921 and 1930, the figure of the refugee was reinvented and intensely regimented in a statist sense. The regimentations of the figure of the refugee continued through a series of organizations that followed the LNHCR in the 1930s and 1940s. The last of these organizations, the UNHCR, was established in December 1950 and has since continued to do what the first organization was oriented to do: to refashion and preserve a field of statist regimentation under the sign of the refugee.

In familiar terms, this international governmentalization, particularly since the advent of the UNHCR, represents a refugee regime that is oriented primarily to help displaced humans. Yet in this study I have tried to show that the international refugee protection regime bespeaks as much of a desire to make individual refugees relevant to "the state's preservation, the state's expansion, and the state's felicity" (Foucault, 1988a: 148) by pointing to specific problems and dangers in refugee events and conditioning possible responses as it does of a desire to help displaced humans—the refugees—by pointing to their humanity.

WHAT IS AT STAKE IN THIS WORK?

To recall the historical problematizations of the refugee is to highlight what is at stake in this study, both theoretically and practically. Theoretically, I have shown that the subject of the refugee, conceived as stateless, is made to partake in statecraft, that is, in the articulation and practical empowerment of the state. But I am interested in more than just showing how refugee problematizations work in statecraft. I am also interested in the question of the normative effects of the discourse.

The study shows that the effect of the refugee discourse is a problematization of the refugee that both erases the refugee's agency and effaces the refugee's humanity under the sign of the refugee in order to privilege the state's territorial order. Facing this double estrangement, is it possible to theorize the refugee from a standpoint that does not so territorialize the refugee, from a theoretical attitude just as nomadic as the refugee and statist responses to the refugee? My study works within this field of discourse, examining how the discourse simultaneously announces itself as a redemptive discourse regarding the refugee yet manages to effect multiple estrangements for the refugee.

It is in contemplating this question in history that this study acquires its normative dimension. In showing how problematizations work to produce such an effect, the study responds to the perennial questions "What then?" and "What is the alternative?" My response in this book to these questions is in the spirit of the genealogical attitude expressed best in the following words:

> Critique does not have to be the premise of a deduction which concludes: this is then what needs to be done. It should be an instrument for those who fight, who resist and refuse what is. Its use should be in process of conflict and confrontation, essays in refusal. It does not have to lay down the law for the law. It isn't a stage in a programming. It is a challenge directed to what is, [or] what counts as being self-evident, universal and necessary. (Foucault, 1991: 84)

A genealogical attitude takes seriously the complexities and difficulties of refugee situations and attempts to theorize the refugee from the standpoint of the refugee herself. Its answers to the question of how refugee problematizations produce what counts as the self-evident and universal may, but only may, become the instruments for those whose displacement is made to engender specific statist effects in local and global politics. Its critique may enable knowledgeable resistant responses to practices through which the refugee is inscribed as voiceless and without effective agency. It highlights the ways in which displaced people can come to the discourse on the refugee and begin to explore openings in this discourse through which effective strategies may be formulated and undertaken to afford the refugee a voice, an agency.

The study represents a critical orientation, one that answers certain questions but, in line with a genealogical attitude, eschews the issuing of truth statements on the subject of the refugee. For instance, on a normative and theoretical plane, it shows that refugee regimentations are not neutral, ephemeral, or transitory practices designed merely to handle "the challenges of the day" emanating from mass migratory movements of refugees. Beyond that, practices of regimentation establish "ground rules" of theory and praxis regarding human displacement. These ground rules in turn affect the trajectories and patterns of life in a multitude of areas, from democracy and welfare to human rights, stability, and security. They participate in determining how human displacement does or does not figure in these areas. They shape the content and contours of normative orientations in "the public at large," such as the orientations in the morality of dealing with human displacement. In the words of Ashley,

> They instruct an *aesthetics of existence* whose values and criteria dispose people to understand [refugees as either objects of compassion or agents of dangers and uncertainties] and to willingly support the state, its laws, its technologies of violence, its administrative resources, and its international regimentation . . . of policies as means by which [the problems and uncertainties of refugee events] might be brought under control [in the name of the citizen in a domestic community in France, Germany, or England]. They define the questions [people] need to respond to and the solutions [they] are compelled to search for. (1993: 9; emphasis added)

I have shown how governmental and intergovernmental refugee regimentations delimit the real possibilities of life for the people who are written (or in some cases, are not written) as refugees. The consequences of these practices might be deadly serious for those who are "refugeed," whether in their inertia, as are the people of Bosnia, imprisoned in putative safe havens, or in their mobility, as are millions of people who traverse the world in search of safety and well-being.

On another plane, however, the study shows the syncretism of identities, images, and desires prevalent in refugee events and experiences and in their links to the relations and institutions of governance. For example, in the study of humanitarian interventions and democracy, it shows how refugees are capable of initiating resistant responses to statist regimentations, resistances that enable refugees to recast the statist, territorializing limits on their lives in ways that afford a living space. In certain instances, they simply contest and manipulate the "aesthetics of existence" that informs the regimentation, and move on with living, even if living is a difficult task. "We work. We are here to stay," remarks Garip, a refugee from Turkey now living in France (qtd. in Range, 1993: 113). At other times, refugees show a willingness to internalize the territorializing proddings of the aesthetics of existence; they wait their turns to be citizens once again, either in their "country of origin" or in a new country. Consider the case of Dikita, formerly of Mali, now living in France: "We came here to be French. Where can we go?" (qtd. in Range, 1993: 114). In all cases, however, refugees' presence is implicated in and implicates the making and remaking of processes of statist territorial governance. Sometimes refugees are problematized to make possible more or less stable, normatively effective articulations of relations, institutions, and subjectivities that get recognized as those of the sovereign territorial state. At other times their presence works as a vehicle of change and transformation of the ways, relations, and institutions by which men and women govern themselves and others.

Several years ago, a policy analyst advised me to find another topic for examination. His reason was that the topic of refugees had already been exhausted theoretically and that writing a study on the refugee would be reinventing the wheel. Now this study, quite to the contrary, attests to how the subject of the refugee has been and continues to be an understudied subject and to how the wheel that gets recognized as the refugee is still being invented day in and day out.

Recognizing this production as something that has practical implications for refugees, it is possible to suggest that, normatively, one of the purposes of this book is to go beyond simply saying that refugee discourse, a discourse on displacement, seems strange. It is to begin to question and disrupt the self-evidentiality of the refugee category. It is to suggest that the identity of the refugee, like that of the nonrefugee, is open-ended—it "proceeds neither from renunciation nor from frustration regarding a supposedly deteriorated (deterritorialized) situation or a country of origin; it is not a resolute act of rejection or an uncontrolled impulse of abandonment of any place or country" (Glissant, 1997: 34). It is an identity of survival and resistance against the odds. It is to start saying that "sometimes by taking up the problems of [refugee] others, it is possible to find oneself," realizing that in opposition to one's proper rootedness is one's refugeeness. It is to articulate the self first not to a life of territoriality but to life as "a limitless creolization, a limitless *metissage,* its elements diffracted and its consequences unforseeable . . . [a life that allows] each person to be there and elsewhere, rooted and open, lost in mountains and free beneath the sea, in harmony and in errantry" (Glissant, 1997: 34). It is to foster these thoughts, however difficult that may be to do in this world we have managed to fracture so. It is to begin to highlight and intimate, however tentatively, ways in which people such as I, a refugee, can come to the discourse on the refugee and begin to explore openings in it through which effective strategies may be formulated and undertaken to afford the refugee an agency, a voice, and a face.

Notes

INTRODUCTION

1. Julie Peteet suggests that "the term 'refugees' (laja'een) was rejected because it implied a passive acceptance of the status quo and suggested the possibility of the Palestinians' resettlement elsewhere. . . . In vehemently rejecting the imposed term of reference and consciously choosing to refer to themselves as 'returners,' they were constructing a lexicon of both refusal and resistance" (1995: 177).

2. For example, see the collection of essays in Bammer (1994); Daniel and Knudsen (1995); and Lavie and Swedenburg (1996).

3. For such accounts of refugee lives, see Malkki (1992); Appadurai (1991); Gupta and Ferguson (1992); and Daniel and Knudsen (1995).

4. These studies include, but certainly are not limited to, Hope-Simpson (1939); Stoessinger (1956); Vernant (1953); Robinson (1953); Grahl-Madsen (1972); Gordenker (1987); Gallagher (1989); Dacyl (1990); Rogers (1992); Guest (1991); Aleinikoff (1991); Ferris (1993b); and Skran (1988; 1995). I am not saying here that these studies are all identical. No doubt they are richly varied in their orientations. No doubt, too, much more is to be said and written along the lines they pursue. Still, for all their variety, these studies share something in common in their conceptualization of the refugee. My purpose in pointing out this commonality within the diversity of their inquiries is not to diminish their usefulness or value. It is not to say that before my work, every approach to the question of the refugee has been conservative, reactionary, bourgeois, statist, or anything of the sort. In fact, many of these studies do speak to and highlight the immense difficulties and hardships

that millions of refugees have to endure day by day, and I borrow much from them in this study. Rather, my purpose in highlighting the commonality is to establish something of a general background (discourse) against which it may be possible to glimpse what is perhaps somewhat distinctive about my orientation, my own way of interpreting the proliferating activity around the question of the refugee in global politics.

5. The imagined possibilities of the distant places for building new homes give rise to refugees' willingness to reevaluate loyalties of all sorts, including that to the native land. Surely, it may be that the new homes are seen as mere imitations or even transplantations of some beginning or original place like India, Turkey, Algeria, or Mexico. But, as it is seemingly the case with the Kurdish refugees, the sight of the Swedish coastline may be perceived as a new beginning based on a willingness for a complete "forgetting" of the past. Whatever the case may be in such scenes, what is significant is that individuals simply move across identity borders and boundaries, blurring the differences between the strange and the familiar, the refugee and the citizen, and the home and exile (Soguk, 1995c).

6. For another reading of Foucault's notion of problematization as a strategy, see Castel (1994).

7. This study focuses on Euro-Mediterranean experiences in history, particularly the interface of human displacement and the emergence and intensification of the practices and projects of the sovereign territorial state in Europe since the seventeenth century. There are several reasons for this focus. The first is already obvious: Europe affords a peculiarly rich history in territorial statecraft, the complex and multiple practices of which have been brought to bear on Europe's people, nomadic or sedentary, with revolutionary (e.g., in France) and not-so-revolutionary (e.g., in England) zeal over the centuries, resulting in substantial human displacement. There is, in other words, a rich historical convergence of human displacement, including refugees, and practices of statist territorial governance in Europe. The second reason is less obvious but perhaps more compelling. No substantial body of literature exists on early human displacement in non-European spaces, let alone a body of work on human displacement and sovereign statecraft. Most of the studies on refugees in non-European, non-Western spaces, for example, deal with contemporary histories and are few and far between. This creates an insurmountable difficulty in incorporating them into this study without diffusing the study's core interest in the instrumentality of human displacement in statecraft in history. So, non-European histories do not generally figure in this study except for chapters 5 and 6, which deal with the contemporary processes of displacement and territorial statecraft. This study should therefore be taken to be a study of statecraft in European histories.

1. THEORIZING REFUGEE PROBLEMATIZATIONS AS PRACTICES OF STATECRAFT

1. There is, in all of these processes, an activity of double silence, each indispensably anticipating and implicating the others. The first silence is about arbitrariness of the constitution of a domestic community of citizens throughout activities of statecraft. The second silence is maintained in the face of the activities that arbitrarily produce the effects of the sovereign state as a sovereign state. The activities of statecraft do not refer to any source of self-evident authority that exists in itself beyond history. Rather, the sovereign state itself is manufactured as both a narrative and a practice in the very activity of producing the citizen-subject. Seeming circularity of the activities should not obscure the fact that the activities of statecraft (of producing the domestic community) are themselves activities by which the images, identities, and powers of the state are produced. The state has a practical, historical power-effect that, in Dipesh Chakrabarty's words, "can mobilize tremendous and effective instruments of violence" (1993: 43).

2. Although the border is "violated" daily, its significance stems not so much from its ability to be a barrier as from its being a discursive reference around which a multitude of actors, refugees, and immigrants, as well as the state, organize their activities. It is the "presence" of the border that makes an economy of activities possible. Put another way, on the one hand, the statist activities are dependent upon the constructed threat of refugees and immigrants. On the other hand, the particular articulation and activation of migrant and refugee activities are developed as a reaction to the statist claim "to stamp or not to stamp" one's papers bestowing proper subjectivity. At this level, "the border is a word game by reference to which a routinization and a ritualization of life activities are achieved" (Soguk, 1995c: 299; Langewiesche, 1992: 55). According to Kearney (1991), then, it is plausible to argue that the practice of stopping a person at a border pass to stamp one's papers is a practice of statecraft. So is the practice of declaring the presence of a line that imposes a perceived or physical discontinuity (the border), signifying the end of one "national space" and the beginning of another. Furthermore, getting people to stop at the border to affirm or agree to the claim of discontinuity is an equally concrete, if not always successful, practice of statecraft. It is even plausible to argue that a specific landscaping or architecturing of border passes is a practice of sovereignty designed to convey an image of particularity and difference of the territory entered.

3. For instance, according to Carter, in 1885, "the first medical survey of Italy sought to map the layout of the medical geography of the nation. This survey, once representing the nation as a document, providing a statistical profile of the nation, worked as a nexus of complex underlying cultural significations and classificatory practices that give life to the art of the state"

(1994: 73–74). Similar profiles of the nation and of the citizen are constructed through interventions, numerations, and classifications around refugee and immigrant bodies nowadays.

4. Mitchell studies the transformation in the landscape of agricultural work before and after the Wheatland riots—the building of model camps, the designing of model tenements, the institution of modern latrines, the construction of recreational facilities—in all of which the California Commission of Immigration and Housing (CCIH) played a leading role. He argues that dynamics of landscape production afforded a specific field of activity for practices of statecraft—in activities of agencies like CCIH—that helped produce the reality of the state as an effective agent of representation, protection, and harmony in the affairs of the domestic community. The state, Mitchell notes, was centrally implicated in landscape production and transformation (1993: 91–97). The results, however, were more than just changes in the conditions of the landscape of work. The process of change, manifested in a series of events, was also the reproduction of the state itself in the production of "harmony" in the work field. Also see Jessica Chapin (1994), whose observations on the organization of the tourist landscape in the San Antonio region corroborate the linkages between interventions in the material landscape and the narrative construction (*representation*) of historico-social and cultural identities, entities, and subjectivities.

5. Herzfeld argues that "statists" are well aware that both the nation and the state are not real entities but metaphorical constructions. Knowing this in full, they simply start with the premise that "both the nation and the state are 'real' entities, not metaphorical ones." However, they exploit and appropriate the power of everyday "ethnic" discourses—those that, for instance, differentiate a Greek identity from a Turkish identity—to generate from a plurality of local discourses "timeless truths" about Greek community and identity, into whose ethnic truth and identity canons they then readily insert the name of the state as if it had always been there (1988: 75–93).

6. For discussion of various aspects of the process of globalization, see R. B. J. Walker (1991b); Held and McGrew (1993); Cerutti (1994); Cumings (1993); Duara (1993); and Appadurai (1996).

7. This, of course, is not to suggest that one could not speak of or refer to a pure acting subject, agent, or entity invested with a multitude of contingent interests and identities that might in fact prod her to kill or to run away from killing, to exploit or torture or to protest against torture, and so on. Rather, it is to accentuate that none of these agents, entities, or subjects nor their interests and identities exist in a fixed and stable form impervious to temporal and spatial changes and transformations. The only permanent fixture to history—living—seems to be the act of "becoming," which is in constant change as the resources for and technologies of becoming this or that—

a refugee, an immigrant, a border patrol agent, a police officer, a judge, a scholar, a president, a Rwandan, a Kurdish Australian, or a *Gastarbeiter* (guest worker)—undergo changes.

8. For various discussions of the current state and future trajectories of the sovereign territorial state in the nexuses of globalization, see Thomson (1989); Barkin and Cronin (1994); Chen (1996); Barry (1993); Shapiro (1991); Walker (1991b); Connolly (1991); Inayatullah and Blaney (1995); and Weber (1995).

9. Ashley (1993) suggests that this is a concern of fundamental importance for activities of statecraft, for it implicates the difficulty of the coordination of activities across multiple localities in the absence of a central coordinator. In agreement with Ashley, this study suggests that the "coordination problem" necessitates a continuous orchestration and management of activities, images, identities, and meanings such that they could be appropriated in the inscription of boundaries attesting to the normality and necessity of the citizen/nation/state hierarchy.

10. A manifestation of the marginalization of gender issues can be seen in the fact the UNHCR did not formulate its first conclusion specifically on the problems of women refugees until 1985 and did not develop its "Guidelines on the Protection of Refugee Women" until 1991 (Bhabha and Shutter, 1994: 255).

2. REFUGEES, HUMAN DISPLACEMENT, AND STATECRAFT

1. See also Furetiere (1690). In this dictionary, *réfugié* is defined as one "who has escaped to some refuge or asylum." The following examples provided in the dictionary (translated from the original French text) indicate the early meanings of the term: "There is always a refugee prince on the court of France"; "This place is for poor refugees." Also see Partridge (1988).

2. Once integrated into the English language, the term *refugee* came to refer generally, but not always, to the Huguenots fleeing the French kingdom of Louis XIV. In fact, three successive editions of the *Oxford English Dictionary* (1888, 1933, and 1989) give 1685, the date of the revocation of the Edict of Nantes, as the commonly accepted date for the first written record of the term *refugee* in the English language. They ground the term *refugee,* similarly, as having originally applied to the French Huguenots who came to England after the revocation of the Edict of Nantes in 1685, though they also introduce the generalized meaning of the term *refugee.* The three successive editions define the refugee identically as "one who, owing to religious persecution or political troubles, seeks refuge in a foreign country; originally applied to the French Huguenots who came to England after the

revocation of the Edict of Nantes." As early as 1708, in the *Dictionarum Anglo-Britannicum*, the refugee is defined as "a French Protestant, fled from the late persecution in France." Different editions of dictionaries and encyclopedias in the late eighteenth century, including the 1771 edition of the *Encyclopedia Britannica*, continued to use the term *refugee* as designating the Huguenots. This meaning remained unchanged until almost the beginning of the nineteenth century. An indication as to the extension of the scope of the term to other incidents of displacement came toward the end of the eighteenth century. In 1780, in *A General Dictionary of the English Language*, Thomas Sheridian defined a refugee briefly, as "one who flies to shelter or protection." More than a century after the Huguenot event, the extension was finally articulated in 1797 in the third edition of the *Encyclopedia Britannica*, which extends the scope of the term to cover "all such as leave their country in times of distress."

3. See Defoe ([1709] 1964) for his use of all of these terms, including the term *refugee*, to discuss the Huguenot displacement from France into other European countries.

4. Colin Holmes, for instance, observes that "for two centuries after the arrival of the Huguenots in the seventeenth century no major influx of immigrants or refugees took place, although the flow of individuals and groups into England continued" (1988: 8).

5. This permissive practice of naming was prevalent even in attempts by founding international relations scholars such as Hugo Grotius, Christian Wolf, and Emmerich Vattel to produce a precise typology of human displacement. See Soguk (1995b: 65–95) for a full discussion of attempts at typologies by Grotius ([1642] 1925), Wolf ([1764] 1934), and Vattel (1820). An instructive example of the permissiveness is exemplified in Vattel, for example, who writes of the Huguenot refugees not as refugees but as "Protestant emigrants" "who implored the protection of the power who would receive them. Thus we have seen Frederick William, King of Prussia, grant his protection to the *emigrant Protestants* of Saltsburg" (1820: 165; emphasis added).

6. As Michel Foucault (1988), E. J. Hobsbawm (1992), and Perry Anderson (1984) suggest, the desire behind the interventions might have been as simple as to raise taxes necessary for the craft and play of the state. Ongoing changes in the absolutist French state toward becoming a territorial sovereign state are adumbrated and the promise of future metamorphosis observed even in the articles of the Edict of Revocation itself. The edict outlines a number of incentives in education, taxation, religious practices, property rights, and commercial privileges that, the king promises, the state would deliver to those Huguenots who would convert to Catholicism and remain in the country. This is significant for at least two interrelated reasons. First, the array of privileges promised by the edict attests to the extent

of government involvement in the "public" sphere. Second, the expulsion represents increasing state power in community interventions conceptualized along the logic of population. The effect was the triumph of biopolitics in terms of the claims on people as constituting populations with certain qualities: homogeneous/heterogeneous, male/female, healthy/sick, Catholic/Protestant, literate/illiterate, and so on. The act could indeed be one of crafting the state as a site of activity.

7. For a convergent reading of the state as a "rational and political unifier," see Henri Lefebvre (1995: 280–82). "The state," writes Lefebvre, "subordinates and totalizes the various aspects of the social practices—legislation, culture, knowledge, education—within a determinate space; namely, the space of the ruling class's hegemony over its people and over nationhood that it has arrogated. Each state claims to produce space wherein something is accomplished" (281).

8. Interestingly, in her study of the emergence of the notion of "Britishness," Linda Colley (1992a; 1992b) advances the same argument on the consequential role of religion in the construction of the British identity. I shall write more on this later in this chapter, but it is instructive to hear Colley suggest that the Huguenot displacement by Catholic France was instrumental in identity construction in the largely Protestant Britain: "France attempted to expel its Protestant population in 1685, and many of these Huguenot refugees settled in Britain, living reminders to their new countrymen of the enduring threat of Catholic persecution" (1992a: 320; see also 1992b: 55). In later years, increasingly, the Britons, she propounds, "defined themselves in terms of their common Protestantism as contrasted with the Catholicism of Continental Europe. They defined themselves against France" (1992a: 316; see also 1992b: 88–91). They could refer to "the poor French refugees, the exiles of the principality of Orange, the Palatines heretofore, and half starved Saltzburgers, driven from their native country in the depth of winter" (1992a: 321; see also 1992b: 24) and say, "Oh Britons let us prize our privileges" (1992a: 319).

9. The Huguenot episode, then, could be seen to have been part of a larger process in Western Europe starting from the late seventeenth century, in which the reasons and projects of the sovereign territorial state were formulated in and introduced into the lives of individuals, however inceptively and tentatively. Eric Hobsbawm points to the later stages of this process of the modern territorial state, stages anticipated in the unfolding of the Huguenot displacement. The territorial state "was defined as a territory over all of whose inhabitants it ruled, and separated by clearly distinct frontiers or borders from other such territories. Politically it ruled over and administered these inhabitants directly and not through intermediate systems of rulers and autonomous corporations. It sought, if at all possible, to

impose the same institutional and administrative arrangements and laws all over its territory. . . . In short, the state ruled over a territorially defined people and did so as the supreme national agency of rule over its territory, its agents increasingly reaching down to the humblest inhabitants of the least of its villages" (1990: 80–81).

10. For instance, starting from as early as the eighteenth century, the question of demarcating the boundaries of the terms *stranger* and *foreigner*—two positions of otherness—was useful in projecting an "England with borders and with a distinct community of non-foreigners," in spite of the fact that "foreigners and strangers" had been entering the country without hindrance, passports being unknown, and settling with little cost save occasional local resistance and/or resentment (Kiernan, 1978: 40). For further critical elaborations of the notion of sovereignty, see Ashley (1988, 1989b); Ashley and Walker (1990); Walker (1990, 1991b); and Shapiro (1992, 1993).

11. See Morrisey (1993: 130–32).

12. See Weiner for the original full list of "Parliamentary Grants to French Refugees" from 1794 to 1810 (1960: 223).

13. In addition to uncovering original permissive references to displaced people (as being "refugees," "exiles," and/or "émigrés" simultaneously), these authors themselves employ such terms simultaneously to speak of specific displacements. See, for example, Marrus on the Polish nationalists of the 1830s, whom he calls "political outcasts first to define a distinct refugee identity for themselves" (1985: 15). In fact, in his analysis of human displacement in the nineteenth century, Marrus comprehends exile as a form of refugeehood, hence the exile as a refugee (14–27).

14. The 1799 French revolutionary constitution inaugurated under Napoleon demonstrates the imperative of this task, as well as the productive capacity of statecraft. The constitution posits and awards centrality to the national citizen as if the citizen is already there in the very act of "constituting" the boundaries of citizenship. The first article of the constitution, for example, declares that "the French Republic is one and indivisible. Its European territory is divided into departments and communal *arrondissements.*" While the constitution starts by positing the existence of a community of citizens, in the next fourteen articles it actually "writes" or "inscribes" the qualities of a "true" French citizen vis-à-vis foreigners. The "open secret" of the modern state remains intact. For the full text of the constitution, see Arnold (1994: 22–34).

15. Colley writes: "What most enabled Great Britain to emerge as an artificial nation, and to be superimposed onto other alignments and loyalties was a series of massive wars between 1689 and 1815. . . . Britons defined themselves in terms of their common Protestantism as contrasted with the Catholicism of Continental Europe. They defined themselves against France

throughout a succession of major wars with that power" (1992a: 316). She also points out that the religious rivalry between Great Britain and France contributed directly to the "strengthening of the machinery of the state [in Great Britain], necessitating the creation of an efficient and nationwide bureaucracy and inexorably inflating the armed forces" (322). For Colley, both institutions were instrumental in heightening Britons' sense of Britishness, "the sense of solidarity with their [British] tribe" (322).

16. Popular stereotypical images were largely negative, as they referred to the Scots as "backward, provincial, and overbearing, scarcely better than penniless savages"; to the Dutch as "lazy except when their own interests are concerned, slippery and possessing an inferior sort of cunning and a vulgar stolidity"; or to the French as "French dogs." With the French, they could get humorous as well; they ridiculed errors in English grammar and pronunciation by the French, as in, "It but three weeks since me came from France" (Statt, 1995: 186–90). See also Porter (1979); Garrard (1971: 15–20); and Panayi (1994: 10–22, 140–48).

17. Exiles became objects of practices of modern statecraft, working "to enframe [l]ife, to differentiate a sphere of 'men in domestic society' by setting it in opposition to things fearsome beyond," which can be taken to mean that exiles were considered exterior to men in domestic society and whose exteriority served to enframe the domestic society (Ashley, 1988: 302). The exiles represented the other within.

18. Consider the following poem, written in support of "unnaturalizing the French in England": "Wretched and Tatter'd, full of wants; / Forlorn and friendless, hunger bit, / Hither he comes to ply his Wit, / A Beggar first, and then a Thief / If you deny the ask'd relief; / If you relieve his starving Need, / Soon he'll requite the friendly deed; / Either he will your Pocket pick, / or shew you some worse scurvy Trick" (qtd. in Statt, 1995: 190–91).

19. The instrumentality of the foreigner also produces a normative effect that goes to the heart of the rights discourse that I briefly discussed earlier in this book.

20. The full text of the Edict of Potsdam is reprinted in Baird (1895: 85).

21. See also Green (1987: 580) for a parallel discussion.

22. In the height of mercantilist economic strategies, the importation of labor and wealth was a common practice. In the mercantilist era, "skilled foreign workmen who could introduce new trades or new methods were to be encouraged by every means possible to settle in the country. Foreign craftsmen were attracted by tempting privileges such as tax-exemption, free dwellings, or a monopoly for a certain number of years on the manufacture of their products. . . . When they could not be induced to come of their own free will, then occasionally governments resorted to kidnapping them. Colbert [who held many cabinet posts in seventeenth-century France] was

particularly eager to get foreign craftsmen to live and work in France. He stationed agents in other countries whose sole job it was to recruit laborers" (Huberman, 1937: 127). Bernard Cottret bespeaks the same mercantilist phenomenon in an earlier time when he cites the coming to England of the Dutch and Walloon weavers in 1571: "The most important event in the industrial history of the sixteenth century was the coming of Dutch and Walloon weavers. Their immigration constitutes the second great landmark in the history of the English Cloth trade, just as the influx of Flemish weavers in the fourteenth century was the first. . . . The exiles were welcomed by the English Government both as religious refugees and as a valuable accession to the economic resources of the country" (1991: 57). Also see Statt (1995); Holmes (1988); and Garrard (1971).

23. See, for example, the proclamation of Henry VIII of 16 May 1544, ordering all Frenchmen to depart the kingdom (in *Typographical Antiquities*). See also "The Parliamentary Act regarding Englishmen Living Abroad," enacted in 1572, meting out penalties to those Englishmen living abroad without the queen's leave (in *Status of the Realm*, vol. 4: 13, qtd. in Loomie, 1963: 9).

24. At one level, such were the activities of dealing with practical questions as to the control of the movements of people, attempting to manage "who comes in . . . from outside" (Porter, 1979: 3). At another level, however, they had implications in terms of the transformations of the forms of governance in larger fields of politico-social and politico-economic activities. In that sense, the significance of these practical developments was unique. It lay not so much in their successes or failures to manage or control the movements of people across (imagined or real) borders and boundaries, as in their facilitation of the emergent discourse of territorial sovereignty of inside versus outside (Walker, 1993)—the emergence of the notion of territoriality of sovereignty predicated on an image of the world as consisting of territorial inside (the site of "national") and outside (the site of "international"). In short, they were of the very activities by which the inside/outside difference was gradually produced. They represented some of the earlier interventions in the realm of people as populations, and populations as domestic communities of citizens—as nations—subsequently establishing the alien politics as a field of activity for territorially grounded statecraft.

25. See Colley on the strengthening of the powers of the state, in n. 15 of this chapter.

26. The full text is reprinted in Jones (1956) and quoted in Porter (1979: 3). The 1793 act was presumably designed to empower the queen's government to expel any "aliens" living in England: "Aliens were required to assign a good reason to their presence in England, to register themselves, and to produce their passports when called upon. At first, these laws were used

in fact to deport some prominent Monarchist individuals including Charles Talleyrand, the Monarchist Bishop of Autun in France who had to flee France after the French Revolution. But, the deportations did not represent a comprehensive move against immigration. Rather, they were few in numbers, due largely to the pressure from the French government, requesting that the Queen's government deny refuge to such eminent dissidents. In his memoirs Talleyrand points to the practical power of such enactments when he wrote that 'I was expelled in order to prove that the alien act was no dead letter'" (qtd. in Cunningham, 1897: 257).

27. See Cottret (1991: 52) for an elaborate mapping of the status of alien vis-à-vis the citizen-subject by the end of 1870.

28. Article 3: "The principle of all sovereignty lies essentially in the nation; no group, no individual may have any authority that does not expressly proceed from it." Article 4: "The law is the expression of the general will; all citizens have the right to work towards its creation; it must be the same for all, whether it protects or punishes" (qtd. in Kristeva, 1991: 148–50; also see Arnold, 1994).

29. "While the term passport has been used for centuries, its meaning has undergone considerable changes in the course of time. Its first use in an English statute was 1548, where it applied to a license given by a military authority to a soldier to go on furlough. In a treaty between Great Britain and Denmark of July 11, 1670, the word is used to connote 'sea briefs' issued for ships, but it is stated in the treaty that 'letters of passport' might be required to be produced on land by men traveling. Under a statute of 1793, aliens were required to obtain a passport from the local authorities of their place of residence. It would seem that in the eighteenth century the term mainly was used for documents issued to aliens by the sovereign of the territory in which the documents were effective. In the course of the nineteenth century the practice of issuing passports to aliens for travel in the issuing country seems to have fallen into disuse. During the French Revolution, while passports were at first abolished in accordance with the proclaimed right of individuals to freedom of movement, a number of laws were enacted which prohibited the departure from France without passports" (Weis, 1979: 222–23).

30. For the full text of the 1799 constitution and the 1803 civil code in English, see Arnold (1994).

31. The original title of the foreigner-refugees law was *Loi relative aux Étrangers réfugiés qui résideront en France,* 21 April 1832.

32. Translated from the original French text quoted in Grahl-Madsen (1972: 95).

33. Even in an assimilationist tradition, the constructing of the foreigner (in this case the refugee, in laws and regulations pertinent to refugees) posits

the "already thereness" of the nation into which the foreigner can then be assimilated. In this sense, the foreigner discourse affirms the statist hierarchy as a priori, for it functions as an alibi for the citizen/nation/state ensemble. That regimenting those who are deemed foreigners amounts to statecraft of the first order goes unnoticed. As Ashley calls it in chapter 2 of this book, the "open secret" of the state remains intact.

34. For a study examining a slice of this historical process in France, the first anticlerical campaign of the Third Republic between 1789 and 1889, see Acomb (1967).

35. The full text of the law appears in Garcia-Mora (1956: 75).

36. This is a partial list compiled from Jones (1956); Grahl-Madsen (1966); Weis (1979); Garcia-Mora (1956); and Booth (1980).

37. "According to the article 6 of the institute's proposals in 1892," Plender writes, for example, "the free entrance of aliens into the territory of a civilized State should not be curtailed in a general and permanent manner other than in the interest of public welfare and for the most serious reasons" (1988: 72). Basing his opinion on this proposal, Johann Bluntschli, a prominent jurist in the late nineteenth century, wrote: "The state may for reasons of public welfare expel certain named foreigners and . . . public welfare alone entitles a State to prohibit foreigners from entering its territory" (qtd. in Plender, 1988: 72).

3. REFUGEES, INTERGOVERNMENTALIZATION, AND STATECRAFT

1. In fact, that the coordination of efforts at all levels, whether between governments or between private organizations, was seen as the primary function of the high commissioner not only was clearly written in the founding resolution but also was repeatedly articulated on different occasions in the ensuing years. See League of Nations (1921i: 37) for the original phrase defining the task of the commissioner as "the coordination of the actions taken in various countries, whether by the governments or by private organizations." For repeated articulations of the "nature" of the task, see League of Nations (1922a). Also see League of Nations (1922b).

2. Thus, it seemed a modest initiative in terms of both its scope and its mandate; its scope was limited, at least initially, to Russian refugees, and its mandate was declared to be primarily humanitarian, oriented to tackle the "unforeseen" phenomenon of the refugees, "people driven from their country by Bolshevik excesses" (League of Nations, 1921i: 37). This objective was again accentuated in the League of Nations Conference on the Question of the Russian Refugees in August 1921: "The conference is of the opinion that, as a problem of interest to the entire world, it would not be just to

leave the burden of relieving Russian refugees to the few nations which have hitherto borne it alone for philanthropic reasons and by reason of their geographical situation, a course which might involve them in sacrifices beyond their power; and that not only all the states belonging to the League of Nations, but all the states of the civilized world, ought to be invited to contribute support in proportion to their resources for this urgent and essential task in the common interest of mankind" (League of Nations, 1921a: 902).

3. In recent years, informed more systematically by the recent literature on international regimes, a somewhat "revisionist" view on the "beginnings" of an effective refugee regime has been advanced (Skran, 1988; 1995; Marrus, 1985; Loescher, 1993). This view commences by identifying the League of Nations High Commissioner for Refugees as the starting point of the modern refugee regime. It then proceeds to recount the evolution of the refugee regime through the establishment and transformation of a number of refugee organizations and the development of an international legal and institutional framework underlying the activities of these organizations. According to this view, all of these organizations—the High Commissioner for Refugees, the Nansen International Office for Refugees, the Intergovernmental Committee on Refugees, the United Nations Relief and Rehabilitation Agency, the International Refugee Organization, and the United Nations High Commissioner for Refugees—represent progressive steps in the evolution of the international refugee regime.

Even when such a view on continuity is advanced, however, the "revisionist" studies also point to certain periods of discontinuities and even breaks in the historical continuity of the refugee regime. In general, they understand the development of the refugee regime, in the political and legal sense, in terms of two successive periods of regime formation (Loescher, 1993). The first period starts with the establishment of the League of Nations High Commissioner in 1921 and ends with the liquidation of the successor organization—the Nansen International Office for Refugees—in 1938. The regime formations during this period are designated under the rubric of "the interwar refugee regime" built around successive League of Nations organizations. In these studies, the first period still represents a series of ad hoc attempts undertaken in response to refugee emergencies in Europe. As such, they constitute but a patchwork of responses, lacking continuity and universality. In other words, the legal and institutional arrangements around which their activities are organized lack universality, temporally and geographically, as well as organizationally.

The second period commences with the founding of the United Nations High Commissioner for Refugees in 1951 and continues to the present. The regime formations that have occurred since 1951 are subsumed under the rubric of "the modern refugee regime." Contrary to the representation of regime activities during the interwar period, the second period is generally attributed the characteristics of an effective international regime: a universal applicability of the arrangements that govern the relations of the parties involved across time and place. Let me say that this view is closer to the arguments of this study on the "origins" of the refugee regime. But, to the extent that the proponents of this view still operate within the statist paradigm and, say, comprehend regimes as tertiary responses by already fully established states, as well as argue that the post-1951 era is the decisive era in the formation of the refugee regime, paradigmatic-epistemological and historical-interpretive differences remain between their reading of refugee histories and the reading in this study. Such differences notwithstanding, this "revising" view, as evidenced most lucidly in the studies by Gil Loescher (1993) and Claudena Skran (1988, 1995), represents a certain clarity in the discourse on refugees.

4. In this analysis, intersubjectivity is not the intersubjectivity of knowledge but the intersubjectivity of regimentation, the controlling of the space of the refugee. It does not posit the presence of an environment that is simply there to be acted in, but it refers to an active fashioning of the environment within which the figure of the refugee is shaped and acted upon, both conceptually and practically.

5. Among the multitude of forces and actors active in postwar politics—the bourgeoisie, nationalists, communists, socialists, republican-monarchists, and militarists—coalitions of bourgeois-nationalist movements led by the Young Turks uprooted more people in what had been the territories of the Ottoman, Russian, and Austria-Hungarian Empires, in effect adding to the millions already displaced as a result of the preceding wars.

6. E. J. Hobsbawm argues that this nineteenth-century principle of territorially conceptualized hierarchy in life "triumphed at the end of World War I," even if only momentarily (1992: 131). However, while even only temporary, the triumph of such a conceptualization proved very costly in human lives.

7. Generally, in the implementing of these projects, the displaced people were seen as necessary casualties of what was perceived as an inevitable unfolding of history in favor of imagined nations and their representative agents, sovereign territorial states. As Mocsy suggests, "The social structure was in need of revision" to create homogenous populations rooted in clearly delineated homelands (1983: 8).

8. This difficulty was compounded by yet another contemporaneous practical problem, an impasse arising out of the imagined organization of space in a global state system that had left no "neutral" space into which the undesirables and unwanted could be expelled. In other words, it became impossible to expel the unwanted into a neutral space, unless it would be

the depths of the oceans or the heights of the skies, the only two remaining neutral spaces.

9. In the territorial articulations of the state, "beyond" the state lies the site of anarchy.

10. These intensifications in the regimentation of human displacement, however, did not represent an ontological change in the task of statecraft from the times of, say, the French Revolution. The task remained continual "people production," as Appadurai (1996) might put it, or the continual "invention" of the territorially bound nation, as Brubaker (1992) or Hobsbawm (1990) might prefer to say. As I have already discussed (in chapter 2), the effecting of the images and identities of a figure of externality—the alien or the foreigner-other—is intimately instrumental to this task. In this sense the task did not change from the nineteenth century to the twentieth. Instead, what changed were the strategies by which this task of statecraft was carried out in relation to the shifts in historical circumstances. The new strategy was the active intergovernmentalization of refugee regimentations.

11. The High Commissioner for Refugees has come to occasion and to embody the intergovernmentalization or internationalization of efforts to regiment human displacement under the sign of the refugee into what has been recognized as the modern refugee regime.

12. The count offered the Greek government's efforts for refugees as worthy of praise, reaffirming that "in redoubling its efforts on behalf of refugees, the government at Athens is contributing to the maintenance of the peace of the world" (League of Nations, 1924: 149).

13. See Vattel (1820) on a similar conceptualization of aliens as threatening to others.

14. For a list of governmental representatives to the commissioner's office and the commissioner's agents appointed to governments and other organizations, see League of Nations (1922d: 394–95). For a list of the organizations belonging to the Special Joint Committee, see p. 387.

15. The Special Joint Committee is identified as the "Permanent Consultative Committee" in Hope-Simpson (1939: 200).

16. For the rendering of the refugee event as an abnormality, see League of Nations (1921a). The first resolution reads as follows: "The conference has considered with great care the difficulties which have been encountered by refugees as regards their juridical status in the law of the countries in which they are. It is of the opinion that each government must solve these difficulties by adapting its own legal regulations to prevent *abnormal* conditions" (901; emphasis added).

17. Giovanna Procacci similarly argues à la Foucault, saying that "procedures of exclusion [the constructions of a refugee category as abnormalcy] in the end [are] a way of including" through "procedures of inclusion, through

juridical as well as scientific norms" (1994: 212). Beyond the refugee identity lies a process of refugee normalization, a process attempting to constitute a "normal" relation between the categories of the refugee and the citizen, where the refugee category signifies the abnormal or the aberrant while the citizen category stands for what is normal.

18. According to Skran, similar developments took place progressively to constitute the basis of the modern refugee regime as written into the 1951 United Nations convention (1988: 281).

19. The governments became instruments of objectification, as Foucault (1984, 1988) understands the idea, creating objects of intervention—the citizen and the refugee—already invested with signs of inclusion and exclusion. The refugee category was written and formalized, and the state identified as the issuing authority, thus putting the state at the center of life. This again is in concert with the earlier logic of the sovereignty, or as Michael Shapiro (1993) put it, the sovereignty impulse, oriented to create identities of inclusion and exclusion under the control of the state, thus bringing under state control as much of life as possible. In Foucault's terms, this was the creation of a legal object of governance already wedded to a specific economy of governance.

20. These practices took various forms. The strategic dispersion of refugees throughout the country so as not to allow them to constitute a refugee majority was one practice of diffusing the "Asia Minor culture" of the refugees. In fact, Renee Hirschon notes that in regions where refugees were in the majority, "electoral districts were gerrymandered to prevent refugee majorities" (1989: 44). Another practice was through schooling, which, according to refugees, was not only insufficient but also unsatisfactory. For decades, dropout rates among the children of refugees were very high as compared to the "mainlanders." Hirschon holds that the refugees from Asia Minor "worked continually at constructing boundaries that would preserve a sense of separate identity from the metropolitan Greek society" (4–5). Citing her encounters with them in the 1980s, Hirschon writes of refugees embracing and cherishing their refugeeness through succeeding generations: "Referring to themselves, people would say, 'We are refugees' (*prosphyges*) or 'We are *Mikrasiates*' (Asia Minor people). Significantly, not only the original refugees, survivors of the exodus, used these terms, but also younger people of the second and even third generation, born in the locality or elsewhere in Greece" (45). For an excellent analysis of the experiences of Asia Minor refugees in Greece, see chapters 1–4 and 10 of Hirschon (1989). See also Herzfeld (1991).

21. Another Greek representative, M. Andreades, had expressed similar sentiments in 1924. "I desire to offer the grateful thanks of my Country to the League for the patronage which it has given to the work of Greek

Government. . . . As was said just now, there are a million and a half refugees deserving our compassion, since they are in no way responsible for the hardships that have befallen them. . . . Had they been abandoned to their fate, they would probably have given way to despair and become a cause of social unrest, the effects of which might have been felt beyond the frontiers of Greece" (League of Nations, 1924: 151).

22. In effect, the high commissioner helped produce and stabilize a specific imagination of the world as a world of states. It did so by making possible the emergence of a number of institutions and techniques of normalization—the procedures of camps, the transfer from camps, and so on—all of which were predicated on the posited, unproblematically prevailing relations and institutions of the state.

23. An Armenian refugee was understood as "any person of Armenian origin, formerly a subject of the Ottoman Empire, who does not enjoy or who no longer enjoys the protection of the Government of the Turkish Republic and has not acquired another nationality" (Hope-Simpson, 1939: 227).

24. The phrases "no longer enjoys the protection of the government of" and "has not acquired another nationality" in the 1926 LNHCR definitions of a refugee have continued to be the bedrock of subsequent attempts to define the refugee, thus placing the sovereign state in the center of refugee practices. In fact, the Convention Relating to the Status of Refugees, which was signed in 1951, simply reiterated the principle of the state-centeredness of refugee issues by defining the refugee. See chapter 4.

25. Both letters are printed in League of Nations (1927b: 68–69).

26. Some of the displaced people saw the refugee status as a category of resistance to incorporation into particular forms of governance with which they disagreed. The refugee status afforded them a neutral ground from which to wage their revolutionary or not-so-revolutionary struggles. However, even the perceived neutral ground had been made possible through continuous practices of statecraft. That is, the refugee status as a perceived "neutral ground" had been defined in accordance with the logic of the territorializing state system as the logic of governance in local and global affairs. For the final salvation, the refugee had either to step back into a territorial space of governance—the original domestic community there—or to step into a new one here, which would be yet another territorially bound community of citizens.

27. There were hundreds of nongovernmental organizations, of a local, regional, and global variety. Some of these organizations were immensely powerful financially and politically. The International Red Cross Committee, the American Red Cross, Near East Relief, Caritas Internationalis, and the American Jewish Distribution Committee were more effectual in active relief work than most other entities, governmental or nongovernmental.

There were also a number of smaller organizations with specific target populations. Zemgor, the Russian Red Cross, the Jewish Colonization Association, the Hebrew Immigrant Aid Society, and Matoetti Socialist Funds were among such organizations that were operating during the tenure of the LNHCR, between 1921 and 1930 (Hope-Simpson, 1939: 172–90; Tabori, 1972: 312–26).

28. See Hope-Simpson (1939: 566–94) for the full text of the convention.

4. CHANGE AND CONTINUITY

1. As I try to clarify in the introduction, the designation "conventional studies" is meant to imply not that such studies are all identical in their interpretations, but that there is a peculiar commonality to their interpretations, a certain common ambiguity on the temporal and spatial origins of the refugee regime that, for heuristic purposes, enables me to subsume them under the "conventional" designation. Consider, for example, the following narrative, which, I think, exemplifies this ambiguity well: "Today's international refugee regime . . . was created in the early post–World War II years and has been further developed since then, but it has its roots in the early 1920s" (Rogers, 1992: 1114). Here, what is symptomatic of the common ambiguity is that the period of the 1920s, while being acknowledged in terms of its place in the history of the refugee regime, is simultaneously marginalized relative to the post-1945 era. It is this marginalization that I contest in this chapter, arguing that the early regimentations of refugee events were cardinal formative regimentations central to the subsequent regime activities.

2. The nine signatory states were Belgium, France, Bulgaria, Egypt, Norway, Denmark, Italy, Czechoslovakia, and the United Kingdom. Also, "certain governments which did not ratify the internationally binding convention have stated that the provisions of the convention are, in practice, applied to refugees in their countries. This was the case as regards the governments of the United States, Estonia, Finland, Greece, Iraq, Latvia, Sweden, Switzerland, and Yugoslavia" (Hope-Simpson, 1939: 244). This convention is significant for our discussion of the LNHCR, for, as I shall show, the 1933 convention is an uncanny anticipation of the 1951 Geneva Convention on Refugees, which is the cardinal canon guiding the activities of the UNHCR.

3. For a descriptive account of the subordinate position of the UNRRA and other refugee organizations to the military authorities, see "Supreme Headquarters Allied Expeditionary Force, Administrative Memorandum, Number 39 (Revised—16 April 1945). Displaced Persons and Refugees in Germany" (qtd. in full in Proudfoot, 1956: 461).

4. Michael Marrus and Leonard Dinnerstein both argue that this view of refugees was widespread among military administrators, who were driven more by the exigencies of occupation than by humanitarianism. Whether willful or not, the military's control of the refugee camps led to accusations against the U.S. military of the mistreatment of refugees in the camps. Some military leaders, such as George S. Patton, were charged with willful mistreatment of refugees and displaced people (Dinnerstein, 1982: 17). Patton had ordered all refugees and displaced people (DPs) to be forcibly interned in camps where subsequently, observers argued, abuses allegedly occurred. Dinnerstein writes that "when confronted with the issue, Patton explained that the DPs should be treated as prisoners and put behind barbed wire. If not, they would not stay in the camps, would spread over the country like locusts, and would eventually have to be rounded up after quite a few of them had been shot and quite a few Germans murdered and pillaged" (1982: 17). While Patton's remarks might reflect an extreme interpretation of the military exigencies of the day, Marrus writes that the view of displaced people as obstacles was "not uncommon" among soldiers (1985: 322).

5. The full text of the memorandum is published in Proudfoot (1956: 461).

6. The number of displaced people assisted by the UNRRA differs from one source to another. In Marrus (1985: 320), the number is given as millions, while in Ferris (1993b: 6) it is two million.

7. The IRO's founders believed that the European refugee phenomenon was a temporary occurrence that could be remedied with rational and austere management, of which the IRO was to be the embodiment. Between December 1946 and September 1948, a preparatory commission for the IRO executed the functions of the organization. After fifteen states had acceded to the constitution of the IRO in September 1948, the IRO succeeded the preparatory commission as the primary intergovernmental refugee organization. Once operational, in the first year of its tenure, the IRO succeeded in resettling the majority of refugees it had inherited from previous refugee organizations, such as the UNRRA. While these efforts strengthened the belief that the refugee phenomenon was ephemeral, the belief was not to last. The founders of the IRO would have to realize, to their disappointment, that the refugee phenomenon was a condition of statecraft to begin with, so that it would be as ephemeral or perennial as practices of statecraft were.

8. The resolution adopted by the United Nations General Assembly on 12 February 1946 (document a/45) declares: "(i) This problem is international in scope and nature; (ii) No refugees or displaced persons who have finally and definitely, in complete freedom and after receiving full knowledge of the facts, including adequate information from the Governments of their countries of origin, expressed valid objections to returning to their countries

of origin and do not come within the provisions of (d) below shall be compelled to return to their country of origin. The future of such refugees shall become the concern of whatever international body may be recognized or established . . . ; (iii) the main task concerning displaced persons is to encourage and assist in every way possible their early return to their countries of origin having regard to the principles laid down in Paragraph (c) (ii) of the resolution. Such assistance may take the form promoting the conclusion of bilateral arrangements for mutual assistance in the repatriation of such persons, having regard to the principles laid down in paragraph (c) (ii) above" (full text is in Holborn, 1956: 588–89).

9. "During its four and a half years of existence, the IRO developed more formalized and closely intertwined cooperation among partners. . . . The cooperation of international and national governmental and nongovernmental agencies which had begun with the efforts of Dr. Nansen in the League of Nations and became more formalized under the UNRRA, was deepened under the efficient leadership of [the] IRO Director-General . . . and his staff" (Holborn, 1975: 32–34).

10. See the Constitution of the International Refugee Organization, annex 1, part 1, section A, "Definition of Refugees." The full text is printed in Holborn (1956: 575–89).

11. The full text of the 1933 convention is published in Hope-Simpson (1939: 566–94).

12. Particularly the mechanisms that regimented the civil, administrative, and juridical rights of refugees were very similar, if not identical, in the scope and nature of the rights and duties of both states and refugees. It is instructive to note that out of twenty-three articles in the 1933 convention and twenty-five articles in the 1938 convention, eleven were identical. Consider one of the articles that is not identical—the 1933 article on *nonrefoulement,* which demonstrates the overlaps in the two conventions not only in terms of the rules (of, say, *nonrefoulement*) but also in the content of the rules. The 1933 convention article 3(1) reads: "Each of the Contracting parties undertakes not to remove or keep from its territory by application of police measures, such as expulsions or non-admittance (refoulement), refugees who have been authorized to reside there regularly, unless the said measures are dictated by reasons for national security or public order." The 1938 convention article 5(2) reads: "Without prejudice to the measures which may be taken within any territory, refugees who have been authorized to reside therein may not be subjected by the authorities to measures of expulsion or reconduction unless such measures are dictated by reasons of national security and public order." Full texts of both conventions are reprinted in Hope-Simpson (1939: 566–98).

13. The Statute of the Office of the United Nations High Commissioner for Refugees was adopted by the General Assembly on 14 December 1950 as

an annex to General Assembly Resolution 428 (V). See UNHCR (1950) for the full text of the statute.

14. For a discussion of the functions of the UNHCR as interpreted by the first high commissioner, see "Refugees and Stateless Persons and the Problems of Assistance to the Refugee" (UN General Assembly, 1952).

15. United Nations Economic and Social Council, *Ad Hoc Committee on Statelessness and Related Problems: Status of Refugees and Stateless Persons: A Memorandum by the Secretary General,* 3 January 1950 (E/AC.32/2), in Takkenberg and Tahbaz (1989: 22).

16. Juridical status: The 1933 convention, article 4(1): "The personal status of a refugee shall be governed by the law of the country of his domicile or, failing such, by the law of the country of his residence" (in Hope-Simpson, 1939: 576). The 1951 convention, article 12(1): "The personal status of a refugee shall be governed by the law of the country of his domicile or, if he has no domicile, by the law of the country of his residence" (UNHCR, 1951).

17. Adminstrative status: these measures regulate identity papers and travel documents for refugees. In both conventions, identity and travel documents are guaranteed for refugees under different names: article 2(1) of the 1933 convention calls travel documents "Nansen Certificates" (in Hope-Simpson, 1939: 570), whereas article 28(1) of the 1951 convention calls them "Travel Documents" (UNHCR, 1951).

18. Employment: The 1933 convention, article 7(1): "The restrictions ensuing from the application of laws and regulations for the protection of the national labor market shall not be applied in all severity to refugees domiciled or regularly resident in the country" (in Hope-Simpson, 1939: 578). The 1951 convention, article 17(1): "Restrictive measures imposed on aliens or the employment of aliens for the protection of the national labor market shall not be applied to a refugee who was already exempt from them at the date of entry into force of this convention for the Contracting States concerned" (UNHCR, 1951).

19. Education: The 1933 convention, article 12: "Refugees shall enjoy in the school, courses and universities of each of the Contracting Parties treatment as favorable as other foreigners in general" (in Hope-Simpson, 1939: 582). The 1951 convention, article 22(1): "The Contracting states shall accord to refugees the same treatment as is accorded to nationals with respect to elementary education." Article 22(2): "The Contracting States shall accord to refugees as favorable as possible, and, in any event, not less favorable than that accorded to aliens in the same circumstances, with respect to education other than elementary education" (UNHCR, 1951).

20. The United States did this by establishing an alternative network of agencies and organizations working in the refugee field. These organizations,

such as the Intergovernmental Committee for European Migration (ICEM) and the United States Escapees Program (USEP), both established in 1951 and generously funded by the United States in the 1950s, relegated the drastically underfunded UNHCR to a status of practical inconsequence in the early 1950s. In addition, the U.S. representatives either blocked in the General Assembly the approval of requests by the UNHCR to raise emergency funds or did not contribute to such requests when they were approved in the assembly. The United States saw the UNHCR as a futile, if not a naive, enterprise in the context of the cold war. It channeled its financial and political energies through the organizations that it could fully control (such as the United Nations Refugee Fund). The unrelenting U.S. attitude discouraged many other countries from lending full-fledged support to the UNHCR. The powerlessness of the UNHCR was manifested in 1952 when the commissioner tried to establish an emergency fund in the amount of $3 million to help the "most needy groups" of refugees. As James Read points out, the international community was largely indifferent to the plea (1962: 10). From 1952 to 1955, only a little more than $1 million was collected (Holborn, 1975: 146). During the same period, the United States contributed more than $45 million to the ICEM and the USEP (Loescher, 1993: 65).

21. After lengthy debates in the General Assembly of the United Nations in 1953, the mandate of the UNHCR was extended for five years starting from January 1954. The conventional studies do not give any clear explanation for this extension, given that, they argue, the UNHCR did not have the support of most governments. One reason that the UNHCR's term was extended might have been to facilitate the entering into force of the 1951 UN Convention on Refugees as an instrument of international law (UNHCR, 1971: 32). This event took place in 1954, three years after the adoption of the convention in the General Assembly, with its formal ratification by Australia, the sixth country to ratify it. The convention explicitly designated the UNHCR as the agency in charge of facilitating its objectives. Coupled with this practical necessity was the perception by some members that the UNHCR's "nonpolitical" coordinative role could be useful in engendering collaboration across Europe. The general secretary of the United Nations, Dag Hammarskjöld, underscored this perception in 1953 by contending that "there remains a need for a central international organization concerned with the problem" (qtd. in Holborn, 1975: 142).

22. On 9 November 1956, the UN General Assembly, in Resolution 1006 (ES II), called upon the high commissioner's office to "consult with appropriate international agencies and interested governments, with a view to making speedy and effective arrangements for emergency assistance to refugees from Hungary" (qtd. in Zarjevski, 1988: 16).

23. In 1957, the General Assembly asked the high commissioner to "use

its good offices" to mediate between the People's Republic of China (PRC), Taiwan, and Great Britain in determining the status of refugees from the PRC in Hong Kong. The practice of the "good offices" represented further expansion of the refugee regime of 1951, in this case by disregarding the clause in the convention restricting the UNHCR's activities to Europe. Loescher maintains that the UNHCR involvement in China through its "good offices" "set an important precedent that led to a steady expansion of the High Commissioner's authority to mount assistance programs throughout the developing world during the next decade" (1993: 72). The UNHCR help to Algerians in refuge in Morocco and Tunisia in 1958 was just a start in this process.

24. Organization of African Unity Convention Governing the Specific Aspects of Refugee Problems in Africa, adopted by the Assembly Heads of State and Government at the OAU's 6th Ordinary Session, Addis Ababa, Ethiopia, 10 September 1969. For the full text, see UNHCR (1979).

25. Cartagena Declaration, adopted at the Colloquium about the International Protection of Refugees in Central America, Mexico, and Panama: Problems of Humanitarian Rights, held 19–22 November 1984 in Cartagena, Colombia. See UNHCR (1993b).

5. HUMANITARIAN INTERVENTIONS AS PRACTICES OF STATECRAFT

1. From April 1991, which marks the date of the Kurdish refugee crisis in northern Iraq, to early 1995, many scholarly as well as policy-oriented studies have been produced (including Lewy, 1992; Garigue, 1993; Nanda, 1992; Delbruck, 1992; O'Connell, 1992; Nafziger, 1991; Adelman, 1992; Arnison, 1993; Whitman, 1994; Jackson, 1993; Roberts, 1993; Fisher, 1994; Rodley, 1992; Donnelly, 1993; Minear and Weiss, 1993; Weiss and Minear, 1993; UNHCR, 1993b; and Heilberg, 1994).

2. In 1579, at the time of religious wars in France, Stephanus Junius Brutus, in *Vindiciae contra Tyrannos* (The grounds of rights against tyrants) affirmed "the right and duty of princes to interfere in behalf of neighboring peoples who are oppressed on account of adherence to the true religion or by any obvious tyranny" (qtd. in Dunning, 1913: 55). Writing in 1642, Hugo Grotius arrived at the same conclusion. As regards the question of "whether a war on the subjects of another be just for the purposes of defending them from injuries inflicted by their ruler," Grotius argued, "If a tyrant like Busiris, Phalaris, or Diomade of Thrace practices atrocities towards his subjects, which no just man can approve, the right of human social connection is not cut off in such a case. So Christians took arms against Maxentus and Licimus: and several of the Roman emperors took or threatened to take

arms against Persians, except they prevented the Christians being persecuted on account of their religion" ([1642] 1925: 439–40).

Vattel referred to a similar notion of humanitarian intervention as unequivocally and categorically as Grotius did: "If a prince, by violating the fundamental laws, gives his subjects a lawful cause for resisting him; by his insupportable tyranny, he brings on a national revolt against him, any foreign power may rightfully give assistance to an oppressed people who ask for its aid" (qtd. in Nafziger, 1991: 21). "Prudence," Vattel wrote elsewhere, "will suggest the times when it [a foreign state] may interfere [in the constitutional government of a state] to the extent of making friendly representations" (Vattel, 1820: 490).

3. In the late nineteenth century, E. R. N. Arntz characterized humanitarian intervention as a rightful "collective" measure exercised by states "when a government, although acting within its rights of sovereignty, violates the rights of humanity, either by measures contrary to the interest of other states, or by an excess of cruelty and injustice" (qtd. in Stowell, 1921: 53). Early in the twentieth century, Ellery C. Stowell defined humanitarian intervention in the same sense, as "the reliance upon force for the justifiable purpose of protecting the inhabitants of another state from treatment which is so arbitrary and persistently abusive as to exceed the limits of authority within which the sovereign is presumed to act with reason and justice" (1921: 52). The eminent jurist-scholar Lassa Oppenheim conceptualized the issue likewise in the aftermath of the terrible Nazi legacy in Europe: "There is a general agreement that by virtue of its personal and territorial supremacy, a state can treat its nationals according to discretion. But there is a substantial body of opinion and practice in support of the view that there are limits to that discretion; when a state renders itself guilty of cruelties against and persecution of its nationals in such a way as to deny their fundamental rights and to shock the conscience of mankind, intervention in the interest of humanity is legally permissible" (1948: 279–80). In the words of another observer, "such intervention, however, was justified only in extreme cases . . . where great evils existed, great crimes were being perpetrated, or where there was great danger of race extermination" (Nanda, 1992: 309).

L. F. E. Goldie suggests that "humanitarian intervention should be seen as a gratuitous act to prevent the continuation of genocidal activities or policies of foreign governments against minorities which are their own (and not intervening states') nationals" (qtd. in Lillich, 1973: 46). Howard Adelman tailors his commentary on the issue in view of the developments since the early 1990s: "Humanitarian intervention refers to the use of physical force within the sovereign territory of another state by other states or the United Nations for the purpose of either protection or the provision of emergency aid to the population within that territory" (1992: 18). Finally, reflections by Fernando Teson are instructive in underscoring the crux of the issue: "I argue that the assertion of a right of humanitarian intervention is the best interpretation of international legal materials. My main argument is that because the ultimate justification of the existence of states is the protection and enforcement of the natural rights of the citizens, a government that engages in substantial violations of human rights betrays the very purpose for which it exists and so forfeits not only its domestic legitimacy, but its international legitimacy as well" (1988: 15).

4. See, for instance, the latest debate on humanitarian intervention in the special issue of *International Political Science Review* (1997).

5. For instance, when the philosopher John Dunn (1994) speaks of an imperative to do something in the face of massive human suffering, he is highlighting the significance of the issue of ethics in humanitarian interventions. Similarly, when Jim Whitman (1994), Adam Roberts (1993), and a number of others point to the dangers of unchecked interventionism, they are emphasizing the importance of the legal aspects of humanitarian interventions from the standpoint of the customary relations and institutions of the territorial state system.

6. Studies of state sovereignty from the standpoint of various theoretical orientations have proliferated in the last decade. Efforts to reconceptualize state sovereignty on the heels of dramatic changes subsumed under such terms as *globalization, interdependence,* and *transnationalization*; postmodern and poststructuralist countercritiques of the state and state sovereignty; and numerous studies in the interfaces of realism, neorealism, liberal institutionalism, poststructuralism, and postmodernism have all contributed to this proliferation. The debate on state sovereignty is richer and more interesting than ever. (For a critical sample of such works, see Bull, 1984; Keohane and Nye, 1977; Thomson and Krasner, 1989; Thomson, 1995; Ruggie, 1993a; 1993b; Barkin and Cronin, 1994; Walker, 1990; 1991a; 1991b; Ashley, 1988; 1989a; 1993; and Shapiro, 1993.)

7. For a discussion of the issue from both perspectives, see Rodley (1992).

8. See chapter 2 for a discussion of what Certeau means by awarding centrality.

9. U.S. Secretary of Defense William Perry argued that the humanitarian intervention in Bosnia must be judged in light of its success in saving the lives of hundreds of thousands of people. He asserted that as of June 1995, only about one thousand people in that year had been killed because of the war, contrasted with one hundred thousand dead in 1992 (National Public Radio, 19 June 1995).

10. The analysis here focuses on the intervention in Iraq following the collapse of the Kurdish uprising. Although the study explores a few other cases, such as interventions in the former Yugoslavia and in Somalia, these

explorations remain preliminary. Inasmuch as this is the case, I am keenly aware of the study's empirical and theoretical limits in terms of "generalizability." It offers only a series of general arguments and hypotheses on humanitarian interventions and statecraft for further consideration in the scholarly field.

11. In a similar fashion, Nigel Rodley speaks of "transboundary implications" as a possible "necessary" condition for undertaking humanitarian intervention (1992: 34).

12. Such imagery conjured through the memorandum and other practices runs in the face of the realities "on the ground." As a Turkish columnist put it, "The border between Turkey and Iraq looks as though it disappeared. Although the border is officially closed, unofficially it is open, as several hundred thousand people have taken refuge on the Turkish side already" (Cemal, 1991; my translation). The Turkish daily *Cumhuriyet* (9–11 April 1991) also reported the frequent ministerial- and ambassadorial-level consultations between Turkish and Iraqi representatives. The reports indicated that the government of Iraq was an integral part of the policies devised at the time. For an extensive analysis of how the allied countries placated Iraq through the United Nations, see Rodley (1992) and Freedman and Boren (1992).

13. For elaborations on the international refugee regime, see Gordenker (1987); Guest (1991); Dacyl (1990); Aleinikoff (1991); Loescher (1993); Ferris (1993b); and UNHCR (1979, 1993b).

14. The U.S. Committee for Refugees (USCR) reported that those people who were forced to remain "close to home" became victims of war in ways other than dying. A report by the committee, for instance, chronicles the events by which thousands of Bosnian Muslim refugees were deported from Croatia into areas in Bosnia held by the Croatian Defense Council, where the refugees were imprisoned, to be used in prisoner exchanges with the Bosnian government army (USCR, 1993b: 9). According to another report (Argent, 1992: 11–12, 18), refugees were forced by both the Bosnian government forces and Croatian Defense Council forces to populate certain areas in order to keep control of those areas. The rape of thousands of women, too, could be attributed to that purpose. Furthermore, the USCR reports allude to hundreds of thousands of women, men, and children who were forced to remain in Bosnia to be ethnically cleansed, raped, or murdered (USCR, 1993a: 12; see also Frelick, 1992b).

15. Stjepan Mestrovic is quoted by Sabina Eleonori (1997: 29) in her excellent study of intervention in the Bosnian refugee crisis. "Suffering-waching" is adopted from Eleonori's use (1997: 2).

16. The hypothesis of the centralization of the refugee as the object of humanitarian intervention in Iraq is a specific hypothesis drawn from a general one. The general hypothesis insists that humanitarian interventions are

orchestrated practices of intergovernmental statecraft, oriented to produce, empower, and privilege the territorially bound images, identities, and relations of the citizen-subject (in domestic community) from which the state gets its sovereign powers and which the state in turn represents. The important point is the problematization of the object in various fields of activity, including that of humanitarian intervention, through which the modern state is crafted into existence day in and day out.

17. Boutros-Ghali (1994) referred to six specific contradictions in world politics as the Achilles' heel of efforts for peace and security in the world. They are systemic contradiction, structural contradiction, psychological contradiction, political-military contradiction, crisis and the contradiction of development, and contradiction in communication. According to him, "enlightened multilateralism" through the United Nations is the answer to these contradictions.

6. REFUGEES, PREDICAMENTS OF TERRITORIAL DEMOCRACY, AND STATECRAFT IN EUROPE

1. In this chapter, at times I use the terms *refugee* and *immigrant* interchangeably, though the chapter purports to examine "refugee" events. This, however, is not an arbitrary practice or an ontological slippage. Rather, it reflects the state of displacement discourse in popular and institutional discourses. In recent years, in both governmental and nongovernmental discourses on human migrations, the generic term *immigrant* or *immigration* is increasingly employed to refer to human migration in the broadest sense, including refugeeism and asylum as forms of human displacement and replacement. For example, efforts by the EU in the 1990s to harmonize its "immigration" policies were carried on under the general rubric of "immigration," which subsumed references to asylum or refugeeism. Often, references to refugees by government officials or the representatives of international organizations conflate various terms, thus blurring whatever distinctions among instituted categories exist. The World Council of Churches, for example, writes of "refugees, migrants, foreigners and unregular migrants" in one sentence (1995: 1). The Refugee Studies Program at Oxford University refers to refugees as "forced or involuntary migrants" as opposed to voluntary migrants. The distinct terms *economic refugees* and *political refugees* have been part of the public and official cant for a long time. One of the seminal collections of international instruments regulating international migration includes refugee movements under international migration (Plender, 1988). Similarly, other scholars writing on issues of "migration" to Europe (whose works are cited in subsequent notes) use the generic term

immigration to refer to what are otherwise categorized as refugee movements as defined in the 1951 UN Convention on the Status of Refugees, as well as to people they consider to be migrants. To this confounding collection of terminology, President Clinton added the term illegal refugee in 1994, referring to "Cuban immigrants." With this field of terminology in mind, in this chapter I use the term *immigrant* along with or in substitution of the term *refugee*. Such usage is employed generally in cases where it is contextually clear that the term *immigrant* in the reference denotes or connotes the term *refugee*. In the final analysis, however, these conflations are also strategically intentional in showing how displaced humans—refugees, immigrants, and others—become commonly instrumental in statecraft.

2. In this book, I make no attempt to define what democracy should be, though in the broadest sense I provisionally understand democracy to mean an organization of relations and institutions in a polity that allow for the production and preservation of capacities to participate in the shaping of the polity. However, in the final analysis, I agree with R. B. J. Walker that "the meaning of democracy has become more obscure and contentious, because the interpretation of specific events, claims about grand philosophies of history, and accounts of what democracy has now become are all caught up in fundamental uncertainties about the direction and significance of contemporary trajectories" (1991a: 247). See also Walker (1991b).

3. One of the most interesting and certainly most significant effects of the ongoing problematizations is the continuous reaffirmation of the citizen-oriented meanings and practices of democracy by further reformulating and renegotiating the contextual and thematic scope of the original exclusionary practices of democracy. To the extent that the possibility of "true" citizenship is predicated on the exclusionary presence of a space of particularity patrolled and represented by the state-agent, the contemporary practices and meanings of democracy reflect the limits and prejudices of the modern territorial state, most specifically in organizing life experiences along the dichotomy of "inside" versus "outside." The citizen remains the undisputed legitimate or privileged agent of democracy who links the possibilities of democracy to the claims of the modern territorial state.

Although the globalizing challenges of recent times—radical extraterritorial and supraterritorial democratic movements of environment, human rights, and so on—are exposing these limits and prejudices to new tests, the proponents of these limits too are busily devising counterstrategies of new problematizations to respond to these challenges. In fact, the citizen-orientedness of democratic practices and meanings remains as intact as ever. Furthermore, practical indications are such that space for tolerance for diversity within the space of the citizen-oriented democracy is dwindling, subject to the interplay of a variety of alarmisms and chauvinisms of the territorial nativist movements. The intensity of such movements seems also to be correlated with the intensity and vitality of the deterritorializing post-modern pressures that attenuate the practical power and relevance of the postulated symbiotic relationships among the state, the nation, and the citizen. Put differently, while the meanings of the citizen-orientedness of the original exclusions are oscillating between ascriptive (learned) and hereditary (acquired) rights to citizenship and democracy, the space in between these two orientations is becoming ever more intolerant of the presence of any subjectivity other than that of citizenship. Increasingly, less tolerance for refugees and immigrants is becoming the reality in the space between the two orientations of citizenship. An appropriately symbolic manifestation of intolerance is reported to have taken place in 1993 in the city of Dolgenbrotdt, near Berlin, where the "native" German people allegedly hired an arsonist to burn down a designated refugee house even before the refugees had arrived (*New York Times,* 25 August 1993).

The fervid activities all across Europe, but especially in Germany, France, and Great Britain, are generating ever more restrictive and exclusionary policies and positions with a view to further sharpening the contrasubjectivity of citizenship vis-à-vis refugee and immigrant subjectivities. Put in the simplest terms, contingent and protean problematizations of democracy are attempting to write (construct and circulate) more exclusionary, more repressive, and more intolerant versions of democracy grounded in the hierarchy of the citizen/nation/state than ever before. In the midst of this reaction are refugees and immigrants who, in search of better and safer places, continue to navigate the spaces presumably designed and reserved for the citizen-subject and her or his versions of democracy (Tololyan, 1991: 4).

4. Surely, such objectives might be part of statist problematizations, since problematizations are reconsiderations of the difficulties of a particular practice or set of practices. It may, for instance, be absolutely imperative to deal with the rise of violent neoracism and xenophobia for any form of democracy to remain viable. So, my argument is not that reconsiderations of the emergent difficulties of "democratic practices" have nothing to do with the viability of democratic practices and projects, however nebulously they might be articulated.

5. It is then plausible to argue that the discourse on democracy and its transformations, whether more restrictive or more open and less territorial, as Connolly (1991) would desire to see, could be understood as the problematization of the notion of state sovereignty, since the notion of democracy is predicated on the presence, or at least the representation, of a well-bounded territory of the state within which the simultaneous formulations of the notions of security (i.e., national security, of which the citizen is the supposed primary beneficiary) and community (i.e., nation, of which the

citizen is a supposed constitutive member) are realized. Thus, the ongoing problematizations of democracy discourse constitute yet another field of statecraft replete with practices of incitement, statization and destatization, and regimentation.

6. These reports appeared in the following sources, respectively: Reuters, 8 June 1993; Reuters, 21 November 1990; Reuters, 14 May 1991; *Los Angeles Times,* 15 December 1990; *Irish Times,* 4 June 1993; Agence France Presse, 31 May 1993; *Independent,* 27 May 1993; *Independent,* 20 March 1993; Reuters, 29 June 1993; *Guardian,* 2 June 1993; *Australian Financial News,* 3 June 1993; *Atlanta Journal and Constitution,* 26 May 1991; *Seattle Times,* 21 March 1993; Inter Press Service, 28 August 1992; *Reuters European Community Report,* 26 February 1993; *Economist,* 5 December 1992; *Washington Post,* 20 December 1992; *Independent,* 19 June 1993; *Fortune,* 13 July 1992; Reuters, 7 May 1993; Agence France Presse, 16 March 1993; Reuters, 24 May 1993; Reuters, 16 March 1993; *Toronto Star,* 19 June 1993; and *Los Angeles Times,* 23 February 1992.

7. Visualize, for instance, the case of a French manager of a variety store creatively impelled to invest refugees and immigrants in the store business in order to enhance security. Miro Rizvic says, "I hire local people, a Moroccan for the vegetables, a Tunisian for the canned goods, a Turk for the cash register. That way, they know just about everybody who comes in here. It is better than hiring security guards" (The New York Times News Service, 15 June 1995).

8. The following report from the *Irish Times,* on 4 June 1993, on efforts by the EC to harmonize asylum and immigration procedures among the member countries might perhaps be insightful as an example of "statizing" activities that attempt to stabilize a specific representation of the state, its territory, and the nature of practices within it: "The review of immigration policy [by EC officials] was the culmination of several months' work. . . . The review was originally seen by officials as a polite exercise, but one stressed that the whole thrust of EC immigration policy has changed since the election of the centre-right government in France. 'The French basically rewrote this report,' said the official. 'In some ways it simply restated what we are already doing to curb illegal immigration. But for French domestic reasons, there is much stronger language. The French want to show that they are getting tough and the Germans are ready to row in.'"

It is clear that the rewriting of the review was done not simply to address the announced primary problem, that is, curbing immigration, or preventing "bogus" asylum, but also to rearticulate or reinscribe the image of France as a territory of a community of citizens, entry into which can and must be permitted only by the presumed legitimate agent of that territory, the state. Since the countries are already doing all they can to "regulate" immigration to serve a variety of interests and needs (to address the perennial labor shortage for labor-intensive and service industries and so on), what other purpose for rewriting could one think of than to project an "alignment" between what is claimed by the participants of statist democracies—Germany or France as a space of the citizen organized around and by the state—and what is real out there—Germany and France considered as possible new homes for a multitude of desiring subjects? A report in the *Independent* on 6 June 1993 points to the alignment aspect of statist practices exemplified in the collaboration of the European Community countries: "A prominent refugee advisor says he was told by EC officials that the recent agreement on immigration was 'mainly for show,' and there are doubts about its effectiveness and legality."

Interestingly, as the foregoing report adumbrated, the French had intensified their efforts on the "home" front. The country's National Assembly passed restrictive laws putatively to discourage immigration. The goal of the new laws was stated by then Interior Minister Charles Pasqua as "zero immigration." Coming in the immediate aftermath of changes in the Nationality Act, which had already narrowed the interpretation of French citizenship, the immigration laws further racialized the political-cultural identity plane. Germany "rowed in" fast, following the French example, as the report had predicted. The German constitution was amended to restrict drastically the refugee and asylum law. An editorial in the *Frankfurter Rundschau* instructively called the changes a "big mistake" that "[turns] a blind eye to the truth of immigration." The editorial went on to argue that "the major parties have not linked their policy on foreigners to the fact that millions of people have already immigrated [to Germany] and that the mechanism . . . must continue to run so that society remains capable of functioning. For many reasons, including racial ones, targeted and planned immigration did not appear on the agenda" (qtd. in *The Week in Germany,* 28 May 1993).

9. On the issue of German constitutional changes, see Reuters, 2 March 1993, "Germany Says Refugee Increase Justifies New Laws." On bilateral and multilateral agreements, see Reuters, 24 May 1993, "Germany, Poland Sign Agreement to Curb Refugee Flow"; and Agence France Presse, 16 March 1993, "Six Central European Countries to Sign Migration Pacts." Finally, on the said compilation by the Inter-governmental Secretariat, see Kumin (1995: 13).

10. See also Nair (1996: 78) on the limiting of long-term residency permits.

11. As I indicated in chapter 5, the otherwise cautious UNHCR repeatedly "expressed concerns" on the new policies erecting impervious legal walls to refugee movements. Similarly, other refugee advocacy agencies and human rights organizations, including the World Council of Churches, the

European Consultation on Refugees and Exiles, and Amnesty International, pointed to these issues (J. Bhabha, 1993a; 1993b; Fernhout, 1993; Rudge, 1992; Ferris, 1993a).

12. Measures that have been introduced as a result of the Schengen Agreements (1985 and 1990) and the Dublin Convention (1990) include "(1) Internal Controls: the introduction of identity cards and the obligation to identify oneself; the introduction and/or reinforcement of hotel registers; the introduction and/or reinforcement of employment registers and controls; the increased use of intelligence and high-tech detection equipment, such as detectors; intensified interagency cooperation and the exchange of information; the introduction of more and tougher police powers in view of an extended system of internal controls; (2) International Instruments of Controls: the introduction of international computerized databases, such as the Schengen Information System and the European Information System; the fingerprinting of refugees; the introduction and/or reinforcement of carrier sanctions; technological cooperation between European law enforcement agencies to combat immigration fraud; the creation of special police units and surveillance forces against 'man' smugglers" (Den Boer, 1995: 95–96).

13. For excellent analyses of how the refugee and immigrant presence is lent to such practices of "securitizing," see Den Boer (1995); Huysmans (1995); and Lister (1995). For example, Monica Den Boer notes that "perception of migratory flows often slips into the vocabulary of internal security considerations. Use is made of a simple rhetoric, which usually starts with 'of course we should not confuse the concepts of terrorism, drugs, organized crime with that of immigration, but . . .' The placing of the fight against terrorism and drugs on the one hand, and that of the control of migratory flows on the other, facilitates the transfer of illegitimacy across the board. The European parliament Committee on Racism and Xenophobia accused Trevi [groups] of an 'unacceptable amalgam' across various Trevi Groups, which deal with criminals on the one hand and with migrants and refugees on the other" (1995: 96–97).

14. See Kristeva's "Open Letter to Harlem Désir" (1992: 49–64), in which she responds to Désir's critical reflections on the constructs of "nations" and "national."

15. For example, "The unsettling ramifications of the Proposition 187—the illegal immigration measure—in California, USA attest to the substantive linkages between international migration and internal peace and stability. The condemnatory logic that nowadays dominates the public discourse on international migration has allowed the Governor of California, Pete Wilson, to point to an 'illegal immigrant invasion' as the source of economic and social problems in California. His maneuvers resulted in the passage of a measure that is purportedly intended to arrest illegal immigration into

California. The questions on the popularity, legitimacy, or ethics of the measure notwithstanding, what must be appraised are the alterations the measure is forcing in the socio-cultural and political economic landscapes of California. Right or wrong, the measure already seems to be working to achieve one of its main aims, which, in the words of a columnist, 'was to make the conditions of life unbearable' for the illegal immigrants. Ironically, the societal 'side-effects' of the measure might de-stabilize the already fractured symbiotic ethnic, political, and economic balance that is California. This danger is already manifest in a number of symbolic yet telling incidents. One is the alleged 'Pizza Incident' where a pizza parlor cashier requested that three 'Hispanic' girls produce immigration papers before he served them. In another case, a restaurant customer in California allegedly attempted to citizen-arrest a cook on the account that he might be an illegal alien. Furthermore, the measure had ramifications across the border in Mexico. After the approval of the measure, popular feelings of displeasure with the measure took the form of mass demonstrations against it. In one case in Mexico City, these feelings turned violent resulting in the destruction of a McDonald's fast food restaurant" (Soguk, 1995a: 112–13).

16. In a special issue of the *International Journal of Sociology* on the question of "European identity," John Fells and Josef Niznik (1992) suggest, based on their findings from a nine-country survey including France, Germany, the United Kingdom, Poland, Lithuania, Austria, Australia, the United States, and the Netherlands, that "European identity is a fact without doubt," although the basis of European identity is difficult to define. However, values such as "civil liberties," "democracy," and "tolerance" are considered to be the most important constitutive elements of an imagined European identity. According to the survey results, three countries—Germany, France, and the United Kingdom—constitute the core of Europe, with the other European Community countries forming an outer circle around that core. An interesting indication of the survey results is that on the Europeanness of Russia, those from Western European countries such as the United Kingdom, France, and Austria were ambivalent, and they hardly considered the former Eastern European countries as party to that "European identity."

17. UNHCR Refugee Information Network, BVerwG 2 BvR 1497/90, 4 April 1991; emphasis added.

18. In many cases, implications of such asylum proceedings for democracy and democratic processes are painfully clear, prodding one to ask the question, What are the objectives of a "due process" if even the most basic ground rule of democracy—fairness—is not observed? In the case of *Ali Celik and Hanife Celik v. Secretary of State for the [British] Home Department* (25 May 1990, CA [Civil Division]), the rule of fairness turned into a rule of indifference to the plight of people. In refusing the asylum request of

the Celiks, the Court of Appeal ruled that "unfairness of procedure per se, is not grounds for judicial review. There are many cases in which judicial review has been refused as a matter of discretion even though there had been impropriety in the procedural or decision making process."

In another case, *Sabri Akdag v. Secretary of State for the [British] Home Department* (21 October 1991 Court of Appeal [Civil Division]), a Turkish man's asylum application was refused by the home secretary, and the applicant was ordered to be removed to Turkey. Upon this decision the applicant "became a suicide risk and commenced a hunger strike" and subsequently applied to the Court of Appeal, arguing that the secretary of state should have made inquiries in Turkey to verify his story. The Court of Appeal dismissed the application, and the applicant was removed to Turkey. In its decision, the court wrote: "(1) The Secretary of State had no obligation to make inquiries in Turkey to verify the applicant's claim. His duty is to consider the application and to use his experience of similar applications and conditions in the country of origin, which are obtained from the Foreign Commonwealth Office; (2) Deportation does not constitute inhumane or degrading treatment. The mere removal of the applicant from the country can not amount to inhuman treatment even if, as a result, the applicant suffers some mental and physical disorder." Similar instances seem to be the rule rather than the exception, and they fly in the face of the 1951 Geneva Convention, for they violate the cardinal principle of *nonrefoulement,* due process, and consideration of individual applications on their own merits (rather than rendering judgments by reference to similar applications from the same country or region) (UNHCR Information Network, 21 October 1993).

CONCLUSION

1. That the agency in this hierarchy, particularly the constitutive agency invested in the citizen, has historically been constructed as male agency is certainly true and must be further examined, especially in relation to refugee histories. Such an examination would amount to a genealogy of problematizations that have worked to gender-neutralize statecraft in refugee events. Such a task, while urgently needed, is beyond the primary interests of this study.

2. Here is an example of refugee experience that a government would want forgotten: "Hamdija Suhonjic, a Bosnian Muslim, came to Britain after being rescued from a detention camp. The home office told him that his wife Safija, could join him but his two adult daughters—Azra and Mirzeta—could not. Safija refused to leave Bosnia without her daughters and in May 1993 she and Mirzeta were captured by Serbs, raped and murdered" (Bhabha and Shutter, 1994: 230–31).

Bibliography

Acomb, Evelyn M. 1967. *French Laic Laws, 1879–1889, the First Anticlerical Campaign of the Third French Republic.* New York: Octagon.

Adelman, Howard. 1992. "Humanitarian Intervention: The Case of the Kurds." *International Journal of Refugee Law* 4 (1): 4–38.

Aleinikoff, T. A. 1991. "The Refugee Convention at Forty: Reflections on the IJRL Colloquium." *International Journal of Refugee Law* 3 (3): 617–25.

———. 1995. "State-Centered Refugee Law: From Resettlement to Containment." In *Mistrusting Refugees,* edited by E. Valentine Daniel and John Chr. Knudsen. Berkeley and Los Angeles: University of California Press.

Alverez, Robert. 1984. "The Border as Social System: The California Case." *New Scholar* 9 (1–2): 119–31.

Amin, Ash. 1997. "Placing Globalization." *Theory, Culture, and Society* 14 (2): 123–37.

Amnesty International. 1993. "Europe Must Open Its Doors to Take More Bosnian Refugees." 16 June. <ACTIV-L%mizzoul.bitnet@umd.cso.uiuc.edu>.

———. 1997. "Refugees, Human Rights Have No Borders." Baltimore: Amnesty International.

Anderson, Benedict. 1992. *Imagined Communities: Reflections on the Origins and Spread of Nationalism.* London: Verso.

———. 1994. "Exodus." *Critical Inquiry.* 20 (2): 314–27.

Anderson, Perry. 1984. "The Absolutist States of Western Europe." In *States and Societies,* edited by David Held et al. New York: New York University Press.

Appadurai, Arjun. 1988. "Putting Hierarchy in Its Place." *Cultural Anthropology* 3 (1): 36–49.

———. 1991. "Disjuncture and Difference in the Global Cultural Economy." In *Theory, Culture, and Society,* edited by Mike Featherstone. Bristol, England: Arrowsmith.

———. 1996. "Sovereignty without Territoriality: Notes for a Postnational Geography." In *The Geography of Identity,* edited by Patricia Yager. Ann Arbor: University of Michigan Press.

Arboleda, Eduardo, and Ian Hoy. 1993. "The Convention Refugee Definition in the West: Disharmony of Interpretation and Application." *International Journal of Refugee Law* 5 (1): 67–90.

Arendt, Hannah. 1958. *The Origins of Totalitarianism.* New York: Meridian.

Argent, Tom. 1992. *Croatia's Crucible: Providing Asylum for Refugees from Bosnia and Hercegovina.* Washington, D.C.: U.S. Committee for Refugees.

Arnison, Nancy D. 1993. "International Law and Non-Intervention: When Do Humanitarian Concerns Supersede Sovereignty?" *Fletcher Forum of World Affairs* 17 (2): 199–211.

Arnold, E. A. 1994. *A Documentary Survey of Napoleonic France.* New York: University Press of America.

Ashley, Richard. 1988. "Untying the Sovereign State: A Double Reading of the Anarchy Problematique." *Millennium: Journal of International Studies* 7 (2) : 227–62.

———. 1989a. "Imposing International Purpose: Notes on a Problematic of Governance." In *Global Changes and Theoretical Challenges: Approaches to World Politics for the 1990s,* edited by Ernst-Otto Czempiel and James N. Rosenau. Lexington, Mass.: Lexington Books.

———. 1989b. "Living on Border Lines: Man, Poststructuralism, and War." In *International/Intertextual Relations,* edited by James Der Derian and Michael J. Shapiro. Lexington, Mass.: Lexington Books.

———. 1993. "Statecraft as Mancraft." Unpublished manuscript.

———. 1995. Interview by author. Tempe, Ariz.

Ashley, Richard K., and R. B. J. Walker. 1990. "Speaking the Language of Exile: Dissident Thought in International Studies." *International Studies Quarterly* 34 (3).

Bader, Veit. 1995. "Citizenship and Exclusion: Radical Democracy, Community, and Justice; or, What Is Wrong with Communitarianism?" *Political Theory* 23 (2): 211–46.

Baird, Henry M. 1895. *The Huguenots and the Revocation of the Edict of Nantes.* New York: Scribner's.

Baker, K. M. 1994. "A Foucauldian French Revolution." In *Foucault and the Writing of History,* edited by Jan Goldstein. Oxford: Blackwell.

Bammer, Angelika, ed. 1994. *Displacements: Cultural Identities in Question.* Bloomington: Indiana University Press.

Barkin, J. Samuel, and Bruce Cronin. 1994. "The State and the Nation: Changing Norms and the Rules of Sovereignty in International Relations." *International Organization* 48 (1): 107–30.

Barrientos, G., et al. 1984. "What Drives Illegal Border-Crossers into the U.S.? A Psychological Perspective." *New Scholar* 9 (1–2): 87–99.

Barry, Andrew. 1993. "The European Community and European Government: Harmonization, Mobility, and Space." *Economy and Society* 22 (3): 314–26.

Bartelson, Jens. 1995. *A Genealogy of Sovereignty.* Cambridge: Cambridge University Press.

Basch, Linda, Nina Glick Schiller, and Christina Szanton Blanc. 1995. *Nations Unbound: Transnational Projects, Postcolonial Predicaments, and Deterritorialized Nation-States.* Luxembourg: Gordon and Breach.

Bell, G. K. A. 1939. *Humanity and the Refugees.* London: Jewish Historical Society.

Bentwich, Norman. 1936. "The League of Nations and Refugees." *Yearbook of International Law,* 114–28.

Berthiaume, Christina. 1995. "Asylum under Threat." *Refugees* 101: 3–10.

Bhabha, Homi K. 1983. "The Other Question." *Screen* 24 (6): 18–36.

———. 1993. "DissemiNation: Time, Narrative, and the Margins of the Modern Nation." In *Nation and Narration,* edited by Homi K. Bhabha. London: Routledge.

———. 1994. "Frontlines/Borderposts." In *Displacements: Cultural Identities in Question,* edited by Angelika Bammer. Bloomington: Indiana University Press.

Bhabha, Jacqueline. 1993a. "Harmonization of European Immigration Law." *Interpreter Releases: Report and Analysis of Immigration and Nationality Law,* January 70 (2): 49–59.

———. 1993b. "Letter from London: Recent European Immigration Developments." *Interpreter Releases: Report and Analysis of Immigration and Nationality Law,* May 70 (18): 605–13.

Bhabha, Jacqueline, and Sue Shutter. 1994. *Women's Movement: Women under Immigration, Nationality, and Refugee Law.* Staffordshire, England: Trentham.

Bodin, Jean. 1992. *On Sovereignty: Four Chapters from the Six Books of the Commonwealth.* Cambridge: Cambridge University Press.

Bohlen, Celestine. 1996. "Italians Contemplate Beauty in a Caribbean Brow." *New York Times,* 10 September, sec. A, p. 3.

Booth, V. E. H. 1980. *British Extradition Law and Procedure.* Germantown, Md.: Sijthoff and Noordhoff.

Bourdieu, Pierre. 1977. *Outline of a Theory of Practice.* Translated by Richard Nice. Cambridge: Cambridge University Press.

———. 1986. *Distinction: A Social Critique of the Judgment of Taste.* Translated by Richard Nice. London: Routledge and Keagan Paul.

Boutros-Ghali, Boutros. 1994. Gabriel Silver Memorial Lecture, at Columbia University, New York, N.Y. SG/SM/5220, 7 February.

Braudel, Fernand. 1977. *Afterthoughts on Material Civilization and Capitalism.* Translated by Patricia M. Ranum. Baltimore: Johns Hopkins University Press.

———. 1988. *The Identity of France.* Translated by Siân Reynolds. Vol. 1. New York: Harper and Row.

Brett, Rachel, and Elaine Eddison. 1993. "Migration, Refugees, and Displaced Persons: Report on the CSCE Human Dimension Seminar on Migration, Including Refugees and Displaced Persons." Colchester, England: Human Rights Centre, University of Essex.

"Britain to Crack Down on 'Bogus' Asylum Seekers." 1995. Reuters, 25 October.

Brubaker, Rogers. 1992. *Citizenship and Nationhood in France and Germany.* Cambridge: Harvard University Press.

Bryce, James. 1916. *The Treatment of Armenians in the Ottoman Empire, 1915–16.* London: His Majesty's Stationery Office.

Buijs, Gina. 1993. *Migrant Women: Crossing Boundaries and Changing Identities.* Oxford: Berg.

Bull, Hedley. 1984. *Intervention in World Politics.* Oxford: Clarendon.

Carter, Donald. 1994. "The Art of the State: Difference and Other Abstractions." *Journal of Historical Sociology* 7 (1): 73–102.

Carvel, John, and Paul Webster, 1993. "Europe Cracks Down on Immigrants." *Manchester Guardian Weekly,* 6 June.

Castel, Robert. 1994. "'Problematization' as a Mode of Reading History." In *Foucault and the Writing of History,* edited by Jan Goldstein. Oxford: Blackwell.

Cemal, Hasan. 1991. "Insan bunlar insan" (They are human beings). *Cumhuriyet,* 7 April.

Certeau, Michel de. 1984. *The Practice of Everyday Life.* Translated by Steven F. Rendall. Berkeley and Los Angeles: University of California Press.

———. 1988. *The Writing of History.* New York: Columbia University Press.

Cerutti, Furio. 1994. "Can There Be a Supranational Identity?" *Philosophy and Social Criticism* 2 (18): 147–63.

Chadwick, Alex. 1992. "UN Debates National Sovereignty and Human Rights." National Public Radio, 11 May.

Chakrabarty, Dipesh. 1992. "Postcoloniality and the Artifice of History: Who Speaks for 'Indian' Pasts?" *Representations* 37: 1–26.

———. 1993. "Marx after Marxism: History, Subalternity, and Difference." *Meanjin* 52 (3): 421–34.

Chapin, Jessica. 1994. "From IRCA to Orca: Apprehending the Other in 'Your San Antonio Experience.'" *Journal of Historical Sociology* 7 (1): 103–12.

Chartier, Roger. 1994. "The Chimera of the Origin: Archaeology, Cultural History, and the French Revolution." In *Foucault and the Writing of History,* edited by Jan Goldstein. Oxford: Blackwell.

Charvet, John. 1997. "The Idea of State Sovereignty and the Right of Humanitarian Intervention." *International Political Science Review* 18 (1): 39–48.

Chen, Kuan-Hsing. 1996. "Not Yet the Post-colonial Era: The (Super) Nation-State and Transnationalism of Cultural Studies: Response to Ang and Stratton." *Cultural Studies* 10 (1): 37–70.

Childs, Lawford S. 1937. "Refugees—A Permanent Problem in International Organization." In *War Is Not Inevitable: Problems of Peace,* edited by Geneva Institute of International Relations. Freeport, N.Y.: Books for Libraries Press.

Chorlton, David. 1994. *Outposts.* Exeter, England: Taxus.

Christiensen, A. R. 1966. *Fridtjof Nansen: A Life in the Service of Science and Humanity.* Geneva: United Nations High Commissioner for Refugees.

Church, William F. 1969. "Louis XIV and the Reason of the State." In *Louis XIV and the Craft of Kingship,* edited by John C. Rule. Columbus: Ohio State University Press.

Cirtautas, K. C. 1963. *The Refugee.* New York: Citadel.

Colbert, Jean-Baptiste. [1863] 1969. "The Regulation of Commerce and Industry." In *The Impact of Absolutism in France: National Experience under Richelieu, Mazarin, and Louis XIV,* edited by William F. Church. New York: Wiley.

Colley, Linda. 1992a. "Britishness and Otherness: An Argument." *Journal of British Studies* 31 (3): 309–29.

———. 1992b. *Britons: Forging the Nation, 1707–1837.* New Haven, Conn.: Yale University Press.

Collinson, Sarah. 1994. *Europe and International Migration.* London: Pinter.

Congar, Yasemin. 1991. "BM derhal Irak'a gitmeli" (UN must immediately go to Iraq). *Cumhuriyet,* 24 April.

Connolly, William E. 1989. *Political Theory and Modernity.* Oxford: Blackwell.

———. 1991. "Democracy and Territoriality." *Millennium: Journal of International Studies* 20 (3): 463–84.

Conover, Ted. 1987. *Coyotes: A Journey through the Secret World of America's Illegal Aliens.* New York: Vintage.

"Convenient Cracks in Wall: European Governments Can't Admit 'Illegals' Serve Useful Purpose." 1993. *Financial Times,* 15 April, sec. 1, p. 59.

Cotgrave, Randle, comp. 1611. *A Dictionarie of the French and English Tongues.* London: Adam Islip.

Cottret, Bernard. 1991. *The Huguenots in England: Immigration and Settlement, c. 1550–1700.* Translated by Peregrine Stevenson. Cambridge: Cambridge University Press.

Cumings, Bruce. 1993. "Global Realm with No Limit, Global Realm with No Name." *Radical History Review* 57: 46–59.

Cunningham, W. 1897. *Alien Immigrants to England.* London: Swan Sonnenschein.

Cydejko, Grzegorz, with Andrzej Koziara. 1993. "Illegal Aliens in Transit." *Warsaw Voice,* 21 May.

Dacyl, Janina W. 1990. "A Time for Perestroika (Restructuring) in the International Refugee Regime." *Journal of Refugee Studies* 3 (1): 26–46.

Daniel, E. Valentine, and John Chr. Knudsen, eds. 1995. *Mistrusting Refugees.* Berkeley and Los Angeles: University of California Press.

De Boer, Gerard C. 1992. "Trends in Refugee Policy and Cooperation in the European Community." *International Migration Review* 26 (2): 668–75.

Defoe, Daniel. [1709] 1964. *A Brief History of the Poor Palatine Refugees.* London: Augustinian Reprint Society.

Delbruck, Jost. 1992. "A Fresh Look at Humanitarian Intervention under the Authority of the United Nations." *Indiana Law Journal* 67 (4): 887–901.

de Lusignan, Guy. 1994. "Global Migration and European Integration." *Indiana Journal of Global Legal Studies* 2 (1). <http://www.law.indiana.edu/glsj/vol2/delusign.html>. Accessed April 1996.

Den Boer, Monica. 1995. "Moving between Bogus and Bona Fide: The Policing of Inclusion and Exclusion in Europe." In *Migration and European Integration: The Dynamics of Inclusion and Exclusion,* edited by Robert Miles and Dietrich Thranhart. Madison, N.J.: Fairleigh Dickinson University Press.

Deng, Francis. 1993. *Protecting the Dispossessed: A Challenge for the International Community.* Washington, D.C.: Brookings Institution.

Der Derian, James. 1993. "Genealogy, Semiology, Dromology: Towards a Nietzschean Theory of International Politics." Paper presented at 34th Annual Convention of the International Studies Association, Acapulco, Mexico.

Derrida, Jacques. 1976. *Of Grammatology.* Translated by Gayatri Chakravorty Spivak. Baltimore: Johns Hopkins University Press.

———. 1994. *Specters of Marx: The State of the Debt, the Work of Mourning, and the New International.* New York: Routledge.

Desbarats, Jacquiline. 1992. "Institutional and Policy Interactions among Countries and Refugee Flows." In *International Migration Systems: A Global Approach,* edited by M. M. Kritz, L. L. Lim, and H. Zlotnik. Oxford: Clarendon.

Dillon, Michael. Forthcoming. "The Scandal of the Refugee: Some Reflections on the 'Inter' of International Relations and Continental Thought." In *Moral Spaces,* edited by Michael J. Shapiro and David Campbell. Minneapolis: University of Minnesota Press.

Dinnerstein, Leonard. 1982. *America and the Survivors of the Holocaust.* New York: Columbia University Press.

Donnelly, Jack. 1993. "Human Rights, Humanitarian Crisis, and Intervention." *International Journal* 48: 607–40.

———. 1994. "Human Rights and International Organizations: States, Sovereignty, and International Community." In *International Organization: A Reader,* edited by Friedrich Kratochwil and Edward D. Mansfield. New York: HarperCollins College.

Donnelly, Michael. 1992. "On Foucault's Uses of the Notion of Biopower." In *Michel Foucault, Philosopher,* edited by Timothy Armstrong. New York: Routledge.

Donner, Ruth. 1994. *The Regulation of Nationality in International Law.* Irvington-on-Hudson, N.Y.: Transnational.

Dowty, Alan. 1987. *Closed Borders: The Contemporary Assault on Freedom of Movement.* New Haven, Conn.: Yale University Press.

Dreyfus, H. L., and Paul Rabinow. 1983. *Michel Foucault: Beyond Structuralism and Hermeneutics.* Chicago: University of Chicago Press.

Duara, Prasenjit. 1993. "The Displacement of Tension to the Tension of Displacement." *Radical History Review* 57: 60–64.

Dunn, John. 1994. "The Dilemma of Humanitarian Intervention: The Executive Power of the Law of Nature, after God." *Government and Opposition* 29 (2): 248–61.

Dunning, W. A. 1913. *A History of Political Theories: From Martin Luther to Montesquieu.* London: Macmillan.

Eleonori, Sabina. 1997. "Beauty and the Beast: The Dialectics of Humanitarianism and Politics." Department of Political Science, York University, Toronto, Ontario.

Farquhar, Elizabeth C. 1967. "A Study of the Debates and Legislation on Sanctions Enacted against Émigrés by French Revolutionary Assemblies, 1791–1794." Master's thesis, American University.

Febvre, Lucien. 1973. "Frontière: The Word and the Concept." In *A New Kind of History and Other Essays,* written by Lucien Febvre, edited by Peter Burke and translated by K. Folca. New York: Harper and Row.

Fells, John, and Niznik, Josef. 1992. "Conclusion: What Is Europe?" *International Journal of Sociology* 22 (1–2): 201–7.

Fernhout, Ross. 1993. "'Europe 1993' and Its Refugees." *Ethnic and Racial Studies* 16 (3): 492–506.

Ferris, Elizabeth. 1993a. *Beyond Borders: Refugees, Migrants, and Human Rights in the Post–Cold War Era.* Geneva: WCC Publications.

———. 1993b. "The Politics of Containment: Asylum in Europe and Its Global Implications." In *World Refugee Survey, 1994.* Washington, D.C.: Immigration and Refugee Services of America.

Fijalkowski, Jurgen. 1993. "Aggressive Nationalism, Immigration Pressure, and Asylum Policy Disputes in Contemporary Germany." *International Migration Review* 27 (4): 850–69.

Finer, S. E. 1997. *The History of Government from the Earliest Times: Empires, Monarchies, and the Modern State.* Vol. 3. Oxford: Oxford University Press.

Fisher, David. 1994. "The Ethics of Intervention." *Survival* 36 (1): 51–59.

Flores, Richard R. 1993. "History, 'Los Pastores,' and the Shifting Poetics of Dislocation." *Journal of Historical Sociology* 6 (2): 164–87.

Ford, Caroline. 1993. *Creating the Nation in Provincial France: Religion and Political Identity in Brittany.* Princeton, N.J.: Princeton University Press.

Forrest, Alan. 1995. *The French Revolution.* Oxford: Blackwell.

Fortin, A. J. 1989. "Notes on a Terrorist Text: A Critical Use of Roland Barth's Textual Analysis in the Interpretation of Political Meaning." In *International/Intertextual Relations,* edited by James Der Derian and Michael Shapiro. Lexington, Mass.: Lexington Books.

Foucault, Michel. 1972. *The Archeology of Knowledge and the Discourse on Language.* New York: Pantheon.

———. 1978. *The History of Sexuality.* Translated by Robert Hurley. New York: Pantheon.

———. 1984. *The Foucault Reader.* Edited by Paul Rabinow. New York: Pantheon.

———. 1988a. "The Political Technology of Individuals." In *Technologies of the Self,* edited by Luther H. Martin, Huck Gutmand, and Patrick H. Hutton. Amherst: University of Massachusetts Press.

———. 1988b. *Politics, Philosophy, Culture: Interviews and Other Writings.* Edited by Lawrence Kritzman and translated by Alan Sheridan et al. New York: Routledge.

———. 1991. "Why the Prison?" In *The Foucault Effect: Studies in Governmentality,* edited by Graham Burchell, Colin Gordon, and Peter Miller. London: Harvester Wheatsheaf.

Freedman, Lawrence, and David Boren. 1992. "'Safe Havens' for Kurds in Post-war Iraq." In *To Loose the Bands of Wickedness: International Intervention in Defence of Human Rights,* edited by Nigel S. Rodley. London: Brassey's.

Frelick, Bill. 1992a. "The False Promise of Operation Provide Comfort: Protecting Refugees or Protecting State Power?" *Middle East Report,* May–June, 22–27.

———. 1992b. *Yugoslavia Torn Asunder: Lessons for Protecting Refugees from Civil War.* Washington, D.C.: U.S. Committee for Refugees.

———. 1993. "Closing Ranks: The North Locks Arms against Refugees." In *Altered States: A Reader in the New World Order,* edited by Phyllis Bennis and Michel Moushabeck. New York: Olive Branch.

Furetiere, Antoine. 1690. *Dictionarie universal, mots francois.* Rotterdam: Arnout and Reinier Leers.

Gallagher, Dennis. 1989. "The Evolution of the International Refugee System." *International Migration Review* 23 (3): 578–98.

Garcia-Mora, M. R. 1956. *International Law and Asylum as a Human Right.* Washington, D.C.: Public Affairs.

Garigue, Philippe. 1993. "Intervention-Sanction and 'droit d'ingérencé' International Law." *International Journal* 48: 669–86.

Garrard, John A. 1971. *The English and Immigration, 1880–1910.* London: Oxford University Press.

Gellner, Ernest. 1993. *Nations and Nationalism.* Ithaca, N.Y.: Cornell University Press.

"Germany, Poland Sign Agreement to Curb Refugee Flow." 1993. Reuters, 7 May.

Glissant, Edouard. 1997. *Poetics of Relation.* Translated by Betsy Wing. Ann Arbor: University of Michigan Press.

Golden, Richard M. 1988. *The Huguenot Connection: The Edict of Nantes, Its Revocation, and Early French Migration to South Carolina.* Dordrecht, Netherlands: Kluwer.

Gómez-Peña, Guillermo. 1996. "Warrior for Gringostroika." In *The Late Great Mexican Border: Reports from a Disappearing Line,* edited by Bobby Bird and S. M. Byrd. El Paso, Tex.: Cinco Puntos.

Gordenker, Leon. 1987. *Refugees in International Politics.* London: Croom Helm.

Gorman, Robert F. 1994. *Historical Dictionary of Refugee and Disaster Relief Organizations.* Metuchen, N.J.: Scarecrow.

Grahl-Madsen, Atle. 1966. *The Status of Refugees in International Law.* Vol. 1, *Refugee Character.* Leiden, Netherlands: Sijthoff.

———. 1972. *The Status of Refugees in International Law.* Vol. 2, *Asylum, Entry, and Sojourn.* Leiden, Netherlands: Sijthoff.

Gramsci, Antonio. 1987. *Selections from the Prison Notebooks.* Edited by Quintin Hoare and Geoffrey Nowell Smith. New York: International.

Grass, Günter. 1993. "On Loss: The Condition of Germany." *Dissent* 40 (2): 178–88.

Green, L. C. 1987. "Refugees and Refugee Status Causes and Treatment in Historico-legal Perspective." In *Thesaurus Acroasium.* Vol. 13, *The Refugee Problem on Universal, Regional, and National Level,* edited by D. S. Constantopoulos. Thessaloniki, Greece: Institute of Public International Law and International Relations of Thessaloniki.

Greenhouse, Carol J. 1994. "Democracy and Demography." *Indiana Journal of Global Legal Studies* 2 (1). <http://www.law.indiana.edu/glsj/vol2/greenhouse.html>. Accessed April 1996.

Greer, Donald. 1951. *The Incidence of the Emigration during the French Revolution.* Cambridge: Harvard University Press.

Grotius, Hugo. [1642] 1925. *De Jure Belli ac Pacis Libri Tres.* Oxford: Clarendon.

Guest, Iain. 1991. "The United Nations, the UNHCR, and Refugee Protection: A Non-specialist Analysis." *International Journal of Refugee Law* 3 (3): 585–605.

Gupta, Akhil, and Ferguson, James. 1992. "Beyond 'Culture': Space, Identity, and the Politics of Difference." *Cultural Anthropology* 7 (1): 6–23.

Haas, Ernst. 1994. "Why Collaborate? Issue-Linkage and International Relations." In *International Organization: A Reader,* edited by Friedrich Kratochwil and Edward D. Mansfield. New York: HarperCollins College.

Haas, Peter M. 1994. "Do Regimes Matter? Epistemic Communities and Mediterranean Pollution Control." In *International Organization: A Reader,* edited by Friedrich Kratochwil and Edward D. Mansfield. New York: HarperCollins College.

Habermas, Jürgen. 1992. "Citizenship and National Identity: Some Reflections on the Future of Europe." *Praxis International* 12 (1): 1–19.

Haggard, S., and B. A. Simmons. 1987. "Theories of International Regimes." *International Organization* 41 (3): 491–517.

Hall, Stuart. 1996. "The West and the Rest: Discourse and Power." In *Modernity: An Introduction to Modern Sciences,* edited by Stuart Hall, David Held, Don Hubert, and Kenneth Thompson. Oxford: Blackwell.

Hansson, Michael. 1972. Nobel Lecture on behalf of the Nansen International Office for Refugees, 10 December 1938. In *Nobel Lectures: Peace, 1926–1938,* edited by Fredrick W. Haberman. Amsterdam: Nobel Foundation.

Harder, Peter. 1993. "Migration: A New International Dimension." *International Journal of Refugee Law* 5 (1): 101–9.

Harvey, David. 1995. "From Space to Place and Back Again: Reflections on the Conditions of Postmodernity." In *Mapping the Futures: Local Cultures, Global Change,* edited by John Bird, Barry Curtis, Tim Putnam, George Robertson, and Lisa Tickner. London: Routledge.

Heilberg, Marianne, ed. 1994. *Subduing Sovereignty: Sovereignty and the Right to Intervene.* London: Pinter.

Held, David. 1996. "The Development of the Modern State." In *Modernity: An Introduction to Modern Societies,* edited by Stuart Hall, David Held, Don Hubert, and Kenneth Thompson. Oxford: Blackwell.

Held, David, and Anthony McGrew. 1993. "Globalization and the Liberal Democratic State." *Government and Opposition* 28 (2): 261–88.

Helton, Arthur C. 1992. "The Legality of Providing Humanitarian Assistance without the Consent of the Sovereign." *International Journal of Refugee Law* 4 (3): 373–79.

Herrero, Miguel. 1993. *Emerging Security Challenges, NATO Rapid Reaction Force: A Report to the North Atlantic Assembly, Political Committee.* Brussels. October.

Herzfeld, Michael. 1988. "Of Definitions and Boundaries: The Status of Culture in the Culture of the State." In *Discourse and the Social Life of Meaning,* edited by P. Chock and Jurer Wyman. Washington, D.C.: Smithsonian Institution Press.

———. 1991. "Displaced: The Spaces of Refugee Identity in Greece." *Anthropological Quarterly* 64 (2): 92–95.

Hill, Peter. 1993. "Nations and Nationalism." *Meanjin* 52 (1): 98–106.

Hirschon, Renee. 1989. *Heirs of the Greek Catastrophe: The Social Life of Asia Minor Refugees in Pireaeus.* Oxford: Clarendon.

Hobbes, Thomas. [1651] 1962. *Leviathan.* New York: Macmillan/Collier.

Hobsbawm, E. J. 1990. *Nations and Nationalism since 1780: Programme, Myth, Reality.* Cambridge: Cambridge University Press.

———. 1992. *Nations and Nationalism since 1780: Programme, Myth, Reality.* 2d ed. Cambridge: Cambridge University Press.

Hobsbawm, Eric, and Terence Ranger. 1992. *The Invention of Tradition.* Cambridge: Cambridge University Press.

Hockenos, Paul. 1994. "German Churches Buck State on Asylum Issue." *National Catholic Reporter,* 9 December.

Hoffman, Mark. 1993. "Agency, Identity, and Intervention." In *Political Theory, International Relations, and the Ethics of Intervention,* edited by Ian Forbes and Mark Hoffman. New York: St. Martin's.

Holborn, Louise W. 1956. *The International Refugee Organization: A Specialized Agency of the United Nations.* London: Oxford University Press.

———. 1975. *Refugees: A Problem of Our Time: The Work of the United Nations High Commissioner for Refugees, 1951–1972.* Vol. 1. Metuchen, N.J.: Scarecrow.

Hollifield, James F. 1992. "Migration and International Relations: Cooperation and Control in the European Community." *International Migration Review* 26 (2): 568–95.

———. 1994. "Immigration and Republicanism in France: The Hidden Consensus." In *Controlling Immigration: A Global Perspective,* edited by Wayne A. Cornelius, Phillip L. Martin, and James F. Hollifield. Stanford, Calif.: Stanford University Press.

Holmes, Colin. 1978. "Introduction: Immigrants and Minorities in Britain." In *Immigrants and Minorities in British Society,* edited by Colin Holmes. Boston: Allen and Unwin.

———. 1988. *John Bull's Island: Immigration and British Society, 1871–1971.* London: Macmillan.

Hope-Simpson, John. 1939. *The Refugee Problem: Report of a Survey.* London: Oxford University Press.

Huberman, Leo. 1937. *Man's Worldly Goods: The Story of the Wealth of Nations.* London: Victor Gollancz.

Hunt, Alan, and Gary Wickham. 1994. *Foucault and Law: Towards a Sociology of Law as Governance.* London: Pluto.

Huysmans, Jef. 1995. "Migrants as Security Problem: Dangers of 'Securitizing' Societal Issues." In *Migration and European Integration: The Dynamics of Inclusion and Exclusion,* edited by Robert Miles and Dietrich Thranhart. Madison, N.J.: Fairleigh Dickinson University Press.

Hyslop, Beatrice F. 1968. *French Nationalism in 1789, according to General Cahiers.* New York: Octagon.

Inayatullah, N., and D. Blaney. 1995. "Realizing Sovereignty." *Review of International Studies* 21: 3–20.

International Political Science Review. 1997. "The Dilemmas of Humanitarian Intervention." Special issue, 18 (1).

Jackson, Peter, and Jan Penrose, eds. 1993. *Constructions of Race, Place, and Nation.* London: UCL Press.

Jackson, Robert H. 1993. "Armed Humanitarianism." *International Journal* 48: 579–606.

Jacobson, David. 1996. *Rights across Borders: Immigration and the Decline of Citizenship.* Baltimore: Johns Hopkins University Press.

Jameson, Fredric. 1981. *The Political Unconscious.* London: Methuen.

Jolly, Danielle, et al. 1993. *Refugees: Asylum in Europe?* London: Minority Rights Group.

Jones, Fortier. 1916. *With Serbia into Exile: An American's Adventures with the Army That Cannot Die.* New York: Century.

Jones, John Mervyn. 1956. *British Nationality Law.* Rev. ed. Oxford: Clarendon.

Kamm, Henry. 1993. "People Smugglers Send New Tide of Refugees onto Nordic Shores." *New York Times*, 15 February, sec. A1.

Kearney, Michael. 1991. "Borders and Boundaries of the State and Self at the End of Empire." *Journal of Historical Sociology* 4 (1): 52–74.

Keely, James F. 1990. "Toward a Foucauldian Analysis of International Regimes." *International Organization* 44 (1): 83–105.

Keohane, Robert, and Joseph Nye. 1977. *Power and Interdependence*. Boston: Little, Brown.

Kersey, John. 1708. *Dictionarium Anglo-Britannicum*. Menston, England: Scolar.

Kiernan, V. G. 1978. "Britons Old and New." In *Immigrants and Minorities in British Society*, edited by Colin Holmes. Boston: Allen and Unwin.

King, J. E. 1967. "The Making of the Ancien Regime." In *The Fulfillment and Collapse of the Old Regime: 1650–1815*, edited by Norman F. Cantor and Michael S. Werthman. New York: Crowell.

Kirisci, Kemal. 1991. "Kürt mülteciler ve Türkiye" (Kurdish refugees and Turkey). *Cumhuriyet*, 15 April.

Klusmeyer, D. B. 1993. "Aliens, Immigrants, and Citizens: The Politics of Inclusion in the Federal Republic of Germany." *Daedalus* 122 (summer): 81–114.

Knutsen, Torbjörn L. 1992. *A History of International Relations Theory*. Manchester, England: Manchester University Press.

Kofman, Eleonore. 1995. "Citizenship for Some but Not for Others: Spaces of Citizenship in Contemporary Europe." *Political Geography* 14 (2): 121–37.

Kohn, Hans. 1967. *Prelude to Nation-States: The French and German Experience, 1789–1815*. Toronto: Van Nostrand.

Koydi, Wolfgang. 1995. "Germany Sees E. T. as Perfect Asylum-Seeker." *Washington Times*, 13 November.

Krasner, Stephen D. 1982. "Regimes and the Limits of Realism: Regimes as Autonomous Variables." *International Organization* 36 (2): 497–510.

———. 1994. "Structural Causes and Regime Consequences: Regimes as Intervening Variables." In *International Organization: A Reader*, edited by Friedrich Kratochwil and Edward D. Mansfield. New York: HarperCollins College.

Kratochwil, Friedrich. 1993. "Norms versus Numbers: Multilateralism and the Rationalist and Reflexivist Approaches to Institutions." In *Multilateralism Matters: The Theory and Praxis of an Institutional Form*, edited by John Gerard Ruggie. New York: Columbia University Press.

Kratochwil, Friedrich, and John G. Ruggie. 1994. "International Organization: A State of the Art on an Art of the State." In *International*

Organization: A Reader, edited by Friedrich Kratochwil and Edward D. Mansfield. New York: HarperCollins College.

Kriegel, Barret. 1992. "Michel Foucault and the Police State." In *Michel Foucault, Philosopher*, edited by Timothy Armstrong. New York: Routledge.

Kristeva, Julia. 1991. *Strangers to Ourselves*. New York: Columbia University Press.

———. 1992. *Nations without Nationalism*. Translated by Leon S. Roudiez. New York: Columbia University Press.

Kulischer, E. M. 1948. *Europe on the Move: War and Population Changes, 1917–47*. New York: Columbia University Press.

Kumin, Judith. 1995. "Protection of, or Protection from, Refugees?" *Refugees* 101 (3): 11–13.

Kusch, Martin. 1991. *Foucault's Strata and Fields: An Investigation into Archeological and Genealogical Science Studies*. Dordrecht, Netherlands: Kluwer.

Laclau, E., and C. Mouffe. 1985. *Hegemony and Socialist Strategy: Towards a Radical Democratic Politics*. London: Verso.

Ladas, Stephen P. 1932. *The Exchange of Minorities: Bulgaria, Greece, and Turkey*. New York: Macmillan.

Langewiesche, William. 1992. "The Border." *Atlantic Monthly*, May, 53–92.

Lavie, S., and T. Swedenburg, eds. 1996. *Displacement, Diaspora, and Geographies of Identity*. Durham, N.C.: Duke University Press.

League of Nations. 1921a. "Conference on the Question of Russian Refugees: Resolutions Adopted by the Conference on August 24th, 1921." *Official Journal*, October, 899–902.

———. 1921b. *Memorandum as to the Right of Option of Refugees in Vienna from the Eastern Glacier*. 21/68/61(XIII), 10 March.

———. 1921c. "Memorandum from the Committee international de la croix-rouge at Geneva to the Council of the League of Nations." *Official Journal*, March–April, 225–29.

———. 1921d. *Polish Complaint on the Expulsion of Jews from Austria*. 21/68/61(XIII), 10 March.

———. 1921e. "The Question of Russian Refugees." *Official Journal*, November, 1006–27.

———. 1921f. "The Question of the Russian Refugees." *Official Journal*, September.

———. 1921g. "Records of the Second Assembly: Meetings of the Committees II." *Official Journal*, September.

———. 1921h. "Records of the Second Assembly: Plenary Meetings." *Official Journal*, special supplement, October, 101–8.

———. 1921i. "Resolutions Adopted by the Council of the League of Na-

tions at Its Thirteenth Session in Geneva, June 17th–28th, 1921." *Official Journal*, 5 July, 37.
———. 1922a. "Minutes of the Seventeenth Session of the Council Held at Paris from March 24th to March 28th." *Official Journal*, May, 375–82.
———. 1922b. "Records of the Third Assembly: Meetings of the Committees." *Official Journal*, September.
———. 1922c. "Report by Dr. Fridtjof Nansen, High Commissioner of the League of Nations, to the Fifth Committee of the Assembly." *Official Journal*, November, 1134–39.
———. 1922d. "Russian Refugees: General Report of the Work Accomplished up to March 15th, 1992, by Dr. Fridtjof Nansen, the High Commissioner of the League." *Official Journal*, May, 385–95.
———. 1922e. *Russian Refugees: Report of the Fifth Committee as Submitted to the Third Assembly*. A.129. 1922 IV-1, 25 September, 2–5.
———. 1922f. "Special Report by the High Commissioner of the League, Requesting the Assistance of the Governments of Members of the League in the Accomplishment of His Work." *Official Journal*, May, 396–401.
———. 1924. "Records of the Fifth Assembly Plenary Meetings: Text of the Debates." *Official Journal*, special supplement 23, 25 September, 144–59.
———. 1926a. *Armenian and Russian Refugees: Arrangement Relating to the Issue of Identity Certificates to Russian and Armenian Refugees, Supplementing and Amending the Previous Arrangements Dated July 5th, 1922, and May 31st, 1924*. A.44. 1926, 3 September, 4–23.
———. 1926b. "Records of the Seventh Ordinary Session of the Assembly: Text of the Debates." *Official Journal*, special supplement 44, 86–139.
———. 1927a. "Measures in Favour of Armenian and Russian Refugees: Draft Report of the Fifth Committee to the Assembly." Minutes of the Fifth Committee (General and Humanitarian Questions). *Official Journal*, special supplement 59, 14–18.
———. 1927b. "Records of the Eighth Ordinary Session of the Assembly." Minutes of the Fifth Committee (General and Humanitarian Questions). *Official Journal*, special supplement 59, 1–72.
———. 1927c. *Report to the Eighth Ordinary Session of the Assembly by the High Commissioner of the League of Nations*. A.48. 1927.VIII, 1–33.
———. 1928. "Measures in Favour of Russian, Armenian, Assyrian, Assyro-Chaldean, and Turkish Refugees." Records of the Ninth Ordinary Session of the Assembly. Meetings of the Committees. Fifth Committee. A.33.1928.VIII. *Official Journal*, special supplement 69, 84–109.
———. 1933. *Official Journal*, special supplement 115.
Lefebvre, Georges. 1964. *The French Revolution*. Vol. 2, *From 1793 to*

1799. Translated by John H. Stewart and James Friguglietti. London: Routledge and Kegan Paul.

Lefebvre, Henri. 1995. *The Production of Space.* Oxford: Blackwell.

Leitner, Helga. 1995. "International Migration and the Politics of Admission and Exclusion in Postwar Europe." *Political Geography* 14 (3): 259–78.

Lewis, Paul. 1992. "Ideas and Trends: The Right to Intervene for a Humanitarian Cause." *New York Times,* 12 July.

Lewy, Guenter. 1993. "The Case for Humanitarian Intervention." *Orbis* (fall): 621–32.

Lillich, Richard B. 1973. *Humanitarian Intervention and the United Nations.* Charlottesville: University Press of Virginia.

Lister, Ruth. 1995. "Dilemmas in Engendering Citizenship." *Economy and Society* 24 (1): 1–40.

Loescher, Gil. 1992a. *Refugee Movements and International Security.* Adelphi Papers, no. 262, Oxford.

———. 1992b. "Refugees and the Asylum Dilemma in the West." In *Refugees and the Asylum Dilemma in the West,* edited by Gil Loescher. Philadelphia: University of Pennsylvania Press.

———. 1993. *Beyond Charity: International Cooperation and the Global Refugee Crisis.* Oxford: Oxford University Press.

———. 1994. "The International Refugee Regime: Stretched to the Limit?" *Journal of International Affairs* 47 (2): 351–63.

Loescher, Gil, and Laila Monahan, eds. 1990. *Refugees and International Relations.* Oxford: Clarendon.

Loomie, Albert J. 1963. *The Spanish Elizabethans: The English Exiles at the Court of Philip II.* New York: Fordham University Press.

Luke, Timothy. 1996. "Nationality and Sovereignty in the New World Order." *AntePodium,* vol. 3. <http://www.vuw.ac.nz/atp/>. Accessed October 1996.

Macartney, C. A. 1929. *Refugees: The Work of the League.* [London]: League of Nations Union.

Malkki, Liisa. 1992. "National Geographic: The Rooting of Peoples and the Territorialization of National Identity among Scholars and Refugees." *Cultural Anthropology* 7 (1): 24–44.

———. 1996. "Speechless Emissaries: Refugees, Humanitarianism, and Dehistoricization." *Cultural Anthropology* 11 (3): 377–404.

Marrus, Michael R. 1985. *The Unwanted: European Refugees in the Twentieth Century.* New York: Oxford University Press.

Marsh, David. 1992. "Keep Out, This Is Western Europe." *Financial Times,* 9 May.

Marshall, Andrew. 1992. "The Long-Term Future for Hatred in Europe." *Independent,* 11 April.

———. 1993. "Immigration: Europe's United Front." *Independent,* 6 June.

Marshall, Ruth. 1995. "Refugees, Feminine Plural." *Refugees* 100 (2): 3–9.

Martin, Susan F. 1991. *Refugee Women.* London: Zed.

Martiniello, Marco. 1995. "European Citizenship, European Identity, and Migrants: Towards the Post-national State?" In *Migration and European Integration: The Dynamics of Inclusion and Exclusion,* edited by Robert Miles and Dietrich Thranhart. Madison, N.J.: Fairleigh Dickinson University Press.

Mayer-Rieckh, Elisabeth. 1993. *"Beyond Concrete and Steel": Power Relations, and Gender: The Case of Vietnamese Women in the Detention Centers in Hong Kong.* The Hague: Institute of Social Studies.

McDonald, James G. 1935. *Letter of Resignation of James G. McDonald, High Commissioner for Refugees (Jewish and Others) Coming from Germany.* London: Hedley Brothers.

———. 1944. "Refugees." In *Pioneers in World Order: An American Appraisal of the League of Nations,* edited by Harriet Fager Davis. New York: Columbia University Press.

Meissner, Doris M., et al. 1993. *International Migration Challenges in a New Era: Policy Perspectives and Priorities for Europe, Japan, North America, and the International Community.* New York: Trilateral Commission.

Mennel, S. 1990. "The Globalization of Human Society as a Very Long Term Process: Elias's Theory." In *Global Culture,* edited by Mike Featherstone. London: Sage.

Migration News. 1994–. <http://migration.ucdavis.edu/mn/mntext.htm>. Accessed 10 July 1998.

Migration World. 1994. *Dateline Migration* 22: (4) 3–11.

Minear, Larry. 1992. "Humanitarian Intervention in a New World Order." *Policy Focus,* no. 1.

Minear, Larry, and Thomas G. Weiss. 1993. *Humanitarian Action in Times of War: A Handbook for Practitioners.* Boulder, Colo.: Reiner.

Minh-ha, Trinh T. 1997. "Other than Myself/My Other Self." In *Travellers' Tales: Narratives of Home and Displacement,* edited by George Robertson et al. London: Routledge.

Mitchell, Don. 1993. "State Intervention in Landscape Production: The Wheatland Riot and the California Commission of Immigration and Housing." *Antipode* 25 (2): 91–113.

Miyoshi, Masao. 1993. "A Borderless World? From Colonialism to Transnationalism and the Decline of the Nation-State." *Critical Inquiry* 19 (4): 726–51.

Moch, Leslie P. 1992. *Moving Europeans: Migration in Western Europe since 1650*. Bloomington: Indiana University Press.

Mocsy, Istvan I. 1983. *The Effects of World War I: The Uprooted: Hungarian Refugees and Their Impact on Hungary's Domestic Politics, 1918–1921*. New York: Columbia University Press.

Moote, Lloyd A. 1969. "Law and Justice under Louis XIV." In *Louis XIV and the Craft of Kingship*, edited by John C. Rule. Columbus: Ohio State University Press.

Morley, Felix. 1932. *The Society of Nations: Its Organization and Constitutional Development*. Washington, D.C.: Brookings Institution.

Morrisey, Robert. 1993. "Whose Home Is This? Feeling at Home with the Past." In *Home and Its Dislocations in Nineteenth Century France*, edited by Suzanne Nash. New York: State University of New York Press.

Mortimer, Edward. 1993. "Convenient Cracks in Wall: European Governments Can't Admit 'Illegals' Serve Useful Purpose." *Financial Times*, 15 April.

Moussa, Helene. 1993. *Storm and Sanctuary: The Journey of Ethiopian and Eritrean Women Refugees*. Toronto, Ontario: Artemis.

Mukerji, Chandra. 1997. *Territorial Ambitions and the Gardens of Versailles*. Cambridge: Cambridge University Press.

Nafziger, James A. R. 1991. "Self-Determination and Humanitarian Intervention in a Community of Power." *Denver Journal of International Law and Policy* 20 (1): 9–39.

Nair, Sami. 1996. "France: A Crisis of Integration." *Dissent* 43 (3): 75–78.

Nanda, Ved P. 1992. "Tragedies in Northern Iraq, Liberia, Yugoslavia, and Haiti—Revisiting the Validity of Humanitarian Intervention under International Law—Part I." *Denver Journal of International Law and Policy* 20 (2): 305–34.

Nansen, Fridtjof. 1927. *Adventure and Other Papers*. London: Hogarth.

———. 1972. "The Suffering People of Europe." Nobel Lecture, 19 December 1922. In *Nobel Lectures: Peace, 1901–1925*, edited by Fredrick W. Haberman. Amsterdam: Nobel Foundation.

Nietzsche, Friedrich. 1969. *On the Genealogy of Morals*. Translated by W. Kaufmann and R. J. Holingdale. New York: Random House.

Noiriel, Gérard. 1996. *The French Melting Pot: Immigration, Citizenship, and National Identity*. Translated by Geoffroy De Laforcade. Minneapolis: University of Minnesota Press.

Norwegian Refugee Council and Refugee Policy Group. 1993. *Norwegian Government Roundtable Discussion on United Nations Human Rights Protections for Internally Displaced Persons*. Nyon, Switzerland: Refugee Policy Group.

O'Brian, R. 1992. *The End of Geography*. London: Routledge.

O'Connell, Ellen. 1992. "Commentary on International Law: Continuing Limits on UN Intervention in Civil War." *Indiana Law Journal* 67: 903–12.

O'Halloran, Patrick J. 1995. *Humanitarian Intervention and the Genocide in Rwanda.* London: Research Institute for the Study of Conflict and Terrorism.

Oppenheim, Lassa. 1948. *International Law: A Treatise,* edited by H. Lauterpacht. London: Longmans, Green.

Panayi, Panikos. 1994. *Immigration, Ethnicity, and Racism in Britain, 1815–1945.* Manchester, England: Manchester University Press.

———. 1995. *German Immigrants in Britain during the Nineteenth Century.* Oxford: Berg.

Partridge, Eric. 1988. *Origins: A Short Etymological Dictionary of Modern English.* London: Routledge and Kegan Paul.

Pasqua, Charles. 1994. "Facing the Facts: An Evaluation of Immigration Policy." *Harvard International Review* 16 (3): 32–33.

Pastusiak, Longin. 1994. *Threats to Security in Central and Eastern Europe.* Draft special report to North Atlantic Assembly, International Secretariat.

Pawloski, Witold. 1993. "Polish-German Refugees Dispute." *Polish News Bulletin,* 25 February.

Peteet, Julie M. 1995. "Transforming Trust: Dispossession and Empowerment among Palestinian Refugees." In *Mistrusting Refugees,* edited by E. Valentine Daniel and John Chr. Knudsen. Berkeley and Los Angeles: University of California Press.

Peterson, Spike V., and Anne S. Runyan. 1993. *Global Gender Issues.* Boulder, Colo.: Westview.

Pieterse, J. N. 1997. "Sociology of Humanitarian Intervention: Bosnia, Rwanda, and Somalia Compared." *International Political Science Review* 18 (1): 71–93.

Plender, Richard. 1988. *International Migration Law.* Dordrecht, Netherlands: Nijhoff.

Porter, Bernard. 1979. *The Refugee Question in Mid-Victorian Politics.* London: Cambridge University Press.

Procacci, Giovanna. 1994. "Governing Poverty: Sources of the Social Question in Nineteenth-Century France." In *Foucault and the Writing of History,* edited by Jan Goldstein. Oxford: Blackwell.

"Protesters Spotlight Discussion over Anti-Immigration Bill." 1997. Agence France Presse, 25 February.

Proudfoot, Malcolm J. 1956. *European Refugees: A Study of Forced Population Movements.* Evanston, Ill.: Northwestern University Press.

Range, Peters R. 1993. "Europe Faces an Immigrant Tide." *National Geographic* 83 (5): 94–126.

Rapaport, Carla. 1992. "Them." *Fortune,* 13 July, 96–97.

Read, James M. 1962. *The United Nations and Refugees—Changing Concepts.* Geneva: Carnegie Endowment for International Peace.

Rees, Elfan. 1959. *We Strangers and Afraid: The Refugee Story Today.* Geneva: Carnegie Endowment for Peace.

Ring, Hans. 1995. "Refugees in Sweden: Inclusion and Exclusion in the Welfare State." In *Migration and European Integration: The Dynamics of Inclusion and Exclusion,* edited by Robert Miles and Dietrich Thranhart. Madison, N.J.: Fairleigh Dickinson University Press.

Robert, Paul. 1985. *Le Grand Robert de la langue française.* 2d ed. Paris: Le Robert.

Roberts, Adam. 1993. "Humanitarian War: Military Intervention and Human Rights." *International Affairs* 69 (3): 429–49.

———. 1994. "The Road to Hell: Humanitarian Intervention." *Current* 363 (June): 24–28.

Robinson, Eugene. 1992. "Refugees Challenge a Continent's Stability." *Washington Post,* 20 December.

Robinson, Nehemiah. 1953. *Convention Relating to the Status of Refugees: Its History, Contents, and Interpretation.* New York: Institute of Jewish Affairs.

Rodley, Nigel. 1992. *To Loose the Bands of Wickedness: International Intervention in Defense of Human Rights.* London: Brassey's.

Rogers, Rosemary. 1992. "The Future of Refugee Flows and Policies." *International Migration Review* 16 (4): 1112–43.

Rose, Nikolas, and Peter Miller. 1992. "Political Power beyond the State: Problematics of Government." *British Journal of Sociology* 43 (2): 173–205.

Rosenau, James N. 1990. *Turbulence in World Politics: A Theory of Change and Continuity.* Princeton, N.J.: Princeton University Press.

Rouse, Roger. 1991. "Mexican Migration and the Social Space of Postmodernism." *Diaspora* (spring): 8–23.

Rudge, Philip. 1988. "Fortress Europe." *World Refugee Survey,* 5–12.

———. 1992. "The Asylum Dilemma—Crisis in the Modern World: A European Perspective." In *Refugees and the Asylum Dilemma in the West,* edited by Gil Loescher. Philadelphia: University of Pennsylvania Press.

Ruggie, John Gerard. 1993a. *Multilateralism Matters: The Theory and Praxis of an Institutional Form.* New York: Columbia University Press.

———. 1993b. "Territoriality and Beyond: Problematizing Modernity in International Relations." *International Organization* 47 (1): 139–53.

———. 1994. "Multilateralism: The Anatomy of an Institution." In *International Organization: A Reader,* edited by Friedrich Kratochwil and Edward D. Mansfield. New York: HarperCollins College.

Ruhl, Arthur. 1917. *White Nights and Other Russian Impressions.* New York: Scribner's.
Rystad, Göran. 1992. "Immigration History and the Future of International Migration." *International Migration Review* 26 (4): 1168–99.
Said, Edward. 1979. *Orientalism.* New York: Vintage.
———. 1993. "Nationalism, Human Rights, and Interpretation." *Raritan* 12 (3): 26–51.
———. 1994. "Reflections on Exile." In *Altogether Elsewhere: Writers on Exile,* edited by Marc Robinson. Boston: Faber and Faber.
Salomon, Kim. 1991. *Refugees in the Cold War: Toward a New International Refugee Regime in the Early Postwar Era.* Lund, Sweden: Lund University Press.
Savoy, Michelle. 1994. "Steamed: Crossing Borders." *Java Monthly,* November, 9.
Schnapper, Dominique. 1991. "A Host Country That Does Not Know Itself." *Diaspora* 1 (3): 353–63.
Scouloudi, Irene, ed. 1987. *Huguenots in Britain and their French Background, 1550–1800.* Hong Kong: Macmillan.
Shapiro, Michael J. 1988. *The Politics of Representation: Writing Practices in Biography, Photography, and Policy Analysis.* Madison: University of Wisconsin Press.
———. 1991. "Sovereignty and Exchange in the Orders of Modernity." *Alternatives* 16: 447–77.
———. 1992. *Reading the Postmodern Polity: Political Theory as Textual Practice.* Minneapolis: University of Minnesota Press.
———. 1993. *Reading Adam Smith: Desire, History, and Value.* Newbury Park, Calif.: Sage.
Shaw, George Bernard. 1924. *Saint Joan.* London: Constable.
Silverman, Maxim. 1992. *Deconstructing the Nation: Immigration, Racism, and Citizenship in Modern France.* London: Routledge.
Sinha, Prakash S. 1971. *Asylum and International Law.* The Hague: Nijhoff.
Sirmen, Ali. 1991. "Dünyada bugün" (Today in the world). *Cumhuriyet,* 14 April.
Sjoberg, Tommie. 1991. *The Powers and the Persecuted: The Refugee Problem and the Intergovernmental Committee on Refugees (IGCR), 1938–1947.* Lund, Sweden: Lund University Press.
Skran, Claudena M. 1988. "Profiles of the First Two High Commissioners." *Journal of Refugee Studies* 1 (3–4): 277–96.
———. 1995. *Refugees in Inter-war Europe: The Emergence of a Regime.* Oxford: Clarendon.
Soboul, Albert. 1974. *The French Revolution: From the Storming of the Bastille to Napoleon.* London: New Left Books.

Soguk, Nevzat. 1995a. "Politics of Resistance and Accommodation: Managing Refugee and Immigrant Movements in the Post–Cold War Era." *Current World Leaders: International Issues* 38 (2): 102–18.

———. 1995b. "Refugee Matters: Refugee Regimentations as Practices of Statecraft." Ph.D. diss., Arizona State University.

———. 1995c. "Transnational/Transborder Bodies: Resistance, Accommodation, and Exile in Refugee and Migration Movements on the U.S.-Mexican Border." In *Challenging Boundaries: Global Flows, Territorial Identities,* edited by Michael J. Shapiro and Hayward Alker Jr. Minneapolis: University of Minnesota Press.

Soysal, Yasemin. 1994. *Migrants and Postnational Membership in Europe.* Chicago: University of Chicago Press.

Spivak, Gayatri C. 1988. "Can the Subaltern Speak?" In *Marxism and the Interpretation of Culture,* edited by C. Nelson and L. Grossberg. Urbana: University of Illinois Press.

Spurr, David. 1996. *The Rhetoric of Empire: Colonial Discourse in Journalism, Travel Writing, and Imperial Administration.* Durham, N.C.: Duke University Press.

Statt, Daniel. 1995. *Foreigners and Englishmen: The Controversy over Immigration and Population, 1660–1760.* Newark: University of Delaware Press.

Steger M., and F. P. Wagner. 1993. "Political Asylum, Immigration, and Citizenship in the Federal Republic of Germany." *New Political Science* 24–25 (spring–summer): 59–73.

Stewart, Alasdair. 1992. *Migrants, Minorities, and Security in Europe.* London: Research Institute for the Study of Conflict and Terrorism.

Stoessinger, John. 1956. *The Refugee and the World Community.* Minneapolis: University of Minnesota Press.

Stowell, Ellery C. 1921. *Intervention in International Law.* Washington, D.C.: Byrne.

Suhrke, Astri. 1993. "A Crisis Diminished: Refugees in the Developing World." *International Journal* 48 (2).

Tabori, Paul. 1972. *The Anatomy of Exile: A Semantic and Historical Study.* London: Harrap.

Tactaquin, Cathi. 1994. "Reframing Borders." *Racelife* 2 (5): 4–20.

Takkenberg, Alex, and Christopher C. Tahbaz. 1989. *The Collected Travaux Preparatoires of the 1951 Geneva Convention Relating to the Status of Refugees.* Amsterdam: Dutch Refugee Council.

Tartakower, Aryeh, and Kurt B. Grosmann. 1944. *The Jewish Refugee.* New York: Institute of Jewish Affairs of the American Jewish Congress and World Jewish Congress.

Teson, Fernando R. 1988. *Humanitarian Intervention: An Inquiry into Law and Morality.* Dobbs Ferry, N.Y.: Transnational.

Thompson, Dorothy. 1938. *Refugees: Anarchy or Organization?* New York: Random House.

Thomson, Janice E. 1989. "Sovereignty in Historical Perspective: The Evolution of State Control over Extraterritorial Violence." In *The Elusive State: International and Comparative Perspectives,* edited by James A. Caporoso. Newbury Park, Calif.: Sage.

———. 1995. "State Sovereignty in International Relations: Bridging the Gap between Theory and Empirical Research." *International Studies Quarterly* 39 (2): 213–33.

Thomson, Janice E., and Stephen Krasner. 1989. "Global Transactions and the Consolidation of Sovereignty." In *Global Changes and Theoretical Challenges: Approaches to World Politics for the 1990s,* edited by Ernst-Otto Czempiel and James N. Rosenau. Lexington, Mass.: Lexington Books.

Tololyon, Khachig. 1991. "The Nation State and Its Others: In Lieu of Preface." *Diaspora* 1 (1): 1–5.

"A Treaty of Peace between the Empire and Sweden, Concluded and Signed at Osnabrück, 24th of October 1648." [1648] 1969. In *The Consolidated Treaty Series,* edited by Clive Parry. Dobbs Ferry, N.Y.: Oceana.

United Nations (UN). 1988. *Human Rights: A Compilation of International Instruments.* New York: Center for Human Rights in Geneva.

———. General Assembly. 1946. *Plenary Meetings of the General Assembly.* Official Records, Verbatim Record, 2d Part, 1st Session.

———. General Assembly. 1952. 6th Session. *Report of the High Commissioner for Refugees.* Supp. 19 (A/2011). Official Record, Paris.

———. General Assembly. 1957. 12th Session. *Report of the High Commissioner for Refugees.* Supp. 11 (A/3585/Rev. I). Official Record, New York.

———. General Assembly. 1959. 14th Session. *Report of the High Commissioner for Refugees.* Supp. 11 (A/4101/Rev. I). Official Record, New York.

———. General Assembly. 1986. 41st Session. Special Political Committee. *International Co-operation to Avert New Flows of Refugees.* 9 October (A/SPC/41/L. 5).

———. General Assembly. 1992. 43rd Session. Executive Committee of the High Commissioner's Programme. *Note on International Protection.* 25 August (GA, A/AC. 96/799).

———. General Assembly. 1993. 44th Session. Executive Committee of the High Commissioner's Programme. *Note on International Protection.* 31 August (GA, A/AC. 96/815).

———. Security Council. 1992. "Text of Resolution 688 on Iraqi Human Rights Abuses." Reuters, 26 August.

United Nations High Commissioner for Refugees (UNHCR). 1950. *Statute of the Office of the United Nations High Commissioner for Refugees.* 14 December (UNHCR/INF/1/Rev. 3).

———. 1951. *Convention and Protocol Relating to the Status of Refugees.* 28 July (UNHCR/IP/10/Eng).

———. 1971. *A Mandate to Protect and Assist Refugees.* Geneva: UNHCR.

———. 1979. *Collection of International Instruments concerning Refugees.* Geneva: UNHCR.

———. 1991. *Draft Report of the Working Group on Solutions and Protection to the Forty-Second Session of the Executive Committee of the High Commissioner's Programme.* 24 July (Excom/WGSP/15).

———. 1993a. "Ethnic Conflict and Refugees." *Refugees* 93: 4–9.

———. 1993b. *Information Paper.* March. Geneva.

———. 1993c. *The State of the World's Refugees, 1993: The Challenge of Protection.* New York: Penguin.

———. 1995. *The State of the World's Refugees: In Search of Solutions.* Oxford: Oxford University Press.

"United Nations–Republic of Iraq Memorandum of Understanding." 1992. *International Journal of Refugee Law* 4 (1): 113–16.

United States Committee for Refugees (USCR). 1988. *World Refugee Survey.* Washington, D.C.

———. 1992. *World Refugee Survey.* Washington, D.C.

———. 1993a. *Refugee Reports,* 31 May.

———. 1993b. *Refugee Reports,* 30 November.

———. 1993c. *World Refugee Survey.* Washington, D.C.

———. 1994. *World Refugee Survey.* Washington, D.C.

———. 1995. *World Refugee Survey.* Washington, D.C.

Vattel, M. D. 1820. *The Law of Nations; or, The Principles of the Law of Nature Applied to the Conduct and Affairs of Nations and Sovereigns.* Northampton, Mass: Buttler.

Vernant, Jacques. 1953. *The Refugee in the Post-war World.* New Haven, Conn.: Yale University Press.

Vita, Mathew C. "West Discards Welcome Mat for Refugees." *Atlanta Journal and Constitution,* 26 May.

Vuilleumier, Marc. 1989. *Immigrants and Refugees in Switzerland: An Outline History.* Saint Gall, Switzerland: Stehle Druck.

Walker, R. B. J. 1989. *One World, Many Worlds: Struggles for a Just World Peace.* Boulder, Colo.: Reiner.

———. 1990. "Security, Sovereignty, and the Challenge of World Politics." *Alternatives* 15: 3–27.

———. 1991a. "On the Spatiotemporal Conditions of Democratic Practice." *Alternatives* 16: 243–62.

———. 1991b. "State Sovereignty and the Articulation of Political Space/Time." *Millennium: Journal of International Studies* 20 (3): 445–61.

———. 1993. *Inside/Outside: International Relations as Political Theory.* Cambridge: Cambridge University Press.

Walker, R. B. J., and S. H. Mendlowitz, eds. 1990. *Contending Sovereignties: Rethinking Political Community.* Boulder, Colo.: Reiner.

Walsh, James N. 1993. "Migration and European Nationalism: France, Germany, and the United Kingdom." *Migration World Magazine* 20 (4).

Walters, F. P. 1952. *A History of the League of Nations.* London: Oxford University Press.

Walzer, Michael. 1983. *Spheres of Justice.* New York: Basic Books.

———. 1993. "Exclusion, Injustice, and the Democratic State." *Dissent* 40 (1): 55–64.

———. 1995. "The Concept of Civil Society." In *Toward a Global Civil Society,* edited by Michael Walzer. Providence, R.I.: Berghan.

Warner, Daniel. 1992. "We Are All Refugees." *International Journal of Refugee Law* 4 (3): 365–72.

———. 1994. "Voluntary Repatriation and the Meaning of Return to Home: A Critique of Liberal Mathematics." *Journal of Refugee Studies* 7 (2–3): 160–73.

Weber, Cynthia. 1995. *Simulating Sovereignty: Intervention, the State, and Symbolic Exchange.* Cambridge: Cambridge University Press.

Weiner, Margery. 1960. *The French Exiles, 1789–1815.* London: Murray.

Weiner, Myron. 1993. "Security, Stability, and International Migration." In *International Migration and Security,* edited by Myron Weiner. Boulder, Colo.: Westview.

Weis, Paul. 1979. *Nationality and Statelessness in International Law.* Germantown, Md.: Sijthoff and Noordhoff.

Weiss, Thomas G., and Larry Minear. 1992. "Groping and Coping in the Gulf Crisis: Discerning the Shape of a Humanitarian Order." *World Policy Journal* 9 (4).

———, eds. 1993. *Humanitarianism across Borders: Sustaining Civilians in Times of War.* Boulder, Colo.: Reiner.

Wendt, Alexander. 1994. "Anarchy Is What States Make of It: The Social Construction of Power Politics." In *International Organization: A Reader,* edited by Friedrich Kratochwil and Edward D. Mansfield. New York: HarperCollins College.

Whitman, Jim. 1994. "A Cautionary Note on Humanitarian Intervention." *GeoJournal* 34 (2): 167–75.

Wicks, Margaret C. W. 1968. *The Italian Exiles in London, 1816–1848.* Freeport, N.Y.: Books for Libraries Press.

Williams, Robert C. 1972. *Culture in Exile: Russian Émigrés in Germany, 1881–1941.* Ithaca, N.Y.: Cornell University Press.

Wittke, Carl. 1952. *Refugees of Revolution: The German Forty-Eighters in America.* Philadelphia: University of Pennsylvania Press.

Wolf, Christian. [1764] 1934. *Jus Gentium Methodo Scientifica Pertractium* (The law of nations treated according to a scientific method). Oxford: Clarendon.

Wolf, Eric. 1982. *Europe and the People without History.* Berkeley and Los Angeles: University of California Press.

World Council of Churches. 1995. "Migration Experts Press Rights Issue at Summit." *Ecumenical Refugee and Migration News,* no. 2.

Xenos, Nicholas. 1992. "The State, Rights, and the Homogenous Nation." *History of European Ideas* 15 (1–3): 77–82.

———. 1995. "Refugees: The Modern Condition." In *Challenging Boundaries: Global Flows, Territorial Identities,* edited by Michael J. Shapiro and Hayward Alker Jr. Minneapolis: University of Minnesota Press.

Zarjevski, Yefime. 1988. *A Future Reserved: International Assistance to Refugees.* Oxford: Pergamon.

Zolberg, Aristide. 1985. "The Formation of New States as a Refugee-Generating Process." In *Refugees and World Politics,* edited by Elizabeth G. Ferris. New York: Praeger.

———. 1989. "The Next Waves: Migration Theory for a Changing World." *International Migration Review* 23 (3).

Zolberg, Aristide, et al. 1986. "International Factors in the Formation of Refugee Movements." *International Migration Review* 20 (2): 151–69.

———. 1989. *Escape from Violence: Conflict and the Refugee Crisis in the Developing World.* New York: Oxford University Press.

Zubrzycki, Jerry. 1956. *Polish Immigrants in Britain.* The Hague: Nijhoff.

Zucker, A. E. 1967. *The Forty-Eighters: Political Refugees of the Revolution of 1848.* New York: Russell and Russell.

Index

Nevzat Soguk is assistant professor of political science at the University of Hawai'i at Manoa.